SAN DIEGO'S FIRST PADRES and "THE KID"

THE STORY OF THE REMARKABLE
1936 SAN DIEGO PADRES
and
TED WILLIAMS' PROFESSIONAL
BASEBALL DEBUT

Authored by

Tom Larwin

Carlos Bauer

Dan Boyle

Frank Myers

Larry Zuckerman

San Diego, California

1936 SAN DIEGO PADRES

Back row, left to right:
    (1) James Kerr, (2) George Hockette, (3) George McDonald, (4) Ray Jacobs, (5) Cedric Durst, (6) Fred Vaughn, (7) Eddie Mulligan, (8) George Myatt, (9) Wally Hebert, (10) Gene (Bud) Tuttle, (11) Ernie Holman

Middle row:
    (12) Ed Wells, (13) Bobby Doerr, (14) Gene Desautels, (15) Vince DiMaggio, (16) Bill Lane (owner), (17) Frank Shellenback (manager), (18) Herm Pillette, (19) Ashley Joerndt, (20) Archie Campbell

Front row:
    (21) Vance Wirthman, (22) Jack Hile, (23) Ken Iverson, (24) Berlyn Horne, (25) unidentified (in Hollywood uniform), (26) Joe Berkowitz

Inset:
    (27) Ted Williams

Published by
Montezuma Publishing
Aztec Shops Ltd.
San Diego State University
San Diego, California 92182-1701

619-594-7552

www.montezumapublishing.com

Copyright © 2019
All Rights Reserved.

ISBN: 978-0-7442-7230-7

Copyright © 2019 by Montezuma Publishing and the authors Tom Larwin et al. The compilation, formatting, printing and binding of this work is the exclusive copyright of Montezuma Publishing and the authors Tom Larwin et al. All rights reserved. No part of this work may be reproduced, stored in a retrieval system, or transmitted in any form or by any means, including digital, except as may be expressly permitted by the applicable copyright statutes or with written permission of the Publisher or Author.

Major League Baseball trademarks and copyrights are used with permission of MLB Advanced Media, L.P. All rights reserved. http://www.mlb.com/

Publishing Manager: Kim Mazyck
Cover Design: Lia Dearborn
Design and Layout: Lia Dearborn
Formatting: Lia Dearborn
Quality Control: Joshua Segui

Names:	Larwin, Thomas F., author. | Bauer, Carlos, author. | Boyle, Dan, author. | Myers, Frank, author. | Zuckerman, Larry, author.
Title:	San Diego's First Padres and "The Kid": The Story of the Remarkable 1936 San Diego Padres and Ted Williams' Professional Baseball Debut/ authored by Tom Larwin, Carlos Bauer, Dan Boyle, Frank Myers, Larry Zuckerman.
Description:	[San Diego, California] : Tom Larwin, [2019] | Includes bibliographical references and index.
Subjects:	LCSH: San Diego Padres (Baseball team : Pacific Coast League)--History. | Pacific Coast League--History. | Williams, Ted, 1918-2002. | Minor league baseball--West (U.S.)--History. | Baseball players--United States--Biography | San Diego (Calif.)--History--20th century.

ABOUT THE AUTHORS

CARLOS BAUER published several books on Pacific Coast League baseball, including the *Coast League Cyclopedia* and the *Early PCL Statistical Record, 1903-1957*. His non-baseball related books have been reviewed in the Sunday *New York Times*, *Chicago Tribune* and *Los Angeles Times*, among others.

DAN BOYLE grew up in the Bronx and hates the Yankees. He moved to San Diego in 1995, just in time for the Padres' unexpected Western Division title in 1996 and NL Championship in 1998. Since then, rooting for the Padres and the Mets has been mostly an exercise in character building. Researching the 1936 Padres season has been a welcome respite. He highly recommends poring over microfilm of old newspapers because you'll never know what you'll find.

TOM LARWIN was born and raised on Chicago's south side as a die-hard Cubs fan, but after moving to San Diego in 1976 he now shares his allegiance with the home-town Padres. He has written on "The 1907 Pacific Coast Baseball Championship Series" (*The National Pastime,* 2000) and heads up SABR's San Diego Ted Williams Chapter. He, along with Carlos and Dan, participated as authors in the book *The Kid: Ted Williams in San Diego* (Rounder Books, 2005).

FRANK MYERS grew up in Pittsburgh getting the last autograph from Bill Mazeroski before he announced his retirement. He shares Dan's deep and abiding antipathy for all things Yankees. He also has season tickets for the Padres demonstrating his deep baseball masochism.

LARRY ZUCKERMAN was the premier ballpark researcher. His *Ballparks of the PCL* remains a classic. A Viet Nam era chopper pilot, he held ratings for most every type of aircraft from seaplanes to 747s. He worked as a social worker (MSW) for the State of California. He died at 56 years old.

CONTENTS

LIST OF TABLES vii

FOREWORD ix

CHAPTERS

   1 — INTRODUCTION 1

   2 — HISTORY OF THE FRANCHISE LEADING UP TO 1936 5

   3 — JANUARY 1936 THE STARS MOVE SOUTH 19

   4 — FEBRUARY 1936 DEVELOPMENT OF THE ROSTER AND SPRING TRAINING 29

   5 — MARCH 1936 LONGSHOT PADRES BEGIN MAIDEN SEASON 39

   6 — APRIL 1936 POSITIVE SIGNS!? 59

   7 — MAY 1936 2ND DIVISION GETS COMFORTABLE 69

   8 — JUNE 1936 "THE KID" DEBUTS 79

   9 — JULY 1936 RIOTS, THE FIRST AMENDMENT, AND LIGHTS AT LANE 91

  10 — AUGUST 1936 A REAL PENNANT RACE DEVELOPS 105

  11 — SEPTEMBER 1936 DEFECTION AND DENOUEMENT 117

  12 — THE GOVERNOR'S CUP 127

  13 — EPILOGUE: POST-1936 135

  14 — REFLECTIONS ON THE 1936 SAN DIEGO PADRES— FROM THOSE WHO WERE THERE 151

APPENDICES

   A — 1936 SAN DIEGO PADRES SEASON STATISTICS 163

   B — TED WILLIAMS GAME-BY-GAME SUMMARY 165

   C — 1936 TEAM ROSTER 167

   D — KEY DATES AND GAME-BY-GAME RECORD 169

E — NOTABLE 1936 PADRES: THOSE HONORED AS
   MEMBERS OF BASEBALL HALLS OF FAME.. 175

F — THE REAL AND TRUE HISTORY OF THE FRANCHISE
   THAT BECAME THE SAN DIEGO PADRES 181

G — A BIOGRAPHY OF H.W. "BILLY" LANE (AS HE WAS CALLED
   IN SALT LAKE CITY) 197

H — BIOGRAPHIES OF THE 1936 SAN DIEGO PADRES 201

REFERENCES 255

PHOTO CREDITS 259

ENDNOTES 261

LIST OF TABLES

Table 2.1. Franchise Annual Records: 1906-1935 13

Table 2.2. Final PCL Standings -1935 14

Table 5.1. Batting and Pitching Totals for March 57

Table 6.1. Batting and Pitching Totals for April 67

Table 7.1. PCL Standings on May 1, 1936 70

Table 7.2. Batting and Pitching Totals for May 78

Table 8.1. PCL Standings on June 1, 1936 80

Table 8.2. Batting and Pitching Totals for June 89

Table 9.1. PCL Standings on July 1, 1936 92

Table 9.2. Batting and Pitching Totals for July 103

Table 10.1. PCL Standings on August 1, 1936.. 106

Table 10.2. PCL Standings on Sunday, August 23, 1936... 112

Table 10.3. Batting and Pitching Totals for August 116

Table 11.1. PCL Standings on September 1, 1936 118

Table 11.2. PCL Standings on Tuesday, September 8, 1936 122

Table 11.3. Final PCL Standings—1936 125

Table 11.4. Batting and Pitching Totals for September 125

Table 12.1. Batting and Pitching Totals for Governor's Cup 133

Table 13.1. Year-by-Year Record of San Diego Padres PCL
   Franchise (1936-1968) 141

SAN DIEGO'S FIRST PADRES and "THE KID"

FOREWORD

We want to set the record straight: we are researchers, not authors. However, bear with us...this does not mean a boring book. On the contrary, we uncovered numerous fascinating stories, and have strung them together into what we believe you will find to be an interesting read.

The other matter we better come clean on is this: as researchers we are joined by a common interest in baseball. It was around the year 1999, when as members of the San Diego Ted Williams Chapter of the Society for American Baseball Research (SABR), we got the idea for the book. Much of our research was conducted in preparation for a March 2003 symposium held in San Diego on the subject of "The Kid from San Diego, Ted Williams."

San Diego is not our original home, we hail from, New York City, Chicago, Los Angeles and Pittsburgh. But San Diego is our adopted home and we agreed that 1936 would be a most interesting year to review...and once we got into the effort we found that to be true.

March 29, 2003 Symposium

The 1936 San Diego Padres of the Pacific Coast League had some very good ball players (20 of the 34 on the roster during the year played in the major leagues at one time or another during their professional baseball careers. Two of them—Bobby Doerr and Ted Williams—became members of the National Baseball Hall of Fame.

They had a DiMaggio roaming the outfield, a player-manager who eventually won 318 games in the minor leagues, another pitcher who won 264 games, a vice president who won 342 games in the minors, an outfielder who played alongside Babe Ruth on the 1927 Yankees, an infielder who collected over 3,000 hits in his minor and major league career, and a colorful owner who was reputed to be one of the "shrewdest" men in baseball. To quote Bobby Doerr "...it was quite a team."

There were the nicknames, too, but not just the normal ones: "Old Folks," "Spider," "Ever Ready," "Preacher," "T-bone," "Trader," "Hardrock," "Doodle," "Foghorn," 'Gyp," "King Tut," "Hardluck," and..."The Kid." It was a colorful team of characters who also were able to team up and play some terrific baseball, almost winning the league title in their first year in San Diego.

We had many partners on the project. Personal interviews with several people who were there in 1936 provided first-person descriptions: players Bobby Doerr and George McDonald, the team's mascot, Ralph

Thompson. There were important research contributions—including photographs and publications—from people who know much more about certain aspects of what we wrote: all-around baseball aficionado Andy Strasberg; San Diego baseball historian Bill Swank; baseball biographical expert James D. Smith III...plus Denis Donley, Bob Hoie, Autumn Durst Keltner, Mark Macrae, Bill Nowlin, and Alan O'Connor. Biographical and statistical information on the players—all 61 of them---was the product of Carlos Bauer's research. Numerous libraries were consulted but none more often than the City of San Diego's Central Library and its Sullivan Family Baseball Research Center managed by the able Section Supervisor Peter Miesner.

One member of the author team, Larry Zuckerman, passed away while we were working on the project, but left his notes and extensive ballpark research documents with Bauer. Carlos was then able to turn Larry's incredible material into a unique story about San Diego's ballpark history.

Finally, but not least, we express our appreciation to our families and our spouses for letting us be boys again! Thanks, Kathleen, Norma, Judith, and Kathy!

Ted Williams and Bobby Doerr

CHAPTER 1
INTRODUCTION

San Diego County had a population of 265,000 in 1936 with about 165,000 of that within the city of San Diego jurisdiction. The busiest traffic location was between 6th and 10th Avenues along University Avenue at 48,000 cars a day while the busiest location outside of the city of San Diego was between Oceanside and Carlsbad on Coast Highway with slightly over 12,000 daily.[1]

Three primary newspapers covered the local scene: the *San Diego Union, San Diego Evening Tribune,* and the *San Diego Sun*. Every once in a while a fourth local paper contributed a story, too, the *San Diego Herald*. Competition for stories was intense and accuracy with facts and names often neglected. So, it was a ripe time for watching events unfold as San Diego's political and civic leaders chased professional baseball...something that had become an on-going hobby of sorts.

The Great Depression had been underway for over six years with signs of recovery building by 1936.

Some sample prices in the ads of April 1936 included one from the Globe Furniture Co. at 12th and Broadway for a Gibson refrigerator for $79.50, no cash down, and three years to pay. At the Thearle Music Co., 640 Broadway, one could buy a mahogany Chickering Piano for $450. Double S&H stamps were available Wednesdays at Walker's located at 5th and Broadway. The cigarette ad from Luckies noted that "each puff less acid, a light smoke of rich, ripe bodied tobacco." At the El Cortez Hotel, one could try a cocktail room "repast" for 65¢.

A gallon of gas was 10 cents and a loaf of bread 8 cents.

The highest paid baseball "figures" at the time were managers:[2]

Joe McCarthy, manager, New York Yankees	$35,000 annually
Mickey Cochrane, manager/catcher, Detroit Tigers	$30,000
Bill Terry, manager/1st baseman, New York Giants	$27,500
Joe Cronin, manager/shortstop, Boston Red Sox	$25,000
Jimmie Foxx, 1st baseman, Boston Red Sox	$23,000
Lou Gehrig, 1st baseman, New York Yankees	$23,000
Lefty Grove, pitcher, Boston Red Sox	$22,500
Charley Grimm, manager, Chicago Cubs	$22,000
Frank Frisch, manager/2nd baseman, St. Louis Cardinals	$20,000
Carl Hubbell, pitcher, New York Giants	$18,500

An editorial in the *San Diego Evening Tribune* was titled "A Dictator's Victory" and covered the 99% vote in support for Adolph Hitler in Germany. Given that there was only one square on the ballot and it could only be voted as a "yes," the editorial noted that the Nazi election was "merely a gesture, typical of a dictator."[3]

Good news! The March 31, 1936, *Sun* had an article headlining that "Sally Rand to Dance at Expo." Also, Alf Landon, Governor of Kansas was to visit on May 17. On the sour side, Bruno Richard Hauptmann–condemned kidnapper and alleged murderer of Charles Lindbergh Jr.–was about to be executed.

April 1936 movies at local theatres included:

The Prisoner of Shark Island at the Fox Theater, starring Warner Baxter

Petrified Forest at the Orpheum, starring Leslie Howard and Bette Davis

Modern Times at the Seville in Chula Vista, starring Charles Chaplin

Early 1936 was also a time in San Diego when west coast baseball was being discussed. Seemingly an annual topic around spring time of the year was whether San Diego could have, or would have a professional baseball team.

There had been attempts at Class D baseball in 1913 and 1929 but both failed to last an entire season.

It took seven years before there was another minor league baseball venture in San Diego. What follows is a story that covers the events that led to the team coming to San Diego, and the people who were involved at the local level, with team ownership, and on the field. This team was named the San Diego Padres and began playing in March 1936.

THE STORY

The franchise that became the San Diego Padres actually had its roots going back to 1906 in Sacramento, California. Eventually the team moved to Hollywood and then was transferred to San Diego in 1936 to play in the Class AA Pacific Coast League (PCL).* The PCL was one step away from being a major league. Many former and future major league players were on each team's roster. There were also players seemingly good enough to play in the major leagues who decided to stay on the west coast, nearer their home, and be able to make a salary comparable to being in the majors.

The story begins with a history of the franchise from that 1906 Sacramento club leading to late 1935 when Hollywood team owner Bill Lane starts looking for possible relocation options. Then, in January 1936 the heart of the story begins and is told, month-by-month, from January through September 1936. While the story naturally focuses on a baseball team, and one season, there are fascinating events and personalities that contribute to a remarkable adventure.

First, there is San Diego itself. Always playing second fiddle to its larger, glamorous neighbor to the north, Los Angeles. "Not big enough to support a high level professional sports team" was a common refrain from outsiders, and even some local folks. "There are too many distractions—and attractions—to draw fan interest in the summer" was another common feeling.

Life in San Diego, an "official" monthly publication of the San Diego Heaven-On-Earth Club was published during the mid-1930s.[4] The Club's President, a Joe E. Dryer, described the "Beautiful Goddess of Fair Weather" stating that "For here I have created Heaven On Earth in this, America's Natural Air-Conditioned Area, which I wish to maintain free from thunderstorms, hot or cold waves, blizzards, tornadoes, hurricanes and earthquake damage." No mention of playing sports, or watching baseball games.

---

* In 1936 Class AA was the minor league highest classification with Class D Being the lowest.

1—INTRODUCTION

San Diego had a rich history of winter baseball San Diego being played in the early part of the 20th century with teams comprised of players from various professional leagues. However, until 1936 there was no professional team that lasted an entire season.

The first team on the scene was in 1913, the San Diego Bears, that played in the Class D Southern California League. They were good enough to be in first place with a 7½ game lead when the league folded on July 20, 1913.

Then, in 1929, the San Diego Aces team was formed to play in the Class D California State League. This team also was good enough to be leading the league by 2½ games when it disbanded on June 17, 1929.[*] When the Orange County club failed, and then were unable to get a park in Pomona, the franchise was shifted to San Diego and given the name, Coronado Arabs, and the city supported two clubs.

In 1936, the developed World was still in the midst of a Depression—what is now referred to as the "Great Depression"—that had started in October 1929 (and would extend to 1939). The worst seemed to be over in 1936 with the economy in recovery. However, there were rumblings of war in Europe. Severe drought conditions in the Great Plains created the "Dust Bowl" and forced tens of thousands of people to abandon their homes and farms and relocate.

The Depression led President Franklin D. Roosevelt to create a federal Works Progress Administration (WPA) in April 1935. The WPA provided a jobs program that would eventually employ 8.5 million people by the time it ended in 1943. There were numerous projects throughout San Diego, including improvements to various schools, Balboa Park, the Zoo, and San Diego County Administration Center. Important to this story is a $25,000 WPA grant that was used to build the Padres' ballpark, Lane Field.

Stimulating San Diego's tourist economy, the California Pacific International Exposition was held for two years, in 1935 and 1936 (May 29, 1935–November 11, 1935 and February 12, 1936–September 9, 1936). The exposition was hosted in Balboa Park and displayed hundreds of exhibits on history, the arts, horticulture, ethnic cultures, science, and industry. There were some exhibits considered a bit unusual, such as a Garden Nudist Colony and the "One Ton Mechanical Man."

U.S. 3¢ Postal Stamp Issued in 1935 Commemorating California Pacific International Exposition

The story plays out over the course of the following 13 chapters.

Chapter 2 traces the history of the franchise from its beginning in 1906 through December 1935. It concludes with a summary of what transpired after the conclusion of the 1935 Pacific Coast League (PCL) season when several teams in the league were "restless."

---

[*] Two interesting side notes: (1) For over a month there were two teams in the San Diego area, the original team from Orange County moved to Pomona on May 8, 1929, and then to the Coronado on May 15, 1929; and (2) another team in the league was from San Bernardino team and its nickname was the Padres.

Chapters 3 and 4 cover the January-February 1936 months when final plans were developed for the team to play in San Diego. The stories about the players begin in Chapter 4 as contracts are mailed out and spring training begins.

Chapters 5 through 12 cover the trials and tribulations of playing 176 games over a 25-week PCL season from late March until The Governor's Cup playoffs in September. This season schedule averages out to seven games a week…typically, Tuesdays through Sunday, with Monday being a "travel day" and doubleheaders played on Sunday.

Chapter 13 provides an Epilogue, a summary of what happened after the 1936 season with the players, the ballpark in San Diego, and the franchise.

Chapter 14 is the concluding chapter and contains verbatim interviews with two players who were there: Bobby Doerr and George McDonald. Plus, a third member of the team, the team mascot, Ralph Thompson, also contributed an interview.

The book is more than a story, it also serves as a research reference. To this end, there are over 90 pages of Appendices. Appendices A-D provide season summaries of the players, roster moves, and game-by-game results. Appendix B provides a game-by-game summary of Ted Williams' season. The research into compiling this summary found two errors in Williams' "official" statistics for the 1936 season, resulting in a slightly lower batting average of .269 (down from .271).

Appendix E introduces those notable Padres from the 1936 team who have been honored as members of baseball Halls of Fame. Appendices F and G provide additional detail on the history of the franchise and the biography of Bill Lane, respectively.

Finally, Appendix H contains 53 pages of mini-biographies of each of the personalities that shaped the team from the beginning of spring training to the conclusion of the season on September 21, 1936.

CHAPTER 2
HISTORY OF THE FRANCHISE LEADING UP TO 1936

When the Hollywood franchise was considering a move to San Diego in late 1935 and early 1936, every schoolboy in San Diego knew that the team was based in Los Angeles, where the team had been known as the Stars. The sharper ones knew—or soon learned--that Hollywood had originally been from Salt Lake City, where the owner, Bill "Hardrock" Lane had started out. That, of course, is only partially true. The real story began some eight years prior to Salt Lake City joining the Pacific Coast League. The San Diego franchise began not in Salt Lake City, and not even in the PCL. The Padres franchise began as an expansion franchise in an outlaw league.*

The franchise history can be traced back to 1906—in Sacramento, California—with a team called the Cordovas in the California State League. It took 30 years, a change from one league to another, and three geographic re-locations before the team found a permanent home in San Diego some 30 years later. The chart on the next page traces this 30-year history.

A more detailed story of the franchise history through 1936 is contained in Appendix F and is summarized in the following sections of this chapter. Chapter 13 includes a discussion of the franchise ownership history from 1936 to 1968.

THE SACRAMENTO YEARS
(CALIFORNIA STATE AND PACIFIC COAST LEAGUES): 1906—1914

— 1906 —

In the spring of 1906, Sacramento was given a franchise in the outlaw California State League, which had formed in 1903. The 1906 league was to comprise six teams: Alameda Grays, Oakland Commuters, Sacramento Cordovas, San Francisco Orphans, San Jose Prune Pickers, and Stockton Millers.

---

* An "outlaw league" is one that does not honor the contracts and agreements of professional Organized Baseball.

Franchise and Ownership History, 1906-1935

1906-1908	1909-1913	1914	1915-1925	1926-1935
Sacramento	Sacramento	Sacramento / Missions (San Francisco)	Salt Lake City	Hollywood
California State League	Pacific Coast League	Pacific Coast League	Pacific Coast League	Pacific Coast League
Bill Curtin (1906)		Harry Wolverton, Lloyd Jacobs (1914)	Frank Murphy (1915-17)	
Curtin, Charlie Graham (1906-10)			Bill Lane becomes member of club's Board of Directors (1915), Lane becomes club president (1917), Lane becomes majority owner (1918)	
	John Irving Taylor (1910-12)			
	Jack Atkin (1913)			

The league awarded the Sacramento franchise to Bill Curtin, who had been field manager of the non-California State League Stockton Distillers in 1905. Curtin stocked his club with former California League-PCL players, and future major leaguers like Charlie Enwright, and well-known players Charlie Graham, Spider Baum, Fred Brown, Jay Hughes, Phil Knell, Bobby McHale, Jimmy Shinn, and Max Muller played for them over the next several years. Basically, the California State League depended on released Coast Leaguers, and local players on the way up. The league scheduled some 30 games apiece for the teams, and all were scheduled for Sundays.

— 1907-1908 —

With the Pacific Coast League weakened by the 1906 Earthquake, its directors decided to drop two teams, Seattle and Fresno, and compete as a four-team circuit for 1907, and continued with four clubs the following season, 1908. As a result, some of the PCL's best players were being snatched up by the Cal State League. Players found the money better, and every team was stocked with Coast League contract jumpers. The PCL countered by having the California State League declared an outlaw league by the National Association.

Sacramento played excellent ball those two years under the management of Charlie Graham, with a number of fine players showing up in the lineup. Hall-of-Famer Harry Hooper roamed the outfield for two years, hitting .301 and .344, respectively. Fred Brown was the stopper with records of 24-6 and 23-12 for the two years. The club in those two years had pitchers who would go on to win over 300 games in the minors, Spider Baum and Jimmy Whalen. Whalen went 31-8 for Sacramento in 1908.

After the 1908 season, the PCL and Cal State leagues made one last stab at resolving their differences. When Graham and his partner, Bill Curtin, saw that the gap between the two leagues could not be breached, they took up a standing offer by Coast League to join that circuit. The Coast League also had an implied threat in that they would place a club in Sacramento if Graham and Curtin didn't jump. Thus, an outlaw league team in Sacramento became, overnight, a stalwart in the Pacific Coast League.

2—HISTORY OF THE FRANCHISE LEADING UP TO 1936

— 1909 —

The PCL decided to expand back to six-team league with two new teams: one from Vernon and the transplanted Sacramento team. On March 30, 1909, the Sacramento Senators faced the Vernon Tigers at Oak Park in Sacramento in what was the first Coast League game for both clubs. With Charlie Graham remaining at the helm, the Sacramento Senators, as they were now called, ended in fourth place with 97 wins.

— 1910 —

After that first year in the PCL, the Senators found itself facing a $5,000 deficit. Charlie Graham, by then the owner of an automobile agency in Sacramento, tried to persuade other businessmen to help the club financially. But when that failed, Graham turned to John Irving Taylor, owner of the Boston American League team, and scion of the *Boston Globe* fortune. Taylor had been looking for a minor league team in the East where he could send his prospects, but Graham persuaded him to buy controlling interest in the team. Taylor bought 12,000 of the 25,000 shares in the club, with Bill Curtin and Graham retaining 4,000. The latter two would control the day-to-day operations, Graham as manager, and Curtin taking care of off-the-field matters. The infusion of Taylor's cash, and a number of Red Sox players did not help, as the Senators finished in the cellar in 1910.

— 1911 —

The 1911 team bounced back on the field, finishing in fourth place but they still didn't draw enough fans to break even. Patsy O'Rourke was brought in to manage the club replacing Graham who decided to run his automobile dealership full-time.

— 1912 —

Manager O'Rourke had a running feud with players on other clubs—as well as on his own team. On June 25 he handed in his resignation. Graham and Curtin installed veteran Deacon Van Buren as manager—he had been a manager in the PCL since 1903. The change in managers did not help as the club wound up dead last.

— 1913 —

On the business side Taylor decided to unload his stock in the club and sold out to Jack Atkin of Spokane, Washington. Atkin came in and decided to spend money and, in so doing, snagged highly respected manager, Harry Wolverton—paying him more than he had made leading the Yankees. To honor the new manager the team was rechristened the Wolves. Atkin's spreading around of so much cash did succeed in making the club competitive on the field, but the club still failed to draw fans. By mid-season, rumors began to spread that Wolverton and a couple of Sacramento insurance men wanted to buy the club and as the season concluded so was the deal. The new owners were manager Harry Wolverton and Sacramento insurance man Lloyd Jacobs. And, on the baseball side, the Wolves were successful finishing second to the Portland Beavers and racking up 103 wins.

— 1914 —

After spending all their cash and credit buying Atkin's shares, the majority owners had nothing left over for player acquisitions. The club started out the 1914 season poorly and the club went downhill from there. The Wolves stumbled out of the gate in fourth place and then settled into fifth, where it remained for the rest of the summer. Fans were not attending games and opponents were losing so much money when playing at Sacramento that they no longer wanted to travel there. In September the team became a "traveling team" playing home games in Oakland and San Francisco. In the middle of the month, the team became known as the Mission Wolves.

Autumn found the team bankrupt with Wolverton and Jacobs having lost their investments. At the PCL Winter Meeting in November, the league announced that the Missions would be sold to the highest bidder. San Jose, Seattle, San Diego and Sacramento submitted formal bids of $25,000 but, almost immediately, San Jose was deemed too small a city to host a franchise, and Seattle too far away leaving San Diego and a newly constituted group in Sacramento as the leading bidders. According to press accounts, the San Diego bid was rejected not much later because of some shady characters who formed part of their group. With seemingly only Sacramento left in the mix, Salt Lake City appeared on the scene with a formal bid.

A group was put together by E. A. Vanderventer, editor of the *Salt Lake City Tribune*. To spearhead the lobbying effort Vanderventer hired Cliff Blankenship whose career in the Coast League began as a player in 1904 and who supposedly knew everybody in the league. League owners were hesitant about Salt Lake City because of travel expenses between California and Utah. In response Vanderventer did two things that put Salt Lake City over the top: (1) he sent a $20,000 deposit to the league (the other bidders only sent promises), and (2) he formally guaranteed each club $2,000 minimum on every series they played in Salt Lake.

At a special meeting on December 18, the league officially awarded the franchise to Salt Lake. One month later, on January 15, 1915, the club met officially and a permanent Board of Directors was elected. The biggest shareholder, lumberman Frank Murphy became president, with Reverend Elmer Goshen as vice president, and George Wasson and Bill Lane as members of the board as directors.[*] Blankenship was named as field manager of the club.

THE SALT LAKE CITY YEARS (PACIFIC COAST LEAGUE): 1915—1925

— 1915 —

The new business manager of the Salt Lake team was Bill O'Connor who had local experience with the Salt Lake club in the Union Association the year before, as business manager and "assistant secretary." One of the first actions O'Connor accomplished was to secure a corner area of Bonneville Amusement Park for a ballpark which would also be called Bonneville Park. Meanwhile, in early February the *Salt Lake City Telegram* ran a "name that club" contest with "Bees" being announced as the winning nickname. Under O'Connor and Manager Blankenship, the 1915 club finished in second place only five games out of first place and proved to be a success financially.[†]

— 1916 —

The 1916 season had the club falling back to third place, three games above .500. There also was internal troubles in the clubhouse with manager Blankenship being undermined by star outfielder Buddy Ryan. On September 5, with the club at 71-70 Blankenship abruptly resigned, saying he couldn't take anymore backbiting. Even though the press speculated that Wahoo Sam Crawford would be offered the job the managerial post went to Ryan…the same player who had led the revolt. Quickly, Ryan found that he couldn't control the club any better than Blankenship, with the team going at a .371 clip before he gave up the reins on October 9, at which time he said he would continue as a player only. On October 10 Bill Bernhard, the former American League pitcher, met with club directors, and was given a contract for the rest of the season and for 1917. Bernhard managed the 1914 Salt Lake City club in the Union Association and had not managed for two seasons working

---

[*] This was the official entry of Bill Lane into the ownership of the franchise. Interestingly, Goshen and Wasson would remain stockholders in the club until the Lane Estate sold the club in 1944.

[†] No data were published by the league on attendance, but during the club's first three years it was well reported that club declared a dividend that was paid out to all subscribers, some 500 shareholders in all.

2—HISTORY OF THE FRANCHISE LEADING UP TO 1936

as a pitching coach and umpire in the Southern Association. The club immediately responded with a 15-4 record for the rest of the 1916 season.

— 1917 —

In late December 1916 the team's business manager, Bill O'Connor, resigned. Within a month Murphy hired William P. "Jack" Cook to take over as business manager. Cook had been in a similar position with the Oakland Oaks. The club made it through the season again turning a profit with another third-place finish. The club had three 20-game winners, and third baseman Morrie Rath led the league in hitting with a .341 batting average.

The off-season proved interesting. Just prior to the November club's directors meeting, Frank Murphy resigned as president of the club, citing his other business interests as requiring his fulltime attention. At that meeting, Bill Lane became president of the club. In short order, he fired manager Bill Bernhard and hired Walt McCredie who had managed the Portland franchise since 1905.

— 1918 —

The 1918 season was a financial disaster for the PCL forcing the league to suspend operations mid-season on July 14. This was during World War I and a "Work or Fight" order from Washington D.C. was the stated reason for closing up shop. However, attendance was way down as a great number of fans felt it unpatriotic to attend baseball games while men went off to war. The Salt Lake club again finished third, this time winning their last game of the season, 5-3, to wind up with 49-49 win-loss record.

Off the field, the club lost money for the first time since the club moved to Salt Lake City. Some shareholders balked at an impending assessment and Bill Lane stepped in to purchase the shares of those stockholders over the course of the next few months.*

— 1919 —

With the war over, the league decided to expand to eight teams for 1919 adding Seattle and bringing back the Portland franchise. The latter addition led McCredie to resign and head back to managing the Portland club. In turn, President Lane wasted no time in hiring St. Louis Cardinal scout Eddie Herr—who was reputed to be one of the best minds in baseball—to take over the reins of the Bees. The club did no better than before, finishing once again in third place. Lane was not satisfied and fired Herr at season's end replacing him with Ernie Johnson as player-manager for the 1920 season.

— 1920 —

This season was confronted with a bribery scandal involving six Bees' players resulting in two of the team's best hitters being suspended. The club went from one percentage point behind league-leading Vernon to fifth place at the close of the season.

Bill Lane...
"The Charlie Comiskey of the PCL"
Salt Lake World Republican, March 31, 1918

---

* Lane had stated that he got control of the club in 1919, which seems correct. He probably began picking up shares in 1918, and gained control in early 1919.

— 1921 —

During the off-season, Ernie Johnson was replaced as manager for the 1921 season with Gavvy Cravath. Subsequently, he was replaced—late in the season—with catcher Butch Byer. The club finished in seventh place with 73 wins

— 1922-1924 —

After having eight managers in a six-year period, the Bees named outfielder Duffy Lewis as manager for the 1922 season. He stayed on for three years accomplishing a fourth place and two fifth place finishes. A good hitter, in 1924 Lewis won the PCL batting title with a .392 average barely edging out teammate Lefty O'Doul by .0002 for the crown. After the close of the 1924 season, Duffy was sent to Portland and another teammate, Ossie Vitt, was named manager.

On the management side the team's business manager, Jack Cook, hired long-time PCL pitcher Spider Baum as a coach and to be his assistant in January 1924.[*] In June 1924, Cook passed away with the result that Baum took over as the club's business manager.

— 1925 —

With Lane and Baum fully in charge of the club for the 1925 season, they named third baseman Ossie Vitt player-manager. The club jumped from fifth place to second. Additionally, Tony Lazzeri set the record for home runs for both the PCL (that still stands) and for Organized Baseball. Also, joining Lane and Baum for the first time was MLB spitballer and PCL veteran, Frank Shellenback. At the time, who would have ever thought that this threesome–Baum, Lane, Shellenback– would be the management foundation for the 1936 Padres?

At the annual PCL Winter Meeting in December, led by William Wrigley, five owners mounted a coup against PCL president William H. McCarthy. Wrigley owned the Los Angeles Angels and the Chicago Cubs and wanted to wrest control from the Bay Area owners and their man, PCL President William H. McCarthy—whose intent it was to install his man, *Los Angeles Times* journalist, Harry Williams. Lane supported Wrigley, and in doing so ingratiated himself with Wrigley.

Wrigley also wanted to get rid of the owner who was sharing his new digs, beer baron Ed Maier. Maier wound up selling the club to a Wrigley confidante, Hebert Fleishhacker. The league, in a special meeting on January 15, 1926, announced approval of the deal, with the Vernon club moving to San Francisco to become the Mission team…and one surprise: The Salt Lake City Bees would be moving to Los Angeles to share Wrigley Field with the Los Angeles Angels.

THE HOLLYWOOD YEARS (PACIFIC COAST LEAGUE): 1926—1935

— 1926 —

On its arrival to Hollywood the club was first to be named the Blues, then Lane thought better of that, and retained the existing name, the Bees. The Hollywood Bees name lasted throughout most of spring training, but at the behest of Hollywood fans and residents, the name was changed officially to Stars. The Stars dropped from second place in 1925 to sixth place in their first year in Los Angeles. However, the Hollywood fans came out in support as season attendance increased from 137,012 in Salt Lake City to 212,813 at Wrigley Field. While the attendance increase was nice, Wrigley's Angels retained all concessions at the park. That, along with Wrigley's insistence on having ladies admitted free to games, did not sit well with Lane.

---

[*] Baum would still be with the club in 1936, and beyond, winding up as president of the club after Lane's death.

2—HISTORY OF THE FRANCHISE LEADING UP TO 1936

— 1927 —

The Stars again found themselves in sixth place and attendance slipped over 20 percent to 164,430. Rumors ran wild that Bill Lane was going to show team manager Ossie Vitt the gate after the club's poor showing, but nothing came of it, and the manager returned for the 1928 season. Starting in 1927, a new nickname began to be used for the team: the "Sheiks." It was used by the local press in the wake of silent movie star Rudolph Valentino's death, though the team was still officially the "Stars." The nickname Sheiks continued to appear in the press until the club moved to San Diego.

— 1928 —

The Sheiks rebounded in 1928 both on the field and at the box office. The Hollywood club finished second in the first half of the split season, and third in the second. The club also outdrew their landlords, the Angels, for the first time. Despite the good news about the gate, Lane still had major financial issues with Wrigley Field's Lady Days' policy which gave free entrance to women on Tuesdays, Saturdays and Sundays. Further, Lane had always claimed that his club should share in the concessions revenue, or at least have a certain percentage of Hollywood home games. At the time it appeared that Lane had limited choices: return to Salt Lake City, or move the club down to San Diego. Given the territorial rights that the Angels possessed the option of Lane building his own park in Hollywood was not feasible. However, Lane's interest in San Diego as a future home base likely was forged around this time with the team deciding to train in San Diego in 1929 instead of Santa Monica.

— 1929 —

Spring training went well, but Lane and Baum were not sure if San Diego was ripe for a berth in the PCL. In the meantime, the team won 112 games finishing tied for second place. To cap off a good season they went on to win the playoffs against the Missions. Fan interest grew and the Stars finished second to Los Angeles in attendance with 314,243 passing through the turnstiles—more than double what was experienced two years earlier.

— 1930 —

The Depression that started in 1929 had not made its full weight felt in Los Angeles and both the Angels and Stars drew fairly well at Wrigley Field. Hollywood's attendance dipped to a still respectable 289,131 while the Angels again led the league. The first half ended with the Angels edging out the Stars by 3½ games, but the second half was all Stars. Hollywood posted a .650 win-loss percentage, and finished eight games ahead of Los Angeles. In the playoffs, Hollywood ran off with the title, winning four of five games.

— 1931 —

This season started off well as the Stars won the first half by a wide margin. But, then they stumbled in the second half and wound up losing in the playoffs to the San Francisco Seals. Yet the club drew over 300,000 fans to Wrigley Field, leading the league by far. The Stars had two outstanding individual player-season that year. Frank Shellenback had his best season ever with a won-loss record of 27-7, and a 2.85 ERA. Outfielder Dave Barbee hit a league-leading 47 home runs to go along with 166 RBIs and a .332 batting average.

— 1932 —

This year found the Stars training in San Diego again for the fourth straight year, though pitchers and catchers reported early to Carlsbad, north of San Diego. On the field, the Stars had another good year as they finished second with 106 wins, five games behind the Portland Beavers. Year three of the Depression was starting to have an adverse impact on PCL attendance and team owners decided to shelve the split season schedule that had been in effect since 1928. After the season concluded, Lane was involved in a new dispute with the Angels' Wrigley, this one having to do with radio broadcasts of games from Wrigley Field. Lane opposed radio broadcasts but it was the park, and not the club, that controlled air rights. So he had no choice.

— 1933 —

Spring training was a rough go for the Stars in 1933. San Diego's Navy Field had been made unplayable by winter motorcycle races and so the club made a deal with Shell Oil in Long Beach to use its field. However, an earthquake damaged the field and the team was forced to move to grounds in Sawtelle located in the west of Los Angeles. The club dropped a notch in 1933, being barely edged out of second place by the Portland Beavers. The team was led by a staff four 20-game winners: Frank Shellenback, Archie Campbell, Tom Sheehan, and Vance Page.

— 1934 —

After the spring training debacle with San Diego and Long Beach in 1933, the Stars decided to train in Riverside at the far eastern reaches of the Los Angeles basin. In the meantime, the league's deteriorating economic condition was a matter of concern and the two non-California teams, Portland and Seattle, seemed to be on the "bubble." However, the eight-team league survived. As the season was to get underway, Lane experienced a heart attack but had recovered by mid-summer. Even so, he would come to be plagued with poor health the rest of his life.

The Los Angeles Angels won the league title with one of the greatest minor league teams ever. They finished 35 games ahead of the second-place Mission Reds, and 39½ games ahead of the third-place Stars. Not long after the season ended, with Lane obviously back on his feet, he changed managers: Ossie Vitt was out after 10 years and long-time PCL pitcher Frank Shellenback was named as the new manager to guide the 1935 Hollywood Stars.

— 1935 —

For spring training this year, the club had concluded that the last year in Riverside was not satisfactory and headed to Fullerton located in the southeast part of the Los Angeles region. During spring training, Lane told the press that he had dropped $61,000 over the preceding three seasons. When asked about his health, he stated that his health had been completely restored. While his health may have been restored, that of his club was not. The Stars ended up in the cellar winning only 73 games while losing 99. Attendance inched up to 135,916 but was substantially under the "salad days" of the late 1920s.

Financial issues lingered between Lane and the Angels' ownership that now included both father William Wrigley and son P. K. Rumors swirled around the league folding up, forcing PCL officials to formally deny the rumors. In November Hy Baggerly resigned as Coast League president. At the PCL Winter Meeting, Bill Lane was elected First Vice President, though the league presidency remained open. Thus, Lane represented the league at the National Association Winter Meetings in Dayton, Ohio. On his way back to Los Angeles, he included a stop in Salt Lake City, ostensibly to ascertain interest in having a team back in town. There were rumors about Sacramento being moved as well as the Hollywood Stars. Plus, the San Francisco Seals faced foreclosure on Seals Stadium, and the Mission team might have to be sold.

With several teams in a state of flux, on December 18, 1935, W. C. Tuttle, novelist, former newspaper reporter and cartoonist, was elected president of the Pacific Coast League.

2—HISTORY OF THE FRANCHISE LEADING UP TO 1936

THE FRANCHISE RECORD FROM 1906 THROUGH 1935

The franchise that would become the San Diego Padres in 1936 had been in existence for 30 years, playing in Sacramento, Salt Lake City, and Hollywood. The team's year-by-year record over this period is shown in Table 2.1.

Table 2.1. Franchise Annual Records: 1906-1935

Year	Club Name	League	W	L	Finished	Manager
1906	Sacramento Cordovas	California State	21	11	3rd	Bobby McHale/Charlie Graham
1907	Sacramento Cordovas	California State	38	18	2nd	Charlie Graham
1908	Sacramento Cordovas	California State	55	20	3rd	Charlie Graham
1909	Sacramento Coyotes/Senators	PCL	97	107	4th	Charlie Graham
1910	Sacramento Senators	PCL	83	128	6th	Charlie Graham
1911	Sacramento Senators	PCL	95	109	4th	Patsy O'Rourke
1912	Sacramento Senators	PCL	73	121	6th	Patsy O'Rourke/Deacon Van Buren
1913	Sacramento Wolves	PCL	103	94	2nd	Harry Wolverton
1914	Sacramento-Mission Wolves	PCL	90	121	5th	Harry Wolverton
1915	Salt Lake City Bees	PCL	108	89	2nd	Cliff Blankenship
1916	Salt Lake City Bees	PCL	99	96	3rd	Cliff Blankenship/Buddy Ryan/Bill Bernhard
1917	Salt Lake City Bees	PCL	102	97	3rd	Bill Bernhard
1918	Salt Lake City Bees	PCL	49	49	3rd	Walt McCredie
1919	Salt Lake City Bees	PCL	88	83	3rd	Eddie Herr
1920	Salt Lake City Bees	PCL	95	92	5th	Ernie Johnson
1921	Salt Lake City Bees	PCL	73	110	7th	Gavvy Cravath/Butch Byler
1922	Salt Lake City Bees	PCL	95	106	4th	Duffy Lewis
1923	Salt Lake City Bees	PCL	94	105	5th	Duffy Lewis
1924	Salt Lake City Bees	PCL	101	100	5th	Duffy Lewis
1925	Salt Lake City Bees	PCL	116	94	2nd	Ossie Vitt
1926	Hollywood Bees/Stars	PCL	94	107	6th	Ossie Vitt
1927	Hollywood Stars	PCL	92	104	6th	Ossie Vitt
1928	Hollywood Stars	PCL	112	79	2nd tied	Ossie Vitt
1929	Hollywood Stars	PCL	113	89	3rd	Ossie Vitt
1930	Hollywood Stars	PCL	119	81	1st	Ossie Vitt
1931	Hollywood Stars	PCL	104	83	2nd	Ossie Vitt
1932	Hollywood Stars	PCL	106	83	2nd	Ossie Vitt
1933	Hollywood Stars	PCL	107	80	3rd	Ossie Vitt
1934	Hollywood Stars	PCL	97	88	3rd	Ossie Vitt
1935	Hollywood Stars	PCL	73	99	8th	Frank Shellenback
	California State League Record=		114	49	.699	
	Pacific Coast League Record=		2578	2584	.499	
	Overall Minor League Record=		2692	2633	.506	

SETTING THE STAGE FOR A FRANCHISE MOVE—
NOVEMBER-DECEMBER 1935

LANE SAYS HE MAY MOVE BALL CLUB TO SALT LAKE

Headline Indicating Lane May Move Club to Salt Lake
Los Angeles Times, November 28, 1935

Soon after the close of the 1935 baseball season rumors filled the air about several PCL teams moving to different cities. Three teams seemed to be prominently mentioned: the Missions, Hollywood, and Sacramento teams. A persistent rumor was the Bill Lane, Hollywood's owner, would move the team back to Salt Lake City; this was especially hot following the minor league meetings being held in Dayton in late November.[5,6] It was "hinted" that, if this move were to occur, then the Sacramento or Mission teams may move to Los Angeles. As an aside, there was wide local news interest in the possible move with three daily Los Angeles area papers engaged—especially the *Los Angeles Times* and *Los Angeles Examiner*. Reporters from at least five newspapers were after stories…chasing the same people. That competition, by itself, made for interesting stories.

In 1935 the PCL was a class AA league (the highest minor league classification at the time) and consisted of eight teams. The final PCL standings for the 1935 season are shown in Table 2.2.

Table 2.2. Final PCL Standings -1935

	W	L	GB
San Francisco Seals	103	70	-
Los Angeles Angels	98	76	5½
Oakland Oaks	91	83	12½
Portland Beavers	87	86	16
Mission Reds	87	87	16½
Hollywood Stars/Sheiks	**83**	**89**	**19½**
Seattle Indians	80	93	23
Sacramento Solons	75	100	29

The 1935 playoffs were won by the San Francisco Seals against the Los Angeles Angels, four games to two. Leading the PCL in RBIs was San Francisco's Joe DiMaggio with 154. Gene Lillard of the Angels led with 56 home runs and Oscar 'Ox' Eckhardt of the Mission team had the highest batting average of .399.

In the *Los Angeles Times* on November 28, 1935, there was an article that indicated that Lane "may" move the ball club to Salt Lake City. The article indicated that Lane was serious about the move given that Salt Lake City was his "first love." Lending credence to the speculation he gave his reasons for the consideration as follows:

> *Salt Lake City hasn't been hard hit as the California towns. I believe…improving conditions here…warrant bringing the Bees back to Salt Lake City. I think it would be a paying proposition. He noted that rail transportation is cheaper and faster than it was in the early 1920s. In addition he cited his health as another factor for the possible move. Spider Baum,*

2—HISTORY OF THE FRANCHISE LEADING UP TO 1936

Lane's club vice president and secretary also noted that the ball park and stands in the Mormon City were in excellent condition.[7]

The "staying" and "going" situation would remain an active topic for the Hollywood club throughout the off season. On December 4, 1935, *Los Angeles Times* published an article under the headline "Lane Keeps Stars Here." Rumors that the team would be transferred to Salt Lake City for the 1936 season were "blasted" by Lane. He said, "The Sheiks would again hold forth at Wrigley Field with a bigger and better ball club."[8]

Within days of this article, Lane was off to Sacramento to make a "personal investigation" of the situation there.[9] His visit fueled reports out of Sacramento that Lane would be invited to move to that city.[10] He said that the purpose of his trip was to obtain firsthand information on the financial status of the club to give to the other owners at the upcoming Coast League meeting. But, in the meantime, the Sacramento Chamber of Commerce called an emergency meeting ostensibly to invite Lane to move his team to Sacramento. The Solons were in poor financial shape and the team had hoped that some major league organization would step in and take them over. After the close of the 1935 season, a San Francisco bank that held the mortgage sold many of the Sacramento club's best players.[11]

Lane apparently did not bite. However, by mid-December, Branch Rickey and the St. Louis Cardinals expressed interest in the team as part of their farm team expansion program. Within days, the local Chamber of Commerce which had purchased the team from the bank for $5,000, turned the club over to the Cardinals.

The "saving" of Sacramento by the Cardinals seemed to give relief to the notion that the Sheiks would move from Hollywood. Bob Ray, in his *Times* article of December 13, 1935, indicated that "it looks as though everything is all set for a great season in 1936."[12] He offered that the Sheiks are rounding up the best team they've had in five years.

Related to San Diego, in an article dated December 13, 1935, *San Diego Union* Sports Editor Ted Steinmann gave his opinion that, if the Cardinals did not go ahead with Sacramento, then there would be the possibility of a Class D league being formed in southern California.[13] He concluded that this might offer San Diego its best chance of getting organized baseball and a ballpark.

THE MISSION REDS COURT SAN DIEGO

On December 16, it was reported that three southern Californians (Wilson Atkins, Eddie "Dunk" Farrell, and John 'Foghorn' Murphy) had obtained an option to buy the San Francisco Mission ball club and move the team to San Diego.[14] Manager of Sports Field, Linn Platner, was pleased and was quoted saying, "If the Mission club does come here, it will fulfill my hopes of more than five years. Although I have not been contacted by any of the gentlemen holding the option, they know the place is ready for them at any time. I will have Sports Field renovated completely, and we will have a field equal to any on the Pacific Coast."[15]

Dampening any enthusiasm in San Diego, this news was met with skepticism from the president of the San Francisco Seals, Charles Graham, who reportedly said, "Murphy has talked of buying a club for years, but I have never heard of any bona fide offers."[16] In the *Sun* Farrell is quoted as saying "the city (San Diego) is a natural. Clubs from the north could play either the Angels or the Sheiks in Los Angeles one week, drop down to the border city for a week, then return to Los Angeles for a series with the other club."[17]

By the next day, *San Diego Union* headlines read that:

"Owner Denies Plan To Bring Missions Here"

The owner of the Missions, Joe Bearwald, disputed reports that there had been any business dealings with the "Los Angeles syndicate."[18] He indicated that the club would not be moved from San Francisco. Local hopes may have dimmed, but in the same article Platner expressed optimism that a PCL franchise would be in San

Diego, if not in the coming year, "it will be almost a certainty the following season." He also suggested that Branch Rickey is favorable toward San Diego and "he might be the one to start a move in this direction."

In the meantime, PCL directors meeting in Oakland on December 16 adopted their initial schedule for the 1936 season. Opening day would be March 28, 1936, with Los Angeles at Hollywood, Seattle at Oakland, Portland at Sacramento, and San Francisco playing the Missions at Seals Stadium (home to both clubs). Further, the owners decided to institute a "Shaughnessy Title Playoff" for 1936. This playoff format, named after Frank Shaughnessy, president of the Montreal baseball team, who borrowed the idea from National Hockey League, and was adopted by International League and the American Association, the other two AA leagues, would put the top four teams into a pennant playoff of two rounds: the first and fourth place clubs facing each other, and the second and third place clubs doing the same. The winners of round one would face off in the final round.

In another action, on December 17 the directors voted to hire William C. Tuttle as PCL President.

Confused reports on what was happening with the Missions continued to flourish in the local San Diego press. Headlines on December 18 read:

"Trio Still Making Plans To Move Missions To San Diego"[19]

Murphy was quoted as saying "all previous reports and denials to the contrary, we positively have an option to purchase the Mission club of the Pacific Coast League and intend to move the team to San Diego or some other California city if we decide to exercise it." He noted that San Diego is "ripe" for PCL baseball but also stated that Fresno and Long Beach were being considered as likely sites. Murphy and his two partners indicated that they were planning to visit San Diego within days to review the local situation prior to making a final decision. In fact, local teams noticed the possibility of their visit. The semi-pro Reuben Verdugo's San Diegans were preparing for an upcoming game against the White King club. They had a workout on Sunday, December 15, in order to ready for the game and show the "'big three' holding an option of the Mission club" who reportedly will be in the stands for the game. Inspired by these reports, the players went through a "snappy" workout.[20]

As expected, on December 19, Murphy, Atkins and Farrell came to San Diego for an inspection tour. A photograph in the next morning's newspaper showed the three, along with Roy Hegg, chairman of The San Diegans (the tourist and sports group of the Chamber of Commerce), in town to "look over San Diego as Coast League site."[21]

The *Sun* proclaimed:

"Magnates Favor San Diego for Mission Ball Club, Consider New Ball Park; Sale of 1,000 Box Seats Would Assure Club Here"[22]

The *Union* had headlines that were equally upbeat:

"City's Chances To Secure Missions Bright"[23]

While in town the group met with Hegg, head of the Chamber and a group of business leaders and other prominent local figures (which included D. W. Campbell, Chamber of Commerce; Henry Cramer, sponsor of several semi pro teams; A. Snyder, American Legion junior baseball; D. R. Minshall; Fred Faddis; Linn Platner; Ewart Goodwin; Fred Kinzel, Junior Chamber president; W. A. Kearns, Rodney McLeod; Joe Rafferty; and Albert Mayrhofer). The discussion covered population figures, availability of suitable sites for a park, and level of civic interest for supporting a team. One of the three, Wilson Atkins, noted that they were favorably impressed but expressed hope that there would be some assurance of an adequate season ticket base.

In its December 20 edition, the *Sun* announced that "Pacific Coast League baseball will come to San Diego if San Diegans show enough interest to assure a seasonal attendance of 125,000; if a good ball park is provided; if San Diego businessmen prove their interest by purchasing 1000 box seats in advance." That is at least what the three Los Angeles businessmen told the chamber group headed by Hegg. Atkins was quoted in the *Sun* that

2—HISTORY OF THE FRANCHISE LEADING UP TO 1936

"I'm sold on San Diego. I like the city, but I want to be sold in dollars and cents. We're in baseball because we love the game but we want to handle it as we do our business – at a profit. If people here show enough interest to purchase, say, 1000 season box seats at $15 each, I believe that'd be enough show of interest."

Following this informal challenge, Ted Steinmann announced in his December 20 column that the paper would begin a "test of San Diego's interest" starting with the next day's paper. Already the *Sun* was staging a contest with theirs beginning on the 20th. The form that was included in the paper specifically referred to the "proposed" arrival of the Missions.

Likewise, a sign-up pledge was included in the Sports section of the *Union* beginning on December 21. Support was to be indicated if the reader would consider taking one or more season tickets (priced at $15) as a "pledge."

These initial pledge requests were to help guide the local civic leaders later on.

What Do You Think About Missions Here?
FILL OUT AND SEND TO THE SUN

San Diego has a chance for a Pacific Coast League baseball club if the men who hold an option on the San Francisco Missions can be assured of adequate attendance.

The Sun, believing a club would be of great civic value, invites its readers to comment on the proposed coming of the Missions.

Below is a form all baseball fans are invited to fill out and mail to The Sun Sports Department, 7th and B Sts.

Bear in mind that there will be some 90 games for the season and that prices are 75 cents for adults in the grandstand and 40 cents for adults in the bleachers. Children are 15 cents.

The form:
- Would you buy a $15 season box?..............
- Would you regularly attend weekends?..........
  (State Sat., Sun., or both)
- What site do you suggest for the park?...........
  (Sports Field only available site now under consideration; Stadium out because no left field; only alternative some new location).

Do You Want Organized Baseball Here?

I want to see Pacific Coast League baseball in San Diego and hereby pledge myself to attend and support the sport.

Signed..

Address...

I hereby pledge myself to purchase a season box seat ticket, which sells at $15 per year.
Signed..

Send no money. These are just pledges. Send them in at once to the sports department, San Diego Union.

Questionnaires in The San Diego Newspapers Gauging Fan Interest in Baseball "Here"
San Diego Sun, December 20, 1935, and *San Diego Union*, December 21, 1935

On the political front, things also were heating up. The December 21, 1935, *San Diego Union* had headlines that read:

"City Makes Plans to Rebuild Field for Coast Club"[24]

Joe Brennan, the City of San Diego's port director, met with the three Los Angeles businessmen on the December 20 and indicated that the city would "gladly" help in converting the Sports Field site into a baseball park. Brennan indicated that they were willing to immediately get underway with plans for a WPA (Works Progress Administration) project. Time already was a big element with opening day—March 28, 1936—only some three months away.

The three Los Angeles "sportsmen" left town and reiterated their interest in bringing baseball to San Diego and all they sought in the way of any guarantee was a "showing a public interest and a baseball park." At the same time, Chamber of Commerce representative Hegg announced a proposal to enlist the support of all local civic and service clubs to assist with the building of the ballpark.[25]

Almost daily newspaper reports covered the return of pledges to the sports department. In the December 23 edition of the *Union,* it was noted they were "deluged" with coupons. On Christmas Day the newspaper clarified what the $15 was for: a "swell seat and one that you can always find whenever you attend the games." However, it "does not entitle you to admission to the park, for you must pay the general admission fee also."[26]

The editor of the *Union* got into the act, too, with this editorial on December 27:

> THESE BALL GAMES
>
> *The crowds at the recent pro ball games in the stadium here ought to furnish a highly encouraging index to the promoters who are said to be considering the possibility of supporting a Coast league baseball team here. The fans want baseball. The rumor of a chance to enter the Coast league has had a good deal to do, we suspect, with getting out the crowds for these winter games. We suggest, though, that Mr. Verdugo's* local club ought to pull itself together, in the interests of future gate receipts. The home fans don't demand that their team always win, but they do insist that it bear down.*
>
> *We believe that San Diego would support baseball – but it would have to be baseball.*[27]

Coupons and letters kept coming into the *Union*: from military personnel, from visitors indicating an interest in moving to San Diego, if there was a Coast League team; and from residents from all corners of Southern California. One individual wrote on behalf of employees at Arden Dairies to commit to 10 season box seats and 50 or more tickets on weekends. He also said that "the city should build a modern plant as near the business district as possible and give free rent to the Mission club for at least five years to give them a chance to get established here."[28]

In the meantime, as the new year arrived in San Diego plans were being developed by The San Diegans (i.e., the Chamber group) to sell box seats to businesses, hotels, and individuals in order to further convince the Los Angeles sportsmen that the move to San Diego would be profitable.[29]

---

* Verdugo was manager of a local semi-pro team.

CHAPTER 3
JANUARY 1936
THE STARS MOVE SOUTH

NOTABLE WORLD EVENTS-JANUARY 1936

1st Stanford University beats Southern Methodist University 7-0 in Rose Bowl

1st A new law in Germany bars women under the age of 35 being employed by Jews

14th Howard Hughes flies from Los Angeles to Newark in a record 9 hours 27 minutes

29th The National Baseball Hall of Fame announced its initial inductees:-Ty Cobb, Christy Mathewson, Walter Johnson, Babe Ruth and Honus Wagner

The year 1935 had ended with a buzz of baseball news in San Diego related to hopes for a relocation of an existing "Coast league baseball team" to San Diego. The newspapers were providing daily reports on the latest hearsay; input was being solicited from locals on their interests to attend games; and business groups were getting behind the effort.

As January 1, 1936, rolled around both the *San Diego Sun* and the *Union* were leading the cause for inviting the Missions to relocate to San Diego. Coupons and letters continued being touted each day in the newspapers. On January 2 the *Union* played up the public relations value to San Diego and quoted one fan (named "A. Fan"!) who wrote that having "...a good, strong club could do more for advertising the city than anything else we have here."[30] The *Union* played up the enthusiasm for "Coast ball" while the *Sun* seemed more pessimistic. The Sports Editor for the *Sun*, Nelson Fisher, reported on January 8 that response "has been none too encouraging on the whole."[31]

Things perked up on January 10 as the *Union* and *The Sun* had headlines that read:

Baseball Moguls Approve San Diego as Team Site,
Quartet Now Here to Make Final Decision on Plans
to Bring Franchise to S. D.[32]

Mark Mensing Announced As General Manager
for Missions Baseball Club, Murphy;
Atkins Name Ventura Oil Man as Associate;
Option Holders Reassure San Diego of Preference for Local Site[33]

Still not final, but with increasing assurances, it appeared that the Missions were on their way to San Diego. On their return trip to San Diego, on Thursday, January 9, Murphy, spokesman for the Los Angeles group, reinforced a feeling that they were about to give the city assurances, but just needed to have a suitable park to rent and a showing of definite fan interest. He was quoted as saying "We have done our part and are ready to step into San Diego, which by all means has the best climate of any city in the country, bar none, for year-around baseball. We must, however, receive assurance of adequate attendance."[34]

During this visit the three men again met with the Port Director Brennan and Sports Field Manager Platner to receive an update on plans for improvements to Sports Field. In addition, they met with Mayor Percy J. Benbough; Sam E. Mason, general manager of the San Diego Electric Railway Company; Arthur Marston of the Marston Company; and Morton Fowler, vice president of the San Diego Gas and Electric Company. Murphy also mentioned his intent to keep the new team in San Diego for spring training in order to acquaint San Diegans with the players. However, on January 11, the *Sun* reported that the Mission Group was "irked" over the tardiness of action by the Chamber of Commerce.[35]

Angels, Sheiks Still "Under Construction"

Cubs and Red Sox Promise Talent to Local Clubs; Lane Expects Six More New Players

BY BOB RAY

Although the start of the 1936 Pacific Coast League race is less than three months away, the present status of our Angels and Hollywood

Los Angeles Times, January 12, 1936

In any event, things were getting serious. By all appearances, San Diego was on the verge of having a new Pacific Coast League team...the Missions. Speculation had it that all the sudden activity had been precipitated by the PCL directors meeting coming up in Los Angeles on January 15-16, 1936?

Well, the PCL meeting came—and went—with league business being conducted within a few hours. The directors adopted the final league schedule for 1936, made some changes to the league constitution, and fired three umpires. Nothing apparently was formally discussed concerning any franchise shifts or sales.

Then another twist to the story developed: that Joe Baerwald, president of the Missions club, was to come to San Diego on either January 16 or 17. But the trip wasn't to discuss details for a transfer of the team because there isn't a "snowball chance" that the Missions club would move to San Diego.[36] Rather, the stated purpose of the trip was to look for a site in San Diego for spring training.

Then, on Friday, January 17, an apparent rumor was reported, first in Bob Ray's column in the *Los Angeles Times*:

Quit Kiddin', Bill
Rumor going around town that Bill Lane is still threatening to move his Hollywood Sheiks out of Wrigley Field. It's lease-signing time and Lane is parrying for cheaper rent. I'll admit that Lane has lost money the past few seasons at Wrigley Field, but it was his own fault. Had

3—JANUARY 1936 THE STARS MOVE SOUTH

he gone out and got himself a good ball club, baseball interest would have been kept alive in Los Angeles. When the Sheiks put losing clubs on the field year after year the Hollywood fans just got too tired of going out to the ball park. And in the past these same Hollywood fans were so rabid that when the Sheiks weren't at home they'd go out just to root against the Angels. Let Hollywood and the Angels both have strong teams and the fans will once more fill the ball park for civil war series.[37]

THE STARS/SHEIKS MAKE THE MOVE

Finally, the news broke on Tuesday, January 21, 1936—San Diego was going to get a PCL team! But—after a month of talks about the Missions moving to San Diego—instead, it turned out that it was going to be the Hollywood Stars/Sheiks!

Three sets of headlines in the dailies blared out the news:

Angel Boss Raps Lane For Moving Sheik Club Here;
Hints Club Should Go To Sawtelle;
Plans Announced For New Park Of 10,000 Capacity[38]

Sheiks Quit Wrigley Field For SAN DIEGO;
Lane Will Move Club; Rent Row Forces Transfer; Hollywood Boss Tentatively Agrees With Border City Officials on Switch[39]

S. D. Gets Hollywood Team;
Stars To Shine Here As Soon As New Park Built;
Lane Agrees to Change Home City,
Bringing Players to Open Season Next March[40]

Lane arrived in San Diego on Sunday, January 19, to begin what amounted to a day of negotiating on the 20th, and the all-important meeting on January 21. A tentative agreement was reached in a Tuesday morning meeting held in port director Brennan's office. In attendance, besides Brennan and Bill Lane, were Linn Platner, Eddie Taylor (an aide to Platner), Joe Reyburn (a director of the Hollywood Ball Club corporation), Emil Klicka (a local banker who also served as a Harbor Commissioner), and Nelson Fisher, Sports Editor of *The Sun*. Brennan opened the meeting by asking: "And now what, gentleman, have you to say after sleeping over the idea of taking Sports Field for your Hollywooders? Has your pencil grown sharper or duller?"[41]

In response, Lane offered: "Yes, we have. We shall take the field. We shall give you thus and so for the first three years, such and such for the fourth and thus and so for the fifth. But provided that you put up a 'respectable' park (meaning grandstands)." Reportedly Brennan smiled and said, "sold!"

All told, the negotiations took all of three minutes!

Of course, there were some details that remained. Getting the WPA financial aid being one of the more significant details. Still, the Stars/Sheiks seemed to be on their way to San Diego. And, in the meantime, this same day it was announced by Missions President Bearwald that he would not make a deal with the trio of Los Angeles businessmen whom were angling to buy the Missions team.[42]

Within a few weeks, events related to San Diego acquiring a professional baseball team turned completely around in the most surprising and quick fashion.

While San Diego officials were basking in excitement, up north in Los Angeles officials were in a "state of high peeve."[43] The Los Angeles Angels were joint tenants with the Stars since 1926 when Lane brought his Salt Lake team there. The president of the Los Angeles Angels, David P. Fleming, indicated that he wouldn't try to talk Lane out of the move, and that all they have ever asked for was "a fair rent." As a slap in the face to Hollywood's recent teams, Fleming indicated that "Lane should move to Sawtelle instead of San Diego. From the looks of the Hollywood clubs of the past few years, the Sheiks would fit in nicely at Sawtelle."*[44] As to the finances at Wrigley Field, the Hollywood club did not pay any rent in 1934 or 1935, but contributed half of the operating expenses and received no cut of the concessions.

The reaction by local residents to the new San Diego baseball club was very positive. Henry Cramer, sponsor of several local semi-pro teams, pledged to do anything "within reason" to cooperate with the new team.[45] In that same article, another local baseball activist, George Harding, was quoted as saying that "it is one of the greatest things, from a sports angle, that ever happened to San Diego." Bert Stratton, who has had a semi-pro team for years, said that he will "be lucky to have half a team ready on Sundays for sandlot ball. They'll all be at the league game, and I'll be there, too."

Up north, there was still a feeling that the deal would fall through. It was reported in the *Los Angeles Times* that the move "is fraught with so many complications that until the deal is sealed it is hard to believe. Not that San Diego can't support a Pacific Coast League ball club, but leaving Los Angeles with only one team is something the directors won't allow inasmuch as a major slice of the season's receipts comes out of this city."[46] The skepticism was based upon the need to get the three-quarters approval from the PCL directors and the belief that the league needed two teams in Los Angeles. If the Stars did move out of Los Angeles, there was speculation that Sacramento would be a good candidate to move in with Branch Rickey now in charge of that team and his being "smart enough to see the chance of cashing in on this city's reputation as a sports center." The other candidate would be the Missions team from San Francisco, given the fact that there were three teams in that region.

Other doubts about San Diego's chances for success were also being expressed. For one, Charlie Graham, president of the San Francisco Seals ball club, doubted that San Diego could support a team.[47] Angels' President Dave Fleming was quoted as saying: "After all, Hollywood didn't have much of a ball club, and it isn't much of a loss."[48] He continued to assert that he only asked for fair rental on Wrigley Field from Lane and that he felt the Mission team would move to Hollywood.

However, while there was dismay in Los Angeles, things continue to progress in San Diego. The *San Diego Herald* urged community leaders to get behind the transfer. In an editorial on January 23, 1936, it exhorted that "It has been the dream of San Diego ball fans to have a Coast league ball club in San Diego. Now is our chance. Let's make the most of it....Let's all pull together and make this dream come true."

On Monday, January 27, Lane and his club secretary, Charles "Spider" Baum, announced that all negotiations with Wrigley Field officials were dropped.[49] Also in that article, PCL president Tuttle was quoted as being "highly pleased with the location of Sports Field and was certain businessmen and fans will turn out in large numbers..."

Introduction to Spider Baum
San Diego Union, June 28, 1936

---

* Sawtelle is located in west Los Angeles.

3—JANUARY 1936 THE STARS MOVE SOUTH

The *Evening Tribune* and *Union* were even more certain with headlines on January 28 that read:

San Diego Assured Coast League Team,
Lane to sign contract for moving stars[50]

Hollywood Baseball Team Will Move To San Diego;
Lane To Sign Formal Papers Today[51]

Apparently, Lane and Baum were certain, too, as the *Union* article pointed out that they were looking for homes in the area! Beat writer Earl Keller, in that day's *Evening Tribune,* noted that the move was "definite."

The key date arrived: on Tuesday, January 28, 1936, Lane signed an "articles of agreement" to bring the Hollywood club to San Diego. The *Union* featured the signing with a photograph of Lane, Brennan, Baum, and Klicka posing with the caption that read: "City's Dreams Materialize As Ball Pact Signed."[52] The paper noted that it was proposed that as an aid to the team in moving that no rent be charged during the first season, but Lane insisted on paying rent in return for obtaining complete control of the park year around. After meeting with Lane, Mayor Benbough and the city council passed a resolution favoring the building of the site at the foot of Broadway into a "first class" baseball park. The resolution called for plans to be rushed by the manager and Harbor Commission. While things were being finalized in San Diego for Hollywood's move, reports out of Los Angeles seemed to indicate that the Missions would indeed move south.

"Missions To Move South" read the headlines in the January 29 *Times*. Angels president Fleming welcomed the possibility and kept up a minor war of words for Bill Lane wishing him "the best of luck, and it may be that San Diego will prove a better baseball city than we think."[53] Fleming noted that Lane was never entirely satisfied with the arrangement at Wrigley Field, and he (Fleming) was "never satisfied with Lane's attitude as a co-tenant…we granted him so many favors that he came to demand them as rights." As for the Missions moving in, Fleming said he was still planning on only one team playing at Wrigley Field in 1936, but that there would "most certainly" be two clubs in Los Angeles in 1937.

Lane, on the other hand, indicated that he and the Angels have had one disagreement after another since arriving in 1926. "First, it was over the ladies-free policy, then it was over night games, as well as the number of major league exhibition games played at Wrigley Field before the Coast season started."[54]

Despite Fleming's assertions that he would not stand in the way of Lane's franchise move, the *Times* indicated that there would be with their headline: "War Looms Over Lane".[55]

The PCL constitution required a three-fourths vote of the directors for approval of any shift. Lane, on the other hand, essentially defied the league to stop him given the status of agreements with San Diego. The article noted that the league's only recourse if Lane does go ahead without consent would be to sue him. PCL president Tuttle was preparing for a telegraphic vote to seek the views of the other team owners to the proposed transfer. A final tally was expected by Sunday, February 2. The *Times* also dampened hopes of having continuous baseball in Los Angeles. In that same article, it was reported that the Mission Reds would not move because they receive a better share of concessions in San Francisco than they could receive from Fleming and the Angels – a familiar refrain to Bill Lane.

The February 1, 1936, edition of the *San Diego Evening Tribune* proclaimed that Lane was expected to receive the "okay" from the directors of the Coast League clubs. Of course, Lane had already gotten things in motion in San Diego, and so the vote seemed sort of perfunctory. Lane was quoted as saying: "If the other club owners were able to stop me from moving, who'd pay the rent at Wrigley Field?…not me. That's why I'm moving to San Diego, where I have a fair chance to make some money rather than lose it."[56]

The next morning's headlines in the Union shouted the good news good, that is, for San Diego: "Loop Moguls Approve San Diego."[57]

San Diego Union, February 2, 1936

The precise details of what happened on the February 1 were a bit sketchy. PCL owners had, apparently, agreed via a telegraphic poll to allow the move of the Hollywood franchise to San Diego. While three-fourths vote was required, the final tally was reported in the *Union* as being 5-1, not sufficient to meet the requirement. However, the speculation in *The Sporting News* February 6 edition was that there were the necessary six votes and that Seattle, Portland, Sacramento, Oakland, and the Missions voted with Lane.

Feelings were running hot in Los Angeles and the rivalry between the two cities heated up with the transfer. Two fans were quoted in the *Times* on February 5. One fan predicted that when the Angels get through with the San Diego team "they're liable to retreat across the border over into Agua Caliente." The other pundit said that "Unless Lane comes up with a lot better ball club than he has now the Angels will personally see to it that his Dons [sic] never get in the play-off." Ted Steinmann, *Union* sports editor, got into it a little bit too in his February 7 column in which he commented that it was "only logical" for the Los Angeles fans to resent Lane's move. Further, he quoted the Angels' manager as insisting that San Diego won't take a series all season!

WHERE TO PLAY?

All the while that the negotiations to get a team in San Diego were going on, so were efforts to make sure a suitable playing field could be provided by the end of March. As early as November 1934, ideas for using Navy Field for professional baseball were taking shape. On November 1, 1934, Port Director Joe Brennan reported to the Board of Harbor Commissioners that negotiations were underway for the St. Louis Cardinals to start a Class C league in southern California. He reported that the Cardinals would want use of Navy Field. The Commission directed that Brennan "cooperate with Mr. Platner with a view to having the Cardinals here if possible." Nothing happened with such a league being formed, but the seed for a downtown ballpark was planted.

In December 1935, active plans for a ballpark in downtown San Diego began taking shape when the three Los Angeles businessmen were expressing interest in acquiring the Missions team and moving them to San Diego for the 1936 season. However, one of the three, Eddie Farrell was blunt in his assessment of the Sports Field: "I don't like the place. In the first place it hasn't a covered grandstand. People also tell me it is a gathering spot for fog. The seats would be wet at night games. It'll have to be improved a lot."[58]

In a meeting on December 20, 1935, Port Director Brennan met with the group and provided optimism that the park could be ready by March 28, 1936, opening day of the PCL season.[59] All along it was expected that Sports Field, originally called Navy Field (or Army-Navy Field or YMCA Field), at the foot of Broadway was the only readily available alternative for a site. As a central sports facility, it had served baseball, football, motorcycle races, soccer, cricket, and numerous other sports venues.

Brennan was quoted in *The Sun* on the December 21, 1935, as preparing a WPA grant application and the "plans of the Wrigley Field baseball plant in Los Angeles will be sent here immediately." He also noted that there would have to be "considerable" work done on the grounds to make Sports Field satisfactory for Coast

League baseball. Mayor Percy J. Benbough also weighed in with a ringing endorsement, stating, "It will be a wonderful thing for the city from a civic point of view...and will be of inestimable value in publicizing San Diego nationally...I'm strongly in favor of it!"[60]

It was on December 26, 1935, when the Board next met to consider the use of Navy Field for professional baseball. The *San Diego Union* ran the news as a headline in the next day's edition. Platner discussed his proposal to erect a grandstand for Coast League games. The Commission agreed to include his proposal in their application for a WPA grant. Then on December 31, 1935, Platner returned to the Board of Harbor Commission and further discussed changes to Sports Field to accommodate the Mission ball club. Brennan was optimistic about using a WPA grant to offset 80 percent of the cost, or $20,000, with the remaining $5,000 to be raised by the city or harbor department. Tentative plans were displayed for alterations to the field and plans for operations.

San Diego Union, December 21, 1935

The plans at that time called for covered grandstand seating for 5,000. Some of the then existing bleacher seats would be kept and attached to the new seating to provide bleacher seating all down the left and right field foul lines. Total seating capacity was expected to be between 8,000 and 10,000.

In late December, it was too early to estimate costs with any precision, but it was reported that the grandstand could be completed "for about $20,000."[61] The Los Angeles trio also weighed in with regard to the design and indicated that they favored a stand with wooden facing rather than a steel base "in order to avoid the cold found in the average concrete stadium, particularly for night baseball."

While the Sports Field location seemed to be the obvious location for a ballpark site, another site, north of Balboa Park, was proposed in early January 1936. This 450-foot by 450-foot site was located bounded by Madison, Boundary, Meade, and Ohio Streets. While the size did not appear sufficient, the project proponents indicated that they would not be "disinterested in turning over the layout to the Mission Reds of the Pacific Coast League, if that club comes to the city."[62]

Information in a Sunday, January 5 column reporting on the status of pledges, noted that general opinion is that "...Balboa Park, preferably the swimming pool area, is the best site for a proposed ball yard, but that in a pinch Sports field at the foot of Broadway would be O.K. as a temporary park while a new one is being built."[63]

With news on January 21, that agreement had been reached to bring the Hollywood team to San Diego, Joe Brennan had his hands full to get the park ready in slightly over two months. To help out, the team agreed to shift its opening date from March 28 to a later date—which turned out to be March 31.

On Thursday, January 23, Brennan announced plans to remove all stands and materials on the then existing playing field in order to install new sod.[64] Further, he was still awaiting approval of the plans and funding by the WPA. The city council was ready, too, with Councilman Harry Warburton indicating his intent to recommend early action on the city's support.[65] Warburton noted that "a good ballpark would be a decided asset to the city's recreational program under any conditions..." That same day's article quoted PCL President Tuttle as saying that "the San Diego park will be ideally located, within easy walking distance of the business section. All streetcars terminate near the site."

Joe Brennan showed he meant business. By Wednesday, January 29, the baseball diamond was beginning to take shape at Sports Field. The crash wall for motorcycle racing had been torn down, the football goal posts were gone, and bleachers moved and being prepared for their overhaul.[66] By then, the estimate of seating was 7,000, with 5,000 still projected to be part of a covered grandstand. The covered portion of the stands was to be in the southwest corner of the field and run along each of the foul lines just beyond first and third bases. The distance down the lines was planned to be 340 feet from home plate.

Getting a ballpark didn't take too long after the good news on Tuesday, January 21, that San Diego would have a team. Nine days later, in fact, on Thursday, January 30, the Board of Harbor Commissioners approved a resolution endorsing the construction of a park for PCL games. A minor league ballpark for San Diego that will be called...what?

WHO'S TED WILLIAMS?

On August 30, 1918, a baby was born to parents Samuel Williams, a photographer, and May (Venzor) Williams in San Diego, California. At the time the family lived at 933 13th Street in what is today the eastern part of downtown San Diego. The baby was named Theodore Samuel.

By the 1930s, the family had relocated to a home at 4121 Utah Street in the North Park neighborhood of San Diego, northeast of downtown. Sam Williams had a photography shop at 820 5th Avenue and May was working full-time with the Salvation Army.

In January 1933, young Ted started high school at Herbert Hoover—the Hoover Cardinals—a relatively new school. Ted also was playing baseball. As early as 1934, about the time he was turning 16 years old, newspaper accounts of 28 games were found mentioning Williams.[67] These games included high school, American Legion and various local leagues.

Even without a professional team in San Diego, baseball was a very active sport in the community. Because of the year-round climate offered in San Diego, baseball could be played all 12 months of the year—and it was. The three major daily newspapers covered many of the games resulting in a rich body of baseball information from area leagues, but also from semi-pro matches and touring professional teams. As a relatively small city, there was significant local news coverage of high school and youth sports, too. In much of the coverage, box scores were provided.

In 1935, now in his junior year at Hoover, Ted played in 50 games that were covered in the papers, in every month but November. Of the 50, games 23 were with his Hoover High team, and the other 27 on American Legion and teams in the local leagues. In the various game accounts, he was occasionally recognized for his hitting but was primarily a pitcher for the Hoover team. Publicly, Williams was beginning to get noticed, as evidenced by this report in April 1935: "Ted Williams, lanky Cardinal chucker, pitched six-hit ball, fanned 16 batters and pounded out four hits in five trips plateward to grab starring laurels."[68] He ended the 1935 season at Hoover with a batting average of .588, 30 hits in 51 at bats.

Despite being a high school junior, Williams, was already attracting interest of major league baseball scouts that included Herb Benninghoven of the St. Louis Cardinals and "Vinegar" Bill Essick of the New York Yankees.[69,70,71]

As a part-time scout, Benninghoven worked for the San Diego Gas Company. Former major league player, and San Diegan, Ray Boone noted that Benninghoven had a Sunday ball club and a lot of local high school and

Ted Williams (back row, left) and Hoover High School 1934 Baseball Team

St. Louis Nine Offers Williams Tryout

Ted Williams Gets MLB Tryout in 1935
San Diego Union, August 6, 1935

college guys played for him. Williams lived only a few doors from Benninghoven and would frequently hang out there.[72]

Essick was from Illinois and came west in 1904. After pitching for a number of years in the minors, with a short stint in the majors, he became a manager in the Midwest, and then in the PCL with the Vernon club, where he achieved much success. After his managing career, he became a scout for the Yankees in Southern California. He had a hand in the signing of Joe DiMaggio in in 1934.[73]

In 1935, Williams was invited to a St. Louis Cardinals tryout camp held in Fullerton, California—along with several hundred other young players. He reportedly did get an offer from the Cardinals but was reluctant to accept due to his fear of getting lost in their huge farm system the team had at the time.[74]

As the new year arrived, now a 17-year old, Williams was awaiting the start of his senior year with the Hoover Cardinals. Additionally, he remained active playing outfield in the city's winter league for Cramer's Bakery in weekend games from January through early March.

On January 12, playing outfield for the Bakery club, Williams hit a two-run home run in support of Elmer Hill's no-hit, no-run game win against Texas Liquor House.[75] Then, on January 18, Williams was back in the news again, but as a pitcher, logging seven innings in a 6-5 win this time against the St. Louis Blues, a traveling negro leagues team.[76]

CHAPTER 4
FEBRUARY 1936 DEVELOPMENT OF THE ROSTER AND SPRING TRAINING

NOTABLE WORLD EVENTS-FEBRUARY 1936

6th *Adolf Hitler presides over the opening ceremony of the winter Olympics opening ceremony being held in Garmisch-Partenkirchen, Germany*

8th *Jay Berwanger, from the University of Chicago, is the first pick by the Philadelphia Eagles in the first National League Football draft*

12th *California Pacific International Exposition opens for a second year in San Diego's Balboa Park*

It's February 1936 and San Diego had its first class AA professional baseball team. While local efforts were focused on readying a suitable ballpark for baseball, Owner Bill Lane was working on building a team for the 1936 season.

Following the 1935 season, Lane was prepared to do some housecleaning. In November 1935 the Stars completed the sale of Shortstop Bobby Doerr and Second Baseman George Myatt to the Boston Red Sox.[77,78,79]

The *Boston Post* noted, in its November 22, 1935, edition that: "Two Coast Stars Tied Up By Sox." In the *Post*, reporter Malaney opined that the Red Sox "demonstrated they are preparing not only for tomorrow but the day after tomorrow."

The *Los Angeles Times* on November 23 reported that Bobby Doerr and George Myatt had been sold to Boston for $75,000 plus two pitchers. The Sheiks' two "keystone kids" would report to the Sox in 1937. As part of the deal, the Red Sox were to turn over a right-hander and a southpaw to Hollywood for the 1936 season.

> **Doerr and Myatt Sold to Boston for $75,000**
>
> Hollywood to Get Two Hurlers for Young Pair; Jolley Sold to Albany Outfit
>
> BY BOB RAY
>
> Bobby Doerr and George Myatt, the Hollywood Sheiks' keystone kids, were sold yesterday to the Boston Red Sox for a reported price of $75,000.
>
> *Los Angeles Times*, November 23, 1935

Red Sox General Manager Eddie Collins attended the Winter Minor League Meeting that year in Dayton, Ohio, and apparently had one thing in mind, and that was to obtain rights to Doerr and Myatt. It was felt that next to Joe DiMaggio (who was just about to begin his career with the New York Yankees) Bobby Doerr was the best prospect in the minor leagues.[80] Already at ages 17 and 19, respectively, Doerr and Myatt, were reputed to be the "finest keystone combination the Coast had seen since the great duet of Lyn Lary and Jimmie Reese." Collins spoke highly of Doerr's polished fielding ability and believed that Myatt had "brilliant" possibilities because of his speed. Ernie Johnson, scout for the Red Sox, saw the two play in 1935 and had raved about them back to Collins. Bill Lane had promised Collins that the Red Sox would be given the first crack at the two players.

Lane kept his word and Collins handed over a check as down payment, plus gave Lane left-handed pitcher George Hockette. The Red Sox received an option for delivery of the two players for the 1937 season. In return, the Sheiks would receive Hockette and another pitcher for 1936, along with the cash. The remainder of the deal depended upon whether the option was exercised in late 1936 and, if so, transfer of a nominal amount of money would then make the players Boston property.

Also in November 1935 the Stars sold outfielder Smead Jolley to Albany of the International League, and traded infielder Jim Levey to Tulsa of the Texas League for Third Baseman Ernie Holman in hopes that they would pick up some slugging ability.[81] Jolley had a good offensive year for the Sheiks, batting .372 in 1935, but was a notoriously bad fielder and slow afoot, the joke being that he would kick in more runs than he would bat in!

Coming back from the minor league convention in Dayton, Spider Baum, Stars' vice president and secretary, reported that the team would "probably" also get pitcher Manuel "Manny" Salvo from the Red Sox as part payment for the Doerr-Myatt transaction.

Continuing through mid-January 1936, Bill Lane was still intent on rebuilding the Sheiks in order to give Hollywood fans a winner. In an article by Bob Ray, there were reports that he was trying to land first baseman Babe Dahlgren from the Red Sox, who lost his starting position when the Sox purchased Jimmy Foxx.[82] For first base, the Stars also had George McDonald, only 18 at the time and was believed to need more seasoning. Ray Jacobs was reportedly on the block to be sold or released. Outfielders Cedric Durst and Vince DiMaggio were expected to return, but Lane wanted two more outfielders and the Red Sox apparently had made promises to help. Vance Wirthman—a "youngster"—was expected to be farmed out. At catcher, Jimmy Kerr and Gene Desautels were viewed as adequate at the position, and Johnny Bassler from the 1935 club would be released.

As for pitching, it was reported that George Hockette and three other pitchers were to be sent to the Stars from the Red Sox. Pitchers returning from the 1935 club included Ed Wells, Wally Hebert, Archie Campbell,

THE SPORTING NEWS

MINORS WORTH WATCHING

ROBERT DOERR, Hollywood   **GEORGE MYATT, Hollywood**
JAMES J. GLEESON, New Orleans

The Sporting News, June 20, 1936

Berly "Trader" Horne, and the manager, Frank Shellenback. Ray's article concluded: "It appears the local clientele will have a lot of new faces and two good ball clubs to look at this year at Wrigley Field."

Two good clubs might be playing perhaps—but not in Wrigley Field in 1936!

CONTRACTS IN THE MAIL

The *Los Angeles Times* reported on February 6 that the Dons* had signed Frank Shellenback to a 1936 contract for a second season as playing-manager for the team. In addition, contracts for the 1936 season were placed in the mail to 24 players:[83]

Joe Berkowitz, util	Larry Gillick, P	George McDonald, 1B
Archie Campbell, P	Wallace Hebert, P	George Myatt, SS
Ritchie Cooper, inf	Jack Hile, P	Eddie Mulligan, util
Gene Desautels, C	George Hockett, P	Herman Pillette, P
Vince DiMaggio, OF	Ernie Holman, 3B	Elmer Stock, C
Robert Doerr, 2B	Berlye Horne, P	Fred Vaughn, inf
Cedric Durst, OF	Ray Jacobs, 1B	Edwin Wells, P
Bill England, OF	James Kerr, C	Vance Wirthman, OF

---

* The reporters were having a difficult time deciding what to call the team. The "Dons" seemingly was the favorite of some of the writers.

By February 13, nine players had signed contracts and club secretary Spider Baum was quoted as saying he expected "little trouble" bringing the remaining players into the fold.[84]

George Myatt (also referred to as Glen by local reporters still trying to become familiar with the new Padres) was still unsigned and apparently the only holdout as the team started camp. Reports were that he received $125 per month in 1935 and was seeking more than $175 for 1936. He had felt that he had a good year batting .311 and the Red Sox had thought enough of his ability to take an option on him. Of course, Lane was famous for being "thrifty" and a request like this must have been upsetting to him.

Years later, here was Myatt's version of the events that led to his eventual signing with the 1936 Padres: "I made $125 a month in '35. Mr. Lane sent me a contract for $200 a month in '36. I held out for $275. 'Spider' Baum, the secretary, talked me into signing a dollar contract for spring training. He said if I wasn't in camp, Mr. Lane would fine me. So I did, had a good camp, and when we went to San Diego to start the season, opening day I had to sign my contract. Mr. Lane was very rough, giving me hell. I got mad and told him I had to have $325. He really raved and said I was robbing him—but he wrote the contract."[85] On February 26 he inked a contract for a raise that was not revealed publicly that Myatt later claimed was for $325 a month.

Nevertheless, Myatt was quoted as saying, "I took a low salary last year to get a chance to make good. I batted .311 and the Red Sox thought enough of my ability to take an option on me. If I can't get more than $175 for being a regular shortstop on a Class AA club, I might as well get an all-year job and give up baseball."[86]

NAMING THE TEAM—THE SAN DIEGO DONS!? TARS!? GAELS!? GOBS!? FLYERS!?

In the *San Diego Sun* article dated January 28 it was reported that a contest was about to begin to name the new team. The next day, the *Sun* ran the following headline: "Lane, Sun Invite Public To Nickname Club; Renovation Of Diamond Under Way; Formal Name To Be San Diego Club But Bill Asks Familiar Handle".

Lane indicated that the team will be known as the San Diego club but is "anxious for a familiar moniker to replace the 'Stars' and 'Sheiks,' their old nicknames."[87] The article noted that a prize would be awarded "the nature of which will be announced later!"

Your Choice?

Get in the contest for picking a new nickname for the Hollywood baseball team which will move to San Diego. Owner Bill Lane invites everyone to vote. Clip this and mail to The *San Diego Sun* Sports Department, 7th and B Streets.

MY CHOICE..............................
My Name................................
Address..................................
Phone....................................

Contest for Readers to Pick a Team Nickname
San Diego Sun, January 29, 1936

4—FEBRUARY 1936 DEVELOPMENT OF THE ROSTER AND SPRING TRAINING

By February 5 the *Union* joined in and invited fans to send in their suggestions for names by February 15. They offered some guidelines: "It should be short enough to fit in newspaper headlines…(and)…also identify the team with San Diego."

In a February 6 *Union* article names were starting to come in: [88]

Dons	Gobs	Flyers	Twirlers
Aviators	Giants	Blues	

The article reported that Dons and Flyers were the leading early contenders. A few days later it was reported that nine out of every 10 fans responding favored the name "Dons."[89]

More suggestions kept on coming in: [90]

Gulls	Admirals	Blue Jays	Eagles
Aces	Bears	Expos	Navarines

Lane started out by implying that he would go with the most popular choice. However, he also announced that a committee would be used to aid him comprising the sports editors of the three local newspapers.[91] The same article reported that it appeared that it was going to be a "cinch" that the team would be named the "Dons" because it far outnumbered any other option. Even the San Diego County Baseball Managers' Association favored the "Dons."[92]

More names continued to come in:

| Gorillas | Tarzans | Tunas | Pointers | Vaqueros | Balboas |

For the first time, the name "Padres" showed up in the list printed on February 10th but the article said that now the "Tars" is also running in the forefront along with the "Dons": [93]

| Padres | Stars | Tars | Destroyers | Lomans | Billy Boats |

The local fans were not through—on February 11 more names poured in: [94]

Gaels	Friars	Sandies	Cli-mates	Tourists	So'westers
Internationals	Mariners	Pilots	Skippers	Cougars	Comet Stars

Union Sports Editor Steinmann noted in his column of February 12 that the "Dons" was still favored but that "it might cause some confusion to have a ball club use the same moniker" as does the University of San Francisco. He also noted that the final choice for the name would be up to Bill Lane, clarifying any confusion that might have existed with regard to how the decision was going to be made. Reports on the 14th indicated that "Contrary to previous predictions, the Dons haven't got it. A week ago it looked like the Dons was the most popular nickname. That was a week ago, however, for the Padres, Gaels, and Flyers now hold the lead, with the Gobs getting a great deal of play."[95]

Finally, in its Tuesday, February 18 edition, the *Union* reported that Lane would make a decision at a meeting of "newspapermen" later in the week.[96] The article noted that being included in the meeting would be new PCL President W. C. Tuttle. On that same day, it was leaked that the "Dons" was selected.

However, the next day, the *Union* quoted Lane as saying that the name had not yet been selected and will be announced at the dinner with Tuttle on Thursday evening February 20.[97] The earlier publication of a name was "unauthorized" according to Lane. On the morning of the 20th the *Union* reported that "as far as possible the judges are to be guided by the votes of the fans but Lane let it be known yesterday that names already used by teams or colleges will be avoided if possible in order to avoid conflict."[98]

The *San Diego Union* headlines pronounced the decision about a team nickname—and a ballpark name—reached on the evening of February 21, 1936:

'PADRES' Picked As Name of San Diego Club, Baseball Park Will Be

Known As Lane Field[99]

The "Gaels" actually was ahead in the vote but St. Mary's University (in the Bay Area) was already using that name. Similarly, and as expected, the "Dons" was discarded as a nickname. So, the "Padres" was selected, on the one hand, because of the conflicts with the two Bay Area colleges, and on the positive side, since the name was "closely identified with the pioneering in this area and would fit in well with the pioneering being done here by Lane."[100] The name of the team and the ballpark were decided upon at a banquet on February 20 and was attended by Tuttle and Lane. There were other league dignitaries in attendance as well and included Harry A. Williams, league director of publicity, and Frank Herman, secretary for the league.[101] Speaking on behalf of the name "Padres" was Howard Morin of the Chamber of commerce who pointed out that it was properly fitting because of its historical association.[102] At the same meeting, Emil Klicka, of the Harbor Commission, made the motion for calling the new park "Lane Field."

The lucky fan who won the team name contest was R. F. Smith who lived at 3755 Front Street in San Diego. Smith was one of eight who had submitted the winning name of the "Padres" and his name was pulled out of the hat to receive a season pass.[103] It was reported that Smith had some baseball in his background as a catcher and reportedly helped major leaguer Ray Schalk among others.[104]

SPRING TRAINING BEGINS IN FULLERTON

The spring training location for the Hollywood team had been in San Diego in 1930-32 but moved to Fullerton in 1933 due to San Diego's Sports Field being used for motorsports events. Because of ongoing construction of the new stands at Sports Field, Lane announced that the team would again train in Fullerton.[105]

The "advance guard" of the San Diego club was described as moving into Fullerton's Erle Hotel on February 18.[106] At the time, the hotel advertised "A home for a day or always" and daily rates of "$1 up."[107] It was located at 115 West Commonwealth Avenue and less than two blocks walk from the club's training facilities at Commonwealth Park.[108] Spring training activities caused a minor disruption to the local Fullerton Firemen winter team which was to be disbanded at the same time.[109]

The five-week training period began on Sunday, February 23, with pitchers and catchers reporting that day. Also in attendance was League President Tuttle, a supporter of the team's transfer to San Diego, who indicated that he "could see nothing but improvement in the move."[110]

"Padres Knuckle Down to Hard Training" read the sports section headline on February 25 in the *Union*. On Monday, February 24, the new San Diego Padres – in Hollywood uniforms (the new ones were being "saved" for the regular season!) -- took the field in Fullerton to begin their initial PCL season. Not all of the players under contract reported that first day.

However, some new recruits – "all said to be brilliant sandlot performers" -- were brought in for tryouts: Elmer Stock, Berkely McDonald,* Al Pignataro, and Joe Monahan.[111] Also joining them were M. K. Jackson, Gene "Bud" Tuttle (PCL President W. C. Tuttle's son), Ed [sic] Vickers from Michigan (son of a famous Coast league chucker of former days), Eddie Ehil from Missouri, Kenneth Iverson from Seattle, Fred Vaughn from Coalinga, Elmer Stock, Richie [sic] Cooper from Van Nuys, and Bill England [sic].[112,113] Five prospective players

---

* Or, was his first name Burt? Or was he Bruce? Subsequent articles had his name as Bruce. Numerous instances of wrong names were noticed in articles from early 1936 as the San Diego sports writers had to become familiar with having a new baseball team in town.

were signed on Boston Red Sox contracts by Ernie Johnson: Harl Maggert, Jr., Ken Storms, Stan Steely, Hub Kittle and Larry Gillick.[114]

As the second day of spring training arrived another new player, John Bladell [sic], showed up, a hurler from the Brooklyn Dodgers organization.[115] Also, the article reported that Ashley Joerndt signed a contract. Joerndt was from San Diego and led the Nebraska State League in hitting in 1935. Two more new players showed up on February 26, Leslie "Red" Williams, a left-handed first baseman/outfielder, and Winfred Pepper, a catcher from Fullerton.[116]

Intra-squad spring training games for the Padres began on February 27 with the veterans being on a team called the "Oranges" and the rookies on the "Lemons." Ash Joerndt had two singles in three at bats in the six-inning game, while Joe Berkowitz was 3-for-3, including a double. Of the pitchers, the one the impressed most was tall right-hander Scaroli. There was one less player at the end of the game when Bruce McDonald, "Yannigan infielder from Wyoming, packed his bags and went home."[117] The Oranges won this first tilt 9-1.

The next day the Lemons won, 8-6. Bud Tuttle pitched three innings of shutout ball but Jack Hile absorbed two straight innings with the Lemons batting around and scoring eight runs. Red Williams and Bobby Doerr hit spring training's first home runs. Future Hall of Famer Sam Crawford umpired the game.

The third intra-squad game on February 29 had the Oranges winning, 5-3. Larry Gillick went four innings for the Oranges and gave up 10 hits but allowed only three runs. Ernie Holman had a home run for the Orange team. George Harris, a local boy from El Centro, pitched two innings for the Lemons and did not allow a hit. Williams had his second home run in as many days, with runners aboard. And, "Myatt and Doerr, as often is their habit, shared the limelight, Myatt with his sweet recoveries and rifle-like tosses to First-Sacker George McDonald, Doerr with several nifty catches, which helped in a double play."[118]

BUILDING THE BALLPARK (...IN TWO MONTHS!?)

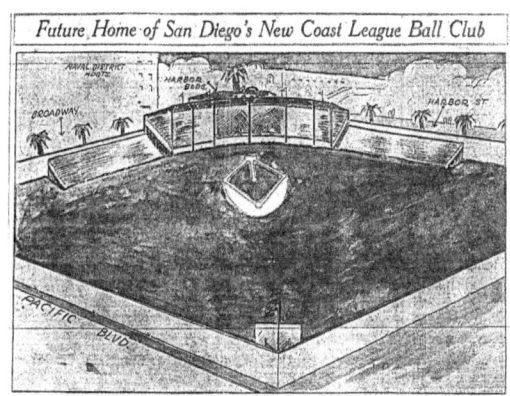

Artist Rendering of Future Lane Field
San Diego Union, February 2, 1936

Reports on February 2 had seating capacity projected to be 11,000.[119] In the same newspaper, another article had the figure was back to 8,000, with 5,000 still being in grandstand seats.[120] A crude sketch of the new ballpark, to be "modern in every detail," was included with the article and was depicted in the *San Diego Union*. The article confirmed the 340-foot distance down the foul lines, and 480 feet to center. The new grandstand would be made of wood and a roof that would be designed so that a "fan sitting in the deepest spot up under the eaves can see the highest of flies and pop fouls." Lights were also included in order to allow for night games. To help local designers, Lane and Baum took one of the Harbor Department engineers to Wrigley Field in Los Angeles to point out improvements that could be copied "to further make the local park attractive to local fans."[121]

By mid-February work on getting a ballpark ready was proceeding even during rains. As February 14 arrived, concrete forms for the grandstand were in place and the infield had been sodded and rolled.[122] And... soon "local fans who travel down to the foot of Broadway park will be able to get a pretty fair idea of what the new layout will look like..."

In the meantime, at the newly named Lane Field, work kept progressing, and as proof, the *San Diego Union* published a photo on February 23 showing that "Lane Field Layout Begins to Take Definite Form as Workmen Rush Construction."[123] The photo showed the grandstand beginning to take shape and stakes in the playing field denoting areas to still be graded. At the same time, players began to be a little concerned about the size of the park, what reputedly would be the biggest in the league, especially after playing in the "crackerbox" Wrigley Field before.[124]

The Board of Harbor Commissioners reviewed the terms of a lease on February 27, 1936, and agreed to lease Sports Field to William Lane and officially change the name to "Lane Field."

WHERE'S "THE KID"?

During the hectic campaign of late December 1935 and early January 1936, when the community was anxiously trying to encourage a team to locate in San Diego, one of the locals voicing an enthusiastic opinion was Wofford Caldwell. Caldwell was Ted Williams' baseball coach at Hoover High School. He was reported to believe that they would have close to 100 boys annually turn out for baseball and be regular supporters of a Coast League team. He was quoted as saying, "There are always a number of young fellows on our teams who hope to make baseball their profession, and the presence of a professional team here in town would give them more incentive."[125]

How prophetic! Ted Williams, a player for Caldwell in 1934, 1935 and, now, in 1936, was one of his players with such hopes. Who knows what might have happened to Williams if the Stars did not move to San Diego in 1936? Looking back, Williams later remembered: "Before the Padres came to town, I didn't have any ambition to play up the coast for the L. A. Angels or for a big league team. My only real concern was just becoming a good hitter. The big leagues were in the next world years ago. It was just the playgrounds. I grew up right by the water tower on Utah Street."[126]

As Caldwell's Cardinals prepared for the new season with eight lettermen returning—including "lanky pitcher Ted Williams"[127]—they had high hopes for a banner season. Training started on February 24 and their first game was scheduled as a March 7 match against Hoover's alumni all-stars. This game was expected to present Hoover with one of their toughest opponents given that many of the alum players were active playing semi-pro or professional baseball.

Ted Williams, Hoover High School, 1936

4—FEBRUARY 1936 DEVELOPMENT OF THE ROSTER AND SPRING TRAINING

Ted Williams (tall player, back row, center-left) and Hoover High School 1936 Baseball Team

SAN DIEGO'S FIRST PADRES and "THE KID"

CHAPTER 5
MARCH 1936
LONGSHOT PADRES
BEGIN MAIDEN SEASON

NOTABLE WORLD EVENTS—MARCH 1936

5th   The Oscar for Best Picture goes to Mutiny on the Bounty

7th   German forces violate the Treaty of Versailles and enter the Rhineland

9th-21st   Record floods hit New England and the east coast of the U.S. resulting in 150-200 lives lost

DEVELOPMENT OF THE TEAM'S ROSTER—SPRING TRAINING CONCLUDES

On Sunday, March 1, the new Padres played a semi-pro team from Fullerton and won 9-6. Red Williams led hitters with a single and a double in three at bats. Fred Vaughn had a home run plus two singles in five at bats. Horne struck out six in three innings. Three pitchers got their release: Allan Whitlock, Eddie Ehil, and M. K. Jackson.[128] Outfielder Vance Wirthman, a holdout, finally joined the club on March 2. Another pitcher that Shellenback was reportedly taking a hard look at in camp was Johnny Donovan. Early reports out of camp were that George McDonald continued to shine around first base but lacks hitting punch. Also, that, Ash Joerndt and Richie Cooper "are getting the most attention."[129]

At the start of week two, it was made clear by Manager Shellenback that spring training would be "all business." The training grind was reportedly much different from 1935 when training was delayed due to movie production. Weather had postponed the filming of the movie called "Alibi Ike," and starring Joe E. Brown...with Frank Shellenback being a technical director for the film. A prior agreement allowed the actor and film crew to have possession of the park for filming and so, while not planned in advance, the players became "extras" for the movie.[130] The players did not suffer too much as they were able to pick up extra movie money. However, the players' attitudes in March 1936 suggested that most were relieved to not have to face the flurry and worry of picture-making which prevailed in 1935.[131]

The Lemons took on the Oranges again on March 3 and shut them down, 5-0. All of the runs were scored in the 1st inning when Richie Cooper, "sawed-off"[132] shortstop, led things off against Horne with a home run. Wally Hebert pitched well for the Lemons, facing only 10 men over the three innings he worked. Cooper ended the day by going 3-for-3.

In early March there were still reports that Lane was hoping to pick up some more players. Rudy York was key on Lane's list but was making a fine impression with the Detroit Tigers.[133] Lane was hopeful of landing York and giving San Diego a "million dollar infield." Speculation in the article was that Lane was also looking for an outfielder from the Red Sox. Ash Joerndt, again this time in *The Sporting News*, was noted for having a fine spring.

By March 5 the *Union* cited the following "youngsters" showing the most promise to date: Red Williams, Bill England, Ken Storms, Joe Monahan, Richie Cooper, Fred Vaughn, Kenny Iverson, George Harris, "Bud" Tuttle, and Ashley Joerndt.[134]

The Oranges took the March 5 game by a score of 4-3. Playing manager Frank Shellenback worked three innings and gave up only two hits. Doerr had his second home run of the spring, and Vince DiMaggio got his first hit of the spring.

The Orange team made it two in a row on March 6 by winning, 9-4. George Myatt hit a home run, his first of the spring. George McDonald and Joe Berkowitz each had three hits. Players in the lineup that were unknowns in any coverage to date were Storms, a left fielder who went 1-for-2 for the Lemons, and Elmer Stock, a catcher who also went 1-for-2 for the Lemons.

On March 7 the Padres took on Lehr's Service of Anaheim and won, 15-10. George Harris went the distance giving up 12 hits. Joerndt and Fred Vaughn led the Padres, each with three hits. Red Williams again was in the middle of the by scoring going 2-for-4 with a grand slam home run.

The next day the Padres took on the Brea Merchants and won, 6-5. Pitching for the Padres were Bud Tuttle and Don Elton and they held the opponents to seven hits. This time Vaughn had a home run and Joe Monahan went 3-for-4. Shellenback continued trying out "rookies" with this line up:

Cooper	SS
Berkowitz	2B
"Red" Williams	RF
Joerndt	CF
Vaughn	3B
Wirthman	LF
Monahan	1B
Stock	CF
Tuttle	P

5—MARCH 1936 LONGSHOT PADRES BEGIN MAIDEN SEASON

Oh boy! The headlines said it all:

Manager Shellenback Puts Padres Through Long Base Sliding Drill[135]

Everyone except the pitchers was put through this lengthy sliding drill on March 9, along with a lengthy batting practice. Also, this date three more players were cut: George Harris, Storms, and England. So far, the team's batting leaders resulting from the spring training games were:

Stock	.571	(4-for-7)
Monahan	.519	(14-for-27)
Wirthman	.500	
Desautels	.417	
Vaughn	.387	
Kerr	.367	
Cooper	.367	
Holman	.357	

The Oranges and Lemons kept up their series on March 10. Herman "Hec" Carroll was brought in from the USS Tennessee to pitch for the Lemons and limited the Orange team to two runs and seven hits over seven innings as the Lemons won, 4-2. Ernie Holman accounted for one of the runs with a home run. Center fielder Harl (also referred to as Carl in some articles) Maggert, in camp "getting in condition to report to the Boston Red Sox,"[136] also homered for the Lemons. Bobby Doerr and Ernie Holman had two hits apiece for the losers.

The two teams played to a 1-1, six-inning tie on March 11. Wally Hebert and George Hockette went the distance for the Oranges and Lemons, respectively. Doerr drove in the one run for the Oranges with a single and Maggert homered for the Lemons' one tally.

The Lemons took the next day's game, 8-1, with Horne limiting the Orange team to one hit by Ray Jacobs. Maggert and Wirthman both had home runs for the Lemon team.

The Padres defeated the Mexico City Aztecas, 5-1, on March 14. Herman Pillette and Hebert limited the Aztecas to four hits. George Myatt went 3-for-3 with two bunt hits and a double. Ray Jacobs clubbed a two-run home run.[137]

The next day the Padres again played the Aztecas and posted a 14-1 win behind Hec Carroll, "prized hurling find of the spring season" and George Hockette.[138] Carroll pitched five innings of no-hit, no-run ball. Vince DiMaggio had a home run and went 2-for-5 and George McDonald and Ced Durst both had three hits apiece.

Manager Shellenback made some more roster moves on March 16 as Larry Gillick and Elmer Stock were released. Max Bryan a recruit from Long Beach was added to the roster at the same time. Shellenback and Lane both were adamant that they would not build the team around local San Diegans or the Navy.

For the game on March 17, the Orange renamed themselves the "Dutch" and the Lemon was the "Irish" in a St. Patrick's Day intra-squad match. The Dutch were the regulars and led by Bud Tuttle who pitched the complete six innings allowing two runs and five hits. It was said that Tuttle "gives the appearance of having less on the ball than any of the pitchers in camp, but his record to date gives lie to that appearance. Bud pitches largely to spots, never giving the batter a good ball to hit and has proved a mighty tough hurler to beat in practice games."[139] The line up in the March 18 *Union* added "O's" and "Mc's" to the Irish team's names. Gene Desautels went 2-for-3 for the Dutch team. Both of the Irish tallies came in on a double by an Irishman: Eddie Mulligan.

As the season was approaching Shellenback was firming up his starting lineup which looked similar to what he finished with during the 1935 season:

George Myatt	SS
Bobby Doerr	2B
Cedric Durst	CF
Ernie Holman	3B
Ray Jacobs	1B
Vince DiMaggio	RF
Ashley Joerndt	LF
Gene Desautels	C

The primary pitchers were: Ed Wells, Herman Pillette, Berly Horne, Archie Campbell, Wally Hebert, and George Hockette.[140]

Shellenback was also quoted as being concerned about the loss of Smead Jolley over the offseason. He offered hope that Ash Joerndt might be able to solve the "Jolley vacancy." Shellenback said, "He's probably better at hawking flies because Jolley would bat in about three runs then give the opposition five on balls that he missed." He also spoke highly of Fred Vaughn, Hec Carroll, and Len Iverson. About the latter he said "he's a left hander, but not a bit goofy."

In the meantime, Vance Wirthman took over the team's batting lead at .533 (8-for-15), followed by Joe Monahan (.429, 15-for-35), Harl Maggert (.417, 5-for-12, plus three home runs), Fred Vaughn (.381, 16-for-42).

The Orange team won again on Wednesday, March 18, 8-7. Vaughn went 4-for-4 for the Lemons with a home run. For the Oranges, McDonald was 3-for-4. Holman also homered for the Orange team and went 2-for-4.

Harl Maggert continued his slugging in the March 19 intra-squad game with his fourth and fifth home runs of the spring. He batted in all three runs in the Lemons 3-1 victory over the Orange team. His last home run being the game-winner with the score tied at 1-1. Fred Vaughn continued his hot hitting, going 2-for-3 and running his streak of hits to 10 in his last 12 at bats. Ernie Holman had two hits for the Oranges.

With about two weeks to go before opening day, several rookies were being touted as possibly staying with the Padres: Joerndt, Cooper, Monahan, and Vaughn.[141] However, Manager Shellenback was still awaiting three players from the Red Sox, an outfielder, a first baseman, and a pitcher.[142] He especially was hopeful of getting fourth and fifth place batters for the lineup.

The Padres beat the Brea Merchants on March 21, 4-0, behind the three-hit pitching of Kenny Iverson. Jacobs drove in all four runs with a home run and a double. George Myatt "turned in a brilliant game at shortstop" with eight putouts and three assists.[143]

Finally, on Sunday, March 22, the Padres played some Coast League competition going up against the Seattle Indians in Fullerton. A single by Vince DiMaggio with two out drove in the winning run in the bottom of the ninth as the Padres won, 3-2. A combination of Pillette, Hebert, and Horne held the Indians to five hits. Another key hit came off the bat of Maggert in the eighth with the bases loaded. He pinch hit and "walloped a cannonball" to the shortstop who could not make the play in time to save the run.[144] After the game Manager Shellenback announced that catcher Max Bryan had been released.

As the final week of spring training wore on, Manager Shellenback was still hoping to hear from the Boston Red Sox. He had asked for an outfielder, a pitcher, and a first baseman. Another plan in the offing was to form a "school" for the Padres at Phoenix in the Arizona State League where rookies would get some experience.[145]

5—MARCH 1936 LONGSHOT PADRES BEGIN MAIDEN SEASON

Later during the week there were reports that the Boston Red Sox would send three of their best replacements to the Padres, two pitchers and an outfielder.[146] These players supposedly would be part of the earlier deal for Doerr and Myatt.

The tentative starting lineup was announced by Manager Shellenback on March 25:

George Myatt	SS
Cedric Durst	CF
Bobby Doerr	2B
Ernie Holman	3B
Vince DiMaggio	RF
George McDonald	1B
Van Wirthman	LF
Gene Desautels	C
Wally Hebert	P

That same day the Padres played a team traveling from Japan, the future Tokyo Giants, losing to them 4-1. Joe Berkowitz went 3-for-4, with a double, and knocked in the only run for the Padres. Hile pitched eight innings and gave up all four runs in the loss.

In the March 26 edition of the *Sun* another roster loss was reported, this time due to the federal government which would not give a discharge to Hec Carroll. Manager Shellenback reportedly had offered a contract to Carroll if the pitcher could secure his discharge from the Navy.[147] It was also reported that Harl Maggert and Don Elton had been sent down to the Rocky Mount club in the Piedmont League.[148]

As opening day approached, help from the Red Sox was still expected. However, neither Lane nor Baum had heard a word from the big-league club. Faced with this uncertainty, the club was expected to keep a few rookies around: Fred Vaughn, Ritchie Cooper, Joe Monahan and Max Bryan.[149] Shellenback also reported some changes to his opening-day lineup, with George McDonald replacing veteran Ray Jacobs and Ed Wells pitching instead of Wally Hebert.[150]

The next day's paper—on Opening Day, March 28—confirmed that help was not on the way from the Red Sox:

Help From Red Sox Now Doubtful for San Diego, Cronin's Club Unable To Send Players To Padres, But Lane's Team Ready For Opener[151]

Eventually, however, Lane and Billy Evans of the Red Sox negotiated a favorable working agreement that would have pitcher Manny Salvo coming to the Padres.[152]

WHAT ABOUT A TEAM MASCOT?

The March 15 *Union* indicated that the "Padres Plan to Select Mascot."

Lane had a uniform all ready for a boy between the ages nine to 12. Any boy interested in the job just had to answer 11 questions and supply a letter in 100 words or less telling how the Padres will benefit San Diego. To aid youngsters, the answers would be supplied in the classified sections of the paper. Here were the questions:

Who are the San Diego Padres?
In what League are the San Diego Padres?
What is the name of the San Diego Padres baseball park?
Where is the baseball park located?
Who is the owner of the San Diego Padres?
Who is the manager of the San Diego Padres?

Name the teams in the Pacific Coast League?
Who is president of the Pacific Coast League?
When is the first home game of the San Diego Padres?
What class baseball is played in the Pacific Coast League?
Who is "Spider" Baum?[153]

On March 24, nine-year old Ralph Thompson was selected as "official" Padres team mascot. Ralph was the son of Mr. and Mrs. J. V. Thompson of 4587 Terrace Drive. According to newspaper accounts, his answers were correct "to the minute" and his letter straightforward and completed in a "neat manner."[154]

Thompson's letter was addressed to Mr. H. W. Lane and read as follows:

Dear Sirs:

It is my desire and my Daddy's wish that I become a great ball player. I think my being mascot for the padres will be very beneficial to my base ball training.

Please return my pictures.

Allen Ralph Thompson

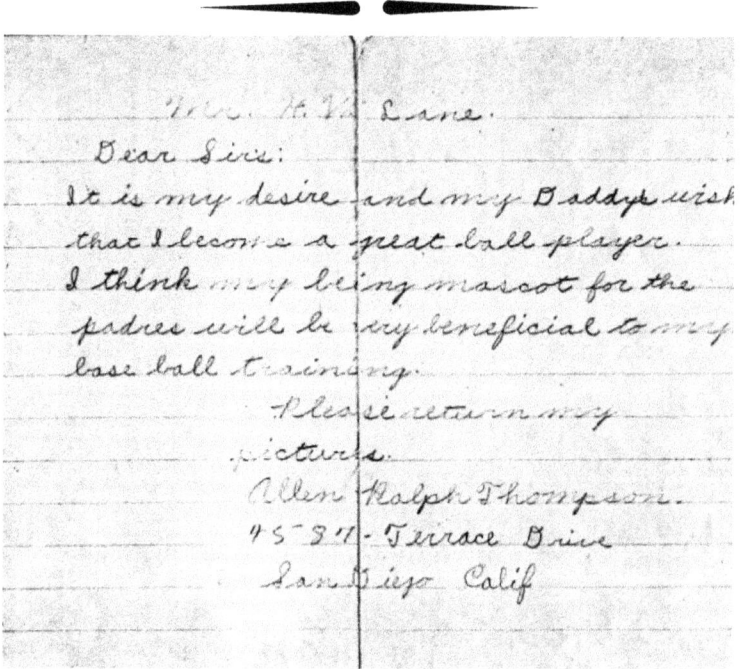

Letter from Ralph Thompson in March 1936

Mascot Ralph Thompson
San Diego Union,
March 28, 1936

There was quite a bit of fanfare surrounding Thompson, as he made news in all the dailies being dressed and ready for the home opener. Thompson was a third-grade student at Benjamin Franklin School.

His first appearance in uniform would be on Opening Day in San Diego. He would wear uniform number 55. In 1936, as mascot, his job was "to take the bats back to the rack, to take the pitcher's coat when he goes to bat and take it back to him when he gets to first base. And you have to root for the team, too, and give the players all your support."[155] In a 2001 interview (contained in Chapter 14) Thompson admitted that he believed the mascot's job to be a "terrific one."[156]

5—MARCH 1936 LONGSHOT PADRES BEGIN MAIDEN SEASON

SATURDAY, MARCH 28, 1936—OPENING DAY IN LOS ANGELES

The Padres would have their first game where they had played home games since the 1926 season…Wrigley Field in Los Angeles. And they expected to do what they did most often…lose. Listed as 7-5 favorites to take the flag, the Los Angeles Angels had to be excited about taking on their old roommates, who were listed at 100-1 longshots to take the PCL crown.[157] Despite the long odds, the *San Diego Evening Tribune's* Earl Keller picked the Padres to finish in the first division, fourth overall. As for pending roster moves, it was reported that Al Pignataro and Dennis Crabb were given their release before the game.

1936 San Diego Padres (Opening Day)
Back row, left to right: James Kerr, George Hockette, George McDonald, Ray Jacobs, Cedric Durst, Fred Vaughn, Eddie Mulligan, George Myatt, Wally Hebert, Gene (Bud) Tuttle, Ernie Holman; *Middle row:* Ed Wells, Bobby Doerr, Gene Desautels, Vince DiMaggio, Bill Lane (owner), Frank Shellenback (manager), Herm Pillette, Ashley Joerndt, Archie Campbell; *Front row:* Vance Wirthman, Jack Hile, Ken Iverson, Berlyn Horne, (unidentified, in Hollywood uniform), Joe Berkowitz

Interestingly, despite the proximity to Los Angeles, the *San Diego Evening Tribune* did not send a reporter north and instead covered the story via the wire services. The *San Diego Union* was not as frugal for this opening series. Los Angeles Mayor Frank Shaw threw out the first pitch of the game. The Padres Opening Day lineup was as reported earlier except Jacobs played first base rather than George McDonald.

The game started promisingly for the Padres scoring two runs in their premier inning off of LA's Fay Thomas. George Myatt led off the game with the first Padres hit, a single, and subsequently scored on a Ray Jacobs' single. Leading off for the Angels was Jigger Statz, the centerfielder for the Angels. He took the first pitch ever thrown from a Padres pitcher, starter Ed Wells.[158] Statz was in the middle of his legendary PCL career at age 38. By the time he hung up his glove after the 1942 season, he would have 3,356 hits in the PCL—all with the Angels. The Angels finished the home half of the first inning with two runs of their own to knot the score, 2-2.

Fay Thomas, who was making a return to the Angels after having pitched for the St. Louis Browns in 1935, held the Padres at bay and was leading, 4-2, going in to the seventh inning. He was able to retire Holman for the first out but the next batter, Jacobs, hit a line drive back toward the mound that hit Thomas's pitching hand…he managed to pick it up and get the out but had to retire from the game. John Campbell came in and retired the side but not until after giving up hits to DiMaggio and Myatt, making the score 4-3 in favor of the Angels.

The Padres starter, Ed Wells, ran into troubles in the bottom of the seventh, walking in a run to give the Angels a 5-3 lead. With two out Berlyn Horne came in and walked in another run before getting the side out, and now the Padres were down, 6-3. The Padres managed to come back with two more runs in the top of the eighth inning on two-run RBI by Jacobs, making it a 6-5 game. Helped by an error in left field by Ash Joerndt, the Angels scored one more run in the bottom of the eighth and held on to win the game, 7-5.

1936 San Diego Padres
Home Uniform
Source: Brandes and Swank, *The Pacific Coast Padres, 1936-1946*

Box Score of Padres' First Game,
March 28, 1936
The Sporting News, April 2, 1936

The matchup, although favoring the home club Angels, did not draw well with fewer than 10,000 fans paying for the privilege of seeing their team defeat Wells and the Padres.

If the first Padres loss failed to draw, the first Padres win was even less attractive to Los Angeles fans. Less than 5,000 people attended the second game of the series, part of a Sunday doubleheader. For San Diego the game was a success with Wally Hebert picking up the club's first win, 9-2, with a five-hitter. Centerfielder Cedric Durst was the hero making a spectacular grab colliding with the wall but hanging onto the ball.

Game two did not go as well with the Padres, losing, 9-6, in a seven-inning game. The Angels scored six runs in the decisive sixth inning after the Padres had scored three in the top half to take a short-lived lead, 6-3. Archie Campbell took the loss in relief of George Hockette who started the game and went 5⅓ innings, allowing three runs. He gave up two singles and was removed by manager Shellenback in favor of Campbell. Campbell faced three batters gave up a single and two walks, forcing in two runs, making the score, 6-5, in favor of the Padres. Shellenback went back to the bullpen and brought in Horne whom promptly allowed a single and double resulting in four more runs, and a final score of Angels 9, Padres 6.

The Padres left Los Angeles with a record of 1-2 and were about to face their inaugural home crowd.

Opening Day in San Diego
San Diego Union, March 31, 1936

PREPARING FOR THE HOME OPENER—LANE FIELD TAKES SHAPE

After San Diego's Board of Harbor Commissioners approved the terms for a ballpark lease on February 27, 1936, the City Council approved a final lease of the 500-foot by 500-foot property on March 3, 1936. Lane was committed to bringing the team here for five years with an option for renewal. The specific terms of the lease were as follows:

Term – five years, to begin April 1, 1936.

Rental – $3,000 per year for the first three years, $3,500 for the fourth year, and $4,000 for the fifth year.

Option – included was an option for a 10-year renewal, and rental to be not less than $4,000 nor more than $7,500 a year for the first five years and not more than $10,000 for the next five years.

Field conditions – to be suitable for playing Class AA ball.

Maintenance – the tenant was responsible for operation and maintenance of the Field.

Conditions – the lease was conditional upon the park being the home of a Coast League ball team and Coast League ball to be played in the park; no leasing or subleasing other than permits for concession privileges.

In addition, the Board approved the payment of $6,000 to Platner for the acquisition of the Field. With this action and eventual confirmation by the City Council, San Diego had a ball club and a park in which it could play.

On March 5 the lease was signed by Harbor Commissioners R. H. Van Deman and Emil Klicka in the office of Port Director Brennan.

Things were moving fast with the new franchise. As an example, a report by Steinmann in the March 18 *Union* indicated that Spider Baum was in town preparing to open club offices at Lane Field on March 24.

The final design of the ballpark was completed and by mid-March it was reported that there were two crews hard at work remodeling the former Army-Navy Field.[159] Welding of the steel trusses for the roof was underway in mid-March, but was not expected to be ready by opening day, but would be by late April. On March 24 Lane announced that the roof and lighting would not be in place until after the Padres complete their first homestand.[160] Final painting of the seats was also underway as of this date.

On March 23 some of the Padres got a chance to see Lane Field for the first time. Catcher Jim Kerr noted that "it's not going to be as easy as Wrigley Field...(but)...it's going to be a nice place to play, though, but oh, that center field fence!"[161]

In time for the opener, three turnstiles were placed at each entrance. Bleacher patrons were encouraged to enter from the Harbor boulevard side due to the fact that 4,000 bleacher seats were accessible from that side and 2,000 from the Pacific Highway-Broadway gate.

The base paths were made 30 feet wide, which was a lot wider than on the other Pacific Coast League diamonds.[162]

With the roof not being completed, many fans attending games in 1936 at Lane Field were going to be subject to injury from foul balls. There was only a sun screen behind home plate and foul balls flew everywhere into the stands causing some broken noses and other injuries.[163] Later,

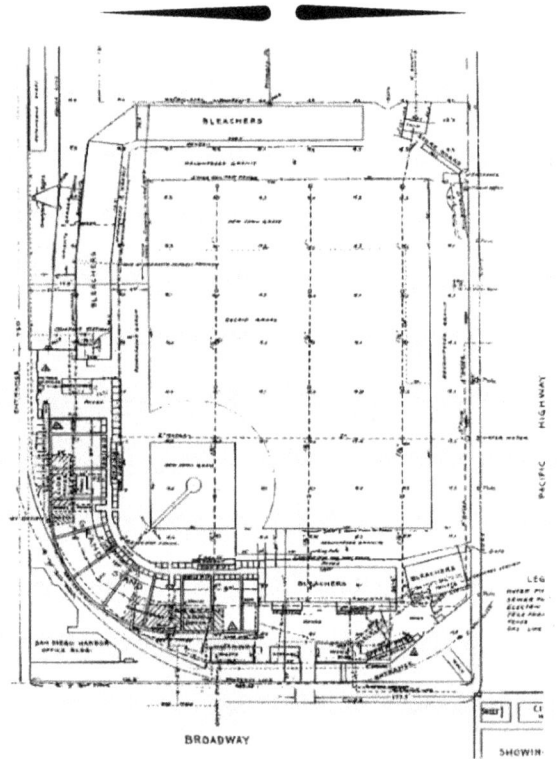

Design Plan for Lane Field

5—MARCH 1936 LONGSHOT PADRES BEGIN MAIDEN SEASON

Earl Keller recalled that "There was only a small little screen behind home plate. I mean foul balls would come back and hit spectators left and right. I can't tell you how many people ended up with broken noses because of that."[164] The press box was also close to the field and located on the first level behind home plate, allowing fans to help the sports writers in scoring games.

Lane Field's groundskeeper for this first season was a veteran from Los Angeles that Lane brought with him, Homer Knight.[165] Knight also assisted during the preparation of the field in advance of the season's home-opener on March 31, 1936.

TUESDAY, MARCH 31, 1936—HOME OPENER

Finally, professional—Double A—baseball had arrived in San Diego!

In addition to the new team, and a new ballpark, Lane also had a new radio announcer by the name of Dan Tobey. Tobey came from Los Angeles where he filled in for Bob Kelley the announcer for the games at Wrigley Field.[166] Ticket prices were also clarified:

Grandstand: 75¢ (tax included), Children (12 years and under) 25¢, Family books (10 admissions) $7.00

Box seats: $1.00, Children 50¢

Bleachers: 40¢, Children 15¢, Family books $4.00

On this first-ever Opening Day in San Diego, were people excited?

After the opening three-game series in Los Angeles, the Padres came home for the team's first-ever home game with a record of 1-2. Beginning Sunday, March 29, and running through Tuesday, the 31st, the local papers were full of articles and advertisements celebrating the impending arrival of opening day in San Diego for its Padres.

The ads were worded like one would congratulate someone you knew personally for their graduation generally wishing Bill Lane and the San Diego Padres "success and best wishes." They were placed by a variety of local businesses:[167]

Special Service Flooring Corp.	The Watts Building
States Café and Buffet	Hotel Casa Loma
Franklin Insurance Service Corporation	H. D. Hubbs, Plumbing
Western Metal Supply Company	Central Sign Studio
Dimitri Senoff Ballroom Studio	Daley Corporation
San Diego College of Commerce	Baybridge Cafe

There was "A Message from 'Bill' Lane," too, in the form of an ad expressing appreciation the "support and well wishes of my San Diego friends." His message also included thanks to community leaders and workers "for their untiring efforts in the building of Lane Field."

San Diego was also getting ready to shed its small-town identity associated with not having a professional baseball team. The *San Diego Sun* had an editorial that stated:

> ...beginning with the opening day game San Diego:
>
> *Will lose its unwanted distinction of being the nation's largest city without organized baseball.*
>
> *Will take its place as one of the sports capitals of the Pacific Coast.*
>
> *Will gain advertising on sports pages throughout the country the summer long.*
>
> *Will boast a baseball field ranking with any in the Pacific Coast League.*

The editorial concluded by noting that "Any city that can support a Class AA baseball team, must of necessity, be an up-and-coming town."[168]

The *San Diego Union* chimed in too with an editorial promoting the notion that San Diego was growing up:

The new venture is only one of many indications that San Diego is growing up. The best means of hastening that development, of bringing here the attractions that only a city can provide, is for the entire town, to turn out and prove that we are ready to take our place among the West's metropolitan communities.[169]

On Monday morning, March 30, there was a slight hiccup. Due to the Lane Field clubhouse not being ready, the team was forced to postpone a scheduled workout. It was reported that the presence of the team at the park on Monday "seemed to spur the workmen" since the field had to be ready the next day.[170] Another hiccup appeared to be a forecast of rain late Monday and perhaps even lingering into Tuesday.

Tuesday came—the day of the home opener—and a baseball luncheon was held, sponsored by the Electric Club in the U. S. Grant Hotel. California's Lt. Governor, George Hatfield, would be there along with Pacific Coast League officials and community leaders. Providing music was Don Igoe's "Little German Band." Following the luncheon, there was a parade to the ballpark that started at 12th Avenue and Broadway. Businesses along Broadway were encouraged by the Chamber of Commerce to decorate their buildings for the occasion.

Fortunately, the rain in the forecast occurred overnight. The afternoon's *Evening Tribune* pronounced that the "playing field was perfect after overnight rains."[171] The field was inspected early in the day and determined to be playable for a 2:15 P.M. start. Mayor Percy Benbough threw out the first ball to Lt. Governor George Hatfield, and it finally was "Play Ball" in San Diego.

Padres' Home Opener
Players by Position
San Diego Evening Tribune,
March 31, 1936

Opening Day Players Shown
by Position:
Wirthman-LF, Durst-CF,
DiMaggio-RF,
Holman-3B, Myatt-SS,
Doerr-2B, Jacobs-1B,
Desautels-C, Pillette-P

5—MARCH 1936 LONGSHOT PADRES BEGIN MAIDEN SEASON

Opening Day is typically a day of optimism and by all accounts, March 31 in San Diego was a success. The starting nine for this inaugural home game were proudly displayed in the *Evening Tribune*.

Good news for the home team! The Padres won their first ever Pacific Coast League home game, and a crowd of 8,178 fans turned out to watch the home team beat the Seattle Indians, 6-2. Right-hander Herman Pillette went the distance, allowing only two runs and fanning three. The San Diego offense picked up six runs chasing the Indians' starter, Kewpie Dick Barrett, before he completed three innings in a rally that would plate five of their six runs.

Home Opener Ticket Stub

Box Score of Padres First Home Game,
March 31, 1936
The Sporting News,
April 9, 1936

March 31, 1936, Lane Field's First Game,
Padres Starting Pitcher Herman Pillette on the Mound
San Diego Padres, *1966 Program*

There were more in attendance than the 8,178, as several hundred construction workers were invited because they were the men who did everything in their power to get the ballpark ready for Opening Day within that short two-month period. All-in-all, a successful beginning.

Despite the not yet completed ballpark, the Padres did not seem worried that only 511 of the attendees were children.[172] These were not the days when professional baseball worried about potentially losing the young boys' interests to other sports. More children and adults watched from across the street sitting on top of the boxcars at the Santa Fe station. The fact that over 8,000 fans could afford tickets for a game being played in the midst of a worldwide economic depression was a point of pride reflected in the San Diego newspapers.

Although the game garnered front-page headlines, coverage was a reflection of the times. Whether the first pitch by and to a Padres batter at Lane Field was a ball or strike was not noted, nor was the first hit at Lane Field deemed worthy of note. What was covered were personalities. Statistics and minutia wouldn't bring fans to the park, but a team of players they knew might. The players obliged.

It's difficult to know if it was from this sense of promotion or Bill Lane's frugalness that garnered the singers for the national anthem. But it was a trio of Padres' players—Myatt, Doerr and Pillette—with their supposedly "sweet tenor voices" who sang the national anthem. Surprisingly, teammates would not list any of them as having the best voices on the team. Years later all would recall that the best voice on the team belonged to Vince DiMaggio. Also of curious note is that when Myatt made the majors a number of years later his nickname was "Foghorn".

The team did have something to sing about because by the end of the game the Padres had their first home victory in hand. Happy fans would grace coverage of each game in a homestand with the "Lucky Fan Wins Ticket" promotion by the *San Diego Evening Tribune*. A circle would be made around one nearly indistinguishable face among the fans. The San Diego audience would see mostly smiling faces in those pictures during the season-long promotion. One can only suspect they never took any pictures of the crowd behind home plate. The region was notoriously dangerous with no screen to protect the crowd from balls coming off the bats at home plate, as many bloody noses were reported.

San Diegans were happy. They finally had a professional team playing at the highest level of the minor leagues. The fans were enthusiastic and the team seemed to have some very good players. The three primary local newspapers were barking, too. Listen to the editorial writer at the *San Diego Evening Tribune*:[173]

The Home Team Wins

Judging from the enthusiasm of the crowd that attended the opening of the Coast League season here yesterday, professional baseball is one of the attractions San Diego has been waiting for. The Padres' victory over Seattle, of course, goes a long way toward sustaining the enthusiasm, but that feature isn't as important as the fact that the team has the full support of the city.

Baseball has been called a good barometer of business conditions. Heavy attendance indicates not merely a surplus of money to be spent for amusement, but it further indicates that men and women can relax and dismiss business while enjoying the sunshine and the clean sport of the diamond. As long as baseball is popular, as long as businessmen can toss off their cares and become excited over a stolen base or a long throw from center, the solution of the more weighty problems of the day will remain in pretty safe hands.

The opening of the season is an occasion for mutual congratulations, for the excellence of Bill Lane's team is matched by the excellence of the field and the enthusiasm of those who wish him well. Every day's crowds probably will not always match that of the premiere skirmish, but Mr. Lane was given ample evidence yesterday that his efforts to put the city on the baseball map will not be single handed. The "gate" always important in the perpetuation of sports events as well as theatrical ventures, shows no indication of slumping as long as the Padres maintain even a semblance of the brilliant showing they made yesterday.

San Diego has needed professional baseball enthusiasm for a long time. The friendship, the relaxation and the keen civic interest that is aroused by a crack team of go-getters often leads to a new spirit of enthusiasm that reflects upon the community in numerous ways. The advertising value of a team of winners, whether in baseball or other ventures, cannot be measured in dollars and cents. It is one of those things that goes on and on, building up from year to year.

San Diego baseball fans, and others as well, congratulate Mr. Lane upon the team he has assembled. The city showed its enthusiasm yesterday, an enthusiasm that is bound to be reflected throughout the community. With home town support, an excellent playing field and an organization spreading the message of San Diego all up and down the coast, it is an investment that should and will bring heavy dividends to all concerned.[174]

Deservedly so, Bill Lane was being given much of the credit for the positive mood in the community with the start of San Diego's first entry into professional baseball. In an otherwise cynical editorial, here's what the *San Diego Herald* had to say:

BILL LANE

If there should ever be erected in the Plaza a monument to San Diego's most useful citizen – a project to which Percy Flage of The Herald once gave a great deal of his attention -- that monument should go to Bill Lane, owner of the San Diego Padres of the Pacific Coast baseball league.

When Bill Lane opened the gates to lane Park at the foot of Broadway last Tuesday noon, he changed San Diego from a second class town to a first class city. His field is the only big-town thing in the city. His ball club is the only thing in this benighted bailiwick that puts us in the classification of Los Angeles, San Francisco, Portland, Oakland and Seattle. Outside of his ball club we are a community of rogue players, of shuffle-board experts and bowling-on-the-green has-beens. If he hadn't come to town with his baseballers the chances are that within a year we would have won the national knitting championship and our sole bid to fame would have been the dollies we had embroidered for the 1936 Exposition.

But Bill Lane has brought us a new hope. Who among us would ever have thought that 8,200 of us would pay real money to see a ball game? Who among us would ever have thought that we could crowd his big grandstand to the limit? But, by gosh, we did just that – and we liked it!....

....They have a new town and a new field – and Bill Lane. And when they take a cut at the old ball they mean business. Look at Wednesday's game – 17 hits. Wham! Bang! Socko! On the nose and out she goes and where she will land nobody knows![175]

Not to be outdone, the *San Diego Sun* also was also on the bandwagon. However, the theme that San Diego needed a boost in spirit, and needed to advertise itself continued:

Well, We Did It

...yesterday they turned out to the opening ball game in droves—the largest opening day crowd in the history of Coast League baseball!...

....Besides, baseball is a whale of a lot of fun. With baseball, fishing, wrestling, boxing, swimming, bowling, football in season and a bang up Exposition there should be a lot of joy and very little depression in this city in a few more weeks.

Looks like nothing can stop San Diego now.[176]

SCORECARDS – CAN'T TELL THE PLAYERS WITHOUT ONE!

The 1936 programs were printed on heavy paper and made a sufficiently hard surface to write on. The program contained numerous ads and little information about the ball club aside from the roster. Probable line-ups for both teams for that day's game were printed on the scorecards. Ads were primarily local ones as would be expected; not expected were the ones for the Hotel Cecil in Los Angeles, Northonia Hotel in Portland, and Hotel Cadillac in New York City.

As was somewhat normal in that period, the scorecard page contained a pre-printed line-up for an early season game:

Contests included lucky numbers (two to a program) with four winners announced during the course of the game that resulted in a pass to a future game. The winner could also get a quart of ice cream from Mountain Meadow Ice Cream (4600 Sixth Avenue).

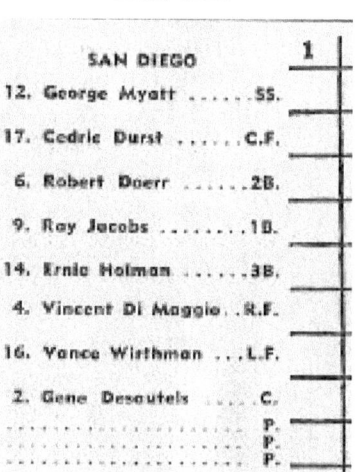

Example of Pre-Printed Lineup in 1936 Padres Program

The price list for items at Lane Field included these items:

Red Hots	10¢	Baby Ruth & Butterfinger	5¢
"Padre" Ice Cream Bars	10¢	Del Cera Cigars	5¢
Peanut (Large) Bags	10¢	"Santa Fe Patties"	10¢
Soda Water	10¢	Ben Hur Coffee	10¢
Maier's Beer	15¢		

Before or after the game, if one felt like eating at the Pullman Cafeteria, 1240 Fifth Avenue, you could get a Top Sirloin with French fried Potatoes for 20 cents. How about one-half Lobster, any style for 20 cents! New Buicks were available at Robt. D. Maxwell Co., Broadway at State, for $1095 – plus sales tax.

Fan information was limited but relevant!

FAN INFORMATION

All single games at Lane Field are called at 2:15 P.M. Double headers on Holidays and Sundays start at 1:30 P.M.

Ladies' Day every Wednesday. Kiddies Day on Fridays.

Patrons are requested to return baseballs hit into the stands. In appreciation a grandstand ticket FOR ANY FUTURE GAME will be given for each ball returned. If the usher does not tender a ticket, please bring the ball to the office for exchange.

On the main concourse there is a Ladies' Rest Room.

5—MARCH 1936 LONGSHOT PADRES BEGIN MAIDEN SEASON

> The management would appreciate the reporting of any discourtesy on the part of any employee of the Ball Club.
>
> Ball Clubs have discontinued the practice of giving scores, or the results of games over the telephone.
>
> Public Telephone Booths east of grandstand.
>
> Physicians or professional men expecting telephone calls are requested to inform our office where they will be seated in the stand so there will be no delay in locating them.

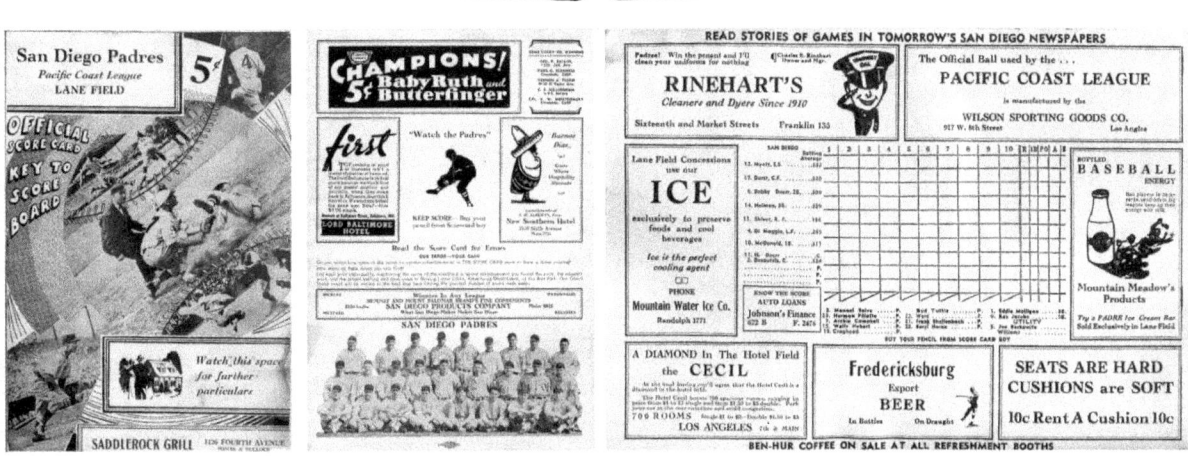

Cover, Sample Page, and Scorecard from 1936 Padres Program

THE KID'S SEASON BEGINS, TOO!

March found the Hoover Cardinals also getting ready for its season. Their first game was played against Hoover alums several of whom had professional experience. The alumni team did win by a score of 5-4. They faced "lanky" Ted Williams who took the loss despite fanning 12 batters and hitting two home runs.[177]

Williams was still getting noticed by professional scouts, too. In a March 7 interview with the school newspaper Coach Caldwell predicted that Williams would sign a contract with a Coast club when he graduates and noted that he was on the St. Louis Cardinals' radar.[178] Also, his photo as a pitcher made the sports page of the *San Diego Union* on March 8.

On March 13-14, Hoover played in the first annual American Legion Interscholastic Baseball tournament. The Cardinals won their first game, 18-0, against Sweetwater with Williams not pitching and scoring two runs in the victory.

The tournament continued on March 14, with Hoover slated to play two games. In the day's first game, a semi-final match against St. Augustine High, Williams batted fourth and played shortstop going 2-for-2 and scoring four runs in a 14-3 win.

Hoover's final tournament game was against its "arch rival" San Diego High. The Cardinals won, 6-1, behind a "brilliant three-hit mound performance by lanky Ted Williams."[179] The *Union* reported that "Williams, a limber-armed right hander who usually shows more at the plate than on the mound, received potent stick assistance..." Williams fanned 13 and went 1-for-3 driving in one run. To cap it off, Williams was unanimously selected as the right fielder for the tourney all-star team, having hit .500.[180]

Ted Williams: One of
"Cardinal Workhorses for Legion Title Tourney"
San Diego Union,
March 8, 1936

A week later, on March 21, Hoover soundly trounced Covina High, 17-0, behind "ace Cardinal chucker" "lanky" Ted Williams.[181] He pitched the entire nine innings and allowed only one hit, no walks, and striking out 13. Williams also helped his cause with a double and a home run.

The wins continued for Hoover. On March 27, they beat Santa Monica High, 4-0, with Williams pitching and going all the way, yielding only three hits.

Williams' first month into his senior high school season was off to a great start. Over the six games, he went 10-for-13 (.769) and, as a pitcher, his record was 3-1 with 51 strikeouts.

The Padres finished their abbreviated first month with a won-loss record of 2-2. The individual player batting and pitching records for March 1936 are provided in Table 5.1. Ray Jacobs was clearly off to a hot start going 7-for-15 (.467) and driving in six runs, with Bobby Doerr on his heels with a 7-for17 (.412). On the pitching side, Wally Hebert and Herman Pillette both had complete-game victories to set the pace. The Padres were ready to bring on April.

5—MARCH 1936 LONGSHOT PADRES BEGIN MAIDEN SEASON

Table 5.1. Batting and Pitching Totals for March

Players	Positions	G	AB	R	H	1B	2B	3B	HR	RBI	SB	AVG
Herman Pillette	p-1	1	2	0	1	1	0	0	0	1	0	.500
Ray Jacobs	1b-4	4	15	4	7	4	2	1	0	6	2	.467
Bobby Doerr	2b-4	4	17	4	7	6	1	0	0	1	3	.412
Cedric Durst	cf-4	4	17	2	6	5	1	0	0	2	2	.353
George Hockette	p-1	1	3	1	1	1	0	0	0	0	0	.333
George Myatt	ss-4	4	17	2	5	5	0	0	0	3	1	.294
Van Wirthman	lf-3	3	11	1	3	3	0	0	0	4	0	.273
Ernie Holman	3b-4	4	15	5	4	3	1	0	0	3	0	.267
Vince DiMaggio	rf-4	4	14	5	3	1	1	0	1	4	1	.214
Wally Hebert	p-1	1	5	0	1	1	0	0	0	0	0	.200
Gene Desautels	c-4	4	13	2	2	1	1	0	0	2	0	.154
Ed Wells	p-1	1	3	0	0	0	0	0	0	0	0	.000
Trader Horne	p-2	2	1	0	0	0	0	0	0	0	0	.000
Joe Monahan	ph-1	1	1	0	0	0	0	0	0	0	0	.000
Archie Campbell	p-1	1	0	0	0	0	0	0	0	0	0	.000
Ashley Joerndt	lf-1	1	0	0	0	0	0	0	0	0	0	.000

Pitchers	G	GS	CG	ShO	Sv	W	L	PCT	IP	H	R	ER	SO	BB	ERA
Wally Herbert	1	1	1	0	0	1	0	1.000	9	5	2	2	2	4	2.00
Herman Pillette	1	1	1	0	0	1	0	1.000	9	9	2	2	3	0	2.00
Ed Wells	1	1	0	0	0	0	1	.000	6⅔	9	5	4	2	2	5.40
George Hockett	1	1	0	0	0	0	0	.000	5⅓	6	3	4	1	1	6.75
Trader Horne	2	0	0	0	0	0	0	.000	2⅔	5	4	3	1	2	10.13
Archie Campbell	1	0	0	0	0	0	1	.000	0	0	1	2	0	2	∞

SAN DIEGO'S FIRST PADRES and "THE KID"

CHAPTER 6
APRIL 1936
POSITIVE SIGNS!?

NOTABLE WORLD EVENTS-APRIL 1936

1st   *Britain assures France and Belgium of support in the event of war with Germany*

11th *The Detroit Red Wings win their first Stanley Cup beating the Toronto Maple Leafs, 3-2*

29th *The first professional baseball game is played in Japan as Nagoya defeats DaiTokyo, 8-5*

The Padres' maiden homestand continued over the first two weeks of April. After their .500 start in March, they faced off against the Seattle Indians for six games, before the San Francisco Seals—the 1935 PCL champs—came into town on Tuesday, April 7, for a seven-game series.

The team then would head north to face Oakland, Seattle, and Portland in succeeding weeks—all told, 30 games in 30 days.

COMPLETION OF THE FIRST HOMESTAND

Home game number two took place on Wednesday, April 1—and was no longer deserving of being front page news. The game was also not the business success that the premier home game was, but for the Padres it would be another game added to the win column.

Only 1,237 paid to see the game, although initial reports in the *Evening Tribune* estimated the crowd at over 2,000. The Seattle Indians started right-hander Howard Craghead, a 6'2" fastball and curve ball artist. To counter Craghead, the Padres manager picked—himself! Frank Shellenback started the game in search of his number 291 win. After a two-hour and 10-minute game, he would have the win in the books. The Padres exploded for 10 runs, including a five-run sixth inning to beat the Indians by a final score of 10-5. If the Indians had anything to be proud of, it was that they had robbed the Padres of a first: Seattle Indian third baseman Dick Gyselman hit the first home run at Lane Field.

If game two had not been as financially successful for the Padres as Bill Lane had hoped, game three turned out to be an even bigger disappointment. On April 2, 1936, in San Diego the rain came and so did the pounding. Only 982 fans braved the weather to see Archie "Iron Man" Campbell take the mound for the Padres. When all was said and done, the scoreboard recorded the first Padres home loss, 7-4. Curiously, the press recorded that the defeat "helped them a lot."[182]

The next day rain and cold would again deter fans attending. It would also delay local high school match-up of Hoover High. A meager gate of 1,229 saw the Padres drop the next game, 8-4, as 23-year old Indian's pitcher Don Osborn dominated the Padres with his curveball. There were some bright spots for the Padres. Padres right fielder Vince DiMaggio uncorked a strike to third base that nailed the Indians' Jerry Donovan. The out kept the game closer. But, as in any eight-run games, the negatives were more notable. With Doerr, Myatt had been part of the "keystone kids" who had been much ballyhooed in the press. The local papers speculated that the team's solid defense up the middle might be capable of setting a new PCL record for twin killings. By the end of the game, however, Myatt had tallied three errors on his line in the box score.

Game five of the series saw the Padres cruising to a 5-1 lead and holding it until the top of the eighth inning when Herm Pillette lost his touch and the Padres allowed six runs to score in the final two innings, taking the loss, 7-5. On top of this bad news, the weatherman was predicting that Sunday's games would be lost to rain.

On Sunday, April 5, the weather held. San Diegans came out to see their new team in droves with 9,332 passing through the turnstiles. They got to see the Padres drop both ends of the twin bill, 7-4 and 2-1. All the breaks seemed to be going the Indians' way. In the second game, Dick Gyselman hit a low liner which Ced Durst snow-coned, but then dropped turning the out into a fatal triple. Shellenback went the distance in the second game after having used three of his pitchers in the first game of the doubleheader.

The series had been a financial success, at least from Seattle owner Bill Klepper's perspective. He announced that his cut for the series was bigger than Seattle's take for every California-based series the year prior.[183]

From the standings perspective, the Padres had more things about which to be concerned. After winning the first two games at home, the Padres had dropped five straight. They finished the Seattle series at 3-7, only a half-game ahead of basement dwelling Sacramento (2-7). It was time for action thought management. First came promotion. The Padres announced Fridays would be "ladies days," charging only 15 cents a ticket for women and providing boutonnieres to match their outfit. Thursday would be "High School Days," allowing students to enter the park late.

The next action was a search for talent. The Padres had to feel good about their batting, they had hit .301 for the series. But, on the pitching side of the equation, they allowed the Indians to hit a torrid .319. The Padres wanted and needed pitching and the Boston Red Sox still owed them a pitcher for Bobby Doerr. Bill Lane made no secret that he wanted the fast-balling Portuguese, Manuel "Manny" Salvo. Although his ethnicity was mentioned, unstated was the obvious hope that this would bring some of the sizeable local Portuguese fishing community out to see him pitch. Lane also indicated that he was owed an outfielder, an obvious reference to the Myatt part of the deal.

6—APRIL 1936 POSITIVE SIGNS!?

HERE COME THE SEALS

The San Francisco Seals were next and came into town with a formidable team on paper. The winners of the 1935 PCL championship, they were undoubtedly weaker given the departure of their star Joe DiMaggio to the New York Yankees. In game one, the Seals would start their ace, the premier pitcher in the PCL in 1935, Sam Gibson. The Padres would go with their lefty fastballer, Wally Hebert.

Before the first game of the series, Tuesday, April 7, Lane invited Hoover's and St. Augustine's high school baseball teams to work out with the Padres. No mention was made if Ted Williams was at the workout, but he was Hoover's star and it seems likely that his absence would have been mentioned. Bobby Doerr might have felt at home among the high schoolers. The Padres had just held a small celebration of his 18th birthday.

Doerr also celebrated on the field, going 2-for-4 with a double and turning his 6th double play of the season with Myatt. Hebert ultimately had to help himself out picking up an RBI and the win in a tightly contested 2-1 game. Hebert remembered his matchups with Gibson well: "His knuckles dragged the ground every pitch. His knuckles on his throwing hand would always skin up. I used to hit him good, because I hit down on the ball and his ball was coming up. I believe I hit him two or three times in the box during my career. I got more hits through the middle than anywhere."[184] The rest of the Padres were not as effective against Gibson, the whole team only picking up seven hits. Wally Hebert accounted for two of the hits.

The April 8 game had to be one of the strangest games from an umpire-manager relationship point of view. Lefty O'Doul, managing the Seals, had placed himself in the third base coach's box. Padres starter Pillette was pitching effectively. The Seals had a runner on and O'Doul announced loudly that he had seen Pillette balk. In the ensuing argument with umpire Crawford, O'Doul found himself ejected. The game proceeded smoothly if not to the Padres favor when a voice questioning various calls could be heard from the Seal's dugout. O'Doul found himself ejected again. Not content with two ejections in one game, Lefty proceeded to take a box seat in the stands. He obviously felt he still had a better view of plays than the umpires otherwise he wouldn't have been questioning them. This questioning resulted in his third ejection from the game. It is not known if he then mounted the boxcars across the street at the Santa Fe station to view the game and question the calls!

O'Doul's riding of the umpire crew may have had some impact, but it was Pillette's fatigue that sealed the game. Down by the score of 3-2 in the ninth inning, Pillette took the mound and was "shelled." The box score reflects only two runs scored in the ninth. Pillette managed to finish the game, but the coverage implied that the pitcher was lucky to have gotten off so easily. Pillette got the "L" in the 5 to 2 game.

At the end of the game, one of the first Padres to have appeared in a regular game was released, Joe Monahan. He was hitting .400 (2-5) with two runs scored and had to be a little surprised when he was given his papers and told to report to San Antonio. Kenny Iverson, Fred Vaughn and Ritchie Cooper remained, but were told they were on the "bubble."

On the next day, April 9, the Padres were unable to go the distance in an extra-inning affair. The Padres had been down, 4-1, in the bottom of the sixth but battled back. After eight innings, they had fought back to a 4-4 tie but then Padres' starter Ed Wells gave up a run to put the home team down, 5-4. The Padres rallied in the bottom of the ninth to again tie the game. However, in relief, "Trader" Horne gave up two runs in the 10th. This time the Padres could only make up one of the runs and lost the game, 7-6.

The third game of the series, on April 10, was a bit more cheerful. Ladies Day saw a crowd of 2,100 attend and included exotic dancer Sally Rand. What game Sally would attend had been cause for much speculation up until that point. The presence of ladies did not deter the "gentlemen" players from engaging in the first on-field fight at Lane Field. George Myatt threw the first punch at Seals' left fielder Joe Marty. The punch came as a result of a rundown Marty was in, with Myatt applying the tag and Marty knocking the shortstop down. Early in the game, Padres starter George Hockette's change-up was working wonders and after six complete innings the Padres led, 3-2, but in the end, the result would be the same, another Padres loss by the score of 6-3.

The loss did feature one bright spot: the first Padres' home run at Lane Field that was hit by first baseman Ray Jacobs.[185] The long ball was not likely to be an integral part of the Padres game with the departure of Smead Jolley and his 29 homers after the 1935 season. Even so, it was a big deal of sorts for Jacobs as he pocketed a prize from Harbor Liquor and Variety Store: a fishing reel with a value of $5.00.

Lane's temper flared after the game when he told the press that he had twice telegraphed the Red Sox demanding pitching help. Help that had yet to arrive.

Manager-pitcher Frank Shellenback took a more positive approach, giving the team a pep talk before the game on April 11. It apparently worked as the Padres exploded for a 23-4 shellacking of the Seals. The Padres scored in every inning and tallied 25 hits. Shellenback had his 292nd PCL victory and had an 11-run lead before he allowed the Seals to get a man across home plate. Bobby Doerr had a six-hit effort. Vince DiMaggio picked up five RBIs in the game. Kenny Iverson pitched the final two innings for the Padres, allowing only one hit. Myatt and Doerr turned their 10th double play in 13 games.

The next day Wally Hebert continued the Padre's success by leading them to a 6-5 win in game one of the Sunday doubleheader. Hebert by then had won three in a row and was one of the few positive signs on the pitching staff. The second game was also a squeaker, the Padres, behind the pitching of Herm Pillette, picked up a 3-2 win. Pillette only allowed the Seals six hits over the seven innings that was played before the game was called because of darkness.

As the series ended, the Padres bats continued hot. The averages to that point showed that first baseman Jacobs was hitting .373. On the other side of the diamond, Ernie Holman, at .224, had less to boast about.

SALVO ARRIVES

Monday, April 13, the travel day, brought the news that Lane awaited: the Red Sox were sending Salvo. The three-straight wins against the Seals had improved the team's record to 7-10. After the doubleheader sweep, the Padres went on the road to Oakland to face the Oaks and their 12-4 record. The Padres hitters led the league in batting average (.304), trailed by the Oaks with .299.

For Manny Salvo, the move to San Diego would be bittersweet. "On opening day in 1936, I was sitting on the bench in Boston. They had made a deal with San Diego for Bobby Doerr and George Myatt. Mr. Cronin called me into his office and said Lane had called and told him 'You either send me Salvo right away or I'm calling this deal off!' Cronin showed me the telegram and asked how I'd like to go. I said I'd prefer to fly. They made arrangements." And so Salvo departed Boston. He had finagled his first flight ever. He nearly missed the flight, which had to be held for him on the rainy tarmac.[186]

The first game against the Oaks on Tuesday, April 14, had "slowball" artist Ed Wells on the mound. Holding Oakland to only two runs on eight hits, the Padres nevertheless needed an error by the Oakland shortstop Bernie DeViveiros to eke out a 3-2 win. The Padres had won four in a row.

The streak would stop there. The offense had shown signs of slowing in game one and all but disappeared in game two, as Oakland pitcher Floyd Olds shut out the Padres on six hits. The Padres never mounted a serious threat, with all of their singles occurring in separate innings.

Meanwhile, back in San Diego, work continued on Lane Field and the press was given a preview of the soon-to-be-completed scoreboard which would record balls, strikes number of outs, and the other scores in the PCL. Later in the week, it was announced that there would be "no night games until the fog season was over" in San Diego.

The Padres hoped to get back on track with Wally Hebert on the mound. He had yet to suffer a loss. However, he would only last 6⅓ innings, losing, 6-2, to Oakland's pitcher McDonald.

For the Padres, Friday, April 17, was no better as they dropped another game to Oakland, its third straight. After 5½ innings the Padres led, 4-1, but once again Pillette ran out of steam. Archie Campbell came in with two outs in the bottom of the sixth to stem the tide. But, in the bottom of the 10th inning he would allow Oakland to plate a run and take the win, 6-5.

The much-anticipated debut of Manny Salvo happened on Saturday, April 18. Salvo showed he was something worth waiting for. Allowing only two runs in a complete game effort, he struck out seven Oaks. The Padres batters also woke up, scoring seven times on 13 hits for a 7-2 win.

Shellenback penciled in his own name to start game one of the Sunday doubleheader. His spitter was effective through seven innings, allowing only one run to match the Padres output to that point. But, in the bottom of the eighth inning, Shellenback got hit hard. Five Oakland players crossed the plate and the Oaks went on to win, 6-2.

In the second game on Sunday, Ed Wells started and pitched a solid nine innings. The game was tied 2-2, when Wells, with the bases loaded, let go a wild pitch that catcher Kerr could not handle and the winning run for Oakland scored.[187] With that loss, the Padres left Oakland having lost the series, five games to two. The Padres ended the series hitting .289 with not one batter in the top five of the PCL.

ON TO SEATTLE

The Padres headed north from Oakland to Seattle for a seven-game series. At the time, the Indians (18-13) were in second place behind Oakland (22-8). The Padres had put a few games between the last-place Los Angeles Angels (9-20) and themselves (12-19) but still were the second worst team in the league.

The road was not a fun place for the Padres. Bill Lane, after losing money for three straight years, developed a number of cost-minimizing actions. Among them was putting his team up at the cheapest and seediest of hotels…a fact that was memorable for many of the Padres.[188]

The starter for the series was Herm Pillette, who had developed an interesting coping mechanism for the road trips. His roommate, Padres first baseman George McDonald, recalled, "Every morning, he'd take a shower, brush his teeth and fill a water glass half full of 100 proof whiskey. He called it mouthwash, but I never saw him drunk."[189]

Pillette steadied by his morning breakfast of champions pitched strongly through eight innings. Ten thousand Seattle fans watched as he took a 4-3 lead into the ninth. But then the walls fell in and Pillette allowed two runs without retiring a batter in the bottom half of the ninth inning. Pillette had not pitched and won a full nine-inning game since the home opener. The only bright spot was that DiMaggio had two hits and was starting to show signs of coming out of his slump.

Two firsts happened to the Padres on April 22. They played their first night game and they won their first night game. Manny Salvo took the mound for San Diego and, while not quite as effective as he was in his debut, still had a complete game victory and five strikeouts to show for his efforts. A six-run fourth inning and a four-run seventh sealed the Indians fate in this 12-5 Padres romp. DiMaggio picked up five RBIs on the night with his homer, the first by a Padres in a night game, and a triple also the first by a Padres in a night game. Gene Desautels missed the end of the game, getting tossed after arguing a call over a foul ball.[190]

The Padres must have begun to think Seattle night games were to their liking because the next night they again beat the Indians under the lights. DiMaggio homered, again, this time it was the game-winner in the eighth. Trader Horne allowed only three runs over nine innings, taking the win, 4-3. Dutch Reuther, manager of the Indians, started Howard Craghead. Ruether was still occasionally playing, and also acting as road secretary, and general manager. In this game, he inserted himself into the lineup in the bottom of the ninth as a pinch hitter, which put two members of the famous 1927 Yankees on the field. The other was Padres center fielder Cedric Durst.

Ced Durst had to be happy about some of the news coming out of San Diego. Homer Knight, groundskeeper at Lane field, had finally managed to catch the gopher that had been digging holes in centerfield!

Friday, April 24, was the third night game in a row. But this game was not to San Diego's liking. The Padres tallied one run in the first inning and would not score again as Indians pitcher Paul Gregory bore down, only allowing the Padres four hits. In fact, the Padres would not have scored at all if it had not been for an error by the pitcher who threw wildly on an attempt to pick off George Myatt.[191] The Indians were not troubled by a lack of run production, tallying seven runs against Padres pitcher Archie Campbell. Shellenback was obviously saving his pitching staff for the three weekend games left in the series.

Frank Shellenback started the Saturday game. He would not need help from anyone in finishing his five-hitter against the Indians. The Padres had four runs to show against the Indians one. But it was not a pretty game. Both the Indians and Padres shortstops had two errors apiece. Myatt was not alone on the Padres with two errors, as first baseman Ray Jacobs also posted a pair. Ernie Holman contributed another error to make it a total of five for the error-prone infield.

The wrap-up games on Sunday, April 26, 1936, turned out to be even worse for the Padres. Going into the doubleheader, the Padres were up three games to two and had the inside track at winning the series. The Padres would start off with Pillette in the morning game. Unlike his starts to date, he ran into trouble early and before he had eight outs, he found himself watching the game from the bench. George Hockette came in to relieve, but the eight runs he gave up did nothing to calm the Padres' concerns about his arm. By the time the first game was over, the scoreboard told the tale of Padres frustration, 13-1 in favor of the hometown Indians.

The Padres turned to Salvo in the afternoon game, and he pitched five strong innings of shutout ball, but lost it in the sixth, surrendering four runs. The Padres would score two runs in the game while the Indians would add another run in the seventh inning making the final score, 5-2. One somewhat remarkable occurrence for the Padres was another stolen base for Jacobs. He was described by the San Diego press as the slowest of the Padres but he got his fifth base tying him with Myatt, the fastest man on the team.[192]

Despite the disappointing end to the series, the Padres still had some hope. Vince DiMaggio hit .308 for the series, up from his .249 average going into it.

As April was nearing its end, back home the San Diego press was looking for news other than the 12-19 Padres, despite the fact that the club was only a half-game behind Sacramento, and still holding second place in the second division. There was always high school baseball and Lane Field's anticipated final completion. Minor work was getting done on the field, the north end of the field was getting a new fence, one that would be 12 feet high.

The roof was another matter entirely. Work on it had not yet begun and no action was anticipated until the plans were approved. The plan had been sent to Washington but had not yet been approved and returned from the WPA. Hopes were that approval would be quickly forthcoming and that the girders would be placed early in the first week of May.

Earlier in the week, the Padres announced cancellation of the "B" games while the Padres were on the road. These games consisted of Padres who were on the roster but did not travel with the team. The B squad consisted of three players from the spring training roster: Ritchie Cooper, Kenny Iverson and Fred Vaughn. The team was supplemented with other locals and played other local teams. The reason cited for cancelling the games

6—APRIL 1936 POSITIVE SIGNS!?

Scenes at Lane Field in Spring 1936—Concessions and Outfield Advertising

was complaints about the games impacting the attendance at the other local baseball venues. Since the local papers did not cover these B games, it is difficult to ascertain the veracity of these statements. Nevertheless, now that these games had been cancelled, Bill Lane had three more Padres than he needed and was attempting to place them in a league either in the southwest or south. Lane announced he would release them if he failed in placing them with other clubs.

NEXT STOP: PORTLAND

Tuesday, April 28, 1936, found the Padres in Portland to face the 17-16 Beavers. Wally Hebert started the game for the Padres. Archie Campbell would relieve him, but before the rout was over, the Padres staff would give up 19 hits and have five errors committed behind them. The final score was an 11-4 shellacking.

On Wednesday, however, the Padres returned the favor. Behind a complete-game effort by Trader Horne, who only allowed three runs on six hits, the Padres took the contest, 10-3.

The last game of April found the Padres down 4-0 to start the fourth inning, but home runs by Ernie Holman and George Myatt turned the tide. Manny Salvo pitched another complete game, winning, 6 to 4.

Despite the two wins that week, the Padres ended April only ahead of Los Angeles. Oakland was out front, leading the PCL with a record of 23-10.

WHAT'S "THE KID" UP TO?

Ted Williams was continuing to get attention in the sports pages. After a starring performance in the Pomona tournament, hosted by the 20-30 Club, where he pitched 19 innings, struck out 21, and allowed only nine hits and three runs, he was regarded as the city's finest diamond prospect.[193] On the batting side, he managed to hit four home runs, including two in one inning. However, his four dingers could only lead Hoover High to second place in the competition.

Given his pitching and hitting performance, it was no wonder he was receiving attention. The April 13 *Union* featured a large photo of Williams swinging a bat under the banner of "They'll Be Calling Him Bambino." The caption read "The 'Babe Ruth' of the Herbert Hoover High school baseball team, Ted Williams, pictured above, got three home runs as he pitched the Cardinals to the consolation title in the 20-30 club championship tournament at Pomona Saturday. One of the heaviest hitters in southland prep circles, Williams also startled

Ted Williams of Hoover High School –
First Published Photo Batting
San Diego Union, April 13, 1936

the railbirds with his flinging in the semi-finals and finals."[194]

On that same date, he was recognized by the 20-30 Club with a gold baseball for his four home runs. Ted's four dingers could only give Hoover High second place in the competition.

The Hoover High *Cardinal* newspaper was also getting into the act. The April 17 edition had a story about "N. Y. Yanks Offer Williams Contract." The article indicated that Yankee scout Vinegar Bill Essick had offered Williams a contract for $150 a month plus travel expenses. It also mentioned that Williams "will sign the dotted line when he is graduated from Hoover High."[195] Essick was quoted as saying that Williams has character in his make-up which is the kind of player that the Yankees want.

That same day, April 17, Hoover played Compton with Williams pitching. The Cardinals won 7-1 with "The Kid" pitching a complete game. He went 0-1 and was intentionally walked three times. Yes, his reputation had spread.

The next game for Hoover was against Redondo on April 24. Williams pitched and established himself as one the best prospects in Southern California with a new Bay League record 19 strikeouts in a 5-2 win.

Late in the month, there was a story of Grossmont high school student Bill Gray who was tampered with by a Cardinal scout and lost his eligibility to play in any more high school sports. The *San Diego Union* reported, "Gray is not the only youth being sought. Ted Williams, Hoover High's star pitcher is another marked youngster. His name on a contract is in big demand. The Cardinal organization wants him, so do scouts for the Yankees. But so far school authorities have kept him embroiled in ineligibility difficulties. They hope to keep him clear until his graduation." Ironically, Frank Shellenback, in the paper, would caution against joining the majors too soon.[196]

6—APRIL 1936 POSITIVE SIGNS!?

The Padres played 30 games in April 1936 winning 12 and losing 18. The individual player batting and pitching records for the month are provided in Table 6.1. Catcher Gene Desautels led the team in batting for the month with an average of .373. The other offense leaders for the month were Ray Jacobs with 18 RBIs and Ernie Holman with four home runs. On the pitching side, part-time pitcher, part-time manager, Frank Shellenback and newcomer Manny Salvo set the pace with three wins each.

Table 6.1. Batting and Pitching Totals for April

Players	Positions	G	AB	R	H	1B	2B	3B	HR	RBI	SB	AVG
Joe Monahan	ph-3, pr-1	4	4	2	2	1	1	0	0	0	0	.500
Fred Vaughn	ph-2	2	2	1	1	1	0	0	0	0	0	.500
George McDonald	1b-5, ph-4	9	7	2	3	3	0	0	0	0	0	.429
Gene Desautels	c-25	25	75	13	28	23	4	0	1	16	0	.373
Ray Jacobs	1b-30	30	105	20	33	25	5	0	3	18	4	.314
Cedric Durst	cf-30	30	128	16	39	28	10	0	1	13	1	.305
Ashley Joerndt	lf-3, ph-3, rf-2, 1b-1	9	17	3	5	3	2	0	0	3	0	.294
Frank Shellenback	p-5	5	17	5	5	4	1	0	0	2	0	.294
Archie Campbell	p-7	7	7	0	2	2	0	0	0	0	0	.286
Ernie Holman	3b-28	28	99	15	28	20	3	1	4	17	3	.283
Vince DiMaggio	rf-23, lf-7	30	104	19	29	17	5	5	2	16	3	.279
Van Wirthman	lf-22, rf-5	27	105	11	29	24	4	1	0	9	1	.276
Wally Hebert	p-4	5	11	0	3	3	0	0	0	1	0	.273
Manny Salvo	p-3	4	12	1	3	3	0	0	0	1	0	.250
George Myatt	ss-27, ph-1	28	102	14	25	22	2	0	1	12	5	.245
Bobby Doerr	2b-29	29	112	11	27	21	5	1	0	7	3	.241
Joe Berkowitz	ss-6, 3b-2, rf-1, 2b-1	9	30	7	7	6	1	0	0	1	0	.233
Jimmy Kerr	c-9, pr-1	10	26	2	6	4	2	0	0	4	0	.231
George Hockett	p-4, pr-1	5	5	0	1	1	0	0	0	0	0	.200
Ed Wells	p-5, ph-2	7	13	1	2	1	0	1	0	2	0	.154
Trader Horne	p-6, pr-1	8	8	0	1	1	0	0	0	1	0	.125
Herman Pillette	p-6	6	14	0	1	1	0	0	0	0	0	.071
Eddie Mulligan	ph-3, pr-3, cf-1, 2b-1	8	5	1	0	0	0	0	0	0	0	.000
Jack Hile	p-2	2	4	0	0	0	0	0	0	0	0	.000
Kenny Iverson	p-1	1	0	0	0	0	0	0	0	0	0	.000

Pitchers	G	GS	CG	ShO	Sv	W	L	PCT	IP	H	R	ER	SO	BB	ERA
Kenny Iverson	1	0	0	0	1	0	0	.000	2	0	0	0	1	1	0.00
Wally Hebert	5	4	2	0	0	2	2	.500	27	42	14	9	9	9	3.00
Trader Horne	7	3	2	0	0	2	2	.500	30⅓	35	17	11	13	16	3.26
Frank Shellenback	5	5	3	0	0	3	2	.600	40⅔	35	17	15	17	4	3.32
Manny Salvo	4	4	3	0	0	3	1	.750	33	33	15	13	16	5	3.55
Ed Wells	5	3	2	0	0	1	1	.500	27	30	12	11	5	4	3.67
Jack Hile	2	1	0	0	0	0	1	.000	9	10	4	4	3	5	4.00
George Hockette	4	2	1	0	0	0	2	.000	22⅔	33	16	13	2	9	5.16
Herman Pillette	6	6	3	0	0	1	4	.200	42	56	29	25	6	6	5.36
Archie Campbell	7	2	1	0	0	0	3	.000	25	37	26	22	9	12	7.92

SAN DIEGO'S FIRST PADRES and "THE KID"

CHAPTER 7
MAY 1936
2ᴺᴰ DIVISION GETS COMFORTABLE

NOTABLE WORLD EVENTS-MAY 1936

1ˢᵗ *Starting today every newlywed couple in Germany will receive a copy of Mein Kampf from the Registrar*

3ʳᵈ *Rookie Joe DiMaggio makes his debut with the New York Yankees and goes 3-for-6 in a 14-5 win against the St. Louis Browns*

27ᵗʰ *The Queen Mary departs Southampton (England) on its maiden voyage to New York City*

May 1, 1936, May Day and International Worker's Day, was not to be a day of celebration for the Padres. After their first full month of play, the club was 14-20 and well-entrenched in second division as seen in Table 7.1. The Padres had lost two straight series on the road and now were in Portland. They would not return to San Diego until May 8, a few days short of a month from when the road trip began. With the arrival of big right-hander Manny Salvo in mid-April, it was still too early to see how the dividends would turn out. Would a return home make a difference? Who would have expected that the Padres were a team in the process of being molded into a winner?

Table 7.1. PCL Standings on May 1, 1936

	W	L	Pct.	GB
Oakland	23	10	.697	--
Missions	18	14	.563	4½
Seattle	19	15	.559	4½
Portland	16	15	.516	6
Sacramento	14	17	.452	8
San Francisco	14	17	.452	8
San Diego	**14**	**20**	**.412**	**9½**
Los Angeles	11	21	.344	11½

ON THE ROAD AGAINST THE BEAVERS AND MISSIONS

Ed Wells pitched masterfully on May 1, allowing only four hits. The only run produced was on a homer by Beaver Johnny Frederick. The Padres bats gave Wells no support at all until the ninth inning. The ninth inning began with Padre third baseman Ernie Holman getting on base. Manager Shellenback sent in coach Eddie Mulligan to run for him. Vince DiMaggio followed with an out and Jimmy Kerr was sent in to pinch hit for left fielder Van Wirthman. Kerr got on, but not having any speed and with catcher Gene Desautels coming up, Shellenback wanted to stay out of a double play, so he sent in George Hockette—whose arm was questionable but whose legs were fine—to run for Kerr. Desautels had been carrying a hot bat to that point, but with two strikes against him, Hockette took off for second and he swung at the pitch. Home plate umpire Hood yelled strike three on Desautels and the Beaver catcher Brucker whipped the ball to second where the tag was applied to Hockette. Thus, the game ended, Beavers 1, Padres 0, on the strikeout-throwout double play.

While Lane was looking for help for his second division team, Don Hurst who had been playing with Los Angeles was offered to the Padres for the waiver price of $1,500. Lane declined, and stated that if Los Angeles is releasing him, he "must be through."[197]

Manager Shellenback looked to his own arm with the series knotted at two games each. The Padres bats that had slumbered so peacefully awoke. The Padres had seven runs on the board when Shellenback did not take the mound to start the bottom half of the fourth inning. He had what was described at the time as a "charley horse."

Despite only pitching three innings, the scorer—citing the "overwhelming lead"—gave Shellenback the win as was a scorer's prerogative at the time. Shellenback's 293rd win was closed out by six innings of relief-work by Archie Campbell, who gave up all four of Portland's runs.

By the time the game was over, Ernie Holman had clubbed a home run and three other Padres doubles. The other 17 hits the Padres had were all singles. The Padres won, 15-4.

Conditions had been rainy in Portland the entire series, and by Sunday the field was completely unfit for playing, and so the doubleheader was canceled, giving the Padres an early start to San Francisco to play the Missions. Southpaw George Hockette did travel with the team, as he headed for Los Angeles to see a chiropractor about his failing arm.

Despite the strikeout in game three of the Portland series, Padres catcher Gene Desautels had used the series to boost his batting average to .371, fourth best in the PCL behind San Francisco's Joe Marty (.435), Seattle's Hal Spindel (.400) and Cleo Carlyle of the Angels (.375). Overall, though, the team batting average slumped to the fifth best in the PCL (.287). The average was well off the pace of league-leading Oakland Acorns at .302, but still much better than the lightest hitting team, Sacramento (.265). Manager Shellenback could console himself with the fact that the upcoming Missions were not much better at .290 than his own club.[198]

7—MAY 1936 2ND DIVISION GETS COMFORTABLE

The Padres began the series against the Missions on Tuesday, May 5. Salvo was strong, allowing no walks and only five hits, but in the seventh and eighth innings the Missions managed to push a couple of runs across. Down by two, the Padres finally began to get to the Missions' pitcher, Frank Lamanske, who had held them scoreless till then. The Padres had runners on first and second when Padres batter Gene Desautels hit a screaming liner to Mission first baseman Roy Mort who snagged it in flight, touched first base to double up the runner, and then flipped to Clyde Beck at shortstop who stepped on the bag at second base to complete the triple play.

George Myatt was obviously fading during the game, going 1-for-4 but committing three errors. After the game, he would see Padres trainer Doc Richard, who was the only M.D.-credentialed trainer in the PCL. Myatt was diagnosed with "mild appendicitis" and told to take it easy for a few days.

The news from San Diego was not much more encouraging. Fresh from his triumph over the gopher, Lane Field groundskeeper Homer Knight announced his retirement. Knight had been a staple in San Diego sports facilities and was liked by the written press. It was also undeniable that the roof would not be completed in time for the Padres return, as the WPA had yet to give the go-ahead. This is not to say that progress had not been made. The plumbing was finally complete and so was the wiring. The infield soil which had caused a number of bad bounces in the original homestand was being reworked and "experimented" on.[199]

Because the local papers usually used the wire services exclusively for coverage of the San Diego team on the road, major attention was diverted elsewhere during their road trips. During this Padres road trip, the papers in San Diego kept most of the attention focused on the Bay League championship to be decided on May 8. The Hoover High Cardinals led by a game after coming off a 17-0 win over Inglewood. Hoover High ace Ted Williams would start against Woodrow Wilson High.

On May 6 the Padres presented a lineup without Myatt placing shortstop and hitting lead off. Berkowitz would fill both roles and go 3-for-6 on the day. Wells would be masterful in subduing the Missions, throwing nine innings of five-hit shutout ball. In the beautiful 81 degree weather three Mission pitchers would try and fail to stop the hemorrhaging of runs. The Padres would win, 7-0, alleviating some of the frustration from the first game in the series.

Wally Hebert would extend the shutout-pitching another nine innings, scattering five Mission hits. Hebert was impressive, but the triple and the double by Missions' catcher Joe Sprinz caused some tight spots that Hebert was able to pitch himself out of. This time Berkowitz would not contribute to the offense, going 0-for-4. Instead, it was the number seven and eight hitters, Van Wirthman and Gene Desautels, who would have multi-hit games and help give the Padres their four runs.

On May 8, the series moved south to San Diego. It was a true "David and Goliath" match-up with Trader Horne the shortest man on the Padres facing Lloyd "Eppa" Johnson, a 208 pound 6' 4½" giant on the mound. Horne started off impressively, throwing four more shutout innings, making it 22 innings since the Missions had scored a run. The Padres had a three-run lead after two innings but began to see it slip in the eighth. The Missions had begun the inning with only one run but had pushed another across this inning. Then, with the bases were loaded with still no outs, Horne threw a ball to the batter who connected, lining it in the direction of Padres' shortstop Myatt who had just recovered from his mild bout of appendicitis. Myatt snagged the ball in mid-air for one out, stepped on second for the second, and whipped over to Holman at third who stepped on the bag to snuff out the rally with the triple play. That was the second triple play the Padres had been involved within four days. Nevertheless, Horne appeared to be clearly losing his stuff and, after one out and one more Missions run, he was pulled in the ninth. Manny Salvo came in to close out the ninth, but by then the game was tied. Salvo would give up a run in the 11th inning and it began to look as if Myatt's heroics were all for naught. But, with two outs in the inning, the Padres would push the winning run across, taking the game, 5-4.

On Sunday, May 9, Padres second sacker Doerr got some bad news, as his brother Harold, who had been the second string catcher for the Houston club, had been sent down to Jacksonville of the East Texas League. Padres manager Shellenback was also out with influenza and had to hand over the reins to Eddie Mulligan. Herm Pillette, 41 years old, had not been with the team since his shelling on April 28. First, he had been out sick then his father died in Seattle. Finally, he was back in the starting rotation. "Old Folks" Pillette would pitch effectively, allowing only three runs, all of them coming in the sixth inning. Part of the reason for the three runs the Missions picked up in the sixth was Myatt's errant throw trying to turn a double play. Myatt's error total would be two for the game, two less than the total number of hits Pillette allowed.

Before 9,000 fans at the still incomplete Lane Field, Ed Wells took the mound for the Padres against Missions pitcher Frank Lamanske. Lamanske, who had narrowly escaped a loss the last time he had faced the Padres, did not need a triple play to get the win. He held the Padres to two runs on five hits. Wells pitched eight innings, giving up three runs. Archie Campbell came in to pitch the ninth and surrendered another run.

The back end of the twin-bill saw Manny Salvo take the mound for the Padres. Salvo would allow a run in the second, two in the third and blank the Missions in the fourth. But, with a rally developing, Salvo was pulled so that Mulligan could pinch hit. The rally evaporated as Walter "Boom-Boom" Beck, pitched the Missions out of the jam. Reliever Campbell took over the mound duties for the Padres and allowed only one more run over the last three innings. With darkness falling, Beck got two outs in the seventh but could not get the third as all five Padres runs were scored that inning. The game was then called by mutual consent, giving the Padres a 5-4 victory.

This win put the Padres record at 20-23, ahead of both Los Angeles (15-28) and Sacramento (18-24) and a half-game behind the Missions (20-22). The Padres spent travel-day Monday trying to sign backup catcher Art Veltman who had been released by the Angels due to illness.[200] Catcher Gene Desautels' bat alone was practically carrying the club, so it appeared likely owner Lane was just attempting to pick up a decent pinch hitter. He had released Kenny Iverson, Fred Vaughn and Ritchie Cooper unable to find berths for them in the lower minors.

BEAVERS HIT TOWN

The series against Portland became a celebration of the return of many local heroes. Earle Brucker was the first to be honored; he had been born in Albany, New York, but grew up in San Diego and was catching for the Beavers. May 13 was declared "Earle Brucker Day" and he was given a check at the game by Bill Lane.[201] The same honor would be bestowed on two of the Coscarart brothers, Pete and Steve, of Escondido on Sunday.*

The series began well enough for the Padres. Berly Horne began the game but was pulled in the third inning in favor of Archie Campbell. He had dominated Portland in his career up to that point (7-0), but that day he had given up seven hits and only retired six. Down 4-1 when he came in the game, reliever Campbell would allow only one more Portland player to cross the plate. To start the bottom of the ninth, Manager Shellenback sent Ed Wells up to pinch hit for Campbell. Wells walked and then Shellenback sent Mulligan in to pinch run for him. George Myatt sacrificed Mulligan to second and then Ced Durst received a base-on-balls. Portland at that point made a pitching change, Bobby Doerr ripped a single to left to load the bases. Ray Jacobs, the slowest man on the team, beat out a slow roller to shortstop for an infield hit and picking up the RBI. Ernie Holman hit a fly to

---

* Brother Joe was already playing in the major leagues.

center for an out, but Durst beat the throw to the plate with the winning run. Horne's jinx of Portland did not end, as the Padres picked up the 6-5 win.

Offensively, May 13 would turn out not to be Earle Brucker's day as he went 0-for-3. Portland's star pitcher, George Caster, pitched game two of the series and was masterful through seven innings. In the eighth, up 3-0, Caster surrendered two runs before getting out of the inning. The Padres held the Beavers scoreless in the top half of the ninth. Vince DiMaggio led off the bottom half of the ninth with a hit, but would only get as far as third base, as Caster put out the fire to win, 3-2.

May 14 saw Portland Beavers' pitcher Don French face Padres hurler Pillette. The papers noted that French did not have much on his fastball, but it had incredible movement. The Padres were held to three hits and only 10 balls left the infield. "Old Folks" Pillette faded and was pulled after six innings; he would take the loss, 5-0.

The next day before the game the white paint that had been under the scoreboard was repainted green. The Padres played had complained the white was hurting their eyes.[202]

The repainted scoreboard did seem to have an immediate effect, as Padres hurler Manny Salvo would return the shutout favor to the Beavers on May 15. The game may have been the ugliest shutout ever thrown! Salvo had been with the team just over a month and in his eight starts had given up only 19 earned runs. But a lot of this was luck and had to do with the breaks going his way.

Portland's 30-year old first baseman Johnny Frederick led off the ninth inning with a single. Moose Clabaugh, Portland's star right fielder, followed by hitting another single. Johnny Frederick, who Lane described as one of the two best players he had ever owned, stopped at second. This brought third sacker Fred Bedore to the plate but, before Bedore's at bat, Frederick wandered a bit too far off second base and was picked off by catcher Desautels. Bedore then hit the only extra base hit of the game, a double, and began tearing around the bases with his head down. Clabaugh, not the sharpest of players, headed into second and saw his manager's hands up and assumed the sign was for him. The play ended with two players on second base and both being tagged out.[203] The Padres offense was not in high gear, as the club only managed six hits in the game coupled with three walks. The Padres had taken the lead in the first inning on an almost textbook example of "little ball." George Myatt walked and then stole second. Portland's Bill Cronin, who was catching the game, uncorked an errant throw in trying to catch Myatt stealing second. Myatt advanced to third. Ced Durst failed to advance the runner home, but Bobby Doerr hit a ball to his Portland counterpart at second base, Pete Coscarart, and Myatt came home on the fielder's choice. One run, no hits. The Padres would pick up another run in the third to win, 2-0.

Myatt would make another error in the game, dropping his fielding percentage to .906 compared with his keystone partner's .970. Doerr and Myatt, nevertheless, had turned 21 double plays.

The Saturday game would be a pitching duel between Ed Wells and Portland pitcher Tom Flynn that was not decided until the last at bat of the game. Tied at two with two Padres on board the bases and two outs, Durst, was 0-for-3 when he came to bat. He connected, barely clearing the outreached glove of Portland shortstop Lee. Mulligan, who had pinch run for Shellenback when he had gotten on with a pinch hit, came home to score.

The Sunday twin bill saw 11,000 pack into Lane Field, a record for the Padres.[204] While there were a lot of fans in the seats, there weren't a lot of Padres in the dugout who could play. Frank Shellenback was still sidelined with his "charley horse" and back-up first baseman George McDonald, was still out with a broken finger from batting practice in Seattle. Ash Joerndt was having trouble with his knee. The cut had been made of the roster in Boston on the May 15 but the Padres still had no word as to which two players were being sent to them or when they would arrive.

George Hockette had returned from L.A., saying his arm was fine, so Shellenback sent him out to start game one. His arm was fine...well, fine for warming up on the mound...but not under fire. Of the first five batters he faced, he retired only one, walked one, allowed three hits, and wound up being charged with three runs. Again, Archie Campbell was called in to quell the fire, and later Manny Salvo finished the game, but the damage had been done in the first inning. The Padres dropped the game, 4-3. While the lights were not yet up at the stadium the game had not suffered from a power outage. Campbell hit a home run for the Padres and Portland pitcher Hobo Carson hit one for the Beavers that was described as the longest one hit at the park to date, landing in the left field bleachers, well over 360 feet from home plate.

Game two of the doubleheader, on May 17, was a seven-inning affair. Trader Horne took the mound and the results were typical of a Horne outing against the Portland team. Horne picked up his eighth win against the Beavers in two years, still without a losses. Vince DiMaggio got a round tripper to complete a stunning Sunday cycle (over two games) with seven at bats, four hits (including a home run, triple and double) for three RBIs, plus nine putouts in the field. His blast in the second game made the final score Padres 3, Beavers 1. Pete Coscarart continued the honoree jinx by booting a ball that resulted in a Padres run.

The series moved the Padres to atop the second division, ahead of Portland, Sacramento, and Los Angeles and 2½ games behind fourth-place Seattle.

THE TRAIN TO SACRAMENTO

The Padres rode to Sacramento on May 18. Earl Keller of the *San Diego Evening Tribune* traveled north with the team in anticipation of their debut in the first division.

Herm Pillette started the game going six innings but, after giving up two runs in his last inning of work, he was pulled in favor of a pinch hitter. Rubber-armed Archie Campbell finished the game for the Padres. In the top of the ninth, the Padres took the lead, 3-2, only to have Campbell lose the game in the bottom of the inning. Manny Salvo was sent in to get the final out, but even he failed.

May 20 was the second consecutive night affair. Wally Hebert endured the 2-1 loss in a game that was a study in the Padres players' failure to consummate. In four innings (2, 3, 6 and 8), the Padres got runners to third, but only in the sixth inning did they score. Manager Shellenback was almost ejected for arguing a stolen-base-call; he thought catcher Desautels' throw had gotten to second base in time. With the loss, they were then only one game ahead of the Sacramento Solons.

Manny Salvo, pitching in Sacramento hometown, failed to last three innings in the late contest. "Ever Ready" Campbell once again took over mound duties, completing the game and picking up enough offense behind him to win, 9-6. Jimmy Kerr was ejected from the game for arguing being put out at first base.

Shellenback announced after the game that players would be fined 50 cents for each time they left a runner at third base with less than two outs.[205] The money would be divided up evenly at the end of the season. The manager was also actively shopping George Hockette, showing him off by pitching batting practice in an attempt to entice a trade for an outfielder. Shellenback felt he could shop Hockette, as news had arrived from the Red Sox that the Padres would be receiving pitcher Johnny Welch (2-1 with a 5.51 ERA with Boston).

Back at Lane Field, the base paths between home and first and third and home were having their dirt replaced with clay from the local Rose Canyon area.[206] The rest of the infield (first to third) would remain the same. The dirt in the infield was sufficiently stable to allow the Padres to hold the league lead in double plays with 45, one more than Seattle.

7—MAY 1936 2ND DIVISION GETS COMFORTABLE

A Padres offensive explosion marked Friday night, May 22. The Padres would get 11 runs on 19 hits including two bunt singles by George Myatt. Ed Wells' curveball was working brilliantly, making the Solons go down with their big swings fanning the air. He allowed three runs in his complete-game effort.

The Saturday game was a day game. Both teams probably wished that it had been a night game. The 98-degree heat was oppressive. Berly Horne threw seven innings of five-hit shutout ball but, exhausted from the heat, he could not take the mound in the eighth. Archie Campbell finished the game for him, with two shutout innings. Padres catcher Jimmy Kerr also succumbed to the heat and Gene Desautels was hustled into the game as a replacement. The Padres would win, 5-0. Despite all the changes in personnel the game was finished in just 101 minutes.[207]

The Sunday doubleheader on May 24 saw Wally Hebert get the start for the Padres in game one. He would pick up the win but needed Manny Salvo to relieve him for the final 2⅔ innings. The final score was Padres 7, Solons 2. Three of the San Diego runs came on Sacramento errors and another run on a Vince DiMaggio homer.

Herman Pillette would start the second game and Shellenback had to have been worried, given the state of his bullpen and Pillette's inability to complete games. But "Old Folks" showed he was more than up to the task, allowing Sacramento only one run over 9 innings. Unfortunately, Solons leather would shut out the Padres. Three sensational catches by left fielder Buster Adams made the difference. The only Solons run came on a slow roller by San Diego-native Joe Dobbins up the third baseline with two outs and two strikes on him. Pillette did not get to the ball quickly enough, and Dobbins took off for second. Jimmy Kerr's throw arrived with Dobbins still three feet from second base, but fortunately for Dobbins, when George Myatt applied the tag, the ball was knocked loose. Myatt was not charged with an error. Dobbins would eventually come around to score.

After the game, the Padres announced the release of Ash Joerndt. The reason given was his trick knee. The club also announced that, if George Hockette did not get into shape, in the next week, he would be declared voluntarily retired.[208]

HOME SWEET HOME?

Tuesday, May 26, found the Padres back in San Diego. Manny Salvo took the mound and hurled what his catcher Gene Desautels described as his fastest fastball yet. San Francisco sent Eddie Stutz to the mound and he ended with his sixth loss in a row in a 9-3 lacing. Salvo would use the brushback pitch masterfully and it resulted in a bit of name calling from the Seals' bench. Harley Boss, Seals first baseman, was knocked down twice in one at bat, the first of which missed his head by only an inch. The Padres would get 17 hits, with only Desautels and Myatt going hitless. Ernie Holman would use two bunt singles to take the team batting average led at .342. The win put the Padres' win-loss record at an even .500 (29-29).

The Padres lean roster was getting to be an issue. Johnny Welch, who had been expected to arrive on Sunday, had yet to appear. The outfield situation seemed critical as well, but Earl Keller reported in the *San Diego Evening Tribune* that the Padres would soon sign an unnamed University of California outfielder.

The San Diego press was also upset by stories about the Padres not drawing well. Mainly, ones appearing in the Los Angeles papers. The *Los Angeles Examiner*, for instance, reported only 800 people had shown up for the Tuesday game at Lane Field. The Tuesday gate showed 1,220 (of which 821 paid). Earl Keller in the *Tribune* countered the reason for the showing was because the fleet was out of town. Los Angeles, he noted, was the only town in the PCL that showed gate receipts off for the season compared to the prior year.

Ed Wells was sent to the mound on May 27. Wells' slow curve, following Salvo's blazing heat, was thought to be a genius call by Shellenback. Lefty O'Doul's selection of Win Ballou to pitch was not quite as much of a genius move. O'Doul would even have put himself on the mound after his starter had given up six runs, five of them earned. Seeing O'Doul on the mound had to be bittersweet for owner Lane, who had converted him to an outfielder in Salt Lake City, saying he was too good of a hitter to be a pitcher.[209] Wells would falter in the ninth, giving up four more runs and allowing the Seals to get within one, but Archie Campbell got the call from the pen and he put out the fire...Padres 7, Seals 6.

The Padres were in the first division, but not all the news was good. Lane had spoken with Johnny Welch on the phone and Welch had told the San Diego owner that he had no intention of traveling west, that he was planning on staying in the Midwest. Welch had done this before when he was sent down. A few years before, he had gone to Los Angeles after reassignment but stayed only a few games before going home. To get his attention, Lane Welch was threatened with suspension.[210]

The win put the club into fourth place. The Padres' stay in the first division, however, was short. They dropped the next game, 4-3, to the Seals. Glove work, or lack thereof, was the difference. Bobby Doerr's error in the sixth inning cost the Padres a run and Joe Berkowitz, who came in as a late-inning replacement for Jacobs, committed an error at first that allowed the Seals to win it in the 10th inning. It was the Padres third loss in an extra-inning game.

Friday, May 29, brought the worst Padres pummeling to date. It was difficult to determine which was worse...the Padres pitching? Or, the Padres fielding? Three Padres' errors would mar the first inning. Campbell, who started, gave up two unearned runs in the first and an equal number of earned ones. After two more innings and one more run, he was out of the game. George Hockette then came in for his "swan song" with the Padres, pitching two perfect innings, but in the sixth was touched up for four runs on five hits and a walk. Things became so desperate that even PCL President Bill Tuttle's son, "Bud," who had been on the roster but had not appeared in a game all season was called upon. In his first inning of work, he gave up three runs and five hits. But then Tuttle calmed down and did something no other Padre did in the game; he struck out a batter. Tuttle finished the game, allowing no more hits. During the game Ernie Holman had a single which extended his hitting streak to 11 games in which he is hit .545. The final score was in the Seals' favor was, 12-0.

The Saturday and Sunday double twin-bills would bring out 15,000 fans. The four games started off well for the Padres, with Saturday's first game being won by Wally Hebert, 5-3. The second game looked it was going to be a breeze for Pillette as he was leading 7-0 going into the sixth, but once again his stamina began to falter. Archie Campbell came in but was pulled after he gave up the lead. Berly Horne would complete the game as the Padres lost 12-7.

Sunday found only Ed Wells and Manny Salvo on the staff as capable of pitching. Salvo took the mound in game one against Eddie Stutz. This time would be a reversal of their earlier match-up, with the Seals taking the game, 5-3. Salvo and Lefty O'Doul would have a memorable encounter. Salvo would give a little nick to Seals third baseman Steve Barath, hitting him on the finger. Salvo had already given up three runs in the first. O'Doul in the third base coach's box yelled to Salvo that he better watch out or he might kill someone. Salvo threw off his glove and walked over to O'Doul. Lefty wasted no time and threw a punch that landed on Salvo's right eye. Fists were exchanged, yet neither man was ejected. Salvo finished the game with a loss and a shiner.[211]

After having dropped the first game, 5-3, all Padres hopes rested on Ed Wells. However, he would last only three innings in giving up five runs. Unable to endure anymore from the bench, Shellenback took the mound and completed the game allowing no more runs but it was too late. The Padres dropped the game, 5-2.

At the end of May, the Padres stood in second place in the second division having dropped four of the last seven games against the Seals.

Hopefully, things would only improve.

7—MAY 1936 2ND DIVISION GETS COMFORTABLE

PITCHING AND HITTING, "THE KID" DOES IT ALL

While the Padres were having trouble hitting that was not the case for a local high school player who was hitting a celestial .461 in early May. Playing for Wofford Caldwell's Bay League-leading team Hoover High's Ted Williams was continuing an explosive offensive season.[212]

Position	Games	At bats	Runs	Hits	Average
P/OF	21	61	19	28	.461

During the Padres' road trip in Portland and San Francisco the sportswriters' attention had other baseball goings-on to focus on, the Bay League championship to be decided on May 8. The Hoover High Cardinals led by a game after coming off a 17-0 win over Inglewood. There was that name again, Hoover High "ace" Ted Williams would start against Long Beach's Woodrow Wilson High on the eighth.

What followed was 14-1 romp over Wilson. Williams allowed only three hits and struck out 13.

After the game, Coach Caldwell was asked to talk about scouts and their impact on his players. In the discussion, Caldwell spoke of his two best prospects and how they became ineffective by listening to advice from big leaguers. In the article, it was obvious that the coach was not referring to Ted Williams as one of his two best prospects he had coached. Caldwell's mind was not on other things, as his next competition, Beverly Hills High, was expected to forfeit as they had not won a game all season and were not eager for the trip to San Diego.[213] Years later some would speculate this was part of Caldwell's and Lane's efforts to get Ted to sign with the hometown team.

Whatever. There was no distraction as Hoover finished its league season with a 9-1 win over Beverly Hills. Next up was Escondido High on May 22.

The *San Diego Union* called it a "startling upset" as Escondido won the championship game over Hoover and Williams, 8-3.[214] Ted Williams took the loss, allowing nine hits, while the Cardinals were able to muster only five hits.

His high school career over, Williams was honored by being one of the two pitchers selected for the All-League Team. His league record was 5-0 with 66 strikeouts in 39 innings. Not bad, but he probably would have preferred to be recognized for his hitting ability.[215]

The end of May provided some tantalizing news regarding Williams. Owner Lane reportedly had offered Ted Williams a contract. Lane made it clear he would not give him a tryout as a pitcher. He would be an outfielder and "...if he can hit he might get a regular berth." Lane promised not to send him out for seasoning and he would report as soon as he graduates. His parents had yet to consent but it was known that they favored him playing baseball at home.[216]

Contracts have been waved in front of the Williams' family in the past. The Yankees, the Cardinals...and now the Padres.

The Padres played 31 games in May 1936 winning 17 and losing 14. The individual player batting and pitching records for the month are provided in Table 7.2. Having a very good month Ernie Holman batted an even .400, and Van Wirthman was close behind with a .383 average. The pitchers were led by Wally Hebert and Ed Wells, each with four wins.

Table 7.2. Batting and Pitching Totals for May

Players	Positions	G	AB	R	H	1B	2B	3B	HR	RBI	SB	AVG
Ernie Holman	3b-31	31	115	16	46	39	4	2	1	19	3	.400
Van Wirthman	lf-31	31	115	13	44	33	9	1	1	16	3	.383
Frank Shellenback	p-2, ph-1	3	3	1	1	1	0	0	0	0	0	.333
Cedric Durst	cf-31	31	124	18	41	30	10	1	0	18	0	.331
Bobby Doerr	2b-31	31	126	14	41	34	5	2	0	13	4	.325
Vince DiMaggio	rf-31	31	111	19	34	19	11	2	2	13	3	.306
Gene Desautels	c-25	25	85	7	25	19	5	1	0	8	1	.294
George Myatt	ss-27, ph-1	28	111	22	30	25	3	2	0	8	3	.270
Jimmy Kerr	c-11, ph-3	14	28	1	7	7	0	0	0	4	1	.250
Ray Jacobs	1b-27, ph-1	28	106	11	25	18	7	0	0	20	0	.236
George McDonald	1b-5	5	17	2	4	4	0	0	0	2	1	.235
Ed Wells	p-7, ph-5	12	22	2	5	4	1	0	0	1	0	.227
Archie Campbell	p-11	11	14	1	3	2	0	0	1	2	0	.214
Joe Berkowitz	ss-4, 1b-2, ph-2, lf-1, cf-1	10	19	3	4	3	0	1	0	3	0	.211
Manny Salvo	p-10	10	15	1	3	3	0	0	0	1	0	.200
Wally Hebert	p-6	6	17	0	2	2	0	0	0	1	0	.118
Herman Pillette	p-5	5	11	2	1	1	0	0	0	2	0	.091
Trader Horne	p-6, pr-1	7	12	1	1	1	0	0	0	0	0	.083
Ashley Joerndt	ph-2	2	2	0	0	0	0	0	0	0	0	.000
Bud Tuttle	p-1	1	1	0	0	0	0	0	0	0	0	.000
George Hockett	p-2, pr-1	3	1	0	0	0	0	0	0	0	0	.000
Eddie Mulligan	pr-9, ph-1	10	0	4	0	0	0	0	0	0	2	.000

Pitchers	G	GS	CG	ShO	Sv	W	L	PCT	IP	H	R	ER	SO	BB	ERA
Frank Shellenback	2	1	0	0	0	1	0	1.000	7	2	0	0	2	1	0.00
Wally Hebert	6	5	4	1	0	4	2	.667	46⅓	46	11	10	11	7	1.94
Ed Wells	7	7	4	1	0	4	3	.571	54⅔	53	20	19	17	11	3.13
Manny Salvo	10	6	4	1	1	3	2	.600	49⅔	46	18	18	19	9	3.26
Trader Horne	6	5	2	0	0	2	1	.667	35⅓	37	15	13	15	15	3.31
Herman Pillette	5	5	2	0	0	1	2	.333	32⅓	29	13	13	13	7	3.62
Archie Campbell	11	1	0	0	3	2	3	.400	39	39	25	19	8	12	4.38
Bud Tuttle	1	0	0	0	0	0	0	.000	3	5	3	3	1	3	9.00
George Hockette	2	1	0	0	0	0	1	.000	3⅓	8	7	7	0	4	18.90

CHAPTER 8
JUNE 1936
"THE KID" DEBUTS

NOTABLE WORLD EVENTS-JUNE 1936

1st *The Queen Mary arrives in New York City in 4 days, 12 hours, 24 minutes*

11th *Alf Landon, the Governor of Kansas, receives the nomination as the Republican Party's candidate for President of the United States*

19th *Max Schmeling knocks out Joe Louis in the 12th round at Yankee Stadium before 39,878 spectators*

The "slugging" of Manny Salvo and Seals' manager Lefty O'Doul at the end of the first inning of game one on Sunday, May 31, did little to lift the Padres' spirits in the wake of a doubleheader loss at Lane Field. As the team headed into June, the Padres barely held fifth place in the PCL, one-half game ahead of Portland, as seen in Table 8.1.

The morning *San Diego Union* noted that the Seals series pointed out a club weakness, that the Padres still are battling with only three outfielders and could use another slugging outfielder.[217]

Table 8.1. PCL Standings on June 1, 1936

	W	L	Pct.	GB
Seattle	37	29	.561	
Oakland	37	29	.561	--
Missions	35	29	.547	1
San Francisco	34	30	.531	2
San Diego	**31**	**34**	**.477**	**5½**
Portland	29	33	.468	6
Sacramento	28	35	.444	7½
Los Angeles	26	38	.406	10

While they prepared for the arrival of the last-place Los Angeles Angels at Lane Field, the Padres were still awaiting word from Johnny Welch, the Red Sox hurler who still refused to report to San Diego and, thus, remained under threat of suspension. Welch was released by the Red Sox on May 21 but continued his refusal to join the Padres. He had become a problem player for Red Sox manager Joe Cronin, who reportedly wanted him as far away as possible, and San Diego seemed to satisfy that objective.[218]

After the Angels' series, the Padres would head to the Bay area for a weeklong series with the Seals before returning home to host Oakland and Sacramento.

THE RIVALS

Truck Hannah, acting manager in place of Jack Lelivelt, led the Angels south to Lane Field. The timing of Lelivelt's scouting trip back east may not have been a coincidence since Lelivelt had boasted during the off-season that the Angels had driven the Hollywood Stars to San Diego from Los Angeles and that the city would be much better off for their departure.[219] While perhaps not on the level of Bill Terry's comment regarding Brooklyn still being in the National League, the comment received prominent play in the morning paper. The Angels were leading the PCL in batting, but pitching troubles kept them in the cellar. Prior to the series, Bill Lane bolstered the Padre pitching staff with the acquisition of Dick Ward, a former Angel standout, from the Cardinals. Ward had posted a 2-3 record for Sacramento in 1936 before reporting to St. Louis.

Just before the beginning of the series, a newspaper report at the bottom of the last sports page further confirmed that Bill Lane had offered a contract for the remainder of the 1936 season to Ted Williams.[220]

The Angels drew first blood with a 5-4 win on Tuesday, June 2, behind starter Jack Salveson. The bespectacled pitcher also delivered the game-winning blow, a two-strike, two-out double in the sixth inning. The Padres got the tying run as far as third base in the seventh, but pitcher Archie "Iron Man" Campbell was tagged out when he lost his footing after rounding third base. Starter Trader Horne took the loss for the Padres.

Wally Hebert threw a five-hitter to even the series on Wednesday with a 5-1 win.

Off the field, owner Lane agreed to allow delinquent Johnny Welch to report to the Pittsburgh Pirates instead of the Padres in exchange for a "player to be named" from the Pirates. Since Welch had refused to report to San Diego, this arrangement was the best that Lane could manage.* In an attempt to address the need for a power outfielder, Lane made an offer to Indianapolis for Ivy Shiver. The Indianapolis club had recently

---

* Welch finished the year with Pittsburgh, getting into nine games. His last full season was 1937 with the Chicago White Sox farm club in St. Paul. That turned out to be the end of his baseball career. In February 1938 he once again refused a contract that would have sent him to the PCL and Welch ended up being on the suspended list. He died at age 33 in September 1940 after battling tuberculosis for several years. Source: Nowlin, Bill, "Johnny Welch," SABR Baseball Biography Project, https://sabr.org/bioproj/person/a0d79463.

acquired Oscar Eckhardt, who had led the PCL in batting in previous seasons, and Lane hoped that that would make Shiver available. Finally, in the aftermath of the Lefty O'Doul–Manny Salvo fisticuffs on Sunday, league president W. C. Tuttle said he had no plans to legislate against the beanball because of the difficulty of enforcing such a rule.[221]

The Angels turned around their season-long struggle in the middle games of the series. Thursday was an 11-2 rout, with Padres pitchers Ed Wells, Manny Salvo, and George Hockette absorbing the blows. After earlier attempts to trade Hockette went nowhere, he was given his release after the game. The only bright spot for the Padres was Ernie Holman's third straight multi-hit game. Dick Ward made his Padres debut on Friday but did not survive the third inning. A five-run seventh took Ward off the hook and knocked out Los Angeles ace Fay "Scow" Thomas, but the Angels rallied for a run in the eighth inning. Then, in the ninth, Padres left fielder Van Wirthman fell over the netting in left field while chasing a ball over his head, resulting in a fluke home run and an 8-7 victory for the Angels. Wally Hebert took the loss in relief, and Vince DiMaggio's home run was the offensive highlight. Skipper Frank Shellenback took the mound on Saturday, but a four-run second inning led to a 5-2 loss, despite three hits from DiMaggio. Shellenback tried regular shortstop George Myatt, just coming back from an injury, in left field for this game, but the shakeup did not awaken the Padres' hitting attack. The heading of the box score for the game read "Cellar Bound!"[222]

The Angels won their fourth in a row in the Sunday opener behind Jack Salveson, who again helped himself with a seventh-inning triple in a 4-2 win. Perhaps reflecting club frustration, the Padres lost several disputes with the umpiring crew. Hebert salvaged the finale with a six-hitter and contributed a home run to a 7-2 Padre victory. Despite the headline of the previous day, the Padres dropped only to sixth after losing five of seven to Los Angeles, while the Angels climbed past Sacramento out of the cellar.

Work was slated to continue on Lane Field during the upcoming road trip. Improvements included replacing the sandy infield soil with brickyard clay and erecting girders and cross members on the roof to support lights.[223] Infield work would end up being delayed until after the next homestand.

THE CITY BY THE BAY

The Padres hoped to erase the disappointment of the Angels series in San Francisco, and sent Salvo to the mound in the opener against Lefty O'Doul's team. The Seals lost four of seven to their hometown rivals, the Missions, during the previous week and held fourth place, three games over .500. Lane continued to pursue the Red Sox for two players owed to his club and discovered that Indianapolis was unwilling to part with slugging outfielder Shiver in the immediate future. On the bright side, Herman Pillette was recovered from a finger injury and ready to take his place in the rotation later in the week.

Manny Salvo raised his won-lost record to 7-3 by pitching the Padres to a 7-3 win over the Seals in the series opener. Vince DiMaggio led the way with three hits, including a home run and a double.

The offense continued on a roll Wednesday afternoon, as Myatt returned to shortstop and laced four hits to lead a 15-hit attack in an 8-3 victory. Ward pitched into the eighth inning to earn his first win as a Padre. Archie Campbell finished the game for San Diego without any runs being scored. Myatt's return to shortstop was hastened by a finger injury suffered by utility infielder Joe Berkowitz before the game. The injury was serious enough that the team sent Berkowitz back to San Diego.

The Padres won their fourth straight game on Thursday as Bobby Doerr singled home Myatt in the ninth for a 5-4 win. Wally Hebert notched his 10th win of the season in a complete game effort.

Bill Lane continued his efforts to improve the team by trading pitcher Ed Wells, a southpaw, to Seattle in exchange for Howard Craghead, a tall right-hander. Wells posted a record of 5-6, including several one-run losses. A change of scenery was in order for Craghead, 2-7 with the Indians, who had just taken over first place. Preliminary reaction suggested that Seattle got the best of the deal,[224] although it was noted that Craghead was only in his twenties, while Wells was approaching his middle thirties. The deal left San Diego with only one lefthander, Wally Hebert, after starting the season with three southpaws in the starting rotation.

Meanwhile, a dispute erupted between the Oakland club and PCL president Tuttle over how the pennant winner would be decided. Tuttle, after conferring with the Seals' owner the previous week, had announced that the winner of the playoff would be crowned as PCL champ, but Oakland's president argued that the team in first place at the end of the season would be considered the champion.[225] Tuttle would have his hands full throughout the season with various owners in the league.

The Seals put a resounding end to the Padres' winning streak with a 15-2 drubbing on Friday, June 12. A six-run second inning drove Horne to the showers, and Craghead was less than impressive in his Padre debut, yielding eight earned runs in 6⅔ innings of long relief. Seals starter Sam Gibson struck out 13 Padres in a complete-game effort.

San Diego rebounded behind a fine pitching performance by Manager Shellenback Saturday to defeat the Seals, 6-1. Shellenback, Doerr, and Durst each had three hits as the Padres battered Kenny Sheehan and Bobby Cole for 20 hits in the game.

A superb road trip became only a good road trip on Sunday as San Diego dropped both ends of the doubleheader to San Francisco. Salvo could not hold a three-run lead in the opener as the Seals came back for a 7-3 win behind Win Ballou. Herman Pillette gave up three runs in the first inning of the nightcap, his only inning of work. Then, after San Diego came back to tie the game, Trader Horne was knocked out in a five-run third inning as the Seals went on to a 9-3 victory.

OAKLAND PAYS A VISIT

Usually, the Tuesday morning paper would trumpet the upcoming series for the Padres, but the impending first visit of the year by Oakland was featured in Sunday's paper.[226] Known both as the Acorns and the Oaks, Oakland swept a doubleheader from Seattle on Sunday to regain first place by 1½ games, while the Padres continued in sixth place, a mere half-game ahead of the Angels. Oakland's strengths included good hitting, especially right-handed power tailored to their ballpark, a "perfect outfield"[227] consisting of Jack Glynn, Fern Bell, and Earl Bolyard, and excellent pitching. Wee Willie Ludolph, the staff ace with a 10-1 mark, was termed the "Christy Mathewson of the minors." Jack La Rocca, noted for his fastball, and Jim Tobin, whose self-styled nickname was "The Mighty," were also consistent winners.

The Oaks did not exactly live up to its advance billing in the opening game Tuesday, as Hebert hurled a shutout and San Diego scored 16 runs. Vince DiMaggio triggered the attack with an inside-the-park home run, and Doerr scored four times. Oakland southpaw Ken Douglas had posted 14 consecutive victories against the Hollywood Stars but apparently did not find Lane Field to his liking.[228]

Fastballer Jack La Rocca took the mound for the Acorns on Wednesday, but the Padre offense continued in gear. A three-run fourth inning drove La Rocca from the mound, and Howard Craghead, making his first start at Lane Field as a Padre, notched a complete game 5-3 win. Centerfielder Durst and young first baseman George McDonald both had four hits in the game. Several thousand "feminine fans and their escorts" were on hand for a mid-week Ladies Day game.[229]

Oaks manager Billy Meyer decided to come back with Ken Douglas in the third game of the series on Thursday, but he was again ineffective and did not get past the sixth inning. Manny Salvo struggled early with his control, but settled down to go the distance in a 6-3 Padres victory. The home team collected 12 hits off

Douglas and reliever Jim Tobin, as Ernie Holman led the way with a 3-for-4 day. The loss dropped the Oaks out of first place.

Oakland's ace, Wee Willie Ludolph, had been held out of the series to date with a sore elbow but took the mound against Horne in the Friday matchup.[230] Ludolph lacked his usual fastball but held the Padres at bay except for a two-out rally in the fourth, when Holman walked and raced home on DiMaggio's double into the left field corner. Trader Horne made the run stand up until the sixth when two walks and a single loaded the bases with one out. Horne induced pop flies from the next two batters and sailed through the rest of the game to record a three-hit, 1-0 shutout. Meanwhile, a Missions win and a Seattle loss put both teams in a tie for first. The Padres fourth straight victory over Oakland merited the top headline in the Saturday sports section, even over Max Schmeling's surprising defeat of Joe Louis for the world heavyweight crown.

The Padres outhit the Oaks 11-8 in the Saturday, June 20, game, but left the bases loaded in both the sixth and eighth innings as Jim Tobin escaped with a 4-2 win over skipper Frank Shellenback. The Oaks' outfield showed why they were regarded as the best defensively in the PCL when centerfielder Bolyard robbed DiMaggio of a home run in the second inning. For the locals, George McDonald's 14-game hitting streak came to an end.

San Diego roared back in the Sunday doubleheader, scoring 13 runs in the middle innings of the opener on their way to a 20-4 drubbing, then winning the nightcap when Durst drove home George Myatt in the bottom of the seventh for a 3-2 win. A crowd of more than 9,000 fans was on hand for the twin bill. Myatt led the offense with five hits and four runs in the opener while catcher Gene Desautels drove in four runs to give Hebert an easy 12th win. In the second game, Howard Craghead outdueled screwballer Harold Haid and two relievers. Oaks' pitcher Jim Tobin played left field and had two hits in the nightcap, but it didn't help. Oakland manager Billy Meyer and right fielder Jack Glynn were ejected in the home seventh after a close pickoff play on Myatt at first base following his leadoff base hit. Doerr sacrificed Myatt to second, and Durst's blast to the fence in right field won the game. As noted in the Monday morning paper, "Syd [sic] Durst is top hole when it comes to delivering in those pinches."[231]

The doubleheader sweep and the 6-1 series victory lifted San Diego to the .500 mark and raised them to fifth place, 1½ games ahead of the Seals and just 3½ games from the lead. Oakland, which began the week in first place, slipped to fourth but remained within ½ game of first place as both Seattle and the Missions were also swept on Sunday. Howard Craghead's two victories during the week began to sway skeptics who had questioned the wisdom of the Wells-Craghead trade.

Even before the well-attended Oakland series, the Padres had drawn over 90,000 fans, exceeding the season total for the 1935 Stars at Wrigley Field.[232] Attendance had remained steady for each weekly series, allaying any fears that other PCL owners may have had about San Diego's ability to support a team. The Oakland series drew 17,500, the second highest weekly total for the season.[233]

AN INTERLUDE – AND AN INTRODUCTION TO TED WILLIAMS

With Sacramento due in for a series to start on Tuesday, June 23, the back-to-back home series gave the Padres a Monday off-day at home. Well, sort of an off-day.

To celebrate the local connection with the U. S. Armed Forces the Padres scheduled a benefit game for the Navy Relief Society on Monday, June 22. The rarely used Bud Tuttle, son of the PCL president, got the call on the mound for San Diego. And, to please the locals, Manager Shellenback announced that Ted Williams would be given an opportunity to display his talents in the exhibition.[234] Also, Grossmont High's standout shortstop Bill Gray would also be afforded a chance to play.

To no one's surprise, the Padres jumped out to a 12-1 lead after seven innings in front of 4,000 fans, including some of the highest dignitaries in the Navy. Several young high school and sandlot players then entered the game, including Williams in left field, Gray at shortstop, Benny Simpson in centerfield, and Tom Downey at third base. Padres pitcher Bud Tuttle ran out of gas, giving up nine runs in the last two innings. Williams singled and scored a run in his only at bat in his first appearance in a San Diego Padres box score, albeit an exhibition.

SOLONS SOJOURN SOUTH

The struggling Sacramento Solons, in the PCL cellar with a record 18 games below .500, arrived in town next for a weeklong series. The Solons were the only club out of the pennant race, as noted by *San Diego Union* Sports Editor Ted Steinmann in his column, "This 'N That".[235]

Seven clubs were in the thick of the pennant fight with only six games separating the leader from the seventh place clubs. And Sacramento, off to a slow start, was expected to get tougher to handle with new talent being added as the season progressed.

San Diego's Padres were in an odd spot, after knocking Oakland out of the lead. They were struggling to keep fifth place over San Francisco and Los Angeles, both dangerous clubs, particularly the Angels, who found themselves finally after getting off to a poor start.

For the Padres, the month had begun in the midst of a war of words over Manny Salvo's alleged headhunting tendencies, and the opening game of the series with Sacramento which had Salvo front and center again. He began by hitting Frankie Morehouse, the leadoff man, and a San Diego resident. Later in the inning, Morehouse barreled into catcher Gene Desautels, who recorded the putout but left the game shortly thereafter with leg and back injuries. Salvo drilled Morehouse again in his second at bat, and "the injury was decidedly painful and possibly serious."[236] With the Solons trailing 8-3 in the sixth, starter Cotton Pippen hit Salvo in the face with a pitch that knocked him out of the game. The hometown paper downplayed the beanball battle, noting that Morehouse "ducked into an inside ball."[237] Archie Campbell finished up the 10-4 victory while Bobby Doerr led the offense with three hits, including one of five Padres triples. Jimmy Kerr, who replaced Desautels behind the plate, also collected three hits.

Kerr kept up his timely hitting in the second game of the series on Wednesday, but his two-run homer was the only offense as the Padres fell, 5-2. Berly Horne was the losing pitcher, despite notching eight strikeouts. The game report noted that Horne struck out the leadoff batter, "thereby putting on the oldest jinx in baseball," a reference to a long-disappeared belief that it was bad luck to strike out the leadoff man.[238] In this case, it turned out to be true as the Solons scored three runs in the first and were never behind after that. The training room report took up much of the game story, with Salvo reporting only a slightly bruised cheek and cuts inside his mouth, Desautels out of action for a few more days, and Morehouse, with no broken bones, expected back before the end of the series. The Padres signed a San Diego boy named Elmer Evert for emergency catching duties until Desautels could return.

Wally Hebert's bid for his 13th victory fell short on Thursday as Sacramento pushed across four runs in the sixth inning to break open a pitchers' duel. Robert Ross, making his second start for the Solons since arriving from the Houston club in the Texas League, yielded only five hits, including three infield hits by speedy leadoff man Myatt. Ross also contributed a defensive gem, throwing out Van Wirthman while lying on the ground after slipping on the grass near the mound.

8—JUNE 1936 "THE KID" DEBUTS

THE KID SIGNS! BUT...WITH WHO?

As a pitcher-outfielder Ted Williams batted .583 and .406 in his last two years of high school and .430 for all three years.[239] He also was successful as a pitcher going 10-2 in his senior year and had one game where he struck out 19.[240]

For the past year, there was ongoing speculation about Ted Williams being courted by several major league baseball teams most notably the New York Yankees, by scout Vinegar Bill Essick, and the St. Louis Cardinals, by Herb Benninghoven.

Detroit also got into the act. Williams recalled that the Tigers sent a scout named Marty Krug, a longtime PCL infielder and manager, to watch his last game in high school: "After Marty Krug watched me he came and sat with my mother, they talked and that night she was in tears. He told me I had a lot of good moves, but I was so scrawny a year of professional baseball would kill me."[241]

In his autobiography written with John Underwood, Williams recounted what was going on behind the scenes with various teams in pursuit: "I eventually did get an offer from the Cardinals, but they would have probably sent me to Oshkosh or Peoria or someplace, because they had a huge farm system then and you could get lost. By that time Bill Essick of the Yankees had come around...Essick was as anxious as anybody to get me. I'll never forget what he said: 'Ted, if I didn't think you were going to be a New York Yankee, I'd never sign you.' Maybe he said that to everybody, but that sure impressed me. I think he offered $200 a month, and a $500 bonus if I made the team at Binghamton, New York, but the story is my mother asked for a $1,000 bonus and Essick refused.

"Los Angeles of the Pacific Coast League wanted to sign me. They were the Angels then, a good club, and I might have signed, but by this time my dad was in the act. He had never seen me play too much, but he could see I was getting an awful lot of attention and he got the idea I was the second coming of Ruth...as my spokesman, he made up his mind he didn't like the Los Angeles manager, Truck Hannah."[242]

Now, with Williams's high school career concluded speculation ramped up beginning on June 1 with an article that announced: "San Diego Contract Offered Williams."[243] Not the Yankees, nor the Cardinals, and not Detroit...but San Diego!

San Diego Contract Offered Williams

Headline of Article Announcing Offer to Williams
San Diego Evening Tribune, June 1, 1936

The article indicated that Bill Lane had offered a contract to Williams on Saturday, May 30. Needing consent of his parents Williams was reported to have indicated he would give Lane an answer in a few days. Also, to no one's surprise who had been watching Williams over the past several years, Lane stated that his intent would be to use the kid in the outfield and not as a pitcher.

It's a bit unclear as to the date Williams's family signed a contract. In an interview with Bobby Doerr some 60 years later, he indicated that Williams was on the train ride from San Diego to San Francisco on Monday, June 8. Yet, there was nothing public about any signing. In those days, it wasn't uncommon that a player might play a game or two before being offered a contract.

Here is how Bobby Doerr described events: "Ted came in for a tryout. I was standing on the right side of the batting cage, one of those old cages we used to have. All the players were standing around waiting to hit. Most players in those days were ex-major leaguers…I remember Ted standing probably four or five feet in front of me. Nobody knew who he was. Big gangly kid. He said he was 147 pounds, six foot three. Shellenback was managing the team, and he was also a pitcher. He was pitching batting practice and he said, 'Let the kid get in and hit a few.' All the guys around the cage, I remember they were moaning, 'Oh geez, this guy's gonna take up our time.' Ted got in and hit, I guess I'd say six or seven balls. I don't exactly remember, but he hit at least one out of the ballpark…When he walked out of the cage, some guy standing on the other side of the batting cage, I wish I could remember who it was, said, 'This kid's going to be signed before the week's out.'

"This was on a Thursday.[*] Every Monday was an off day in the Coast League. That Monday night we were taking the train to San Francisco to play either the Seals or the Missions, two teams that played in the same ballpark. And here's Ted down at the railroad depot all excited that he was going on the trip, walking up and down. That was really my first experience of seeing him."[244]

As noted earlier, the Padres were able to have Williams play in its Navy benefit game on June 22nd. The next day there still was no word on a contract.

Then, on Friday, June 26, *Evening Tribune* beat writer Earl Keller reported that the way things look "Williams may not get lined up with any team this year. The Padres, Yankees, and Cardinals still are dickering with him."[245] Was the train trip to San Francisco a diversionary ruse?

Finally, on June 27, San Diego sports fans learned what was going on. That morning's *San Diego Union* pronounced: "Williams, Former Hoover Star, Signed by Padres as Outfielder."

Williams, Former Hoover Star, Signed by Padres as Outfielder

Article Headline Announcing Ted Williams Signs Contract
San Diego Union, June 27, 1936

The story noted that Williams was a pitcher in high school, but would be used in the outfield because of his hitting abilities. Williams was listed as slightly over six feet in height and weighed in at 165 pounds. The terms of the contract kept Williams with the Padres for the remainder of 1936 and all of 1937 without being farmed out.[246]

In his book with Underwood, here is how Williams described how he came to sign with Lane and the hometown Padres: "So finally I went and worked out with the San Diego team, and by now the pressure's on pretty good for me to sign with San Diego. It was a new team. It had been moved to San Diego from Hollywood

---

[*] That would have been Thursday, June 4th

the year before and everybody was getting civic-minded about the San Diego Padres. A few of the politicians got into it, talking to my mother, and my mother liked the idea because she wanted me close to home."

"So I signed with the Padres in 1936, first for my mother's sake, second because when I signed for $150 a month they said they would pay me for the whole month of June, though this was on the twentieth of the month. That was my bonus...Part of the agreement my mother got out of them was they wouldn't sell or trade me, even to a big league team, until I was twenty-one. They eventually broke that agreement."[247]

In an interview some 60+ years later Williams noted: "Before the Padres came to town, I didn't have any ambition to play up the coast for the L. A. Angels or for a big league team. My only real concern was just becoming a good hitter. Here's a funny thing. There's not one hitting picture of me until I signed my first professional contract. All of them in high school were pitching. So the first was in a Padre uniform."*[248]

June 27, 1936, Ted Williams' 1st At Bat as Professional Player
The Sporting News, July 2, 1936

"New Padre"
San Diego Evening Tribune,
June 27, 1936

Williams would make his official professional debut as a pinch hitter for a pitcher, San Diego friend Elmer Hill, in the second inning of the game versus Sacramento on Saturday, June 27. Surprisingly, the local papers made no mention of it, preferring to concentrate on the pre-game festivities. He was retired by Sacramento

---

* As discussed and shown in Chapter 6, page 66, Williams's memory was not quite accurate since there was a *San Diego Union* photo in its April 13, 1936 edition showing him batting with under the banner "They'll be Calling him Bambino."

pitcher Cotton Pippen.* As Ted recalled, "The Manager, Frank Shellenback, sent me in to pinch hit and I took three strikes down the middle. Didn't even swing."[249]

FOOT RACES AND SCORECARDS

When a last place team comes to town, fans can count on interesting and unusual promotions at the ballpark. The Padres scheduled and promoted a 75-yard race between George Myatt and the Solons' Joe Dobbins (a San Diego native).[250] A throwing contest from home to second and a race around the bases were also part of the festivities. Injured catcher Gene Desautels was healthy enough to emerge victorious in the throwing contest, while Buster Adams of Sacramento won the race around the bases. Myatt won the foot race with Dobbins with "yards to spare."[251]

Some fans expressed concerns. An Imperial Valley fan complained about the inaccuracies of the scorecard numbers for the visiting teams. Apparently, PCL clubs were less than vigilant about providing correct information to other teams.[252]

BACK TO BASEBALL

Meanwhile, the Padres and Solons had resumed their series Friday, June 26, with a 3-2 San Diego win. Howard Craghead continued his impressive pitching for the Padres, with the winning run set up by a bad-hop single in the eighth inning.

On Saturday, after the pregame festivities and Ted Williams' professional debut, the Padres blew a lead in the eighth when Herm Pillette gave up a three-run homer to Solon slugger Frank Doljack. Earlier in that same inning, the injury bug struck again as catcher Jimmy Kerr suffered a split-finger on a foul tip and was replaced by Elmer Evert. Vince DiMaggio led off the home eighth with a double and came in to score on a sacrifice fly for a 7-6 Padre win, with Manny Salvo securing the win for Archie Campbell.

Salvo would start the first game of the Sunday doubleheader and come away with 12 strikeouts and a ragged 14-7 complete-game win. Despite his injuries, Gene Desautels was pressed into duty as catcher and led the offense with four hits. In the nightcap, the Padres came back to tie the game with two sixth-inning runs off Robert Ross, but lost in the eighth, 4-3, with Shellenback taking the defeat. The winning hit nicked Shellenback's pitching hand on its way out to center field, forcing his removal from the game.

San Diego finished the week at 47-46, one game over .500 and 4½ games out of first place. After the usual off day on Monday, they would travel to Los Angeles Tuesday morning to begin an eight-game series at Wrigley Field with the sixth place Angels. To address their catching concerns, the Padres signed Bobby Doerr's older brother Harold, who had formerly caught in the PCL for Portland, Hollywood, and Seattle. Elmer Evert, who had signed on with the Padres as an emergency catcher, was released at his request so he could remain in San Diego at his regular job.[253]

Owner Bill Lane was still feuding with the Boston Red Sox regarding players owed to the club in exchange for Boston's option on Doerr and Myatt. Lane threatened to take back the option and trade elsewhere to get the promised outfielder and pitcher, but it was noted "the talent is not available, no matter where you look…

---

* In Williams' 4th game as a major leaguer with the Boston Red Sox on April 23, 1939, he faced Pippen (then with the Philadelphia A's) and had a single and a double in two at bats. In 1938 and 1939, Williams faced Pippen eight times in the majors. For four of those at bats play-by-play records are not available to verify what took place. For the two games with play-by-play records Williams batted 1.000 against Pippen with four hits in four at bats: two of the hits were doubles and one was a home run, accounting for four runs batted in.

8—JUNE 1936 "THE KID" DEBUTS

Too many clubs could use a pitcher or a hard-hitting outfielder right now."[254] The perceived talent shortage of the present day apparently is nothing new.

Los Angeles defeated the Padres on the last day of the month to leave the club with a .500 record for the season entering July.

The Padres played 29 games in June 1936 winning 16 and losing 13. Ernie Holman, who was among the PCL batting leaders, led all regulars with a .380 average during June. Ced Durst had 41 hits for the month, George Myatt led in runs scored with 24, and Vince DiMaggio knocked four home runs and drove home 21 runs. Wally Hebert led the staff with five wins during June, while Salvo recorded four victories and Howard Craghead showed the benefits of a change of scenery by going 3-0 for the month.

While at the time no one could foresee the future, looking back, the most significant event of the month was the professional debut of Ted Williams—so far, 0-1 in his one time at bat. San Diego fans coming out to Lane Field would have the pleasure of watching two future baseball Hall-of-Famers—Williams and Bobby Doerr—hone their craft for the remainder of the 1936 season.

Table 8.2. Batting and Pitching Totals for June

Players	Positions	G	AB	R	H	1B	2B	3B	HR	RBI	SB	AVG
Archie Campbell	p-9	9	6	1	3	2	1	0	0	0	0	.500
Herman Pillette	p-3	3	2	0	1	1	0	0	0	2	0	.500
Frank Shellenback	ph-6, p-4	10	17	1	8	7	1	0	0	2	0	.471
Ernie Holman	3b-29	29	100	17	38	29	7	2	0	19	2	.380
Trader Horne	p-6	6	8	2	3	3	0	0	0	0	0	.375
George Myatt	ss-23, lf-4	27	118	24	40	36	3	1	0	11	10	.339
Cedric Durst	cf-29	29	123	18	41	33	6	2	0	18	7	.333
George McDonald	1b-26	26	99	14	33	29	1	3	0	18	0	.333
Gene Desautels	c-19, ph-1	20	67	11	22	18	3	1	0	9	0	.328
Jimmy Kerr	c-13, ph-1	14	43	6	14	11	1	1	1	7	0	.326
Bobby Doerr	2b-29	29	117	23	38	31	6	1	0	13	5	.325
Joe Berkowitz	ss-6, pr-1	7	19	2	6	5	0	1	0	0	0	.316
Vince DiMaggio	rf-29	29	109	20	34	21	6	3	4	21	5	.312
Wally Hebert	p-8	8	25	5	7	5	1	0	1	5	0	.280
Van Wirthman	lf-25, ph-1	26	94	16	25	19	2	4	0	11	0	.266
Manny Salvo	p-7	7	19	3	4	4	0	0	0	0	0	.211
Ray Jacobs	ph-6, 1b-3	9	17	1	3	2	1	0	0	1	0	.176
Howard Craghead	p-4	4	10	0	1	1	0	0	0	1	0	.100
Dick Ward	p-5	5	6	0	0	0	0	0	0	0	0	.000
Ed Wells	p-1	1	1	0	0	0	0	0	0	0	0	.000
Ted Williams	ph-1	1	1	0	0	0	0	0	0	0	0	.000
Elmer Evert	c-2	2	1	0	0	0	0	0	0	0	0	.000
Eddie Mulligan	pr-4, 2b-1, 3b-1	6	1	0	0	0	0	0	0	0	0	.000
Elmer Hill	p-1	1	0	0	0	0	0	0	0	0	0	.000
Hal Doerr	c-1	1	0	0	0	0	0	0	0	0	0	.000
George Hockett	p-1, pr-1	2	0	0	0	0	0	0	0	0	0	.000

SAN DIEGO'S FIRST PADRES and "THE KID"

Pitchers	G	GS	CG	ShO	Sv	W	L	PCT	IP	H	R	ER	SO	BB	ERA
Elmer Hill	1	1	0	0	0	0	0	.000	2	1	2	0	1	2	0.00
Archie Campbell	9	0	0	0	2	1	0	1.000	22⅓	13	6	3	10	7	1.21
Frank Shellenback	4	4	2	0	0	1	3	.250	31⅓	14	11	11	11	1	3.16
Wally Hebert	8	7	5	1	0	5	3	.625	58⅓	67	26	24	22	12	3.70
Trader Horne	6	5	2	1	0	1	5	.167	36⅓	43	25	15	19	16	3.72
Howard Craghead	4	3	3	0	0	3	0	1.000	31⅓	33	16	14	18	5	4.02
Dick Ward	5	2	0	0	0	1	0	1.000	14⅔	11	8	7	5	12	4.30
George Hockette	1	0	0	0	0	0	0	.000	2	1	1	1	0	3	4.50
Manny Salvo	6	5	3	0	0	4	1	.800	43⅓	53	28	23	21	11	4.78
Ed Wells	1	1	0	0	0	0	1	.000	3⅓	5	3	2	1	0	5.40
Herman Pillette	3	1	0	0	0	0	0	.000	7⅔	11	7	6	4	1	7.04

CHAPTER 9
JULY 1936
RIOTS, THE FIRST AMENDMENT, AND LIGHTS AT LANE

NOTABLE WORLD EVENTS–JULY 1936

7th *The National League beats the American League 4-3 in the All-Star Game played at Braves Field in Boston*

8th *Following the recent flight of the Hindenburg across Britain and accusations of spying the British government announces they will no longer permit German airships to fly over Britain except in weather emergencies*

17th *17-year old Bob Feller makes his major league debut with the Cleveland Indians and pitches a scoreless inning against the Washington Senators*

As San Diego's "June gloom" faded and July got underway, the Padres found themselves in the middle of the PCL pack, in fifth place with a .500 record, but only 5½ games behind league-leading Seattle (see Table 9.1). The Padres had fallen to .500 on June 30 as Wally Hebert, the only pitcher to beat Los Angeles this season to date, lost a 9-5 decision to the Angels in the opening game of the week-long series.

Table 9.1. PCL Standings on July 1, 1936

	W	L	Pct.	GB
Seattle	52	41	.559	--
Oakland	50	40	.556	½
Missions	49	44	.527	3
Portland	45	41	.523	3½
San Diego	**47**	**47**	**.500**	**5½**
Los Angeles	45	48	.484	7
San Francisco	43	50	.462	9
Sacramento	35	55	.389	15½

Following this series, the Padres would move to Oakland for seven games with the Oaks, then come home to host Seattle and Portland in a split-week series, followed by the San Francisco Missions and the Los Angeles Angels. The Padres would tread water for the month, but certain umpiring decisions during the homestand would trigger lots of excitement on and off the field, and the month would conclude with the first night game at Lane Field.

FOURTH OF JULY IN LOS ANGELES

The month started well for the Padres, still in Los Angeles for a Wednesday, July 1st game, as Howard Craghead shut out the Angels on two hits and the team pushed two runs home in the 8th for a 2-0 win. Los Angeles left fielder Wes Schulmerich had both Angel hits against Craghead. Due to injuries to catchers Gene Desautels and Jimmy Kerr, trainer Les Cook, one of the PCL's best catchers with the Hollywood Stars a few years back, donned a uniform for the first time in 1936 and caught the game. Cook even threw out Jigger Statz on a steal attempt.

Padres pitching failed the team in the next two contests, as the Angels posted 6-1 and 14-9 wins. Manny Salvo failed to survive the first inning in the Thursday game, giving up six runs on five hits before Manager Shellenback called for Dick Ward. The former Sacramento pitcher acquired by the Padres in June, Ward shut down the Angels (another former team) for the rest of the match, but the best San Diego's offense could offer was two hits apiece by Bobby Doerr and Vince DiMaggio.

The 14-9 pasting on Friday night provided an opportunity for Williams…to pitch! And, to hit! The Padres started off on the right foot with two runs in the second inning to open a 2-0 lead behind starting pitcher Horne. However, that lead evaporated swiftly as Los Angeles scored nine runs in the fourth inning off Horne and Campbell in relief. The Angels scored another run in the fifth and two in the sixth, and were going into the top of the seventh with a 12-3 lead.

It was time for some of the utility players to get action off the bench, like Ted Williams. After his first appearance on June 27 he sat on the bench and threw some pre-game batting practice, but that was all. So, Williams got another chance when Shellenback had him pinch hit for Campbell. He was facing Angels pitcher Glen Gabler and he singled for his first hit in professional baseball. He was part of a Padres five-run rally to make the game a bit closer, 12-8, going into the bottom of the seventh inning. Williams stayed in the game… as a pitcher in relief of Campbell.

9—JULY 1936 RIOTS, THE FIRST AMENDMENT, AND LIGHTS AT LANE

Lanky Ted Williams, the pitcher, ended up getting out of the seventh without allowing any runs. However, in the eighth inning, the Padres scored a run and pulled even closer, but still trailed by three runs, 12-9. Williams came out for his second inning of relief and was not as fortunate this time around as he gave up two solo home runs, one by Steve Mesner and another by Wes Schulmerich. In Michael Seidel's book, the last home run was described this way: "The left-field blast by Schulmerich tore into a tree 450 feet away and ripped off most of its branches. Shellenback had seen enough. Williams was through as a pitcher, though it looked as though he could hit."[255] Williams did get to bat again, this time facing Joe Berry and got himself a second hit, but the Padres ended up losing the game, 14-9.

Even though it did not help the standings, San Diego outhit the Angels, 18-14, with every regular in the lineup except catcher Hal Doerr collecting at least two hits and Williams, the third of four Padre pitchers, added two more.

In his book (written with John Underwood) Williams remembers his pitching performance this way: "…we got ten [sic] runs behind in the sixth inning of a game with the Angels at Wrigley Field in Los Angeles. With a doubleheader coming up on Sunday, Shellenback was desperate for a pitcher. Eddie Mulligan was one of our coaches and I heard Shellenback say to Mulligan, 'Damn it, Eddie, who am I going to put in there? I'm using up all my pitchers.' When he went out to the coaching line I move in beside Mulligan. 'Tell him to put me in, Eddie. I can pitch. I'm ready.' Mulligan looked at me, then smiled and when Shellenback came in he suggested it. Shellenback nodded and told me to go down and warm up. He didn't have much choice really.

"So I warmed up, then he let me pinch hit. Boom, a double [sic]. A rally starts and by the time the inning is over, we've got five runs. So I go out and hold them an inning, and then I get to bat again. Boom, another double [sic]. Now we've whittled it down to 11 to 12, something like that, and Shellenback's got a *good* relief pitcher working in the bullpen. I go out to pitch again and, and the first four [sic] guys in the next inning score runs. Shellenback's out there like a flash to pull me out, and the way he tells it I kind of shrugged and said, 'Skip, I think you've got me playing in the wrong position.'"[256]

Well, Williams had some of the facts wrong, but the story is essentially correct. Williams gave up two hits, a walk, and two runs in 1⅓ innings, his only appearance as a pitcher in the minor leagues, not really that bad, plus he collected his first two hits in professional baseball. Howard Craghead, the winning pitcher two nights prior to Friday, relieved Williams to finish up the game. The Angels clouted three homers, with DiMaggio adding a home run for the visitors.

The news was not all bad for the Padres on Friday, July 3. Lane culminated a season-long pursuit by purchasing power hitting outfielder Ivey "Chick" Shiver, 29, outright from the Indianapolis club of the American Association. Shiver, who to date was nowhere close to matching his impressive statistics in the 1935 season (.317, 31 home runs, 10 triples, 25 doubles), was reported to need only "a change of scenery…to start him clouting the ball again."[257] Shiver was seen as a much-needed power addition to the Padres lineup. His acquisition would give the regular outfielders (Cedric Durst, Vince DiMaggio, and Van Wirthman) an occasional rest and would also "help Ted Williams break into the lineup now and then for the experience he needs."[258] In fact, Shiver would take Wirthman's place in the lineup and keep Williams on the bench.

Indianapolis had been waiting to complete the deal until the team was assured that it would be able to obtain a suitable replacement from the major leagues. After waiting on Brooklyn for most of the season, Indianapolis finally acquired Hubert "Bud" Bates from the Detroit Tigers, freeing up Shiver. The nature of bargaining and trades between minor league and major league teams was indicated by the newspaper report, which noted that this deal "is not a part of the Red Sox deal. The Boston club still owes Lane two players, a pitcher and an outfielder, but has shown no disposition to live up to the letter of its bargain, although the Red Sox did come through with Manny Salvo early in the season."[259] Nor were the Padres the only PCL team looking for power; later in the month, Oakland would pick up slugger Harlan Pool from Toronto.[260]

San Diego was also looking into signing former major league and PCL catcher, Hugh McMullen, for temporary duty while Desautels and Kerr were on the injured list. Les Cook, the 41-year old Padres trainer who caught Tuesday's game, was not being counted on, despite a history of being able to fill in on short notice for a game or two. Cook had once taken over third base for the Stars at Bill Lane's request and played 49 consecutive errorless games at the hot corner. In 1936, Cook appeared in four games (two starts) between July 1 and July 5. After that, he resumed his duties as trainer and most avid fisherman on the club,[261] until three final appearances off the bench during one-sided games in September.

A fashion note in the sports section on the Fourth of July stated that baseball was introducing summer uniforms made of the same lightweight materials as men's summer suits, replacing the old, heavy flannel uniforms on hot days.* The Angels proved to be the hotter team on the fourth, sweeping a doubleheader at Wrigley Field by identical 4-3 scores to drop San Diego into sixth place. After giving up four runs in the fourth inning of the opener, Frank Shellenback removed himself in favor of Manny Salvo. Salvo came back in the fifth inning of the nightcap and held the Angels scoreless until a fielder's choice ground ball scored the winning run in the bottom of the ninth. Ted Williams started the second game in left field and had a double in four at bats—his first extra-base hit as a pro.

The Angels then finished off a disastrous week for San Diego with a doubleheader sweep on Sunday, July 5, 3-1 and 4-3. Hugh Casey defeated Wally Hebert in the opener. Don Hurst, Angel first baseman and hitting star of the series, hit his third home run of the week off Howard Craghead in the first inning of the nightcap. The Angels took seven of eight games and ended the series with a tighter hold on fifth place. San Diego occupied sixth place, five games under .500, trailing league-leading Oakland by nine games, and on their way to the Bay Area for seven games with the Oaks.

Lane Field was not idle while the Padres were on the road. The annual San Diego-Imperial County semi-pro baseball tournament was underway during the first week of July. Nine teams took part, including Oceanside, the Pala Indians, Mountain Meadows Creamery, Muehlesen's, El Cajon, Fallbrook, El Centro, Cramer's Bakery, and La Jolla. At the last minute, the U.S.S. Dobbin team withdrew "because service units are prohibited from participating in professional events and besides the ship was slated to sail."[262] During the following week, workers would once again rebuild the Lane Field infield and continue work to complete the light towers.

SHUTOUTS GALORE IN OAKLAND

The Padres had knocked the Oaks out of first place two weeks prior by winning six of seven, but Oakland took six of eight from Sacramento to regain first place and were looking to avenge their San Diego defeats. Manager Shellenback's pitching rotation called for Hebert and Craghead to start twice, while he penciled himself in for a Saturday start. Chick Shiver would arrive in time for Tuesday's opener.

Before the series began, Lane claimed catcher Norman Kies on waivers from Oakland only to be informed that Kies was on the injured list. Given the Padres' trouble with healthy catchers, Lane replied that he would take Kies, injury or no. This threw a wrench into the Oaks' plans to ship Kies to the Yankee farm club in Newark. As it turned out, the Padres would acquire neither Kies nor Hugh McMullen, thereby being stuck with the catching tandem of Gene Desautels and Hal Doerr until Jimmy Kerr's return.

---

* Further related to baseball uniforms, years later, the revived Hollywood Stars would wear shorts during the hot months.

9—JULY 1936 RIOTS, THE FIRST AMENDMENT, AND LIGHTS AT LANE

PCL owners had decided on the Shaughnessy playoff plan at season's end, under which the first and third place and second and fourth place teams would meet in seven-game series, with a final seven-game series between the winners. Over the Fourth of July weekend, the owners decided that the playoff winner, and not the team that finished first in the final standings, would be crowned as PCL champions,[263] thus siding with President Tuttle.

Meanwhile, Howard Craghead took the mound for a Monday exhibition game against Fresno of the California State League. Left fielder Van Wirthman also got to make a mound appearance in the 11-7 loss.

The series opened inauspiciously for the Padres as they fell to their 10th defeat in 11 games, 2-0. Oakland extended its streak of shutout innings to 21 with the win. Southpaw Ken Douglas of the Oaks authored the five-hitter, outdueling Horne. Shiver played right field and collected a single in four trips to the plate in his Padre debut.

Wednesday night, an error by Oaks' shortstop Joe "Flash" Gordon (future star with the Yankees and Indians) allowed DiMaggio to score in the fifth inning, and Salvo pitched out of trouble in the eighth and ninth innings to secure a 1-0 victory despite 10 Oakland hits. The Padres snapped their eight-game losing streak in a long (3:05 hours) game. Oakland lost no ground, as the Angels beat Seattle. The Oaks filed a protest with the league after the game, but newspaper details were unavailable.

With the series even, Wee Willie Ludolph took the mound for Oakland and pitched brilliantly. One of the aces of the Oaks' staff, Ludolph gave up only two hits, both to George Myatt, and it was Oakland's turn to take a 1-0 win. Dick Ward gave up only five hits in the loss, and Joe Gordon scored the game's only run after a fourth-inning double. Ward had been a star pitcher with the 1934 Angels (considered by some the best minor league club of all time) but had been slowed by arm troubles since then. Thus, Ward's performance and the absence of arm trouble during the game were bright spots on what was turning into a very long road trip.

The third of what would be four 1-0 duels in the weeklong series went in the Padres favor on Friday as Craghead shut down the Oaks on six hits and Shiver drove in Bobby Doerr with an unearned run. Since the San Diego run in Wednesday's game was also unearned, the Oaks staff now had a streak of 49 consecutive innings without allowing an earned run. The Padres were fortunate to be even in the series.

The streak ended at 50 innings on Saturday as the Padres pounded out a 7-1 victory (the first non-shutout of the week) behind Herm Pillette. Ced Durst led the way with three hits in the romp. San Diego followed this game up with a doubleheader sweep on Sunday. Trader Horne and Ward combined for a 3-2 win in the opener, and Manny Salvo pitched a two-hitter in the nightcap to win his second 1-0 game of the series. Ken Douglas and Hal Hald were the tough-luck losers for the Oaks, with Hald's two errors in the first inning of the second game contributing to the lone unearned run.

San Diego headed south with a 5-2 series win over Oakland, who fell back into second place behind Seattle. For the week, the Padre pitching staff posted a 0.92 ERA* as compared to 5.50 in Los Angeles. San Diego remained in sixth place at 53-55 but trailed the fifth place Angels by only one-half game. Lane cited the Oakland series as the best he could recall in 20 years in the Pacific Coast League.[264]

The newspapers were happy to pass along suggestions to Lane regarding the operation of the ballclub. A "veteran ball fan" offered several suggestions: open up the bleachers in deep left field at 25 cents for adults and 10 cents for children; speed up the ball park wire reports on games in other cities; and allow northern radio stations to broadcast Angel games in San Diego.[265]

---

* Earned runs were reported in the 1936 box scores as "runs responsible for."

PROSPECTS

By mid-July, several young Coast league players had established themselves as major league prospects, with the only question being how soon they would be ready. A midseason list of prospects, by team, included the following, with the names in **bold** indicating those players who made it to the major leagues after 1936:[266]

San Diego	**Bobby Doerr, Georgie Myatt**, and George McDonald (with **Ted Williams** rated as a "comer in another year")
San Francisco	Brooks Holder, **Joe Marty**, Steve Barath, Ted Norbert
Los Angeles	**Bobby Mattick, Steve Mesner**
Portland	the **Coscararts** (Steve and **Pete**) and Fred Bedore
Sacramento	Lou Vezelich, **Buster Adams**, Frankie Morehouse, Andy Andrews, and **Don Ross** (a surprising number of prospects for a dead last team!)
Oakland	**Joe Gordon**, Jack La Rocca, **Jimmy Hitchcock, Fern Bell, Dario Lodigiani**, and **Willard Hershberger**
The Missions	**Eddie Joost**, Ray Mort, and Frnak Lemanski
Seattle	Don French, Dick Gyselman, and **Hal Spindell**

UMPIRE TROUBLE: PART I

An item in a Sunday, July 12, column of the *San Diego Union* proved prescient as the events of the week unfolded. It noted that PCL umpires miss plenty of balls, strikes, and close calls on the bases, but credited the umpires for their wit. It seems that a Sacramento player turned on umpire Sam Crawford after a second called strike with the comment, "You sure missed that one!" Crawford's retort was: "Yeah, well if I'd had that bat in my hand I wouldn't have." Since this was the same "Wahoo Sam" Crawford who patrolled the Tigers outfield with Ty Cobb for years, general opinion sided with the umpire.[267] During the split-week homestand with Seattle (the new first place team) and Portland at Lane Field, umpires' wit would not be in evidence.

The Seattle series began on Tuesday, July 14, as manager Dutch Ruether sent "Kewpie" Dick Barrett (13-8) to the mound to oppose Ward. Continuing to demonstrate a full recovery from prior arm ailments, Ward "muzzled the big berthas of the Seattle batting attack" with a three-hit, 2-0 shutout.[268] Chick Shiver made his debut before the home crowd with a run-scoring triple and a circus catch in the ninth inning to preserve the shutout. Anticipation was building for the following day's game when Howard Craghead would take on the team that traded him to San Diego earlier in the season for Ed Wells. The Padres were hoping that Wells would get the start for Seattle, but Ruether did not oblige. As for Lane Field, the infield work had been completed over the weekend, and the new mixture of clay and sand provided surer footing—finally.

The Wednesday game ended to shouts of "We wuz robbed!" Monroe McConnell led his game story in the *Union* with this introduction aimed at umpire Jack Powell:

Dear Santa Claus:

I have tried to be a good boy, but after what happened yesterday in the ninth inning at Lane Field, the San Diego fans will never believe it, so please do something. If it won't be too much trouble, Mr. Santa, please bring me a nice, big cake of ice for I'm in hot water up to my neck and getting in deeper all the time. Secondly, I could use a pair of gold-rimmed spectacles, bi-focals, if you please, so that I can see at least as far as right field without having to guess what happened out there and can be right on at least half of the balls and strikes. On second thought, maybe you had better change that order for spectacles to one for 10-power field glasses, as things looked pretty foggy out there in the right field garden yesterday, and a

9—JULY 1936 RIOTS, THE FIRST AMENDMENT, AND LIGHTS AT LANE

little eye lotion also might be a big help. Five thousand fans all can't be wrong, so it looks as though someone was. Maybe it was me. Yours in need.

JACK POWELL[269]

With two out in the ninth and Seattle holding a 2-1 lead, George Myatt worked a walk, and Ced Durst followed with a blast to right field that apparently scored Myatt. Umpire Jack Powell, however, summoned Durst back to the plate, ruling that the ball was foul. Durst managed a clean single, but Bobby Doerr was retired with the tying run at third base. The fans then poured onto the field and "promptly erected a barrier of small stakes around the marks in the dust made by Durst's smash. The barrier was inside the playing field by several inches."[270] The paper also criticized Umpire Bill Engeln for two consecutive safe calls on a Seattle player.

Seattle got out of town in first place without further incident after a 3-2 win sparked by Mike Hunt's hitting and outfield play. Hunt, who had a lifetime PCL .326 batting average going into the 1936 season, was apparently known for his sartorial style marked by longer than usual baseball pants. Pitcher Salvo was hurt by two errors (one his own) in the sixth. Van Wirthman made his first start in the outfield since Shiver arrived. Upon Shiver's arrival, Vince DiMaggio had been moved from right to left field, but during the week Shellenback returned DiMaggio to right and stationed Shiver in left field.

UMPIRE TROUBLE: PART II

The Portland Beavers brought Escondido natives, the Coscarart brothers—Pete (second baseman) and Steve (outfielder)—into Lane Field for a weekend series that was to begin on Friday, July 17. "Big Moose" Clabaugh insured a Friday afternoon win with a two-run homer on a full-count pitch in the sixth as the Beavers prevailed, 4-2. Clabaugh (who would finish his career with a lifetime .339 average in the minors) was playing with his 17th professional team, having failed to stick in the majors due to fielding deficiencies in an abbreviated 11-game tryout with Brooklyn in 1926. Wearing eyeglasses improved his fielding notably, but he was considered too old to get another shot with a major league club. Berly Horne struggled with his control and was lifted in the third inning, and the Padre offense continued to struggle. The Padres evened the series on Saturday with a 3-1 win behind Wally Hebert, making his first appearance in two weeks after recovering from a bout of influenza. The victory was Hebert's 13th of the season.

The Saturday paper featured a follow-up story regarding the umpiring uproar. The story quoted published reports in a Los Angeles paper (later revealed to be the *Examiner*) that W.C. Tuttle, President of the PCL, had been besieged by a mob of enraged fans and had to be whisked out of Lane Field and later out of his hotel to safety at Bill Lane's home.[271] The L.A. paper went on to declare that San Diego Mayor Benbough had demanded that the umpires be removed from San Diego. Lane got a good chuckle out of the story, which was viewed as part of an anti-Tuttle campaign in Los Angeles. Umpire Powell was still in San Diego and was still receiving unsolicited fan opinion regarding his visual acuity throughout the week.

Sunday the lid blew off. *Union* columnist Ted Steinmann noted, "From a baseball standpoint, San Diego definitely arrived as a real league city with the demonstrations staged against the decisions of Umpire Jack Powell Wednesday and again Sunday."[272] The second game of the doubleheader with Portland was halted for more than 20 minutes in the fourth inning after Jack Powell called Ced Durst out on a play at first that he appeared to have beaten by several feet. Powell then ejected Durst (his first ejection in 16 years of professional ball) and Manager Shellenback for protesting the call. Lane Field fans responded with a shower of beer bottles, cushions, and flasks. San Diego police finally quelled the uprising with a show of force making six arrests and detaining hosts of fans. In the midst of the uproar, a burly fan walked onto the field and confronted Powell, but players led him away before any blows could be exchanged. After the game, the police escorted the umpires to the train and saw them safely out of town.

Interestingly, Steinmann's July 21 column noted that the players rated Powell as the best umpire in the PCL, but took Powell to task for working with a chip on his shoulder. Following this logic, the Sunday incident, and particularly the first-time-ever ejection of Durst, grew out of the controversy surrounding Powell's call on Durst's ninth-inning drive to right field on Wednesday. The *Los Angeles Times* quoted Powell as ejecting Durst with the words that he had "caused him enough trouble this week."[273]

"Riot Rages as Padres, Ducks Split"
San Diego Union, July 20, 1936

Always eager to join the fray, the *Los Angeles Examiner* ran an "exclusive" from Umpire Powell:[274] "Cedric Durst was out! I called the play as I saw it and I was in a position to see Durst was out by half a step. I think what started the trouble was not today's play, but the ball which I called foul in the game with Seattle Wednesday, and since that ruling players, fans, and officials alike have told me that they saw the play as I did. I called the play today as I saw it, and I think I called it right."

While not perfectly clear in all the stories regarding the near riot, it appeared that the league changed Powell's assignment in the wake of the controversy. The *Times* strongly implied that President Tuttle shifted the umpires from San Diego, the first time this season that umpires had been changed during a homestand of the Padres.[275]

When the smoke cleared, the Padres had a split of the doubleheader and of the four-game series with the Indians. Shiver ignited the offense in the first game with a double, two singles, and a near home run, and the defense sparkled behind Dick Ward for a 7-2 win. In the nightcap, San Diego took an early 3-0 lead, but a six-run third inning knocked out both Howard Craghead and Herman Pillette (the losing pitcher) and the Beavers made it stand up for a 6-4 win.

San Diego finished the week at 56-59, trailing fifth-place Los Angeles by 1½ games and only 1½ games ahead of seventh-place San Francisco. Bobby Doerr and Vince DiMaggio were swinging hot bats, and Shiver showed signs of coming around at the plate. While not as dominant as in Oakland, the pitching held up well through the week of first-division competition. Seattle held first by one game over Oakland and led the Padres by 8½. The third-place Missions were on their way south to face the Padres.

LANE TAKES ON THE FIRST AMENDMENT

During the travel day, Monday, July 20, Bill Lane capped a hectic week by barring sports writers from the *Los Angeles Examiner* from Lane Field.[276] The edict, delivered to Bob Hunter of the *Examiner*, came in direct response to the article alleging an attack on PCL President Tuttle by San Diego fans. The headline in the *Examiner* sports section on Saturday, July 18, had been,

"PADRE FANS PERIL TUTTLE"

while the article went on to recount an allegedly narrow escape from a mob of rabid fans after the Wednesday game with Seattle.[277]

Lane specifically stated that this action was aimed at *Examiner* sports editor John Connolly, who (according to Lane) had launched a campaign to discredit Tuttle. Connolly's reputed motives were to force Tuttle out as President and possibly to succeed him. The *Los Angeles Times* quoted Lane as saying, "Had those distorted statements appearing in the Los Angeles paper Saturday and Sunday not been printed, the fans here probably would not have been so inflamed as to have staged yesterday's demonstration against Umpire Powell."[278] The sportswriters for the *Examiner* indicated that they would pay their way into the park, sit in the stands, and report as usual.

Lane was probably equally displeased with the Sunday headline in the *Examiner*, "Tuttle Through as Coast Loop Head!" The article, under Bob Hunter's byline, cited accurate and powerful sources for this bombshell and noted that Lane was the owner who swung the presidency Tuttle's way.[279] In the article, Hunter also floated the rumor that a telegraphic call for a recall is to be made next week, although he suggested that the rumor was untrue.

The hatchet was buried on the following day just before the Missions series opened when John Connolly issued an apology for the story, and Bill Lane announced that all was forgiven.[280] The *Examiner* ran the story (without mention of an apology),[281] although it had not seen fit to publish the news the previous day that its sports writers had been barred from Lane Field. Sports Editor Connolly appeared bewildered at Lane's actions, saying that the *Examiner*'s only fault was in letting people know that there was a lot of excitement to be had at baseball games in San Diego and that "Uncle Bill" changed his tune "since he has seen those extra shekels rolling in" as a result of the publicity.[282] The *Times*, which ran the original story,[283] had some fun at the expense of its rival paper while quoting extensively from a *San Francisco Chronicle* column critical of Lane.[284] In San Diego, all attention returned to the ball field as the Padres prepared to take on yet another first division team.

THE MISSIONS COME TO TOWN

One of the two San Francisco teams in the PCL, the Missions (or Mission Reds, as they were also known) were managed by Willie Kamm. At the start of play on July 21 they trailed first place Seattle by only four games.

Vince DiMaggio was the hero of the opening game on Tuesday when he scored Bobby Doerr with a double off the right-centerfield fence in the home ninth for a 5-4 win. Ivy Shiver clouted his first home run as a Padre and also belted a triple. Dick Ward retired two batters with the go-ahead run at second base in the top of the ninth in relief of Manny Salvo and was the beneficiary of DiMaggio's heroics. Catcher Kerr, out for several weeks with a broken finger, returned to the team but did not play. Shiver's home run was worth $10 to him, half from Eddie Miller of the Santa Fe Smoke Shop and the other half from Walter Church.

The Missions drew even the next day with a 3-1 win behind sidearmer Walter "Boom-Boom" Beck, sometimes known as the "Great Elmer" (for reasons unexplained in McConnell's game report).[285] Trader Horne did not survive the first inning, but Herm Pillette held the Reds scoreless for 7⅓ innings, despite falling down four times in making fielding plays. On Thursday, Wally Hebert struggled with command of his curve and could not get out of the third inning as the Missions took a 6-5 win on a bases-loaded walk from reliever Archie Campbell in the seventh. Friday looked like more of the same, with the Padres trailing in the home half of the ninth, 3-0, before Shiver's double off the fence in right field triggered a three-run rally and Ernie Holman's double in the tenth inning scored pinch-runner Ted Williams for a 4-3 comeback win.

The Saturday game was decided early, with three Missions errors and four Padres hits resulting in an early four-run lead for Howard Craghead, who posted a complete game 5-2 win. Bobby Doerr and Ced Durst sparkled defensively for San Diego. Then, the Sunday doubleheader was enlivened by another umpiring dispute as the Padres split with the Missions to take the series, four games to three. Umpire Hollis Leake called Doerr out for interference when he was hit by the throw as he was racing to first base after laying down a bunt. Leake then ejected first baseman George McDonald after a vociferous argument on a drive down the line that Leake called fair. No objects were thrown onto the field this time, nor was there any mention of the *Examiner's* take on the incidents. The Missions won the opener, 4-1, but the Padres prevailed in the nightcap behind Pillette (with relief help from Campbell), 3-1.

This marked the fourth consecutive series with a first division club. The Padres won two, split one, and lost one, with a combined record of 12-9. Solid pitching, Shiver's big bat, and the hitting and fielding of Bobby Doerr, Ced Durst, and Vince DiMaggio held out hope for the rest of the season, even though the end of the week found the Padres still mired in sixth place. With a record of 60-62, they trailed the fifth place Angels by 1½ games but led the league with a .291 team average.[286] Seattle held a three-game lead over the second place Oaks and led San Diego by nine. With the return of catcher Jimmy Kerr (although he had yet to appear in a game), Bobby Doerr's brother Hal returned to Los Angeles to accept a position with the telephone company. His final appearance had been on July 15 in the first of the two Umpire Powell games.

"GRUDGE" SERIES

Some things never change…case in point: the rivalry between Los Angeles and San Diego. As the Angels arrived for the final series between the two teams, they were fighting to get out of the second division after a very poor start to the season. The 14-5[287] record versus the Padres was in large part responsible for their resurgence, and they hoped to use this week to put the Padres behind them (1½ games separated the teams) and possibly climb past the fourth place Missions.

Umpire Leake displayed a quick trigger in the series opener, Tuesday, July 28, throwing out three visitors, Jigger Statz, Jimmy Reese, and Angel manager Jack Lelivelt. This was not an idle display of temper: Angel offenses included grabbing Leake by the shirt, ripping off his chest protector, and striking him in the face with a cap. The ejected Angels refused to leave the field and had to be escorted by three local policemen. The *Examiner* wrote up an account of the ejection in a light-hearted fashion, describing the ejected Angels as misdemeanants and Leake as the complaining witness (and also as "a bull-voiced arbiter discovered by President Tuttle in the Los Angeles bushes").[288] Wally Hebert shut out Los Angeles for his 14th win, supported by Shiver, who drove home both Padre runs. The Padres won again on Wednesday, July 29, behind Ward in a 5-1 game that featured Leake's ejection of acting Angels manager Truck Hannah. The occasion this time was a dispute over a sensational diving catch by Durst that turned into a double play, a defensive highlight that paved the way for Ward's pitching. The win propelled the Padres past Los Angeles into fifth place.

As a sidelight, it was reported that Heinie Groh, a former third baseman with John McGraw's New York Giants, took in the game at Lane Field on a visit from his home in Rochester, New York.[289]

Before Wednesday's game, Bill Lane conferred with the umpires.[290] The gist of the discussion was a demand that umpires continue to take action against foul language. Lane Field's stands were closer to the field than those of other PCL parks, and some fans may have learned a few new phrases from the Angels and their manager. PCL President Tuttle supported the umpires quickly and firmly, despite the fact that the Los Angeles club was involved and Los Angeles was a hotbed of anti-Tuttle sentiment. Tuttle suspended Reese for 30 days, Lelivelt for 15 days, and Statz for five days in what he stated was the start of a determined campaign to protect his umpires.[291] Later in the season some of the Angels players would voice feelings that Tuttle's suspension of the three in this crucial series cost them a chance for a first division finish and championship play.[292]

Neither the *Times* nor the *Examiner* was light-hearted regarding the suspensions, considering them as a serious blow to the Angels' playoff hopes. The *Examiner* led with this paragraph:

> *Rising to the defense of law and order – not to overlook the San Diego baseball club, with officials of which he has been on the friendliest of terms since his induction into office – W. C. Tuttle, president of the Pacific Coast League, today took the first and most drastic disciplinary action of his interesting career against Manager Jack Lelivelt, Centerfielder Arnold Statz and Second Baseman Jimmy Reese of the Los Angeles baseball club.*[293]

The *Times* reported that Oscar Reichow, business manager of the Los Angeles club, openly charged that Tuttle, because of his friendship with Padres owner Bill Lane, was trying to cripple his team in the fight for the first division and a playoff berth.[294] The *Times* included Tuttle's statement in response to this charge, in which the PCL president expressed regret at having to take the action against the three Angels because he is friendly with all three. Tuttle also expressed his belief that he was rather lenient in Reese's case, given that he slapped the umpire.[295] Attempting a broader perspective, the *Times* baseball columnist noted that Tuttle has a reputation of being very "pro-San Diego" and that Bill Lane hired Tuttle's stepson as a batting practice pitcher for the Padres.[296] It was true that Bud Tuttle appeared infrequently and so this was an understandable perspective from someone based in Los Angeles. The lack of consistency in punishing this type of infraction made it appear that the Angels were the "fall guys."

An interesting follow-up happened at Lane Field on the afternoon of July 30, when Oscar Reichow of the Angels and Jack James of the *Examiner* were challenged by umpire Sam Crawford upon entering the ballpark. Crawford referred to James as Reichow's reporter and claimed that he never wrote anything unless told to do so by Reichow. Reichow said to James, "Since you write only on instructions, you might say for me that Sam Crawford, who kept completely out of yesterday's arguments, has long been regarded as one of the most incompetent umpires in this or any other league, and that he holds his present position only because Mr. Lane of San Diego insisted that something ought to be done for him because of his past service as big league player."[297]

While the suspensions were front-page sports news in San Diego, they were overshadowed by the long-awaited first game under the lights at Lane Field

NIGHT BALL COMES TO SAN DIEGO

During the Missions series, final wiring for lights at Lane Field was being completed. The first test of the lights was conducted on Friday night, July 24, and was pronounced a success. The lights were also successfully tested on Monday, July 27. Lane announced plans for the first night game sometime during the week of July 27 when the Angels would be in town.[298]

Lane selected Thursday night, July 30, for the first professional night game in San Diego. Adding to the drama of the evening was the Angels choice of starting pitcher, Jack Salveson, who brought a personal 11-game winning streak into the contest. Before 7,000 fans, the Padres smacked Salveson for 15 hits, but the Angels matched that total in turning back San Diego, 10-5. The lights clearly did not bother the hitters, but the fielders had some problems, as the Padres committed a season-high five errors.

Salveson's 12th straight win brought him one closer to the PCL record of 16, set by Frank Browning of the Seals in 1909. Interestingly, the closest challenge to the record was authored by Padres Manager Frank Shellenback with 15 straight in 1931 with the Stars. Shellenback also won 12 in a row in 1930.[299]

The inaugural night game was judged a success, particularly in terms of attendance. The turnout was better than expected, and it was noted that the attendance figure was based on actual paid attendance.[300] The players found the lights satisfactory, although the infield was slightly darker than at other parks. Plans to rectify the problem were contingent upon completion of the grandstand roof. Bill Lane left the prices at the weekday schedule for the night contest. After the home double header on August 2 there were only two weeks of home games left on the schedule, and speculation was that the Thursday and possibly the Wednesday contests would be played under the lights.

The home team atoned for the defeat under the lights with a 2-0 win on the final day of the month, "Spanky Day"* at Lane Field (kids admitted free). Howard Craghead authored the three-hit shutout that restored the Padres to fifth place. The team thus finished at .500 for the month with a 16-16 record. The individual player batting and pitching records for the month are provided in Table 9.2.

Bobby Doerr led the team with 50 hits for the month and batted .403. George Myatt led in runs scored with 19, and Chick Shiver topped the team with 17 RBIs despite a .238 average. Ted Williams batted only 20 times with four hits during July and posted a forgettable 13.50 ERA in 1⅓ innings of work on the mound. Dick Ward was the pitching star, going 5-1 with an 0.98 ERA, while on the other side, Berly Horne struggled to an 0-4 mark (after a 1-5 June) with an ERA of 5.88.

After dropping to sixth place, the Padres ended the month in fifth although only one-half game ahead of the Angels. The series continued with three more weekend home games remaining to complete season play between the clubs.

---

* Named for Spanky a child actor in the *Little Rascals* film comedies, popular at the time.

Table 9.2. Batting and Pitching Totals for July

Players	Positions	G	AB	R	H	1B	2B	3B	HR	RBI	SB	AVG
Bobby Doerr	2b-32	32	124	16	50	41	5	3	1	13	3	.403
Gene Desautels	c-27, ph-1	28	77	6	26	25	0	1	0	7	1	.338
George McDonald	1b-21	21	63	3	21	18	3	0	0	4	0	.333
Ray Jacobs	1b-15, ph-2	17	49	4	15	11	3	0	1	5	1	.306
Cedric Durst	cf-31	31	115	8	31	28	3	0	0	11	1	.270
George Myatt	ss-31	31	123	19	33	29	3	1	0	5	6	.268
Ernie Holman	3b-32	32	110	8	29	25	3	1	0	12	4	.264
Vince DiMaggio	rf-23, cf-2, lf-7	32	115	11	30	20	9	0	1	12	5	.261
Eddie Mulligan	pr-6, ss-1	7	4	0	1	1	0	0	0	0	2	.250
Ivey Shiver	lf-13, rf-10, ph-1	24	80	8	19	13	2	3	1	17	0	.238
Herman Pillette	p-6	6	9	2	2	2	0	0	0	1	1	.222
Ted Williams	lf-5, ph-5, p-1, pr-1	11	20	4	4	3	1	0	0	1	0	.200
Dick Ward	p-9	9	17	1	3	3	0	0	0	1	0	.176
Frank Shellenback	ph-4, p-1	5	6	0	1	1	0	0	0	0	0	.167
Hal Doerr	c-9	9	27	1	4	4	0	0	0	2	0	.148
Vance Wirthman	lf-8, ph-4	12	32	1	4	4	0	0	0	0	0	.125
Manny Salvo	p-12	12	17	1	1	1	0	0	0	0	0	.059
Howard Craghead	p-9	9	15	0	0	0	0	0	0	0	0	.000
Wally Hebert	p-5	5	8	0	0	0	0	0	0	0	0	.000
Les Cook	c-4	4	5	0	0	0	0	0	0	0	0	.000
Archie Campbell	p-7	7	5	0	0	0	0	0	0	0	0	.000
Trader Horne	p-8	8	5	0	0	0	0	0	0	0	0	.000
Joe Berkowitz	pr-5	5	0	0	0	0	0	0	0	0	0	.000

Pitchers	G	GS	CG	ShO	Sv	W	L	PCT	IP	H	R	ER	SO	BB	ERA
Dick Ward	9	5	3	1	0	5	1	.833	55	36	7	6	24	22	0.98
Howard Craghead	9	7	6	3	0	4	2	.667	55	37	12	12	30	17	1.96
Herman Pillette	6	3	1	0	0	2	1	.667	27⅔	28	8	8	8	5	2.60
Wally Hebert	5	4	3	1	0	2	2	.500	29⅔	24	10	10	19	5	3.03
Manny Salvo	11	7	3	2	0	3	5	.375	56⅔	58	23	21	32	19	3.34
Archie Campbell	7	0	0	0	1	0	0	.000	18⅓	17	9	7	9	12	3.44
Trader Horne	8	5	1	0	0	0	4	.000	26	31	18	17	13	14	5.88
Frank Shellenback	1	1	0	0	0	0	1	.000	4	9	4	4	1	1	9.00
Ted Williams	1	0	0	0	0	0	0	.000	1⅓	2	2	2	0	1	13.50

CHAPTER 10
AUGUST 1936
A REAL PENNANT RACE DEVELOPS

NOTABLE WORLD EVENTS–AUGUST 1936

1st *Adolf Hitler presides over the opening ceremony of the Summer Olympics in Berlin*

9th *American Jesse Owens wins his 4th Gold medal of the Olympics in the men's relay*

23rd *17-year old Bob Feller of the Cleveland Indians becomes the youngest player to pitch a complete game victory in major league baseball by beating the St. Louis Browns 11-1 and recording 15 strikeouts*

27th *Fred Astaire and Ginger Rogers star in the musical comedy movie Swing Time that premieres in New York City*

August opened with the Padres having just reclaimed fifth place from the Angels, with three games left to play in the series (refer to Table 10.1 for the standings). Immediately following the Angels series, San Diego would travel north for a split-week series in Seattle and Portland, then play seven games in San Francisco with the Missions, followed by seven games in Sacramento. San Diego would then return home on Tuesday, August 25, to host Oakland for seven games. A 21-day road trip is not necessarily the most desirable means to climb back into the pennant race (the papers were hoping for a chance to hold fifth place) but the 1936 Padres turned out to be a team of surprises.

Table 10.1. PCL Standings on August 1, 1936

	W	L	Pct.	GB
Seattle	71	56	.559	--
Portland	67	57	.540	2½
Oakland	68	60	.531	3½
Missions	66	60	.524	4½
San Diego	**63**	**63**	**.500**	**7½**
Los Angeles	63	64	.496	8
San Francisco	59	68	.465	12
Sacramento	50	79	.388	22

Even with several weeks left in the season, Bill Lane had already concluded that his move to San Diego was the right one. Home attendance was 40,000 more than had been the previous year in Hollywood, with still two weeks of home games remaining. Despite being the second smallest city in the circuit in terms of population, San Diego's home attendance ranked third behind only Seattle and Portland, and first among California cities.[301]

FINISHING OFF THE ANGELS

The archrival Angels for once proved no match for the Padres during the first weekend of August. On Saturday, August 1, George Myatt singled home "Iron Man" Archie Campbell in the 12th inning for a 4-3 win, and San Diego followed with a sweep of Sunday's twin bill, winning by scores of 3-2 and 5-2. The Sunday doubleheader began early (12:30 P.M.) and was played under a curfew of 4:00 P.M. to allow the Padres to catch a bus to Los Angeles where they would board an early train to Seattle. Ivy Shiver singled home Gene Desautels to avert extra innings in the opener and a five-run fourth inning iced the nightcap against Hugh Casey.

During the Saturday game, Lane stepped outside the park and invited the "knothole gang" along Pacific Highway to be his guests for the game.[302] At first, the gang refused the invitation, believing that someone was trying to horn in on their territory, but eventually all but one member accepted Lane's invitation. The lone holdout invited Lane to join him, offering to get a few bricks to build up his guest seat to the right height!

By taking six of seven from the Angels, the Padres moved three games over .500 (66-63) and solidified their hold on fifth place. San Diego trailed league-leading Seattle by 6½ games, but was only one game behind the fourth place Missions and two games back of the third place Oaks.

Before beginning the road trip, there was a bit of non-baseball news. Padres shortstop George Myatt announced he had wedding plans in his near future. His bride-to-be was Georgia Smith, a very successful softball pitcher[303] and resident of nearby National City. The courtship began shortly after the Padres moved to San Diego. The wedding was originally scheduled for August 24, the first off-day after the conclusion of the three-week road trip, but was later switched to Thursday, August 27, with the ceremony to be performed at Lane Field's home plate prior to the game with Oakland.

THE PACIFIC NORTHWEST

The Seattle series would be the Padres' first meeting with umpire Jack Powell since the uproar in San Diego and would prove to be uneventful. The Padres tapped their dormant power source to take the opening game of

10—AUGUST 1936 A REAL PENNANT RACE DEVELOPS

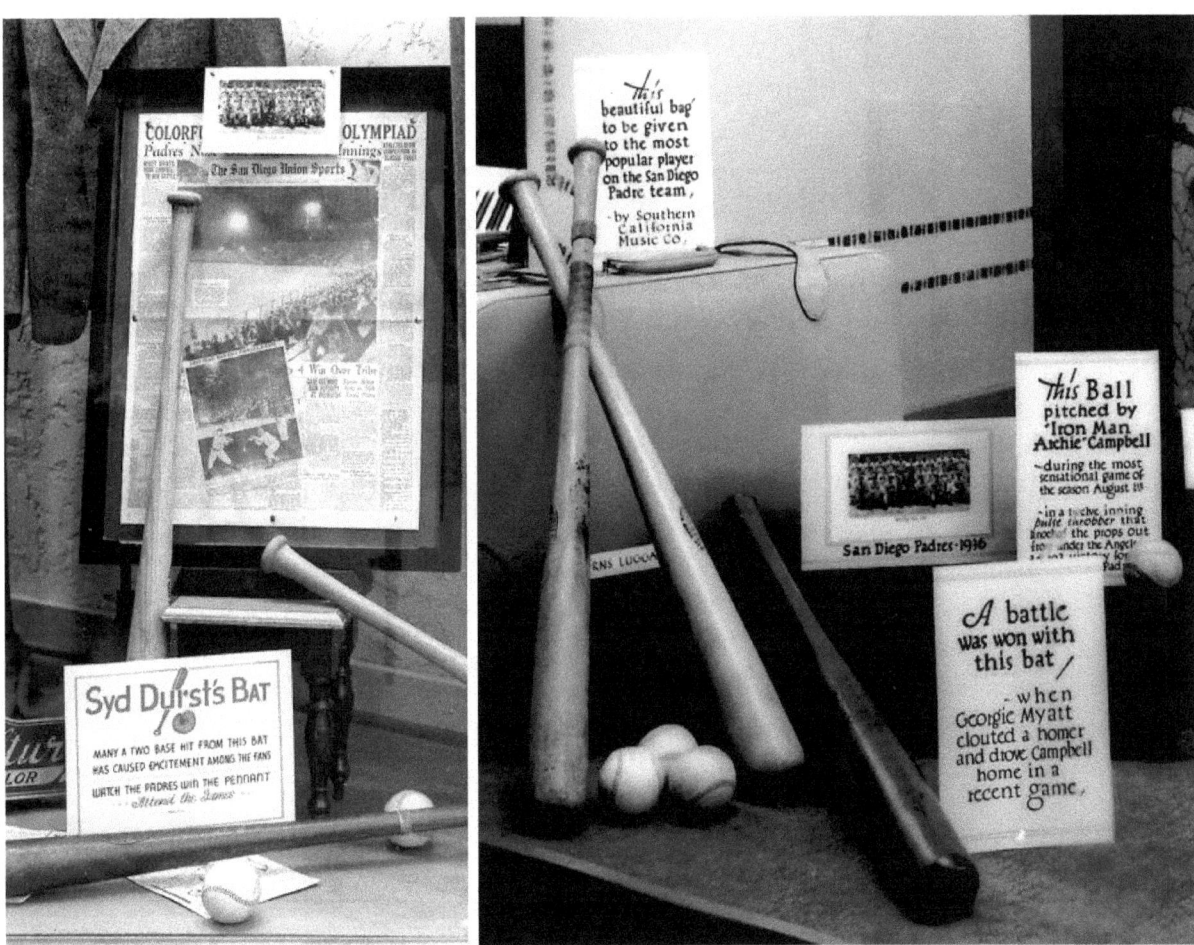

Merchants Supporting The Padres in August 1936
Julius Sturz Men's Store and SoCal Music Co.

the series. With one home run in the previous four weeks, the team offense was clearly not based on the long ball (although doubles and triples were not uncommon). But Chick Shiver and Ray Jacobs blasted back-to-back home runs in the sixth inning and Ernie Holman also homered to lead San Diego to a 7-4 win over the Indians and move the Padres into a tie for fourth place with the Missions. Archie Campbell picked up the win in relief of Manny Salvo.

The Padres took sole possession of fourth place on Wednesday, August 5, as catcher Gene Desautels homered in support of ex-Seattle Indian Howard Craghead, who shut down his former teammates on two hits for a 4-1 win. Thursday was "Ward night" in Seattle, to honor Dick Ward, Padre hurler hailing from the Seattle area. Ward repaid the honor by pitching an 11-inning complete game and scoring the winning run as the Padres swept Seattle out of first place, 5-3. It was the team's (and Ward's) seventh consecutive win. Portland, the new first-place club, would be the next stop.

The San Diego papers' box scores of 1936 did not indicate pitchers' won-lost records, but the *Union* would publish weekly updates of batting and pitching records. Pitchers were ranked in terms of percentage, with wins, losses, and strikeouts reported. Ward's seventh straight win lifted him to seventh place with a record of 9-4.

In terms of wins, Portland's Caster led the circuit with 19, followed by Koupal of Seattle with 18 and the Oaks' Ludolph with 17. Padres pitching marks include:

Ward	9-4	.692
Hebert	14-8	.632 (*sic*, should be .636)
Salvo	13-9	.591
Craghead	9-9	.500 (includes record with Seattle)
Shellenback	5-6	.455
Pillette	5-7	.417
Campbell	5-8	.385
Horne	5-12	.294

Beginning on Friday, August 7, the Padres had a tough three-day stretch awaiting them in Portland with three consecutive doubleheaders making up two earlier rainouts. The Portland club reportedly requested full nine-inning games in both ends of the doubleheader,[304] but under PCL rules both teams must agree, and the Padres did not concur, so the second game remained the normal seven-inning affair. The winning streak, and especially the recent three-game sweep in Seattle, fired up fans. Local sportsmen and civic organizations, including the Chamber of Commerce, the head of the San Diego Motor Vehicle Department, and various San Diegans, sent telegrams of congratulations to the Padres.[305] The Padres were cited for their willingness to put aside personal interests for the team as well as for their success against the top teams in the league.[306]

In the Friday opener, on August 7, the Padres came from behind to tie the Beavers in the ninth, but three hits off Archie Campbell gave Portland a 3-2 win in 10 innings and snapped San Diego's seven-game winning streak. Southpaw Hebert, held out of the Seattle series due to the short left-field wall at the Civic Stadium in Seattle, threw a five-hit shutout in the nightcap to earn the Padres a split, 10-0. DiMaggio had three extra base hits to lead the offense in the second game.

The Saturday twi-nighter did not turn out well for San Diego, as the Beavers jumped out to early leads against Manny Salvo and Herm Pillette in both games and swept the Padres, 9-6 and 8-1. Seven Padres errors, four by the usually sure-handed Doerr, hurt Salvo in the opener. Jimmy Kerr, who made his first appearance since his injury as a pinch-hitter Friday night, caught the Saturday nightcap. But Cedric Durst, star center fielder, sat out both games with a groin injury that had been bothering him for a few weeks. Van Wirthman was not traveling with the club due to an injury but was quickly summoned as a back-up. Ted Williams was inserted into the lineup in left field, with Shiver moving to right and DiMaggio to center.

The Padres rebounded on Sunday, August 9, behind their two most consistent pitchers, Howard Craghead and Dick Ward, to sweep the Beavers by identical scores of 4-1. Craghead allowed eight hits while Ward yielded only four in posting his eighth straight win. Durst was a surprise return to the lineup in both games, but Ted Williams did not return to the bench. Williams started in left field in place of Shiver

"Young" Ted Williams

and collected three hits in seven trips with two doubles and two RBIs in the doubleheader. Referencing "The Kid," McConnell reported: "Young Ted Williams…has been delivering like a veteran and Padre fans probably will see more of him."[307]

The sweep gave San Diego a split of the six-game series with Portland (although the Padres could not knock the Beavers out of first, as they had done earlier to Seattle and twice to Oakland) and a 6-3 mark for the split-week series. The Padres at 72-66 moved into a third-place tie with both the Missions and Oakland (who were swept by the Angels), 3½ games behind Portland and only two games back of second-place Seattle.

Another visitor to Portland this August 8-9 weekend was Boston Red Sox vice president and business manager Eddie Collins, in town as part of a two-week scouting visit to the West Coast. Collins had earlier expressed interest in Bobby Doerr and George Myatt, the Padres keystone combination.[308] This was likely Collins' first sighting of Ted Williams as well. Collins was scheduled to "discuss the weather" with Bill Lane in San Diego later in the week. Hebert, Craghead, and Ward also evinced interest, but because all three had pitched in the majors previously, they were subject to the draft.[309] Their success strongly suggested that they would not return to the Padres in 1937.

The interest in Doerr was not a surprise given that he led all Padres hitters and was tied for 12th in the league with a .326 batting average. However, as it turned out, the "keystone kids" had a game to forget in Saturday's game 1. The two made six errors in the game, four by Doerr. Knowing Collins was watching perhaps they both just had a bad case of jitters.[310] Doerr later recalled: "Of course my goal was to get taken by the Red Sox. I was having a good year and then Eddie Collins came out (I think in July [sic]) and I had a bad day… I think I made three [sic] errors. He called me out between games on Sunday and said, 'Bobby, we're gonna buy your contract. Don't be nervous.' That was real nice…"[311]

Another report had Collins expressing interest to owner Lane for an option on catcher Gene Desautels, and inquired "about the kid in right, that youngster Williams, whose swing looked good and who seemed able to drive in runs. Lane demurred, claiming the kid was just 17 and he had made a deal with his mother. So Collins backed off, but he cajoled Lane into a verbal agreement that the Padres' owner, to his credit, honored. Lane would not peddle Williams to anyone else without first consulting with Collins."[312]

Looking back years later this would turn out to be a pretty good handshake agreement for Collins and the Red Sox!

VISITING THE MISSIONS

The Padres returned to California to start a "make or break" series with the Missions in San Francisco. The two teams would do battle throughout the week while the other third-place team, Oakland, would face the league-leading Beavers and second-place Seattle would try to re-tool against cellar-dwelling Sacramento.

Seattle received bad news before the start of their series when PCL President Tuttle suspended manager Dutch Ruether for the remainder of the season following the run-in with umpire Bill Engeln in which Ruether stepped on his toes and tore his mask off. Not surprisingly, the Angels president protested the decision in a telegram, demanding to know when Tuttle would take action to improve the class of umpiring in the PCL.[313]

Trader Horne posted his first win since June in the series opener on Tuesday, August 11, with a four-hit, 2-0 shutout. George Myatt had three hits, including an RBI triple that plated an insurance run in the eighth. Durst remained in the lineup, but shifted to left field, with Vince DiMaggio in center and Ted Williams in right. Combined with Portland's victory in Oakland, the win put San Diego in sole possession of third place. Wally Hebert faltered the next day as the Missions accumulated 12 hits in a 5-1 win that restored a three-way tie.

Wally Beck, always effective against San Diego, got the win. But Dick Ward and Howard Craghead were next in the rotation.

Craghead was not sharp on Thursday, but the Padres bats rescued him. A four-run fourth put San Diego in the lead for good, and Manny Salvo held on in relief for a 10-9 win. Chick Shiver continued his hot summer start with the Padres and was the big cog in the offense, with four RBIs and four hits, including a double and a home run. Myatt chipped in with another triple for San Diego as the club regained third place alone.

Dick Ward kept them in third by posting his ninth consecutive win on Friday, August 14, with help from DiMaggio's two hits and three RBIs in a 5-1 win that moved San Diego within 2½ games of league-leading Portland. Shiver, clearly hitting his stride in mid-August, and Ernie Holman each contributed three more hits.

Shiver and Gene Desautels blasted home runs to lead the Padres in a wild 15-11 slugfest win on Saturday. Horne was knocked out in the first inning, but Shellenback gave his staff some much-needed relief by pitching 8⅓ innings despite giving up seven runs. This would be the last of Shellenback's 318 career minor league wins.

The Missions turned the tables with a Sunday doubleheader sweep, 15-4 and 6-2. Salvo and Hebert took the losses on Sunday, and Wally Beck picked up another win at the expense of the Padres in the nightcap. Shiver continued his assault with two hits in the opener and Durst showed signs of shaking off his lingering injury with three hits in the nightcap. Bud Tuttle, southpaw son of the PCL President, made a rare appearance in relief in the second game.[314] Despite the double-dip, San Diego ended the week alone in third place with a 76-69 record, 3½ games behind Portland and two back of second place Seattle. Oakland and the Missions were tied for fourth, trailing the Padres by only one game.

With the assault on Padres pitchers by the Missions, it was comforting for Padre fans to read in Sunday's paper that the staff led the PCL in shutouts with 14, eight since July 1.[315] The recent solid performance by the pitching staff (excepting the Missions series) was a primary reason behind the club's surge into the first division and serious contention. Salvo, "Hard Luck" Horne (who seemed to have an uncanny ability to attract nicknames), Hebert, and Craghead each had three shutouts to their credit, with Ward and the departed Ed Wells credited with one each (Ward also had a shutout with Sacramento earlier in the year). San Diego was also the second-hardest club to whitewash, following the heavy hitting Seattle Indians. Eight pitchers had blanked the Padres to date.

Ernie Holman, Padres third baseman and cleanup hitter, moved past Bobby Doerr to top the team with a .324 mark, 14th best in the PCL.[316] Five Padres appearing in 50 or more games posted averages over .300 (McDonald, Desautels, and Durst were the others). Joe Marty of the Seals, who had the unenviable title of "the successor to Joe DiMaggio," led the league with a .350 mark. For the month so far Shiver was hitting .424 with three homers and 14 RBIs.

Bill Lane's Thursday meeting with Collins of the Red Sox was postponed, with the possibility that they would get together over the weekend.[317] The owner recognized that his club had thrust itself into the thick of the pennant race and wanted to avoid any actions that would disrupt his players' focus on the task at hand. Word on the apparent Lane-Collins meeting leaked later in the week but there was not much to report. Boston still had an option, good until October 1, on Doerr and Myatt. PCL managers rated Bobby Doerr as the best bet to stick with the Red Sox with Myatt needing a little more experience.[318] By then it was apparent that the Red Sox would never make good on the promise of two additional players for this season.

10—AUGUST 1936 A REAL PENNANT RACE DEVELOPS

...AND LAST IN THE PACIFIC COAST LEAGUE

The Sacramento Solons were buried in the basement of the PCL, 11 games behind the seventh-place Seals. Although the word "improving" was often attached to the young Solons, the team struggled all season. After weeks of battling first division teams, the Padres welcomed a visit to Sacramento.

The series, beginning on Tuesday, August 18, started with a victory, but San Diego had to withstand a five-run ninth to hold on to a 7-6 win. Craghead staggered in the ninth inning but posted his seventh straight win (5-0 for the month of August). With four hits, Ced Durst was the offensive star. Portland and Seattle both lost, leaving the Padres 2½ games out of first and a game behind the second-place Indians.

San Diego fell back into a tie for third with Oakland on Wednesday as Bill Porter, a local youngster off the sandlots making his first start, went the distance in a 10-8 win, surviving Shiver's ninth inning home run. Berly Horne and Manny Salvo were ineffective against the Senators, as Sacramento pounded three homers. Dick Ward was held back due to a cold.

The Padres were enjoying the winning streaks of Ward and Craghead, but also enjoyed spoiling Cotton Pippen's 10-game winning streak with a 6-1 win over Sacramento Thursday. Herman Pillette, described as the "dean of the Coast league pitchers,"[319] went the distance with a four-hitter. Shiver supported him with three hits, including a triple, and DiMaggio chipped in with a home run. San Diego moved into a second-place tie with Seattle and Oakland with the win. Sacramento announced earlier in the day that all of the players on waivers were withdrawn; the Padres had claimed outfielder Buster Adams and shortstop Frankie Morehouse.

A day later, Seattle owner Bill Klepper asked waivers on nine of his players in the wake of the team's recent struggles. Wally Hebert scattered ten hits on Friday and Shiver collected two more hits, including a home run, as the Padres coasted to a 10-0 shutout. With Portland's loss in their first game of the doubleheader, the Padres were within one-half game of first, but the Beavers won the nightcap.

In response to fan requests, Bill Lane announced that the opening game of the final home stand on the following Tuesday, September 1, would be shifted from day to night.

With Ward still under the weather, manager Shellenback named himself as Saturday's starter. He scattered four hits, but two errors led to four unearned runs as Sacramento took a 4-2 win and dropped the Padres back into a third place tie. Durst sat out his third straight game, with Wirthman taking his place in the lineup.

Sacramento again played spoiler in the opener of the August 22 doubleheader ending Craghead's seven-game win streak with a 7-3 win. Pillette came back with his second strong game of the week for a three-hit, 5-0 shutout to give San Diego the series. The Padres finished the long road trip with a 14-9 mark, in sole possession of third place, and two games out of the lead. The race for first and for a playoff spot had tightened considerably. The standings on Sunday morning, August 23, shown in Table 10.2, found six teams within six games of first place Portland.

The four first-division teams would gain a playoff spot but the playoff format was still up in the air. The league agreement provides that the team with the highest percentage shall decide where the playoff series shall be held, but also holds that the site of the series will be left up to the decision and judgment of the owners.[320]

Table 10.2. PCL Standings on Sunday, August 23, 1936

	W	L	Pct.	GB
Portland	82	70	.539	--
Seattle	81	71	.533	1
San Diego	**80**	**72**	**.526**	**2**
Oakland	79	73	.520	3
Missions	78	74	.513	4
Los Angeles	76	76	.500	6
San Francisco	72	80	.474	10
Sacramento	60	92	.395	22

HOME TO WEDDING BELLS AND PENNANT PRESSURE

A big turnout greeted the Padres' return home on the 12:30 P.M. train Monday, August 24, although manager Shellenback and several players had stopped off in Los Angeles. Cedric Durst, who played right field in both games of the Sunday doubleheader, was in Los Angeles to have his ailing muscle injury in his groin examined. Durst was leading in the voting for most popular Padre. Eddie Mulligan, veteran player/coach who filled in as a pinch runner and backup shortstop, cracked a rib in Sacramento, and Dick Ward was still suffering the effects of what had been diagnosed as influenza.[321] Work on the Lane Field infield was now complete; the dirt portion of the infield was moved back to give infielders a chance to play deep without getting on the grass.[322]

While the Padres and Oaks were preparing to square off, Portland was hosting San Francisco while Seattle was at home facing the Angels. Given the sterling pitching performances the last time these two teams met in Oakland, low-scoring games would not be surprising, but the teams ranked 1-2 in batting in the PCL as well. Before a crowd of over 8,000 fans on Tuesday night, Oakland came back from a 4-1 deficit with four runs in the fifth and went on to a 6-4 win, pulling into a third-place tie with San Diego. Hal Hald got the win in relief, while Hebert took the loss.

Durst was on the sidelines, and would not return to the outfield until the second game of the Sunday doubleheader. Dick Ward was finally healthy and pitched brilliantly on Wednesday afternoon. He shut out the Oaks on three hits for a 1-0 win with Gene Desautels scoring an unearned run in the second inning. The game ended with some "fireworks" between Oakland and umpire Ray Snyder when he called out Joe Gordon on strikes with the tying run on third. Oakland first baseman Roy Anton, in street clothes after an earlier ejection, raced out from the dugout and leaped toward Snyder, only to be intercepted by Ward coming off the mound. The Padres and their fans rushed onto the field as well, but things quieted down quickly as players and umpires left the field.[323] PCL President Tuttle fined Anton $25, viewed as a very lenient sentence.[324]

Thursday, August 27, was another doubleheader of a sort, with George Myatt's wedding night and a baseball game scheduled at Lane Field.

A large crowd of 10,000 (8,342 paid) packed the park. Padres players formed an arch of crossed bats through which Georgie Myatt, his bride Georgia Smith, and the wedding party emerged onto the field. Owner Bill Lane (supposedly a bachelor of 76 years) gave away the bride and Bobby Doerr served as best man. Judge Gordon Thompson of the Superior Court officiated at the wedding ceremony while the San Diego and Oakland teams assembled in the background along with Miss Smith's teammates from the National City softball team on which she was a pitcher. A musical quartet composed of Berly Horne, Archie Campbell, Vince DiMaggio, and trainer Les Cook amused the couple and the crowd with a serenade of three tunes, including "Those Wedding Bells Are

George Myatt's Wedding Night at Lane Field
San Diego Evening Tribune, August 28, 1936, and Private Collection

Breaking Up That Old Gang of Mine," following the ceremony.[325] Reportedly Owner Lane bore no hard feelings from Myatt's spring training holdout and gave the couple a week in San Francisco for their honeymoon on the condition they wed at home plate during the homestand.[326]

At the conclusion of the wedding ceremony, Myatt escorted his bride from the field and proceeded to rap out two hits and score a run on Shiver's seventh-inning home run that put the Padres into the lead. At the end of the night, Howard Craghead had a complete game victory and the Padres moved back into a tie for second with Seattle, staying within two games of Portland. Myatt also contributed a terrific defensive play in the second on Jack LaRocca's hard grounder.

As a side note, Myatt's honeymoon was delayed after the game. According to a 2001 interview with George McDonald, Myatt was "arrested" by San Diego police following the game and taken to jail for a brief stay, the result of a prank pulled off by his teammates.[327]

The Padres' momentum carried over the next day. Facing Wee Willie Ludolph, the league's leading pitcher, San Diego went into extra innings and came away with a 3-2 win.[328] Ernie Holman drove home Van Wirthman with an unearned run in the tenth to give Campbell the win in relief of Herm Pillette. The tenth inning featured some interesting managerial decisions on both sides. Wirthman reached third base with one out, and Oakland manager Billy Meyer elected to walk Doerr intentionally to pitch to Chick Shiver. Shellenback then surprised the Oaks by calling on Durst to bat for Shiver, triggering a long conference on the mound. Ludolph gave Durst nothing good to hit, loading the bases and setting the stage for Holman.

The managerial decisions showed the respect for Bobby Doerr on the part of opposing teams as well as the high regard for Durst by his own manager. While Shiver had been hitless to that point, he was the major power source for the Padres, and had been robbed of a home run on a 450-foot drive by the Oaks' center fielder Earl Bolyard in his previous at bat in the eighth. Yet Shellenback preferred an injured Cedric Durst, who appeared to have "reliable" permanently attached to his name in newspaper accounts throughout 1936. It also bears noting that while Vince DiMaggio would eventually establish himself as an excellent defensive center fielder in the big leagues, Durst was considered his defensive superior in San Diego and started in center field when healthy. DiMaggio picked up some notoriety in the August 13 edition of *The Sporting News* especially citing his arm and 25 assists as of August 1.

With a Portland loss and a Seattle win in later evening games, Saturday morning, August 29, found the Padres tied for second, only one game out of first. The lead in Ted Steinmann's column read, "Try to keep our Padres from going places now."[329] While no one was predicting a pennant or a playoff victory, the acquisitions of Salvo, Craghead, Ward, and Shiver over the course of the season were seen as crucial to overcoming a slow start.

The Saturday matinee started off "...wilder than a tent full of Hopi Indians doing a snake dance on a hill of red ants...Pitchers lasted about as long, during the first three innings, as did the government bonds of the veterans...."[330] The Padres held a 6-5 lead heading into the fourth when relievers Manny Salvo and Tom Conlan restored order on both sides, and a San Diego insurance run in the eighth would be the only other scoring. The victory lifted San Diego into sole possession of second, within a game behind Portland. Paid attendance exceeded 7,000 for the third time this week. Pennant fever was evident everywhere except in the selection of a picture for the front page of the *Union's* sports section. The Sunday sports section featured a large photograph of five local bathing beauties holding up a very big fish, a locally renowned picture reprinted twice in the *Union-Tribune* during the last weeks of 1999.[331]

Oakland showed that it was a resilient ball team in the Sunday doubleheader. Dick Ward and Howard Craghead, the Padres aces, started the two games for San Diego, but the Oaks ended Ward's ten-game winning streak convincingly in the opener, 9-1, and completed a sweep with a 4-3 win in the nightcap (Wally Hebert lost in relief of Craghead). The Padres set a record for series attendance as 8,514 fans paid to watch Oakland revive their playoff hopes. DiMaggio's home run in the first game was one of the few bright spots for the team, but Shiver blasted an even longer blow that bounced over the fence in center, more than 460 feet from home plate. The double defeat dropped the Padres back into a tie for second with Seattle, two games behind Portland. More importantly, Myatt had to come out of the first game with an injured little finger on his glove hand. The injury occurred in pre-game warmups, and Myatt was taken out after the finger began to swell. No x-rays were taken immediately; doctors would examine Myatt on the Monday off-day.

The Padres drew 37,199 fans for the seven game series in what turned out to be the largest crowd for any PCL series in the 1936 season.[332]

Hopes to Join Joe

Vincent DiMaggio
"Hoping to Join Joe"
The Sporting News,
August 13, 1936

10—AUGUST 1936 A REAL PENNANT RACE DEVELOPS

The month ended with a benefit exhibition game sponsored by the Rotary Club on Monday, August 31, against local semi-pro all-stars. With a nine-game series against Sacramento looming, the Padres did not use their first-line pitchers and most regulars played only an inning or two. The local all-stars won an 8-6 game before more than 4,000. Ted Williams was the hitting star, with a home run, a double, and two singles. Bud Tuttle started for San Diego, and a rookie named Blackie Deforth finished up; Deforth would not appear in any PCL box scores for the Padres in 1936. The game earned $1,521 for the Crippled Children's Fund.[333]

August ended with a set lineup for the Padres (barring injuries):

Myatt	SS
Doerr	2B
Durst	CF
Holman	3B
Desautels	C
DiMaggio	RF
Shiver	LF
McDolnald	1B
Pitcher	P

When Ced Durst was out of the lineup, Chick Shiver usually moved up to the third spot and Van Wirthman or Ted Williams would bat seventh. The only other regular substitution was at first base, where Ray Jacobs would spell George McDonald.

Despite a sour ending, August was the most successful month to date for the Padres. They played 33 games in the month, winning 21 and losing 12. They had separated themselves from the middle of the pack and were elevated into the thick of a very tight pennant race.

With two weeks left in the season, the Padres trailed Portland by two games, and were tied with Seattle for second place, with the Missions, Oakland, and Los Angeles all close behind. Injuries to Ced Durst and George Myatt were major concerns. Durst played in the field in the Sunday nightcap against Oakland, but his availability was still day-to-day. The extent of Myatt's injury was unknown. The Padres were entering September with their fingers crossed regarding the health of the team's center fielder and shortstop.

The individual player batting and pitching records for the month are provided in Table 10.3. Dick Ward and Howard Craghead led a revitalized pitching staff with a combined August record of 11-2, while Archie Campbell won three games in relief and Wally Hebert and Herm Pillette pitched effectively, although Hebert was uneven. Chick Shiver batted .364 for the month, with a team-leading six home runs and 26 runs batted in. Bobby Doerr hit .333, scored 21 runs, drove in 19, and contributed 15 extra base hits. Myatt scored 27 runs, while Vince DiMaggio, Durst, and Ernie Holman all hit between .295 and .300 during August.

"The Kid" Williams appeared in 13 games in August, with seven hits in 28 at bats (.250) including two doubles and three RBIs. Manager Shellenback held the rookie back somewhat, even with Durst being hurt during the Oakland series, as he had Van Wirthman fill in with DiMaggio moving to center. While there did not seem to be any doubt regarding Williams's ability, there was an obvious desire to bring him along slowly.

Table 10.3. Batting and Pitching Totals for August

Players	Positions	G	AB	R	H	1B	2B	3B	HR	RBI	SB	AVG
Frank Shellenback	p-3, ph-3	6	12	1	5	5	0	0	0	3	0	.417
Archie Campbell	p-10	10	8	1	3	2	1	0	0	0	0	.375
Ivey Shiver	lf-22, rf-10	30	110	19	40	26	6	2	6	26	1	.364
Herman Pillette	p-6	6	14	1	5	4	1	0	0	0	0	.357
Bobby Doerr	2b-33	33	129	21	43	28	10	5	0	19	2	.333
Vince DiMaggio	cf-23, rf-11, lf-1	33	130	17	39	21	10	4	4	19	4	.300
Trader Horne	p-6	6	10	1	3	3	0	0	0	0	0	.300
Cedric Durst	cf-13, ph-4, rf-3	20	67	7	20	19	1	0	0	10	0	.299
Ernie Holman	3b-33	33	129	19	38	31	6	0	1	20	1	.295
Dick Ward	p-7	7	18	3	5	5	0	0	0	2	0	.278
Gene Desautels	c-32	32	121	15	33	27	3	1	2	13	0	.273
George Myatt	ss-32	32	131	27	35	25	4	6	0	7	2	.267
George McDonald	1b-25	25	87	7	22	18	3	1	0	13	1	.253
Ted Williams	lf-8, ph-3, rf-1, pr-1	13	28	3	7	5	2	0	0	3	0	.250
Ray Jacobs	1b-12, ph-1	13	33	2	8	6	2	0	0	2	1	.242
Van Wirthman	rf-12, lf-5, ph-1	18	52	7	12	10	1	1	0	5	2	.231
Manny Salvo	p-9	9	12	1	2	2	0	0	0	0	0	.167
Wally Hebert	p-8, ph-1	9	16	2	2	2	0	0	0	2	0	.125
Howard Craghead	p-8	8	16	2	1	1	0	0	0	0	0	.063
Jimmy Kerr	c-3, ph-3	6	10	0	0	0	0	0	0	0	0	.000
Joe Berkowitz	ss-2, ph-2	4	4	1	0	0	0	0	0	0	0	.000
Eddie Mulligan	pr-4, ph-2	6	2	1	0	0	0	0	0	0	1	.000
Bud Tuttle	p-1	1	0	0	0	0	0	0	0	0	0	.000

Pitchers	G	GS	CG	ShO	Sv	W	L	PCT	IP	H	R	ER	SO	BB	ERA
Bud Tuttle	1	0	0	0	0	0	0	.000	2	0	0	0	0	0	0.00
Dick Ward	7	6	5	1	0	5	1	.833	43⅔	36	13	11	28	21	2.27
Wally Hebert	8	7	2	2	0	2	4	.333	41⅔	50	18	12	15	8	2.59
Manny Salvo	9	3	0	0	1	1	2	.333	32⅓	37	21	10	22	18	2.78
Frank Shellenback	3	1	1	0	0	1	1	.500	19⅓	22	12	7	8	6	3.26
Herman Pillette	6	5	2	1	0	2	1	.667	39⅔	38	17	15	15	13	3.40
Howard Craghead	8	7	3	0	0	6	1	.857	49⅔	45	24	21	21	20	3.81
Archie Campbell	10	0	0	0	0	3	1	.750	22	26	16	13	11	11	5.32
Trader Horne	7	4	1	1	0	1	1	.500	29⅓	27	19	18	16	17	5.52

CHAPTER 11
SEPTEMBER 1936
DEFECTION AND DENOUEMENT

NOTABLE WORLD EVENTS—SEPTEMBER 1936

3rd *President Roosevelt meets with six state governors, including Governor Landon, in Des Moines, Iowa, to discuss the federal government's actions to combat the draught*

9th *California Pacific International Exposition closes and ends its two-year run in San Diego*

12th *The first non-U.S. player, Fred Perry of the United Kingdom, beats Don Budge in the men's singles finals of the U.S. National Tennis Championship*

September began with the final home series of the year, a nine-game stand with the Sacramento Solons to be followed by a weeklong series against the Seals in San Francisco. The unusual nine-game series featured a Labor Day doubleheader on the usual travel day, Monday, September 7. The schedule appeared to favor the Padres, since their remaining two opponents occupied the bottom rungs of the league as depicted in Table 11.1 showing the standings as of September 1. Spoilers can be the toughest teams to beat down the stretch, however, and Sacramento had a respectable 9-12 record against the Padres to date.[334]

Table 11.1. PCL Standings on September 1, 1936

	W	L	Pct.	GB
Portland	86	73	.541	--
San Diego	**84**	**75**	**.528**	**2**
Seattle	84	75	.528	2
Missions	83	76	.522	3
Oakland	82	77	.516	4
Los Angeles	80	79	.503	6
San Francisco	75	84	.472	11
Sacramento	62	97	.390	24

DEFECTION!

Just as the Sacramento series was about to begin a stunning development took place: the sudden departure of Chick Shiver. A Georgia Junior College had offered Shiver the position of head coach of its football team if he would join them immediately. He took them up on the offer and left town on the evening train on his way to a new job outside of Atlanta, Georgia.[335] The turn of events took the Padre front office completely by surprise. Bill Lane suspended Shiver indefinitely but several players felt that it was Shiver's intention to retire from baseball and so the suspension meant little.

The loss of Shiver, who was red-hot through August, seemingly was a knockdown blow to a team that had fought back to within two games of first place. To make up for Shiver's abrupt departure Manager Frank Shellenback made the decision to replace him in the lineup with Ted Williams, who would be expected to start in left field in the rest of the season.

With the luxury of hindsight (and knowing how baseball history turned out), it is tempting to read more into this startling development. What if Shellenback had decided that Williams was ready and had communicated his plans to insert him in the lineup to Shiver? In the context of 1936, this speculation makes no sense. The much more logical option was summed up by Ted Steinmann's column on September 2: "Tough at this stage of the race, but you don't find many who blame him. Shiver's baseball life was not promising for a long tenure, while a job as a coach, provided that he makes good, will last many more years and at a steady salary the year around."[336]

As Shiver's train wound east—18-year old Ted Williams—all of a sudden found himself with his first starting job in professional baseball, and at the same time as the Padres prepared to try to close the gap between themselves and first-place Portland.

T. SAMUEL WILLIAMS—PUBLIC ENEMY NO. 1!?

The nine-game series with Sacramento began on Tuesday, September 1. The series started on a promising note, as the Padres shook off Shiver's departure and hammered Sacramento, 14-3. Ward struggled with his control (although he issued no walks) but coasted to the easy win behind a 15-hit attack, including four by first sacker McDonald. Williams' debut as a regular featured a double and a triple in three at bats.

Durst answered the starting bell for the first game of this series but switched with Vince DiMaggio in the outfield, indicating that he was not yet 100 percent. Trainer Les Cook made his first appearance behind the plate since July to spell Gene Desautels in the rout, which brought the Padres to within 1½ games of rained-out Portland.

The Padres followed up the first game with an 11-1 pounding on September 2. San Diego gained revenge on Solons' hurler Robert Ross who had stopped the Padres on three hits earlier in the season. Wednesday's

11—SEPTEMBER 1936 DEFECTION AND DENOUEMENT

Public Enemy No. 1 to Floundering Sacs

Ted Williams "Public Enemy No.1"
(Note: The photo was from his Hoover High School days)
San Diego Union, September 7, 1936

beneficiary was veteran Pillette who held Sacramento to four hits. The third base portion of the infield was muddy, due to a hydrant being mistakenly left on overnight, but this did not affect the game. Wirthman again entered the game as a replacement for Durst and stole home on the front end of a double steal to cap the scoring in the seventh inning.

Wednesday was "ladies day" and the newspaper account noted a large number of women in the crowd as the Padres continued to capture the hearts of all San Diegans. San Diego was winning over some experts as well, as PCL publicity chief Harry Williams was quoted as giving the Padres the best chance to finish on top.[337] Lane had begun his quest for a PCL pennant in 1914 and waited 15 years until the Hollywood Stars made three consecutive playoff appearances in 1929-1931. Those clubs had a San Diego connection since the Stars trained in San Diego, but only Shellenback and Les Cook remained from Hollywood's glory days.

Sacramento ace Johnnie Chambers upstaged the Padres in the only night game of the series played on Thursday with a three-hit 1-0 win over Manny Salvo. San Diego native Frankie Morehouse scored the game's only run after Umpire Frank Valerio ruled that first baseman George McDonald missed a swipe tag after being pulled off the bag on a throw from Myatt. Bobby Doerr had two of the three San Diego hits.

The Padre offense put the Lane Field night game jinx behind on Friday afternoon with a 13-1 win. Craghead coasted to his 15th win of the season behind a 16-hit barrage. The Padres continued their weeklong surprising show of speed on the bases picking up three more stolen bases including two by Doerr who now had a total of five on the week. Myatt's fielding struggles, possibly related to his injured thumb, continued with three errors on Friday and a total of five for the week thus far. Ernie Holman, however, continued his sparkling play at third base, and Vince DiMaggio "traveled back to the Orange County line" to make an eighth inning catch.[338]

Heading into the Labor Day weekend with five games to play in three days looming, the Padres remained tied with Seattle in second place, trailing Portland by two games. As with the wrap-up of any PCL season news of next year also made its way into the sports pages and it was announced that Gene Desautels would join Bobby Doerr in the Boston Red Sox spring training camp in 1937.[339] More immediately, Shellenback decided on Ward for Saturday's start, since this would give him two starts in San Francisco during the last week of the season, each with three days' rest. "Slaughter of the innocents continued unabated"[340] on Saturday as Ward cruised to a 10-3 win against sidearmer Pete Landucci who stayed in for the entire game in anticipation of back-to-back doubleheaders on Sunday and Monday. Doerr's inside-the-park home run highlighted the Padre attack, and he added another stolen base as well. Myatt got a day off to rest his thumb with Joe Berkowitz taking his place at shortstop. McDonald drove in four runs giving him 12 RBIs for the five games of this series. To keep Durst as healthy as possible, he continued to be regularly replaced by Wirthman in the late innings.

On Saturday it was also announced that Cedric Durst won a new suit of clothes and a traveling bag as the top vote-getter in the season-long "Most Popular Padres" contest. The ballot was contained inside the scorecard and required the individual to include their name and address. As winner, Durst was to be presented with a "handsome traveling bag" and a suit of clothes (from Julius Sturz, 1059 Fourth Avenue) at the last Saturday game of the season. The final tally showed Durst beating out four other contenders:[341]

Cedric Durst	7,010
Bobby Doerr	6,541
George Myatt	6,462
Vince DiMaggio	6,390
Gene Desautels	5,331

The double-header on Sunday, September 6 demonstrated the Padres' multiple ways of winning. The opener was in line with the rest of the week as San Diego once again pounded the Solons' Robert Ross in a 15-3 victory. The onslaught was highlighted by Vince DiMaggio's inside-the-park home run, his second homer of the series.

In the second game, John Wahonick held the Padres to two hits but was outdueled by "Old Folks" Pillette, 1-0. A good crowd of 6,000 took in the Sunday doubleheader. Among those not in attendance was Solons' southpaw Bill Seinsoth who was scratched from a scheduled start after undergoing an emergency appendectomy Saturday night. Ted Williams made four sensational catches in left field in game one, while Joe Berkowitz again

11—SEPTEMBER 1936 DEFECTION AND DENOUEMENT

filled in for Myatt and collected four hits. When the Angels defeated Portland and the Seals topped Seattle in their respective nightcaps San Diego found itself all alone in second place, only one game out of first.

A crowd of 8,000 turned out for the Labor Day doubleheader, the final regular-season games at Lane Field, and the fans were not disappointed. Johnnie Chambers, the only Solons pitcher to beat the Padres in the weeklong series, started both games due to Seinsoth's appendectomy. San Diego beat him twice behind Manny Salvo and Berly Horne for a sweep and a tie for first with Portland. A four-run eighth, ignited by a Ted Williams double, broke open a tight pitchers' duel for a 5-1 victory in the opener. Horne worked out of a bases-loaded, no-out jam in the sixth inning of the nightcap to preserve a 3-0 win. Ernie Holman continued to sparkle defensively at third with several gems, and Desautels, Doerr, and McDonald combined in the opener to turn a Solon double-steal attempt into a double play.

The Padres rose to the occasion in the nine-game series, outscoring the Solons, 72-13, in taking eight of nine games against an opponent that had played them tough all year. Doerr led the offense with a .457 average for the week while McDonald hit .412 with 14 RBIs. In his first week as a regular, Williams hit .346 with five extra-base hits (leading the team) and six RBIs. Williams also improved the outfield defense (Shiver was not known for his glove), and stole two bases to boot. The pitching staff logged eight complete games, with Ward and Pillette posting two victories apiece.

With 34 professional games now under his belt, Williams was beginning to receive media attention. A photograph of Williams swinging a bat and titled "Public Enemy No. 1 to Floundering Sacs" was featured in the September 7, 1936, *San Diego Union*. The caption with the photograph stated that "T. Samuel Williams, Herbert Hoover High's gift to the San Diego ball club yesterday made himself very much a pain in the neck to Sacramento's Senators, robbing them of hits with his ball snagging activities in left field, and doing better than well at the plate."[342]

The press attention was not limited to San Diego but was also occurring up north in Los Angeles. Witness this bold, but very accurate prediction contained in a full-length Bob Ray column in the *Los Angeles Times*:[343]

> *Mr. Frank Howe, who still holds the 1936 record of being the only fan to pay his way into all five Pacific Coast League ball parks, has taken his typewriter in hand again and I think you'll be interested in what he has to say. From now on, until further notice, Mr. Howe has the floor:*
>
>> "I am just back from watching the Padres massacre Sacramento down in San Diego but, more important, I bring NEWS!
>>
>> "Mr. Shellenback or Mr. Lane have unearthed a second Arnold Statz and Joe DiMaggio combined!
>>
>> "The kid's name is Ted Williams. He is variously reported as 17 and 18 years of age. He is a San Diego High School boy and it is said that Lane has signed him to a two-year's contract which provides he plays only home games. I don't know about that.
>>
>> "This kid is tall, skinny and awkward as hell. Too, he is exceedingly nervous. BUT, he is as sure-fire a future big league sensation as I have seen in this here league since I started watching games in 1908.
>>
>> "Yesterday, playing left field, this Williams turned three sure singles into fly-outs. Then, for good measure, he reached OVER the fence and caught a home run for another out. The ball was actually over the low wire fence in left field when he got it!

"The guy travels like a kangaroo and gets everything from Texas Leaguers to hits like this apparent home run.

"He is a swell hitter, too. He wriggles around all over the place and nearly drives you crazy while he's batting. BUT he lifts the ball high and wide. His double in the first game yesterday was as beautiful a swat as I've seen all season. He contributed some more hits for good measure, also.

"Vince DiMaggio, in center field, apparently has taken a liking to the youngster and seems to be helping him quite a bit. Give him a year's experience under Shelly's management, and he will bring a wad of money. He seems to take kindly to advice.

"And boy, oh boy, are those San Diego fans for him!

"And speaking of Vince Di Maggio, I see the papers failed to relate that he got a home run inside the park on Sunday. No flukes about it—just a mighty poke to center field that enabled him to travel all the way around the bases before the ball was fielded. The first h,r.i.t.p. that I've seen in a long time.

"So—write a piece about this Williams and in a year you can look back and say 'I was the first baseball writer to predict that he would go places.'

"Yours, etc.

"FRANK HOWE"

Heading into the season's final week of the season, the Padres had made it all the way to first place, as they were tied with Portland with a record of 92-76.

Table 11.2. PCL Standings on Tuesday, September 8, 1936

	W	L	Pct.	GB
San Diego	92	76	.548	--
Portland	92	76	.548	--
Seattle	90	78	.536	2
Oakland	89	79	.530	3
Missions	85	83	.506	7
Los Angeles	83	85	.494	9
San Francisco	78	90	.464	14
Sacramento	63	105	.375	29

Oakland's Labor Day sweep of the Missions capped a 7-2 series win and dealt a severe blow to the Missions' playoff hopes. The Missions' chances were further devastated by the sale of star third baseman Eddie Joost to the Cincinnati Reds for immediate delivery. Seattle's sweep of San Francisco enabled the Indians to pick up a game on Portland. The final week featured a battle in Portland between Seattle and the Beavers, while the Oaks were visiting lowly Sacramento and the Missions expected to make up ground in Los Angeles. Oakland was viewed as the most dangerous team since Sacramento was not expected to put up much of a fight. Meanwhile, hundreds of loyal fans gathered at Santa Fe Depot to see the Padres off for San Francisco to take on Lefty O'Doul's Seals.

The home portion of the season was completed without a single rainout or postponement. This feat was noted as unequaled by any other Coast league team.[344] More impressively, attendance at Lane Field was close to 225,000, based on unofficial figures, compared to 87,000 in Hollywood in 1935.[345] Owner Lane also received concession income and had lower upkeep costs, making it likely that he would wipe out the $25,000 lost on his 1935 Stars. Attendance averaged 16,000 per week, with the Oakland series in August drawing 35,000 (helped by two night games and George Myatt's wedding), the final Sacramento series totaling 22,000, and the opening series versus Seattle in April attracting 21,000.

The hitting spree against Sacramento left the Padres with a .293 team average, good for the league lead. Bobby Doerr led all Padres with a .336 mark, tenth in the circuit, while George McDonald, Ernie Holman, Gene Desautels, and Cedric Durst all boasted .300+ averages among players with at least 50 games. The PCL leader was Harlan Pool of Oakland with a .408 average.

The front page of the *Union's* sports section on Wednesday, September 9, promised full coverage of the Padres' fight for the pennant via special wire service from all PCL ballparks. However, the pennant race was not sufficient reason to send a reporter on the road with the team. Speculation as to the possibility of a four-way tie for first as well as possible seedings in the playoffs filled the paper. The league agreement regarding playoff locations specified that the team with the higher percentage shall name the field for the series, unless two widely separated teams opposed each other. In the latter case, "the site shall be left to the decision and judgment of the owners involved."[346]

CLOSING TIME IN THE CITY BY THE BAY

The final Padres series of the season would test their pitching staff. Tuesday, September 8, was an off day to allow the Seals to return from Seattle. Doubleheaders were scheduled for Wednesday, Saturday, and Sunday. By the time the Padres settled into their hotel rooms on Tuesday night, they had taken sole possession of first place by virtue of a Seattle victory over Portland. With Dick Ward and Howard Craghead scheduled to pitch the opening doubleheader Frank Shellenback's troops were confident.

The Seals' travels did not affect their play, as they swept the Admission Day* doubleheader by scores of 6-0 and 3-2. Ward did not survive the third inning in the opener, and San Francisco would have scored more than four runs in that time if not for two sensational throws to the plate to cut down Seal baserunners. Joe Marty homered and singled to drive in the final two runs. Ted Williams doubled and scored the go-ahead run on George Myatt's single—in his first game back in the starting lineup—in the seventh inning of the nightcap, but the Seals pushed the tying and winning runs across in the home half of the inning for the sweep. Portland swept Seattle at home, to re-take the lead by 1½ games over San Diego.

Herm Pillette righted the ship on Thursday with a two-hit, 8-2 win over the Seals. The PCL veteran was staked to a five-run lead in the first inning capped by a DiMaggio home run as the Padre bats warmed up again. Williams was moved from eighth to third in the batting order as Durst got the day off. The win put pressure on Portland but the Beavers defeated Seattle in a night game while Oakland clinched a spot in the playoffs with their second win in three games over Sacramento. The playoff teams were set: it would be Portland, San Diego, Seattle, and Oakland. But the order of finish was still up in the air.

San Diego was unable to maintain its momentum Friday as Manny Salvo, expected to be recalled by the Red Sox for 1937,[347] pitched in hard luck but avoided the loss through an eighth-inning rally. Three Seals errors led to three unearned San Diego runs but relievers Horne and Craghead (on one day of rest) combined to cough up two runs in the home eighth to give the Seals their third win of the series. Portland also lost so the Padres remained 1½ games behind Portland and the same distance ahead of Oakland and Seattle. Oakland could manage only a split of their twin bill in Sacramento. The umpire crew of Jack Powell and Bill Engeln again were involved in

---

* "Admission Day" is celebrated on September 9 in California to commemorate the anniversary of the 1850 admission as the 31st of the Union.

controversy. Engeln ejected Ray Jacobs in the seventh inning following a disputed play at third base and George McDonald entered the game only to drop a third-out throw and allow two runs to score. Bobby Doerr again starred on offense, this time with four hits.

In the final weekend of the season, with playoff opponents already determined, the league made a startling decision. Completely disregarding previous playoff plans based on the Shaughnessy system, league owners announced that, for travel reasons, San Diego would face Oakland, and Seattle would play Portland in the first round of the post-season.[348] The new plan called for the Padres and Oaks to play in Oakland Tuesday and Wednesday to open the series. If the teams split the first two games, then a third game in the best-of-seven series would take place in Oakland Thursday and the series would move to San Diego. If either team won the first two games, the final five games would be played in San Diego. Up north, the teams would play in Portland Tuesday and Seattle on Wednesday.

This action essentially rendered the rest of the season meaningless except for pride of place. On the field, San Diego went 12 innings in the nightcap to defeat San Francisco, 4-1, and gain a split of the doubleheader after a 4-3 loss in the opener. Ward, called on to start the opener with only two days' rest, was not sharp, but Hebert scattered 11 hits in game two. Williams blasted a triple, his third hit of the nightcap, to ignite the three-run twelfth, capped by yet another DiMaggio home run. In both games, Williams maintained his third spot in the batting order, while Durst hit fifth. Catcher Kerr got a rare start in the first game, and replaced Desautels, who had a sore back, early in game two. Given Desautels' iron-man efforts behind the plate over the past several months, it was no surprise that he needed a game off. Up north Seattle defeated Portland later that evening leaving the Padres a game behind Portland and one game ahead of Seattle and Oakland.

On the final day of the season, Pete Coscarart's 10th inning single clinched first place for the Portland Beavers with a 4-3 win over Seattle. The second game was rained out. Meanwhile, the Padres dropped the first of two to the Seals, 5-3, as "Sad Sam" Gibson (who had shut out the Padres on Wednesday) outdueled Howard Craghead. With their season-long sense of drama, San Diego saved the best for last as veteran Herman Pillette came within one out of a no-hitter, giving up a fluke single off his foot to Harley Boss. Pillette posted his sixth straight win, a streak that included three shutouts and only four earned runs and 16 hits. Williams collected three hits in the twin bill while DiMaggio atoned for a misjudged fly ball that landed for a triple in the first game with a home run to support Pillette in the season finale. Oakland swept Sacramento to gain a second place tie with the Padres.

Over the course of the eight-game series, the Padres actually outscored the Seals, 29-28, despite losing five of the games. But unlike Sacramento, the Seals played their spoiler role to the hilt. Bobby Doerr and Van Wirthman both hit .400 for the week, even though Doerr went hitless in both games on Sunday.

For the month of September, the Padres hit .304 as a team with a 2.19 ERA. Doerr led the club with a .429 average for the month, followed by George McDonald at .361 and Gene Desautels at .357. Ted Williams batted .305, with six doubles, two triples, and seven RBIs. Vince DiMaggio stepped up to fill the power gap left by the departure of Shiver with five home runs and 14 RBIs. On the mound, Dick Ward and Howard Craghead slumped from their outstanding performances in July and August, although Craghead posted a respectable 2.63 ERA for September. Herman Pillette was September's pitching star with a 4-0 mark and a scintillating 0.84 ERA, while Hebert came back strong with two wins, no defeats, and a 1.29 ERA.

11—SEPTEMBER 1936 DEFECTION AND DENOUEMENT

Table 11.3. Final PCL Standings—1936

	W	L	Pct.	GB
Portland	96	79	.549	--
San Diego	**95**	**81**	**.540**	**1½**
Oakland	95	81	.540	1½
Seattle	93	82	.531	3
Missions	88	88	.500	8½
Los Angeles	88	88	.500	8½
San Francisco	83	93	.472	13½
Sacramento	65	111	.369	31½

The Padres played 17 regular season games in September, winning 11 and losing 6. Since August 1 the team won 32 games and lost only 18, finishing the season at a .640 clip and on a high note. The individual player batting and pitching records for the month are provided in Table 11.4.

Table 11.4. Batting and Pitching Totals for September

Players	Positions	G	AB	R	H	1B	2B	3B	HR	RBI	SB	AVG
Trader Horne	p-1	1	3	0	2	1	1	0	0	2	0	.667
Bobby Doerr	2b-17	17	70	11	30	25	4	0	1	10	8	.429
George McDonald	1b-17	17	61	8	22	17	4	1	0	14	2	.361
Gene Desautels	c-14	14	42	13	15	13	1	1	0	8	0	.357
Van Wirthman	rf-12, ph-2	14	18	7	6	4	2	0	0	1	1	.333
Wally Hebert	p-2	2	9	2	3	3	0	0	0	2	0	.333
Vince DiMaggio	cf-15, rf-3	17	58	18	19	13	1	0	5	14	0	.328
Ted Williams	lf-17	17	59	11	18	10	6	2	0	7	2	.310
Jimmy Kerr	c-8	8	17	0	5	4	0	1	0	1	1	.294
Joe Berkowitz	ss-7, 2b-2, 1b-1	10	26	4	7	6	1	0	0	4	2	.269
Cedric Durst	rf-12, cf-2, lf-1	14	47	3	12	12	0	0	0	6	0	.255
Dick Ward	p-4	4	12	0	3	3	0	0	0	4	0	.250
George Myatt	ss-12	12	49	9	12	10	0	2	0	2	0	.245
Ernie Holman	3b-17	17	59	11	14	9	4	1	0	12	2	.237
Herman Pillette	p-4	4	13	1	2	2	0	0	0	1	0	.154
Manny Salvo	p-3	3	7	2	1	1	0	0	0	0	0	.143
Howard Craghead	p-4	4	7	0	1	1	0	0	0	2	0	.143
Ray Jacobs	1b-3, ph-2	5	7	1	1	1	0	0	0	0	0	.143
Archie Campbell	p-3	3	2	0	0	0	0	0	0	0	0	.000
Les Cook	c-3	3	2	0	0	0	0	0	0	0	0	.000
Frank Shellenback	ph-1	1	1	0	0	0	0	0	0	0	0	.000
Eddie Mulligan	pr-3	3	0	0	0	0	0	0	0	0	0	.000

Pitchers	G	GS	CG	ShO	Sv	W	L	PCT	IP	H	R	ER	SO	BB	ERA
Herman Pillette	4	4	4	1	0	4	0	1.000	32	10	3	3	17	4	0.84
Wally Hebert	2	2	2	1	0	2	0	1.000	21	17	4	3	9	6	1.29
Manny Salvo	3	3	1	0	0	1	1	.500	24	19	7	4	22	8	1.50
Trader Horne	2	1	1	1	0	1	1	.500	7⅔	9	2	2	7	3	2.35
Howard Craghead	4	3	3	0	0	1	2	.333	24	21	9	7	9	9	2.63
Archie Campbell	3	0	0	0	0	0	0	.000	7⅔	4	3	3	2	3	3.52
Dick Ward	4	4	2	0	0	2	2	.500	27⅓	31	13	13	10	9	4.28

SAN DIEGO'S FIRST PADRES and "THE KID"

CHAPTER 12
THE GOVERNOR'S CUP

Headlines Signal Start of Playoffs
San Diego Union, September 13, 1936

San Diego was ready for the playoffs...but how about the team? The Padres looked ahead to the playoff series with the Oaks with mixed feelings. On the one hand, San Diego had considerable success against Oakland during the regular season (17-11) including going 15-6 over the last three series with the Oaks. However, staff aces Dick Ward and Howard Craghead had looked less than invincible over the final week of the season.

Manager Shellenback named Manny Salvo, who beat Oakland five times during the regular season,[349] as the game one starter, while Oaks manager Billy Meyer did not reveal his choice but was expected to go with staff ace Wee Willie Ludolph, the leading hurler in the PCL with a 21-6 record. Padres fans guessed that Shellenback would try to give both Ward and Craghead, who started on Saturday and Sunday, respectively, as much rest as possible before bringing them back. More than three days' rest for Ward would leave Wally Hebert as the game two starter. Among the regulars, Gene Desautels had been rested in both games of the Sunday twin bill and was expected to be ready.

The PCL assigned three umpires to each of the playoff series. Frank Valerio, Ray Snyder, and the veteran Sam Crawford would call the Padres-Oaks series. Jack Powell was designated to work with the umpire team for the Seattle-Portland series.

The Padres starting lineup for Game 1 looked like this:

Myatt	SS
Doerr	2B
Williams	LF
Holman	3B
Desautels	C
Durst	RF
DiMaggio	CF
McDolnald	1B
Salvo	P

GAME 1, TUESDAY, SEPTEMBER 15, AT OAKLAND— OAKLAND 6 SAN DIEGO 3
Oakland Leads Series 1-0

The Oaks, as expected, sent Wee Willie Ludolph to the mound to oppose Manny Salvo, and Ludolph was up to the challenge. Oakland chased Salvo in the second inning, scoring three times and leaving the bases loaded, and then added two runs in the fourth and one in the sixth off Trader Horne.

San Diego rallied in the eighth; after an error opened the door, George Myatt doubled home a run and Ted Williams homered over the right-field fence. The home run helped make headlines and was Williams' first home run in professional play. Ernie Holman and Gene Desautels followed with singles, but Ludolph got Ced Durst on a fly ball to end the threat. The final score was 6-3 in favor of Oakland. The night crowd was disappointing, with the estimate of 8,000 termed "flattering."[350]

Williams Hits Homer But San Diego Loses First Play-Off Fray

Article Header Touts Williams' Home Run
San Diego Union, September 16, 1936

12—THE GOVERNOR'S CUP

GAME 2, WEDNESDAY, SEPTEMBER 16, AT OAKLAND—
OAKLAND 4 SAN DIEGO 3
Oakland Leads Series 2-0

This second game matched Oakland fastballer Jack La Rocca with southpaw Wally Hebert. Joe Berkowitz replaced Myatt at shortstop due to Myatt's finger injury, which was finally diagnosed definitively as a broken finger.

The Padres hit La Rocca hard, knocking him out in the seventh but the game turned on two calls by home plate umpire Sam Crawford in the seventh inning. After La Rocca had departed in favor of Jim Tobin, "Sleepy Sam… the Optician's friend"[351] pumped his right fist to indicate that Vince DiMaggio was out trying to score on George McDonald's double. Then, in the home half of the inning, Tobin lifted a fly

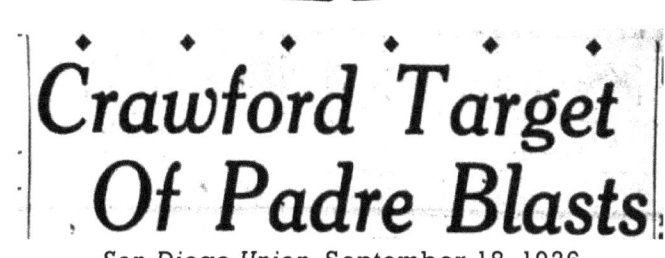

San Diego Union, September 18, 1936

ball to Durst in right field with the bases loaded and one out. Durst's throw home appeared to beat Joe Gordon, and Desautels blocked the plate so effectively that his shin guards were ripped off, but Crawford signaled "safe." Backup catcher Jimmy Kerr was ejected in the subsequent heated argument (supposedly for calling Crawford a "homing pigeon") and reliever Tobin held the Padres in check the rest of the way, to give the Oaks a 2-0 lead in the series.[352]

The sweep meant that the series would move to San Diego. Train schedules prevented the teams from arriving in San Diego until Friday morning or possibly at noon, depending on connections, so the teams would have two days off until play resumed. Up north, meanwhile, Portland swept the first two games at home, then won Game 3 in Seattle on Thursday and completed the sweep on Friday with a convincing 13-3 romp. The Beavers then settled back to await the winner of the California series.

The umpiring was getting a lot attention locally and was the focus of blame for the loss. The teams were at it, too. So keen was the rivalry between the two clubs that the Padres refused to allow the Oaks to practice at Lane Field on their arrival in San Diego on Friday, September 19. And, on the train, both teams were forbidden to mix with each other.[353]

Meanwhile, "The Kid" was continuing to attract notice with his play over the final two weeks of the season and in Game 1. Club secretary Spider Baum predicted that Ted Williams "won't be with the Padres after 1938 if he continues to go at the pace he has been setting since he went to left field."[354]

GAME 3, SATURDAY, SEPTEMBER 19, AT SAN DIEGO—
OAKLAND 5 SAN DIEGO 4
Oakland Leads Series 3-0

Frank Shellenback named Herm Pillette, the hottest Padres pitcher down the stretch as the Game 3 starter on Saturday afternoon at Lane Field. This confirmed pre-series speculation that Dick Ward and Howard Craghead would be held back to get as much rest as possible, although Craghead appeared briefly in relief in Game 2. The Oaks countered with southpaw Ken Douglas.

Oakland jumped out to a 3-0 lead in the second, but the Padres came back to knock out Douglas with three runs in the fourth. The Oaks took the lead in the seventh on an unearned run but Van Wirthman singled home

Ted Williams in the home half to forge another tie. Joe Berkowitz, who was again playing shortstop in place of the injured Myatt, made an error on a ground ball by Dario Lodigiani leading off the ninth inning opening the door for the Oaks, which eventually led to an unearned run.

Vince DiMaggio led off the home ninth with an infield hit and went all the way to third on a wild throw. Ted Williams was up next and grounded out. Ray Jacobs then followed with a grounder that Joe Gordon chose to throw home and was able to retire DiMaggio despite DiMaggio's best efforts to knock the ball loose from catcher Willard Hershberger.

The Oaks' 5-4 win gave them a commanding lead in the series.

GAME 4, SUNDAY, SEPTEMBER 20, AT SAN DIEGO—
SAN DIEGO 7 OAKLAND 1
Oakland Leads Series 3-1

Umpire "Sleepy Sam" Crawford Gets Prize for "Anti-Padre Decisions"
San Diego Union, September 20, 1936

Umpire Crawford was still receiving attention from the local press. However, the Padres had their backs to the wall and facing a well-rested Ludolph. Opposing him would be Dick Ward, finally being called upon to pitch on Sunday. Postal employees honored Gene Desautels and Bobby Doerr before the game to wish them well with Boston in 1937.

San Diego scored seven runs off Ludolph, and Ward held the Oaks to five hits as the Padres finally broke into the post-season win column, 7-1. DiMaggio had an outstanding defensive game who "swarmed all over center field" to account for nine putouts,[355] while Ward pitched a complete game allowing five hits.

Shellenback juggled the lineup a bit, inserting George Myatt back in the lineup despite his broken finger dropping Williams to sixth in the order and moving Ced Durst back into his customary third spot. The combination worked as the Padres rediscovered their offense with four players getting two hits: Durst, Desautels, George McDonald, and pitcher Dick Ward.

The win gave hope that a dramatic comeback was not out of the question.

GAME 5, MONDAY, SEPTEMBER 21, AT SAN DIEGO—
OAKLAND 7 SAN DIEGO 6
Oakland Wins Series 4-1

The offense continued in high gear for Game 5, but Oakland was equal to the task at hand.

San Diego jumped to an early 5-2 lead against the Oaks' Jim Tobin, and Manny Salvo headed into the seventh inning holding a 6-5 edge. After Oakland loaded the bases with two out, Manager Shellenback summoned Game 4 starter Dick Ward from the bullpen and pinch-hitter Fern Bell greeted him with a two-run single to put the Oaks in front. Then the Oakland defense took over. Right fielder Jack Glynn made a sensational one-handed catch of George McDonald's drive with two men aboard to end the eighth, and first baseman Roy Anton knocked down a scorcher by Durst in the ninth with Doerr in scoring position.

With a 7-6 win, Oakland ended the Padres season and moved on to face Portland in the finals (with game locations still to be decided!). Portland would go on win the PCL championship in five games.

PADRES OUT OF PENNANT FIGHT

San Diego Evening Tribune, September 22, 1936

S. D. Players Split $1250, Blow Game To Oakland, Title Chance; Season Ends

By FRANK HAVEN
The Sun's Sports Editor

End of Season Headlines
San Diego Sun, September 22, 1936

Columnist Ted Steinmann summed up the Padres season after the final loss to Oakland in his column as follows:[356]

> *No regrets. San Diego made a spot for itself in the Pacific Coast League in its first season. The support from the fans was far greater than anyone ever expected. And that support helped pep the club up for the drive which carried it to a second place tie with Oakland at the close of the season. Pretty fine for a team experts tagged to finish well down in the second division before the season began.*
>
> *As a team and as individuals, our Padres are a fine bunch. The players gave their best all along and proved themselves a clean, fighting team. There were mistakes, to be sure; mistakes which cost ball games, but they were more the product of over-anxiety than anything else.*
>
> *As to next year, only time will tell. We'll be minus at least two fine players in Gene Desautels, as good a catcher as there is in the league, and Bobby Doerr, top second baseman. Both get a chance with the Boston Red Sox and Padres fans look for them to make good. We might be missing a pitcher or two also. Manuel Salvo has been recalled by Boston; draft might take another, Herman Pillette might quit the game for business, if certain opportunities*

develop. He's been at the game a long time and still a winner. But you can't keep throwing them forever...

A fine club, a fine season.[357]

While the 1936 season ended on a low note with the Governor's Cup series, the Padres in their new home of San Diego were a success. They finished in second place and won 95 games, which proved to be a significant improvement over its 1935 record in Los Angeles when they played as the Hollywood Stars. And, in contrast to the Stars' attendance of 87,000, San Diego's attendance was 225,000,[358] demonstrating that the city could ably support the highest level of professional baseball.

They started 1936 in Hollywood and with no ballpark in San Diego. By the end of March, they had four games under their belt and two wins, and had played their first home game at Lane Field. By late September, it was clear that the team and the ballpark had evolved more than satisfactorily. Now, some 80-plus years later it can be said that the 1936 team and management provided a stable foundation and a lasting baseball franchise, one that actually had its roots in 1906 in Sacramento.

The batting and pitching totals for the five-game series are shown in Table 12.1. Gene Desautels and Ernie Holman led the offense with nine and eight hits, respectively. Ted Williams batted only .188, but was one of two Padres to drive home three runs. Uncharacteristically shaky fielding (eight errors) led to seven unearned runs, including several crucial runs in the one-run games. Dick Ward led the pitchers with his complete-game victory in Game 4.

12—THE GOVERNOR'S CUP

Table 12.1. Batting and Pitching Totals for Governor's Cup

Players	Positions	G	AB	R	H	1B	2B	3B	HR	RBI	SB	AVG
Dick Ward	p-2	2	4	0	2	2	0	0	0	1	0	.500
Manny Salvo	p-2	2	2	1	1	1	0	0	0	2	0	.500
Gene Desautels	c-5	5	20	5	9	8	0	1	0	3	1	.450
Ernie Holman	3b-5	5	20	2	8	6	2	0	0	2	0	.400
George McDonald	1b-4	4	16	0	6	4	2	0	0	2	1	.375
Joe Berkowitz	ss-3	3	12	2	4	3	0	1	0	1	0	.333
Wally Hebert	p-2	2	3	0	1	1	0	0	0	0	0	.333
Vance Wirthman	ph-3	3	3	0	1	1	0	0	0	1	0	.333
Vince DiMaggio	cf-5	5	17	2	5	4	1	0	0	0	0	.294
Bobby Doerr	2b-5	5	21	3	5	4	1	0	0	1	1	.238
Cedric Durst	rf-5	5	21	2	5	5	0	0	0	2	0	.238
Ted Williams	lf-5	5	16	4	3	2	0	0	1	3	0	.188
George Myatt	ss-2, ph-2	4	9	1	1	0	1	0	0	2	0	.111
Ray Jacobs	1b-1	1	3	0	0	0	0	0	0	0	0	.000
Trader Horne	p-1	1	3	1	0	0	0	0	0	0	0	.000
Herman Pillette	p-1	1	2	0	0	0	0	0	0	0	0	.000
Archie Campbell	p-1	1	1	0	0	0	0	0	0	0	0	.000
Eddie Mulligan	pr-1	1	0	0	0	0	0	0	0	0	0	.000
Howard Craghead	p-2	2	0	0	0	0	0	0	0	0	0	.000

Pitchers	G	GS	CG	ShO	Sv	W	L	PCT	IP	H	R	ER	SO	BB	ERA
Howard Craghead	2	0	0	0	0	0	1	.000	4	1	1	0	2	1	0.00
Dick Ward	2	1	1	0	0	1	0	1.000	10	7	1	1	6	2	0.90
Wally Hebert	2	1	0	0	0	0	1	.000	7	10	4	1	3	4	1.29
Trader Horne	1	0	0	0	0	0	0	.000	6⅔	6	3	2	3	2	2.70
Herman Pillette	1	1	0	0	0	0	0	.000	7	9	4	3	4	0	3.86
Archie Campbell	1	0	0	0	0	0	1	.000	3⅓	5	2	2	2	2	5.40
Manny Salvo	2	2	0	0	0	0	1	.000	4⅔	11	8	7	4	2	13.50

SAN DIEGO'S FIRST PADRES and "THE KID"

CHAPTER 13
EPILOGUE: POST-1936

Despite not winning the postseason Governor's Cup, the 1936 San Diego Padres finished the season on a high note winning 95 games and missing out on first place by a game and a half. The team was a balanced mix of well-traveled veterans and exuberant youths. The stories of the team members—both in 1936, and afterward—offer a picture of a remarkable group of personalities and unique baseball legacies.

Beginning with spring training there were 61 players that showed up wearing the San Diego Padres' uniform in 1936, 34 of whom were on the roster during the PCL season. Appendix H contains mini-biographies of 59 of the players, along with their complete professional career playing records.

With the 1936 season concluded, in this chapter there is examination of what happened afterwards: to the players, to Lane Field, and to San Diego's PCL franchise.

WHAT HAPPENED TO THE "FIRST" SAN DIEGO PADRES AFTER 1936?

San Diego Counting Strongly on Young Home-Town Player

SAN DIEGO, Cal.—Frank Shellenback, who will put his name on a 1937 managerial contract for San Diego next month, is going to expect much from an 18-year-old San Diego player, Ted Williams, when next season rolls around. Unless he is nosed out for the job, Williams most likely will be seen regularly in left field for the Padres in the 1937 Pacific Coast League race.

A product of a San Diego high school, Williams was a pitcher at the start, but his

1st Mention of Ted Williams in
The Sporting News
November 26, 1936

It is appropriate to begin with **"The Kid"—Ted Williams**. More than 80 years after this 1936 season it is well known that The Kid did pretty well in the future. Frank Howe's September letter to *Los Angeles Times* writer Bob Ray stated that he wanted to be the first baseball writer to predict Williams would "go places."* Howe may not have been the first writer, but he certainly was first to break the news outside of San Diego.

Later that autumn Williams received his first notice in *The Sporting News*, it came in its November 26, 1936, edition in an article by Earl Keller under the heading "San Diego Counting Strongly on Young Home-Town Player." The article noted that the 18-year old Williams "was a pitcher at the start, but his hitting resulted into a conversion..." However, the article also touted Williams' fielding abilities stating that "when it comes to chasing flies, one would have to look far to find a better ball

---

* Frank Howe's complete letter is contained in Chapter 11, page 121.

hawk..." After 42 minor league games in his initial season of playing professional ball The Kid was beginning to receive national attention, which in retrospect, turned out to be accurate predictors of his future excellence as a professional ballplayer.

In the meantime, after the season Williams went back to Hoover High to finish his senior year and graduate in January 1937. After that he played another year with the Padres, then in 1938 played with Minneapolis in the American Association, and finally, he joined the Boston Red Sox and played with them for 21 years—from 1939 through 1960. He also was a manager of the Washington Senators/Texas Rangers for four years before retiring from baseball for good. **Williams was honored by the National Baseball Hall of Fame, elected in 1966, and is a member of the San Diego Padres PCL Hall of Fame, class of 1966, and the San Diego Breitbard Hall of Fame, inducted in 1954.**

Following is a rundown of what happened to the other 1936 Padres.

After the 1936 season ended, **Joe Berkowitz** was off to Los Angeles looking for a job. He played for the Padres for three more years and his baseball career ended after the 1940 season.[*]

Archie Campbell went to work for the Golden Construction Company in San Diego after the season concluded. Campbell played for the Los Angeles Angels in 1937, then played on and off in the minor leagues form the next 11 years, mostly in the Sacramento Valley League where he managed the Grass Valley club. He played his last season in 1947.

Les Cook joined Bobby Doerr and went hunting and fishing immediately after the season ended. After a month of that, he was planning to be back in San Diego. For all intents, Cook had retired after the 1929 season even though he still had occasional at bats through 1939 with the Padres. He remained as team trainer into the 1950s. **Cook is a member of the San Diego Padres PCL Hall of Fame, class of 2004.**

Howard Craghead abandoned the notion of re-entering Fresno State College and went home to Seattle where he lived at the time. He spent four more seasons with the Padres and won 53 games during that span, retiring from playing in 1940.

Gene Desautels expected to stay in San Diego for a short time and then head back east if he did not find a satisfactory job on the West Coast. Along with Bobby Doerr, Desautels was signed to be on the 1937 Boston Red Sox roster. He played four seasons with the Red Sox, through 1940, and then five seasons with Cleveland and Philadelphia of the American League. He finished his active playing career in 1948 with Williamsport of the Eastern League, and then managed several teams in the 1950s.

Vince DiMaggio was one of several players who was considering an off-season job with May Company in Los Angeles. After 1936 he had a productive major league career lasting 10 seasons with five National League teams through mid-1946. From that point DiMaggio played five more years in the minors retiring in 1951. After his playing career was over, he managed in the minors for a few years during the 1950s.

With Les Cook, **Bobby Doerr** was off to Oregon for a month of fishing and hunting. His winter he planned to spend in Los Angeles with his family. After his one season with the 1936 Padres, Doerr went on to have a 14-year career with the Boston Red Sox before retiring in 1951. He followed his playing career serving as a coach in the majors for eight years. **Doerr was elected to the National Baseball Hall of Fame in 1986 and is a member of the San Diego Padres PCL Hall of Fame, class of 1966.**

Cedric Durst was another May Company employee in Los Angeles where he had worked for several years, and where he had a home. He played another seven seasons for the Padres through 1943, interrupted in 1938 with a brief stint with the 1938 Hollywood PCL team. From 1939-1943 Durst managed the Padres, and then

---

[*] Information concerning what each player did immediately following the conclusion of the 1936 season was obtained from articles in the *San Diego Evening Tribune* on September 5, 1936, and in the *San Diego Union* on September 23, 1936.

managed other minor league teams through 1950. **Durst is a member of the San Diego Padres PCL Hall of Fame, class of 1968.**

Home to Lake Charles, Louisiana, to work in the oil fields was where **Wally Hebert** was off to after the season closed. He played another six years for the Padres before finishing his playing career with the Pittsburgh Pirates in 1943. Hebert won 18 games for the 1936 Padres and then, as a model of consistency, averaged 18 over the next six years—finishing with 126 wins for the team and three 20-win seasons. **Hebert is a member of the San Diego Padres PCL Hall of Fame, class of 2004.**

Ernie Holman, who hailed from Amarillo, Texas, planned to go back there for a short period to take care of some business affairs, then come back to San Diego to sell automobiles for the Robert D. Maxwell Company. He spent the 1937 season with the Padres and part of the 1938 one, too, which was his last season playing.

Like DiMaggio and Durst, **Trader Horne** was set to work at May Company in the off-season having worked there for several years. The 1936 season was his 20th in professional ball and he closed out his playing career with two more years in baseball, one each in the PCL and Western International League.

Salt Lake City native **Ray Jacobs** set off to Los Angeles to find a job during the off-season. After only the one season with San Diego, he continued to play with teams in the Western International and Pioneer Leagues through 1942.

Jimmy Kerr was planning to stay and work in San Diego.

A lumber camp in his home state of Washington is where **George McDonald** was headed—"to gain strength which he believes will fatten his chances of becoming a big leaguer." McDonald continued playing through the 1951 season and never did make it the big leagues. He stayed with the Padres and was "the" first baseman for the team almost exclusively through 1944. **McDonald is a member of the San Diego Padres PCL Hall of Fame, class of 2004.**

Coach/utility player **Eddie Mulligan** continued with the Padres for two more years and then finished his playing career in 1939 with Salt Lake City. Later he served as acting President of the Padres for a short time in 1945, managed several teams, and ended his baseball career as President of the Pacific Coast League from 1956 to 1975. **Mulligan is a member of the Pacific Coast League Hall of Fame.**

Newly married **George Myatt** was to go on a delayed honeymoon to Oregon and then expected to return to San Diego for the winter. He ended up back playing shortstop with the Padres in 1937. In 1938 he split the season in the minors and with the New York Giants. He was back and forth between the minors and the majors until 1943 when he began a five-year tenure with the American League's Washington Senators. Myatt's last year playing was 1949 then had 23 years coaching in the majors and two years managing with the Philadelphia Phillies in 1968-1969.

Herman Pillette was undecided about what he was going to do, but first, was planning to take a vacation. After that, he had to decide between job offers from San Diego Ice and Cold Storage Company and one in Montana with a civil engineering company. It's not sure how that all turned out but for sure he remained a Padre through 1942. Pillette's last three seasons were spent with the PCL's Sacramento's Solon, retiring after the 1945 season. **Pillette is a member of the Pacific Coast League Hall of Fame.**

Manny Salvo returned to Sacramento in the off season and had expected to be on the pitching staff of the Boston Red Sox the next season. However, he played for the Padres for two more years, 1937-1938. Eventually, Salvo did make the majors, with the New York Giants in 1939, and then played with the Boston Braves and Philadelphia Phillies through 1943. His last year playing was 1949 with Sacramento.

Manager **Frank Shellenback** was off to Los Angeles to work for the Warner Brothers Studio where he had worked the previous two off seasons. He kept the managing job with the Padres for another two years—

while pitching an occasional inning or two. From San Diego, Shellenback went into being a coach in the majors through 1955. **Shellenback is a member of the Pacific Coast League Hall of Fame, elected in 1986, and is a member of the San Diego Padres PCL Hall of Fame, class of 1968.**

Along with Campbell, **Dick Ward** went to work for the Golden Construction Company. He stayed with the Padres through the start of the 1939 season and retired at the end of that season finishing with the Los Angeles Angels.

Van Wirthman went north to Los Angeles in search of a job. His 1936 season with the Padres turned out to be Wirthman's last in professional baseball.

WHAT HAPPENED TO LANE FIELD?

Lane Field opened coincident with the Padres' first home game on March 31, 1936, in front of 8,178 fans. As was described in the earlier chapters it had been constructed in two months with a grant of $25,000 from the Depression-era WPA. That first home of the San Diego Padres was constructed on grounds that had been used for both baseball and football for years, but had become a local mecca for motorcycling racing. It was first used for athletics in 1921, and the grounds were used continuously through 1935.

The grounds were variously called YMCA Field or Army-Navy Field. In 1929, when San Diego gained a spot in the four-club California State League, which was a National Association affiliated league, the ballpark was called Navy Field. When the weakest franchise, that had failed in Orange County and Pomona (even before its first game), the league shifted the club to Coronado, but all games were played at the Navy Field venue.

From 1921 through 1935, the park had the same configuration-- except for the 1929 California State League–with home plate located at the southwest corner of the lot. Home plate in 1929 was located in the northwest corner of the lot. Aerial photographs of that ballpark reveal a small grandstand behind home plate, and bleachers extending down both baselines, about some 330 feet. Additionally, there were bleachers running from the left field line to the mid-point of center field.

When Lane Field first opened, the park was still unfinished. The basic plan is shown in the figure on the next page and remained that way until 1945. For the first couple of series, the netting behind the backstop had not been set up, and fans had to duck foul balls. The roof over the grandstand was not completed until May of 1937. The park also incorporated the bleachers for the motorcycle speedway that ran down the right-field line beyond the grandstand. (In 1952, the city condemned the bleachers because of termite damage, which would have cost seating for some 3,700 fans. Quick repairs saved about 2,500 seats.)

Seating for the park had a listed seating capacity of 10,500 in 1936, but official seating capacity over the years ran from 7,500 (its last year) to a high of 12,000 in 1948. Occasionally the club had overflow crowds, and standing room crowds stood around the inner part of the outfield fence and were cordoned off by rope. Balls hit into that area were scored as ground-rule doubles.

Over the years, termites continued to do their damage. First, the stands beyond the outfield fences were condemned, then the bleachers beyond the grandstands down both lines. Ushers would be stationed down the lines to keep kids away from chasing balls in those areas.

Most ballparks that get a reputation as a hitters' park or a pitchers' park remain that way for the length of their life. Not so Lane Field. It had two major configurations: the first, between 1936 and 1944 made Lane Field a definite pitchers park and the second, from 1945-1957, made it a home-run park. From 1936 through 1944, had a home batting average of .270 compared to the league average for those years of .273, and only yielded 39 home runs per season compared to the league average per park of 59 home runs.

13—EPILOGUE: POST-1936

In January 1945, new owner Bill Starr had the left field bleachers moved in and home plate moved out, to make it 330 feet down the left field line.

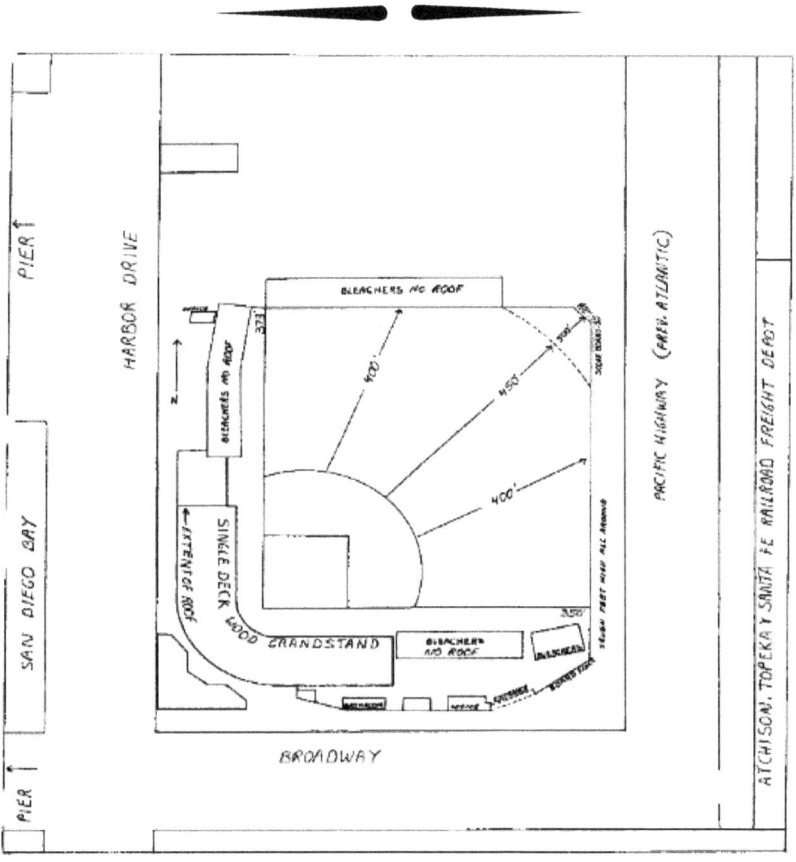

Lane Field from 1936-1945

After 1944, those numbers changed markedly, especially for home runs. Lane Field averaged 113 home runs per season as opposed to 96 home-run-per-park average for those years. The distances in the second rendering are based on the distances given in the *1948 Pacific Coast League Handbook*.

At some point in the 1950s, an inside fence was installed in center field, though the date remains elusive. Nevertheless, there are many photos showing an inner fence, and many without. The inner fence was up in 1956 when Rocky Colavito attempted to set the record for longest throw. According to press accounts, Colavito threw the baseball some 435 feet as measured officially that day. The article also stated that he had thrown the ball over the center field fence; therefore, in 1956 anyway, we know that the inner fence was less than 435 feet from home plate. The record was held at the time by Milwaukee player Don Grate at 445 feet and one inch.

The PCL San Diego Padres used Lane Field for 22 years, though several misconceptions about the park still have traction in books and articles, and then often repeated.

The first has to do with the claim that home plate was only 12 feet from the backstop. In the architectural drawing at the beginning of this chapter, the distance is clearly marked as 31 feet six inches. In aerial photos of the park, one is able to "walk back" the six-foot batter's box to show that the distance could not have been any less than 25 feet.

The other misconception stems from an article published in the *San Diego Tribune* when what was left of Lane Field was being demolished. One of the workers stated that he had measured the distance from home plate to first base and came up with the incredible distance of 87 feet. And, so the myth began.

Regarding the alleged shorter distance to first base, several players were consulted who played from 1936 through 1957 at Lane Field. The players consulted were: Louie Almada, Chuck Stevens, Jack Graham and Roger Osenbaugh. Each of the players said that the shorter length was impossible. Louie Almada went as far as stating that he had walked off everything at the park when he first played there in 1936. He stated disbelief noting that: "Ballplayers are like carpenters, they measure everything in the park. They look for any edge. That wouldn't have remained a secret for very long, that's for sure."

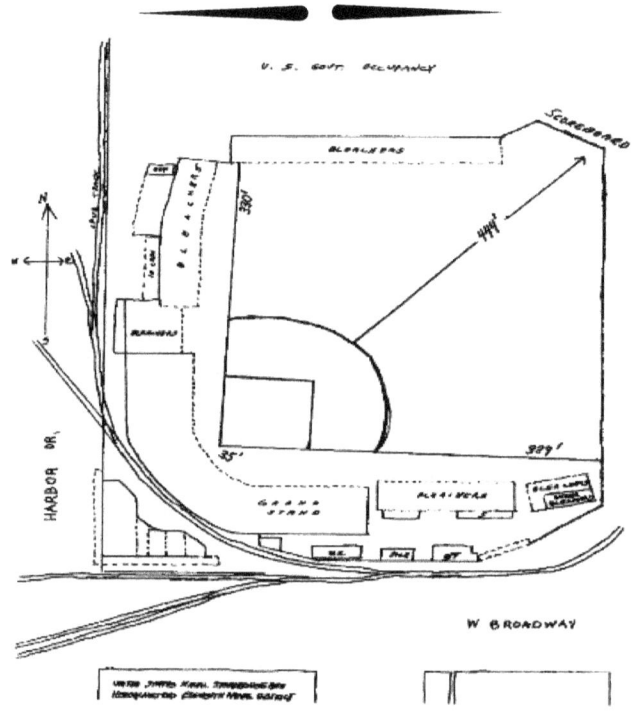

Lane Field Configuration, 1945-1957

Lane Field was never much of a park. Roger Osenbaugh said it had the worse showers in the league. Others merely stated that by the time they got to play there it was outdated. It was also being continually being eaten by termites. First, the bleachers in right field had to be partially saved. Then the ones left field went, followed by the ones down the left field line. Bill Starr several times attempted to get the city to build a new park, but when his 1955 plan failed to be taken up by the city, he sold out. C. Arnholt Smith of the Westgate Packing Company bought the club, then constructed Westgate Park in what was a largely undeveloped part of San Diego, called Mission Valley. Smith had extensive land holdings in the area. When the city built San Diego Stadium (later called Jack Murphy Stadium and still later called Qualcomm Stadium), Smith moved the club for its final 1968 season in the Pacific Coast League to that venue.

Lane Field, nevertheless, will always remain well-etched into the history of San Diego and Coast League ball.

Today there is "Lane Field Park" where Lane Field existed between 1936 and 1957. The San Diego Ted Williams chapter of SABR prepared a plaque commemorating the ballpark's site that was dedicated in 2003 in

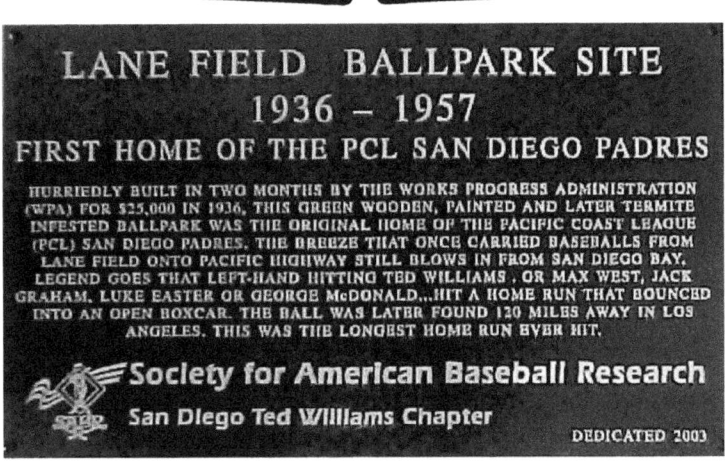

Plaque at Lane Field Park

partnership with the property's owner, the San Diego Unified Port District. The park was opened by the Port District in 2015 and is designed to replicate the infield of the old ballpark with the plaque located in the same corner as where the original home plate existed.

WHAT HAPPENED TO THE PADRES' FRANCHISE?

As shown in Table 13.1, after 1936, the San Diego Padres played 32 more years in the Pacific Coast League. Those years were filled with many great player seasons, and four first-place finishes. The Padres played in three ballparks over those years: Lane Field through the 1957 season; Westgate Park, one of the most beautiful minor league parks of all time, and mostly forgotten; and its final year in Coast League at San Diego Stadium (later named Jack Murphy and Qualcomm Stadium). The franchise had four different owners and two near-owners.

Table 13.1. Year-by-Year Record of San Diego Padres PCL Franchise (1936-1968)

Year	Manager	Wins	Losses	Pct	Finish	Year(s)	MLB Affiliation
1936	Frank Shellenback	95	81	.540	3rd		
1937	Frank Shellenback	97	81	.545	3rd		
1938	Frank Shellenback	92	85	.520	5th		
1939	Cedric Durst	83	93	.472	5th		
1940	Cedric Durst	92	85	.520	4th		
1941	Cedric Durst	101	76	.571	3rd		
1942	Cedric Durst	91	87	.511	4th		
1943	Cedric Durst/George Detore	70	85	.452	7th	1936	Boston Red Sox
1944	George Detore	75	94	.444	8th		
1945	Pepper Martin	82	101	.448	6th	1949–51; 1957–59	Cleveland Indians
1946	Pepper Martin/Jim Brillheart	78	108	.419	6th		
1947	Rip Collins	79	107	.425	8th	1960–61	Chicago White Sox
1948	Rip Collins/Jim Brillheart	83	105	.441	7th		
1949	Bucky Harris	96	92	.511	4th		
1950	Del Baker	114	86	.570	2nd	1962–65	Cincinnati Reds
1951	Del Baker	79	88	.473	6th	1966–68	Philadelphia Phillies
1952	Lefty O'Doul	88	92	.489	5th		

SAN DIEGO'S FIRST PADRES and "THE KID"

Year	Manager	Wins	Losses	Pct	Finish
1953	Lefty O'Doul	88	92	.489	6th
1954	Lefty O'Doul	102	67	.604	**1st**
1955	Bob Elliott	92	80	.535	2nd
1956	Bob Elliott	72	96	.429	7th
1957	Bob Elliott/George Metkovitch	89	79	.530	4th
1958	George Metkovitch	84	69	.549	2nd
1959	George Metkovitch	78	75	.510	3rd
1960	George Metkovich/Jimmie Reese	77	75	.507	4th tie
1961	Jimmie Reese/ Whitey Wietelmann/Bill Norman	72	82	.468	4th
1962	Don Heffner	93	61	.604	**1st**
1963	Don Heffner	83	74	.529	2nd S.
1964	Dave Bristol	91	67	.576	**1st W.**
1965	Dave Bristol	70	78	.473	3rd E. tie
1966	Frank Lucchesi	72	75	.490	5th E.
1967	Bob Skinner	85	63	.574	1st E.
1968	Bob Skinner/Bobby Klaus	76	70	.521	2nd E.
	Totals	**2819**	**2749**	**.506**	

NOTABLE PADRES PLAYERS

The San Diego PCL Padres existed for 33 years. While there were many fine players during this period here are the more notable performances:

1939—Dom Dallesandro led the league with a .368 batting average.

1941—Yank Terry went 26-8 with a 2.31 ERA.

1947—Max West clubbed 43 home runs and batted in 124 runs.

1948—Native San Diegan Johnny Ritchey "broke the color barrier" in the Pacific Coast League playing for his hometown Padres and Jack Graham hit 48 homers.

1949—Max West hit 48 home runs with 166 RBIs and set a league record 201 base-on-balls, while teammate Luke Easter hit 25 home runs, along with 92 RBIs, and a .363 batting average in 80 games.

1954—Harry Elliott's led the PCL with a .350 batting average.

1956—San Diegan Bob Usher came home to battle Steve Bilko for the batting title. Rocky Colavito had an average of .368 with 12 home runs 35 games when he was called up to Cleveland Indians mid-season.

1957—"Mudcat" Grant went 18-7 with a 2.31 ERA.

1958—Earl Averill played every position except pitcher and hitting .347 with 24 home runs.

1962—Jesse Gonder led the PCL in two categories: .342 average and 116 RBIs.

1963—Deron Johnson, another San Diego High product, came home to hit 33 home runs.

1964—Tony Perez' batted .309 with 34 home runs and 107 RBIs.

1965—Lee May hit .321 with 34 home runs and 103 RBIs.

1967—John Tsitouris' pitching record was 17-7 with a 2.58 ERA.

1966-68—Bobby Klaus strung together three seasons of 154, 110, 107 walks.

13—EPILOGUE: POST-1936

The team's "honor roll" also includes Padres who were PCL MVPs:

1941—Yank Terry

1948—Jack Graham

1959—Earl Averill

1962—Jesse Gonder

1964—Tony Perez

1967—Ricardo Joseph

A few of the players who passed through San Diego on the way up to the majors included: Minnie Minoso, Al Rosen, Luke Easter, Rocky Colavito, Tony Perez, Lee May, San Diego High star Floyd Robinson, Walt Dropo, and Al Smith.

On their way down from the majors were Bob Lemon and Herb Score.

There were mainstays on the club too, like: George Detore, Al Federoff, Wally "Preacher" Hebert, Johnny "Swede" Jensen, Bob Kerrigan, George McDonald, Al Olson, Hal Patchett, Buddy Peterson, Earl Rapp, Ray Ripplemeyer, Chico Ruiz, and Milt Smith.

Fan favorites included Minoso and Robinson, plus Del Ballinger, Dane Clay, Cedric Durst, Manny Salvo, Harry "Suitcase" Simpson, and Rupert Thompson.

The Padres suffered through one real tragedy: On April 5, 1953, 27-year-old outfielder Herb Gorman keeled over in left field; he was rushed to Mercy Hospital and was pronounced dead on arrival. There was also one near tragedy: On July 25, 1948, with 45 HRs already in the book and on his way to a PCL record, Jack Graham was beaned by Red Adams, and nearly killed. Graham came back, though, but only hit three more round-trippers the rest of that season. As he admitted years later, his vision never really came back, and a great future turned into only a decent career.

NOTABLE SEASONS

The Padres won pennants in four seasons: 1954, 1962, 1964, 1967.

Of the four pennants, the first in 1954 was the most dramatic. The season ended with the Padres tied with the Hollywood Stars for first place with identical 101-67 records, necessitating a one-game playoff for the pennant. Lefty O'Doul was hired in 1952 to bring a pennant to San Diego, and in his third season of piloting the club, he did just that.

The game was played on Monday, September 13, (the playoffs were to begin the next day), and O'Doul chose lefty Bob Kerrigan to face Red Munger of the Stars. There was an overflow crowd at Lane Field (part of the outfield was cordoned off) of some 11,471. The site was determined by a flip of the coin, San Diego winning.

Bob Elliott, who had finished his major league career the season prior, hit two home runs, driving in five of the seven runs San Diego put on the board. Both were "towering home runs." One was over the left field fence, and the other over the right field fence. Bob Kerrigan pitched a 7-2 complete game, scattering nine hits.

In 1962 the Padres became a Cincinnati farm club, and won two pennants with their farmhands in 1962 and 1964.

The Padres final pennant in 1967 was as a Philadelphia Phillies farm club, with San Diego native Bob Skinner managing the club.

OWNERSHIP

The history of franchise ownership—from 1906 through to the present (2019)—is displayed on the chart below. The period from 1906-1935 is discussed in Chapter 2.

In this section, post-1936 ownership events are traced through the end of 1968 when the PCL Padres baseball club was dissolved. The chart below shows the transition in ownership from 1936 to the present including both the PCL Padres and the National League Padres (from 1968 to the present).

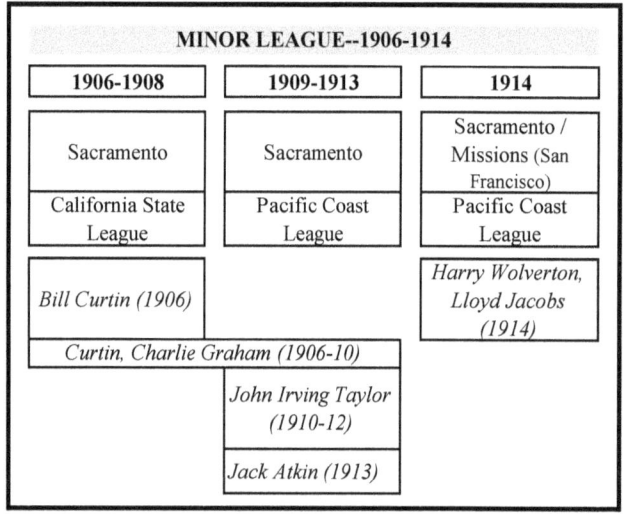

MINOR LEAGUE--1906-1914

1906-1908	1909-1913	1914
Sacramento	Sacramento	Sacramento / Missions (San Francisco)
California State League	Pacific Coast League	Pacific Coast League
Bill Curtin (1906)		Harry Wolverton, Lloyd Jacobs (1914)
Curtin, Charlie Graham (1906-10)		
	John Irving Taylor (1910-12)	
	Jack Atkin (1913)	

MINOR LEAGUE--BILL LANE ERA THROUGH 1968

1915-1925	1926-1935	1936-1938	1938-1944	1944-1955	1955-1968
Salt Lake City	Hollywood	San Diego			
Pacific Coast League	Pacific Coast League	Pacific Coast League			
Frank Murphy (1915-17)			Florence Eastwood (Lane Estate)	Bill Starr	C. Arnholt Smith
	Bill Lane (1918-38)				

MAJOR LEAGUE

1968-1974*	1974-1984	1984-1990	1990-1994	1994-2012	2012-present
San Diego					
National League					
C. Arnholt Smith	Ray Kroc	Joan Kroc	Tom Werner	John Moores	Ron Fowler

*Note: There was a period of time in 1973 when there were two owners. Joseph Danzansky agreed to purchase the club in May 1973 and the sale was approved by the National League owners in December. Danzansky was prepared to move the team to Washington, D.C., for the 1974 season. Due to a pending lawsuit brought by the City of San Diego to prevent the sale and transfer of the team out of San Diego, Smith canceled the deal. In January 1974 Ray Kroc purchased the club with the promise to keep the team in San Diego.

13—EPILOGUE: POST-1936

Bill Lane's ownership had its start in 1918 and continued into 1936 when the club transferred to San Diego. A month after the 1938 season ended, owner Bill Lane passed away. Shortly before his death, he fired manager Frank Shellenback who supplied steady leadership for four seasons, even though he had lost two key players, future Hall-of-Famers in Bobby Doerr and Ted Williams.

Lane died on October 9, 1938, and his Will was read on October 17. In the Will, it was stipulated that the club was to be sold as soon as was possible, and the proceeds given to Miss Florence Eastman (variously called his nurse, his housekeeper, his business manager), and that Vice President Spider Baum was to be installed as President of the club. Lane held 95percent of shares of the club when he died.

The club was not sold as quickly as Lane had envisioned. First, Spider Baum liked being president of the club, and he was in no hurry to sell the club, though other members of the board were, especially Miss Eastman. The club was offered for sale at $100,000, but Baum wanted to hold out for $150,000. But other directors ganged up on Baum, and a stalemate ensued, so two possible sales to the Cincinnati Reds and Chicago Cubs fell through. Not only that, but a brother—unknown until then—showed up and contested the Will. The brother would settle with the estate in 1940.

Spider Baum Exits

In July 1939, Spider Baum was shown the door when he refused the directors' instruction to schedule five night games a week. As Charles Lott, Vice President of the club stated: "We know that Baum does not like night games...but it is not his ball club."

Also in July, Jack L. Corbett, former owner of the Syracuse International League club, put in a bid for the club, after oilman M.L. Clark "temporarily" suspended his offer. In August, Corbett was elected president of the club. However, the deal fell through, and M.L. Clark came back into the picture. On October 9, 1939, the board of directors finalized the sale to Clark at $92,500. On January 12, 1940, executors of Lane will stated that all negotiations had collapsed, and M.L. Clark of Oklahoma City was out of the picture. Or so the executor thought. Clark sued the estate for $114,000. The suit went nowhere, however, and the club was run by the same board of directors until they could find a suitable prospective buyer.

Bill Starr Enters the Picture

The prospective buyer came along right after the close of the 1944 season. Bill Starr, former Padres catcher and real estate developer, put an offer together to buy the club for $120,000. Starr came in with enthusiasm, and baseball knowledge from a player's point of view. Bill Starr would own the club until he sold out after the 1955 season. With no good deed going punished, Bill Starr was drafted two months later. Fortunately, the war ended shortly thereafter, and Starr went back to running a ballclub.

In the years he owned the club, Starr always pushed for a new ballpark for San Diego, even getting the league to kick in money. Most people thought Lane Field was only a stopgap park when it opened in 1936. Over the years, Starr came up with several plans for a new venue for the Padres, but always being turned down by the city.

He made one last stab at getting a new park that would be in a corner of Balboa Park, but the San Diego planning commission rejected his proposal, even though much of the money would be coming from outside sources, including the PCL itself. With that, Starr gave up and announced that he would sell the Padres as soon as he could find someone to buy the club.

Starr Sells to C. Arnholt Smith

In August 1955 the Westgate-California Corporation (owned by San Diego businessman and banker C. Arnholt Smith) bought the Padres.

Smith had one idea for the San Diego: A major league franchise. And that was by any means: hopefully to buy a weak franchise, and move it to San Diego, but he was ready to wait for expansion, if need be.

The first move that Smith made was to sign a big name General Manager, but signed someone had a big name, but no experience in the front office. He signed home run hitter Ralph Kiner, who had retired the year before. Kiner did a very good job, even starting his career as a broadcaster for the Padres' Saturday afternoon TV broadcast. Al Schuss remained the voice of the Padres on the radio. Kiner stayed around through the 1960 season, after which he signed as a broadcaster with the Chicago White Sox. In 1961, Eddie Leishman was hired to take Kiner's place.

The second major project that Smith initiated was building a new ballpark, something that Bill Starr had failed to do. Smith had several advantages over Starr: he was the number one "mover and shaker" in the city, and he owned land in Mission Valley.

In early December 1956, the city council vote 6-1 to rezone the area in Mission Valley where the park would be located. Not all went smoothly, however. In October of 1957, the Padres decided to halt construction because of the uncertain future of the Pacific Coast League. With the Dodgers and Giants moving west, no one knew whether the Coast League would survive the major league expansion to the West Coast.

They did, and work was resumed after the winter meetings guaranteed the continued operation of the league. There was some fear that the park would not be able to open in time for the start of the season, forcing the club to negotiate with the Harbor Commission to use Lane Field. GM Kiner said he thought the park could be finished by opening day, which it was.

Westgate Park was one of the finest minor league parks ever. The plan was to have the park be easily converted to a 42,000-seat park. It probably would have been, had the City of San Diego had not built San Diego Stadium for the Chargers. The 7,500-seat ballpark, with some additional 2,500-seat temporary bleachers, also had a grassy berm around the outfield where any number of fans could, and did, take blankets to view the game.

In 1967, Arnholt Smith decided to grease the skids. He wanted one of the new expansion clubs that would be awarded in 1968 to begin play in 1969. He contacted one of the top baseball executives in the business, Buzzie Bavasi to become president of the Padres. Bavasi at first said that he would have to check with his boss, Walter O'Malley, and added that he would either need a long-term contract, or have an ownership stake in the club.

San Diego already had 45,000-seat San Diego Stadium, where the PCL Padres would begin play in 1968, which put it ahead of the other cities vying for a franchise.

On May 27, 1968, the Westgate-California Corporation was awarded a franchise in the National League. Bavasi got the blessing of Walter O'Malley and became president of the Padres; outgoing President Jim Mulvaney said the only remaining snag was negotiating a lease with the City of San Diego, never an easy deal, but it did come to be.

In the end, the always underdog Padres' franchise went from a humble expansion club in an outlaw league to a mainstay of the National League West. Not too shabby a history.

The PCL Padres played their last game in the Pacific Coast League on September 8, 1968, at San Diego Stadium in front of 10,061 fans.

Box Score or Final PCL Padres' Game, September 8, 1968

September 8, 1968 at San Diego Stadium								
Phoenix	Pos	AB	R	H	BI	PO	A	E
Don Mason	2b	5	1	3	1	3	4	0
Bob Burda	1b	4	1	1	1	8	3	0
Bobby Etheridge	3b	5	1	1	1	2	5	0
Jim McKnight	lf	4	1	1	0	2	0	0
Cesar Gutierrez	ss	5	0	0	0	2	1	0
Angel Rosario	cf	3	2	2	0	4	0	0
Ozzie Virgil	c	3	1	1	2	6	0	0
George Williams	rf	5	0	0	0	0	1	0
William Frost	p	1	0	0	0	0	1	0
Dick Estelle	p	1	0	0	0	0	1	0
Hal Haydel	p	0	0	0	0	1	0	0
Paul Jernigan	ph	1	0	0	0	0	0	0
Larry Miller	p	2	0	0	0	0	0	0
Totals		39	7	9	5	28	16	0
San Diego	Pos	AB	R	H	BI	PO	A	E
Billy Cowan	cf	5	2	1	0	3	0	1
Bobby Klaus	2b	4	1	2	2	1	1	0
Don Money	ss	5	1	1	1	2	4	0
Johnny Lewis	rf	4	1	1	2	3	0	0
Johnny Werhas	3b	5	1	2	0	0	2	0
John Sullivan	c	1	0	0	0	1	0	0
Rich Barry	1b	2	0	2	0	9	1	0
Darrell Peters	ph	0	0	0	0	0	0	0
Stirling Coward	lf	5	0	2	1	0	0	0
Al Raffo	p	3	0	2	0	4	0	0
Doc Edwards	c	3	1	2	0	6	0	1
Jim Gentile	ph	1	0	1	0	0	0	0
Lowell Palmer	p	0	0	0	0	0	0	0
Dick Thoenen	p	2	1	1	2	0	0	0
Larry Loughlin	p	0	0	0	0	0	0	0
Larry Colton	p	0	0	0	0	0	0	0
Bill Edgerson	p	0	0	0	0	1	0	0
William Wilson	p	0	0	0	0	0	0	0
Totals		40	8	17	8	30	8	2

2b: Mason (3), Money, Barry, Williams, Klaus.
3b: Werhas.
HR: Burda (7), Lewis (16), Thoenen (1).

Pitchers	IP	H	R	ER	BB	SO
William Frost	1⅔	6	3	3	1	0
Dick Estelle	1⅓	4	3	3	0	0
Hal Haydel	⅔	2	0	0	2	1
Larry Miller (L 9-8)	4⅓	5	2	2	3	3
Lowell Palmer	1⅔	2	3	3	5	2
Dick Thoenen	3⅔	3	0	0	1	0
Larry Loughlin	1	2	3	2	1	0
Larry Colton	⅓	1	0	0	0	0
Bill Edgerson	⅔	1	1	1	0	1
William Wilson	⅔	0	0	0	0	0
Al Raffo (W 11-7)	2	0	0	0	2	1

Time: 3:02 **Attendance:** 10,061

HERE'S WHAT MAKES THE 1936 PADRES "REMARKABLE"

Two players are in the National Baseball Hall of Fame
    Bobby Doerr
    Ted Williams

SAN DIEGO'S FIRST PADRES and "THE KID"

One player's son is in the National Baseball Hall of Fame
- Larry Gillick, whose son is Pat Gillick, a baseball executive, who is in the Hall of Fame

Three players and two executives are in the Pacific Coast League Hall of Fame
- Spider Baum
- Bill Lane
- Eddie Mulligan
- Herman Pillette
- Frank Shellenback

Seven players, an executive, and one local reporter are in the San Diego Padres PCL Hall of Fame
- Les Cook
- Bobby Doerr
- Cedric Durst
- Wally Hebert
- Earl Keller
- Bill Lane
- George McDonald
- Frank Shellenback
- Ted Williams

One of the team's outfielders played on the famous 1927 Yankees with Lou Gehrig and Babe Ruth
- Cedric Durst

One of the team's pitchers (and its manager) was a former major league spitball pitcher
- Frank Shellenback

One of the three DiMaggio brothers played in the team's outfield
- Vince DiMaggio

Three of the players had sons or fathers who were professional ball players
- Harl Maggert's father was Harl Vestin Maggert who played professional baseball over 15 years including stints with Pittsburgh Pirates (1907) and Philadelphia Athletics (1912)
- Herman Pillette's son Duane played for 15 seasons which included being on four major league teams between 1949 and 1956
- Robert Vickers's father was Rube Vickers (who, in 1906, won 39 PCL games)

Three players became long-time players, coaches, scouts in professional baseball
- Rosey Gilhousen, was a player and manager in the minor leagues (1939-1947) and scouted for several MLB teams from 1947 into the 1970s
- Hub Kittle, was a player, coach, and manager in minor and major league baseball from 1937 through-2004
- George Myatt, was a player, coach, and manager in minor and major league baseball from 1933 through-1972

13—EPILOGUE: POST-1936

Several players from the team remain PCL Record Holders

Most games pitched, Lifetime	708 –	Herman Pillette
Most games won, Lifetime	296 –	Frank Shellenback
Most games lost, Lifetime	235 –	Spider Baum, Herman Pillette
Most innings pitched, Lifetime	4,184 –	Frank Shellenback
Most sacrifice hits, Lifetime	390 –	Eddie Mulligan
Most assists-Pitcher, Lifetime	1,308 –	Spider Baum
Most assists, 3rd Baseman, Lifetime	4,762 –	Eddie Mulligan

Some outstanding career feats by the numbers

- 3,217 Eddie Mulligan had a total of 3,217 base hits in his career including 287 in the major leagues.
- 3,014 Ted Williams had a total 3,014 base hits in his career including 360 in his three minor league seasons.
- 589 Ted Williams had 589 home runs, with 521 in the major leagues.
- 398 Vince DiMaggio had 398 home runs, 273 in the minors and 125 in the majors.
- 342 Spider Baum won 342 games, all in the minor leagues.
- 328 Frank Shellenback had 328 totals wins, with 10 of those in major leagues.
- 298 Herman Pillette won 298 games with 34 of those wins in the major leagues.

SAN DIEGO'S FIRST PADRES and "THE KID"

CHAPTER 14
REFLECTIONS ON THE 1936 SAN DIEGO PADRES—FROM THOSE WHO WERE THERE

More than 80 years have passed by the time this story was written. Fortunately, personal interviews were conducted with Bobby Doerr, George McDonald, and the team's mascot, Ralph Thompson. However, it is only appropriate to lead off with some reflections from Ted Williams about the first Padres. When the season started Doerr was only 17 years old and McDonald was 18. In June, when Williams joined the club, he was only 17. Come September, the three teenagers were starting for the Padres…and each hit over .300 for the month. Doerr and McDonald led the club with .429 and .361 batting averages, respectively.

Following are some of their reflections in their own words.

THEODORE "TED" WILLIAMS, 1936 LEFT FIELDER

From *My Turn at Bat*:

> The San Diego manager was an old spitball pitcher named Frank Shellenback, a big good-looking German with about eight kids. ... He wanted to win, and there were some real established stars in the Coast League.

> But I was just happy to be there, to travel with the team on the train, going places I'd never been, to have new balls to hit, new uniforms. I could order bats. Hillerich and Bradsby paid me fifteen dollars to endorse a bat, which meant I could have all I wanted.

Ted Williams
1936 San Diego Padres

I'd get a box of used balls to take home with me, take them out to the playground for extra batting practice, and after I had hit them until the covers were off I'd ask for more. Shellenback thought I was selling them or something, because he came out to the park one day to see what I was up to.

On the road my roommate was Sid [sic] Durst, who had played with the Yankees during Babe Ruth's days, and he said I woke him up at six A.M., yelling and jumping on the bed and swinging at imaginary pitches and telling him how great it was to be young and full of vigor.[359]

ROBERT "BOBBY" DOERR, 1936 PADRES SECOND BASEMAN

By Bobby Doerr[360]

San Diego in 1936. Oh, I really liked San Diego. God, the weather was great…and we played all day games for a good part of the season. It was just a great place, and the fans were great. That was one of the happiest years I think I had in baseball.

I joined the Hollywood Stars while still at Fremont High School in 1934. I didn't think much about that at the time. It was just another baseball team to me. Only now we were now playing against all professional players. Some might think it put added pressure on me. But, I don't think so. There were three of us younger players, George Myatt, George McDonald and myself. We started playing together in '35. We were all like 19 or 20 years old. George McDonald, who played first, was listed as being five days younger than I was. We sort of grew up together; we played the same kind of ball.

Bobby Doerr, 1936 San Diego Padres

The other thing was, in those days on the Hollywood team in '34, when I joined them, they had practically all players with major league experience on the roster. Fred Haney was the third baseman, Ray Jacobs was our first baseman, from the Cubs, Jim Leavy at short. Frank Shellenback was the manager— and we had Smead Jolley, one of the great minor league sluggers of all time. Any mistakes you made on that team were covered pretty quickly.

I went back to high school in the wintertime. That was one of the conditions my dad made me agree to when I signed. My dad said: "If you do sign, you have to promise that you will go back and get your diploma." Which is exactly what I did.

That winter was when I went up to the Rogue River. Les Cook was the trainer of the club and had been coming up to the river for many years and he brought me up that winter with him.

Then the following winter, in 1935, the Red Sox took out an option to buy my contract and then they would come out in the summertime and decide whether they were going to pick it up. They were interested in both George Myatt and me. At that time Joe Cronin was still playing shortstop, and so Eddie Collins decided he wouldn't take the shortstop, but he'd take me, the second baseman.

What I remember most about Eddie Collins is that he was just a pretty definite kind of person. You know, at the time I had read so much about him and I actually kind of felt like it was quite an honor to get to meet a person who had the baseball background that Collins did. Of course, he never did say too much… I mean, he talked to me a couple of times, but never said a whole lot. And sometimes you didn't even know he was around. For instance, he'd been up there in Seattle and Portland in '36 to watch us play. "We didn't know he was in the stands until probably a week after he was there…he was in Seattle, and then followed us down to Portland. I remember somebody finally spotted him and said "Collins is in the stands." And I think I made three errors in that game…I'm not sure. Back then you hardly ever saw a scout. And when you did, you'd get nervous. Between the doubleheader, he comes to the clubhouse knocked on the door and told me that they were going to pick up my contract. And that to relax a little bit. And, of course, that was at the same time he was looking over Ted Williams. Ted wasn't playing, just hitting batting practice, and Collins wanted to try and buy his contract. That was my understanding, even though Lane said he wouldn't do it, but they wound up shaking hands on the deal.

Which brings me to Bill 'Hardrock' Lane. Well, he was kind of…acted like a grumpy old guy part, you know. I remember one time Ted and I are at the old Leamington Hotel in Oakland, and he pulled Ted over. I remember we were walking in, coming in from a movie and he grabbed Ted and he says, "Hey…" He had a real coarse voice: "You're heading the list." So Ted says, "What list?" Lane grumbles, "Over eaters!" And Ted looked him square in the eye and told him, "I can't eat on that measly…" I don't remember exactly, either $1.50 or $2 a day. And, so he went on giving Ted heck for over spending his *per diem*. Ted told me when we were both up with the Red Sox, "I got up with him my last year…I ate what I wanted to."

I'll never forget the first time I saw Ted. We were standing around the old batting cage at the time and this big, skinny kid was right in front of me not more than four or five feet in front of me. And nobody knew who he was…some 6-foot 3, 147-pound kid. And he was all excited and Shellenback, our manager, was pitching batting practice, and Shellenback yelled, "Let the kid get in and hit a few…" Ted got in and I remember all of the guys around the batting cage started grumbling, "This kid is going to take all of our time for batting practice" and things like that. He hit six or seven balls as I remember, and I seem to recollect that he hit at least one out of the ballpark. Ted hit some hard shots. Somebody on the other side of the batting cage—I don't remember who and I really wish I could have remembered— said "This kid will be signed before the week is out." I'm thinking like that was on a Thursday, and by the Monday he was at the railroad station with us. We were going to San Francisco for a series and he was there to take the train…the team had signed him. And right from the beginning we became close friends…we used to go to movies together. Oh yeah, that was quite a deal being able to (take the train) back then you know…I was playing every day and got a lower berth…and they put Ted in an upper berth because he was riding the bench.

Every night, practically after every game, we would go get a milkshake to try to put on a little weight. My birthday is April and his is August, he's that much younger than I am.

And I can't ever forget Ted's stint on the mound. In Los Angeles we were playing the Angels in Wrigley Field and we were behind by a few runs. Shellenback was trying to figure out who he was going to put in for a relief pitcher cause the game is pretty much lost and Williams is popping off about 'I'm a pitcher.' And so they put him in and I remember Wes Schulmerich hit a home run off of him. But Ted hit a double off the right-center field fence. Later I asked Schulmerich, "What did you think about Ted's swing?" And he replied, "You know, if you ask me, I didn't think he was going to be that good of a hitter…it looked like he was too wiggly up there and not, you know, that good of a hitter." And then he added, "Of course, nobody's ever offered me a scouting job!"

Anyway, they racked Ted up pretty good. My brother was catching him at that time. Desautels, our regular catcher, had a split finger. So my brother joined our club for a month or something like that. Years later he told me that Ted— when he came in off the mound— threw his glove and went over to the dugout and then into the stands. I don't remember that...but Hal, my brother, seemed to think that he saw that...so I imagine he did...sounds just like what Ted might do.

Anyway, Shellenback said, "Well, that's the end of *your* pitching. You're going to be an outfielder from now on!"

Ted pretty much sat on the bench until the regular left fielder, Ivey 'Chick' Shiver left our team in August giving Ted the opportunity to play the last month of the season. He joined the team as a mid-season pick up, moving Wirthman to right. Shiver, who had been an All American at Georgia, got offered an assistant coaching position at his alma mater. The team wasn't upset with Shiver's departure, even though he left right when we were battling our way up through the standings. Ivey was good, yeah, but Ted got in there and did a pretty good job, too. I mean, I don't remember anybody making any great thing out of it. It was a surprise to all of us, but it was no big deal.

Our club, going into the season, was not viewed as any better than also-rans. We finished in the cellar in the second half of the 1935 season, and they didn't figure us to be much better than that in '36. I guess we surprised them, finishing second and making the playoffs.

But, I'll tell you what, we had a bunch of older pitchers— Berly Horne, Archie Campbell, Shellenback... Dick Ward came in later. And they all had good years. I thought Shellenback did a great job in the way he worked his pitchers.

Manager Frank Shellenback was a wonderful man, wonderful man. He had a lot of effect on my life. And he was a very classy person. His morals were great. Discipline was good on the club. Nice guy to play for. Real competitor...and, boy, he was a good pitcher. He'd suck on a slippery elm tablet and he'd have one spot on the ball that he'd spit on and once in a while you'd catch the ball on the ground and you'd throw...and you'd get it on that slick spot and you'd throw a spitter to the first baseman.

MAKES MYTHICAL TEAM

BOBBY DOERR
San Diego's brilliant young second-sacker who is picked as guardian of the keystone position on an Associated Press All-Star team. The story appears in an adjoining column. Doerr is reported sold to the Boston Red Sox, reporting next spring.—(Tribune staff photo.)

Bobby Doerr Named On All-Star Club

San Diego Evening Tribune,
September 9, 1936

Wally Herbert was a good, good pitcher. He kind of had a little fastball kind of away from a right-hand hitter, threw a curve ball. He had good control and mixed his speeds good. Nice guy, real nice guy.

Also in the rotation we had Ed Wells. Wells was another good pitcher who kept everything down. He wasn't overly fast, but he mixed speeds and he really knew how to pitch.

Another good pitcher we had was Herm Pillette. My gosh he was a good pitcher.

All those guys all knew how to mix their speeds real good.

Bud Tuttle, the son of the league president, was also a pitcher on our team. He didn't pitch that much, maybe a few games. He didn't have all that much stuff. I think it must've been a political thing, his being on the club.

Speaking of pitchers, the club secretary was Spider Baum, and he had won well over 250 games in the Coast League. Spider was always a pretty nice sort of guy, but we players didn't have much contact with him, though… we didn't see those guys in the office guys that much.

We also had some good position players on the club. Vince DiMaggio was on the club, and he had a very good season for us. Vince was a real fine person, a great guy to have on the ballclub. When Vince hit straight away on a ball he was a much better hitter. But when he started to pull the ball…why that turned him into a very poor hitter. What would happen was that he'd pull off the ball. But if he hit straight away, which he did more in that ballpark in San Diego, why he was a pretty good hitter.

We also had veteran outfielder Syd[*] Durst on the team. What a nice guy he was. He was great for the young guys on our team. He kind of gave me a lot of confidence; he was the type of player who instilled confidence in you and tried to encourage you— you know, if you weren't hitting he'd try and suggest things to do. A real fine guy on the ball club.

In left, at the start of the season, we had Van Wirthman. He, too, was a pretty solid ball player. He had been a pitcher at one time, and because he was a pretty good hitter they made him an outfielder.

Texan Ernie Holman played third for us. He was a good player who had a great season in 1936.

At first we had George McDonald, who was listed as being a year younger than me at seventeen. Ray Jacobs started the season as our regular first baseman, but he was benched, and George took over there. McDonald never made it to the majors, and I think the reason was that he didn't hit for enough power for a first baseman. But he should have made it up to the majors anyway. He was really a great fielder, and a very solid hitter. He just couldn't hit with much power.

My double-play partner, George Myatt, held down short. We teamed up the year before for Hollywood; the Los Angeles press corps dubbed us "The Keystone Kids." He had a very good in 1935, and the Red Sox picked up an option on him at the same time they did me. George got married at home plate at Lane Field. That last month of the season we did play some night games, and before one of those night games— Lane must have given him a few bucks— had his wedding at home plate. The bride's name was Georgia Smith, and I was George's best man.

Before that, Myatt and I roomed together at the old Broadway Hotel. I think the name of the hotel was the Broadway Hotel…just a little hotel. It was just off Broadway, right across from the U. S. Grant Hotel, a couple, three blocks from the park.

My brother joined the team during the season, after he'd been released by Houston in the Texas League. He was married at that time, so we didn't room together. And then he was released by the club a month or so later.

I also remember a couple of umpires in the league. Hall-of-Famer Sam Crawford umpired in the league when I played. He may have been a great player, but not a real good umpire…kind of hesitant-type umpire. On some plays he seemed very unsure of himself. He just wasn't real good, but I remember him real well. He was an imposing figure on the field.

Another umpire at the time was Jack Powell. I think it was Powell who threw player-coach Eddie Mulligan out of the game for calling him an 'old snot!' For Mulligan that was the worst word that he could say, "old snot!" He never swore. And when that happened, that kind of erupted things. I remember one of the fans broke off

---

[*] Durst's nickname variously showed up as "Ced" or "Syd," and he signed autographs both ways. Discussion with his daughter in November 2001 indicated that "Syd" was generally preferred by Durst, so that is the one used in this book.

one of the pieces off the box seat and threw it out on the field. Powell was a real good umpire. But that day I remember we had a real fan-umpire donnybrook.

Our major rival, of course, was the Los Angeles Angels. They usually had a good ball club and there was always a rivalry there, especially because our team had been the Hollywood Stars before, and shared Wrigley Field with the Angels. They were sponsored by Wrigley of the Cubs. Wrigley Field in Los Angeles was a real modern plant, but Lane Field was a nice ballpark. Yeah, that was a good park. A little rough at first. I remember the infield was a little bit rough. And we didn't play that much night ball that year as the lights weren't installed until well into the season. But it was a beautiful place to play, the weather was always just warm and nice— and the fans were great, and the team responded to that support.

I guess everything about 1936 was great— except the salaries. My best salary was $300 a month that year. Ted, I think, signed for $150.

Looking back on it, it was quite a team and quite a year. We didn't quite win it all, but it was quite a team.

GEORGE McDONALD, 1936 PADRES FIRST BASEMAN

George McDonald,
1936 San Diego Padres

By George McDonald[361]

In 1936 it was nice to come to San Diego because Lane Field was new and a small ballpark, and the fans were real nice and everybody treated you well. I enjoyed it. I really enjoyed it. I believe even with the fleet in the population was about 250,000. So, it was a nice little town. And, the weather...beautiful weather. I lived in Mission Beach, and I lived in Point Loma. I bought a home in Point Loma in 1937, I think, a two-bedroom brand new home for $8,700. We had a beautiful view of the ocean. I heard later on they tore the house down and sold the lot for something like a million.

We all stayed at the Southern Hotel on 5th Street.

In 1933 we had an American Legion team you couldn't believe: Mesner (of the Cardinals) at 3rd, Priddy (of the Yankees) at short, Bobby Doerr at 2nd, I played 1st, Mickey Owen caught, and Dick Conger, a pitcher for Detroit. All went to the big leagues so we all had a shot.

In 1934 Bobby Doerr and I were in the 11th grade at Fremont High and the athletic director from USC came over and offered us scholarships to SC. We thought, 'jeez, that's great.' In 1934 $18 a week was the average pay for everybody. I bought a brand new Chevrolet right off the show room floor for $645. Things weren't very good. I bought that new car in 1934, a brand new Chevy, and I think my next car was bought in 1938. We had an outfielder, Eddie Stewart, and I remember because he had a new car that year, too, I think. If it rained he wouldn't take his car out.

Finally, an old scout from Hollywood, George Stovall, came by and I think it was $150 a month, I'm not sure, I believe that was it. I couldn't spend all of that money. I took all the kids in my neighborhood for strawberry waffles and treated to everything. So, we signed with Hollywood. We were 16 at the time. Today a young player is 22 or 23. About the only difference I can see today is that most of them can't get the ball over. But there are quite a few, 8 or 10 pitchers on every club that can throw 90 or better. In our day there wasn't that many. They are much stronger today, better food, vitamins, and it used to be up to a $50 fine if we lifted weights or went swimming. They said you had to have loose muscles to play baseball. And, it's just the opposite.

Lane Field was all right. Not very good lights. The visiting teams didn't like to come down and play here because of the lights, they weren't very good.

Bill Lane was an old grumpy hard rock miner. Everybody liked him though, he was OK. I was just a little upset when he didn't sell me to the Giants. The Giants then went out and bought Johnny McCarthy, he didn't last very long. He was there a couple of years.

Ted Williams got an awfully bad break when he went to Boston. Right away they thought he was a fresh kid that just was really cocky. But you know we played night games and Ted, Bob (Doerr) and I used to go to the movies in the daytime. Ted always had a couple of tennis balls, and he was squeezing them all the time.

Not in an arrogant way he'd always say about himself, 'you know someday they're going to say there goes the greatest hitter in baseball.' It wasn't in a cocky way it was just that he was very confident. And then he got up there and they (i.e., the writers and fans) took his confidence for being cocky and they started getting on him. And in response, he started getting back at the fans. He got a bad break there. He got a bad break because the fans thought he was a cocky.

In 1937 when Ted went on a streak of hitting home runs and I was hitting behind him, I got caved in on my back every time. That's another thing they don't do in baseball today. Bob Gibson, Sal Maglie, and guys like that would see these guys today digging in at the plate and making a hole for the foot…that's all they would have to see, and wham down they'd go.

It's a different game. I wished I could have played when they had helmets. I used a 35-ounce, 35-inch bat. I tried to hit every ball right at the pitcher's feet. I tried to hit the ball on the line. In fact, I hit a lot of doubles (300 career doubles). I had a hitch in my swing and I'd hit a sinking ball instead of it carrying like a lot of other hitters: Kiner and lot of these guys whose ball would carry, my ball would sink. I just was not a home run hitter. A couple of times watching the games I said 'I wish we would have had helmets…I would have gotten on top of that plate with a 31-ounce bat and swung from my fanny.'

Bobby Doerr's dad bought me my first suit of clothes for $9.00. We were on the 1933 American Legion team in Los Angeles. We played against Ted. He was on a San Diego American Legion team. I never heard Bobby Doerr say a bad word about anybody. If he couldn't say something good, he didn't say it. He is one of the nicest fellows that ever took a breath of air.

Now, Bobby Doerr played 2nd base …my, he was in front of every ball. Today they have this classical going at it backhanded and they're hoping if they don't catch it that it will be called a hit. Just awful. Joe Gordon…he was the same type of fielder as Bobby Doerr. He was great. I watch today's baseball but sometimes it's very upsetting. Especially what's upsetting is when it comes down to the playoffs and the series, there's probably two or three good pitchers on every club and the rest of the 10 or 11 couldn't have made the Coast League.

Frank Shellenback favored Catholic players and, in fact, his daughter was a nun. He was a real strong Catholic. But, he was all right.

Chick Shiver was a free-swinging outfielder, a nice guy. The outfielders we had were Van Wirthman, Hal Patchett. I remember Vince DiMaggio who would sing "O solo mio" at every banquet. He had pretty good voice but that was the only song he knew!

George McDonald

"Old Folks" Pillette, he was a super guy, a really good guy. I roomed with him on the road. Never, never saw him out drinking. For some reason, he just liked the taste of whiskey. But he never drank a lot. If he did he didn't show it.

Howard Craghead, "The Professor," he's the one that gave me my nickname "Doodle Bug." That was my nickname all the time I played here. He used to call me "McDoodle," and then "Doodle," and then "Doodle Bug." Howard Craghead…I don't know if hitters caught on to him. I guess most of them didn't. Howard Craghead was a professor and he pitched backwards. In other words, when he was ahead of a hitter he threw fastballs and when he was behind them he threw curveballs. Like 2 and 0, when they were looking for a fastball, he'd always throw a curveball. And, that's the way he pitched. Nice guy. He died young.

Wally Hebert, a super guy. He just died here recently at 92. I never saw a guy who loved to eat more than Wally Hebert. He loved to eat. He was a nice guy.

I don't remember what year it was, we were in the playoffs…Joe Berkowitz a utility infielder, a good guy. One off day we had a few beers and we dated these two girls. I think it was about the second time we dated them. On the way to the beach, we were going to go to the dance…a name band was there. We stopped at a driving range. He loved to hit golf balls. I said "Aw c'mon, let's go." The girl that I was with wanted to learn. So, I said "well I'll show you." So, I stood behind her and showed her how to grip. She swung around and hit me on the nose. We had to go to the emergency and they put steel things up my nose, and cracked it back. We were playing Portland and I remember the team we're playing, Portland, and I didn't want to say how it happened. So, I told the club that I got hit with a flying golf ball. And it was flying…believe me. I played and I had a big bandage on my nose and every time I went to bat that night everybody went "fore!"

I remember the evening that George Myatt got married at home plate. He was arrested right after the game. We knew a policeman real well and we had him arrested and kept in jail overnight!

Cedric Durst, he was a nice guy. George Detore, a good guy. Del Ballinger, he was a kick…he was a clown, a catcher.

Eddie Mulligan was a real nice guy. I don't think he ever swore.

Umpire Sam Crawford was a nice old guy. There were three umpires I remember when I played: one was a little Italian, Bert Varaillo. It was the offseason, I'm in Big Bear and I go into this place to eat and there he is as a waiter. And he says, "oh…don't you…" I said "why the hell would I?" Well, the next season about the second time he missed a play I had thought I beat out a bunt by a good step. I went to him and I put my hand up like I was carrying a tray and I said "one ham on rye." He threw me out of the game. Threw me out. So, I forget who our manager was but he asked "what did you say to him?" I said "one ham on rye." He laughed. So, I went back in the dugout and I told the guys that he was a waiter and I said: 'I just said one ham on rye and he run me out.' Oh my, did they get on him…they'd say "one hamburger, send it to the kitchen, everything on it."

Another time I'm up in Sacramento and the umpire, Jack Powell, came out drunk. He says "now George, you help me out with these plays at first." The police had to come and take him out of the ballpark. Then we had an old umpire named McGuthrie and he was an ex-football player. He had about a 20 collar and a size 2 head. He was a big, big guy. When you were up hitting, if you looked at a strike and didn't like it, in a real little baby voice he'd say "you can't hit with the bat on your shoulders." You couldn't get mad at him.

The Coast League was pretty good back then…we had Joe DiMaggio, Joe Marty, Joe Gordon…lot of great players.

It was hard in 1934 and 1935 and 1936. In 1937 I had my best year. And old man Lane called me into the office and said 'I can tell you that the Giants want you.' And I said "Gee, that's great." He said, "but I'm not going to sell you." And, I said "why?" He said, "well maybe you will have a bigger year next year and I'll get more money for you. I'll give you part of the purchase price." Well, you know right then, that one time, I think was the turning point in my career. The next year I was "bad."

So, anyway, my life turned out great because I went into the car business and got a Chevrolet dealership. I sold out 22 years ago and I've lived very comfortably since. So, I guess it was supposed to happen that way. My dealership was in Westminster in Orange County. Things seem to work out the way they're supposed to.

A number of times I talked to Casey Stengel in the offseason and he said when he was the manager of the Boston Braves he tried to buy me. They wanted too much money. Joe DiMaggio was the first one sold out here... for $100,000. If it would have been like today big league teams have owned these clubs and if you have a good year they would bring you up. Back then they had to buy you. Maybe to me it's just sour grapes, I don't know. I haven't lost any sleep over it.

Another time I was in spring training in 1947 with the St. Louis Browns. In that spring I hit .400, at least .400. The DeWitt Brothers had owned the team at that time. Seattle offered me more money than the Browns. So, I decided to stay on the coast here where I knew everybody and we didn't have to travel every two or three days.

The International, American Association, and the Coast League...I would venture to say 60% of the ballplayers in the big leagues today could not have made these leagues in the 30s and 40s. In fact, Gene Mauch, who is a friend of mine, told me that 'you can't believe it, George, these guys are getting $2,000,000 hitting .220. They need a map to get to the ballpark.' It's a different game. In those days it was a game. Today it's a business. The worst thing that happened to baseball is when they started 2-3-4 year contracts. You know, you used to get paid the next year on what you done. These guys now that have three- and four-year contracts and Christ, they get a hangnail and they're out a week. They have so many injuries now that we never heard of them. I don't understand it. But, it's life...just like in those days you weren't afraid to open a letter!

I don't like the stage I'm in now because all of the guys I played ball with are dead as are all my friends from my neighborhood, Metkovich, Zarilla, Priddy, Peanuts Lowery...those are all guys I used to run with in LA. We were at the Manchester playground in LA. I got thrilled the other day somebody was old enough that they remembered me. I said 'don't leave me, it makes me feel good!'

Bill Starr, he drove a Ford out here from Chicago, and he said he didn't even have a license he, just bought the car and came out. He turned up owner for a while. He was my first roommate out here. He always was changing suspenders on his suits. He said, "someday I'd like to have enough money to have a pair of suspenders for every one of my pants." That's what I remember about him.

When he was owner I had a good year at Seattle in 1945 (hit .332 with 183 hits). So in 1946, they had a 1st baseman, Torgeson, that was in the service and he had to play in Seattle. So, Bill Skiff says 'stay here George (i.e., in Seattle) and pinch hit or play once in a while, or I'll trade you.' And, I said, "I might as well play all of the time. I'd appreciate it if you would trade me.' Not knowing, for all the world that he was going to trade me back to San Diego. They traded me for Dick Gyselman, a 3rd baseman. So I asked Bill Starr, 'Bill, how could you ever do that? Rip Collins hates my guts." I used to really jockey him with the Angels, and he really did.

Vince Shupe was the first baseman then (i.e., 1947). He (Collins) wouldn't even let me take batting practice on Sundays 'cause they had short times. I'll tell you about this one time, Vince Shupe is up hitting in a Sunday game and I'm sitting between Johnny Barrett and Pete Coscarart on the bench and Shupe gets kicked out of the game with two strikes. Collins gets this big grin and looks around and says "McDonald get a bat." And I say to myself 'that son of a gun." Anyway, I got him mad. It's the 6th inning (it was a seven-inning game and the second game of a doubleheader). And there were two men on and we were one run behind. Tommy Bridges is pitching. He had one of the best curveballs in the big leagues. I go up and I think "I got one strike left, he's going to be thinking I'm going to be looking for his curveball. But I'm going to guess fast ball and if he throws a curveball I will just smile and go back to the dugout." He threw a fastball and I doubled off of the right field fence. Shupe had been hitting about .100 and something. All the guys said you'd be in there Tuesday. We traveled to Oakland the next week and it was 'sit, sit, sit.' Ralph Buxton is pitching for Oakland on Sunday. He had a good screwball that went away from a left-hand hitter. So, Collins calls me up to pinch hit in the last part of the game. I took three swings and then went and sat down. He struck out me out.

I got back from that road trip and I went to Bill Starr and said, "Bill"…then before I could go further, he said, "I know George, I'm not even going to trade you. I'm going to give you your release so you can pick yourself up a little money." So he gave me my release and I signed with New Orleans in the Southern League. And I got a little bonus for signing which wasn't much today but was okay for then.

In 1950 I was in the Giants organization…Minneapolis and Jersey City. I didn't hardly play much. In my last year, 1951, I played for Salem of the Western International League for 52 games.

RALPH THOMPSON, 1936 PADRES MASCOT

Ralph Thompson with George McDonald

Summary of Interviews with Ralph Thompson[362]

In preparation for the start of the Padres' maiden season *The San Diego Union* initiated a contest in mid-March 1936 to help the club select a team mascot. Any boy* interested in the job had to answer 11 questions and supply a letter in 100 words or less telling how the Padres will benefit San Diego. On March 24, 1936 10-year old Ralph Thompson was selected as "official" Padres team mascot. There were several newspaper photos and articles announcing the new team mascot.

His first appearance in uniform was on the Padres' first opening day, March 28, 1936. Thompson indicated that he wore uniform number 55. At the time he was a 3rd grade student at Benjamin Franklin School and would continue to serve the ball club for four more years…until, he said, "…he was bigger than some of the players themselves!"

As mascot, his work was "to take the bats back to the rack, to take the pitcher's coat when he goes to bat and take it back to him when he gets to first base, keep the dugout clean, and help in the locker room. And you have to root for the team, too, and give the players all your support." Ralph admitted that he believed the mascot's job to be a terrific one and felt the cartoon to the right an accurate depiction.

In his interview, Thompson recalled most of the players from 1936. Wally Hebert was one of his

---

* Given the times it was likely that only boys applied for the position. However, it is not known whether there was any specific prohibition against a girl applying. It was likely simply assumed that only boys would apply.

Letter from Lane to Thompson Giving Him a Share of Playoff Proceeds

Newspaper Cartoon about Padres' Mascot
San Diego Union, March 30, 1936

favorites and "...like a father to me...a southern guy who took me under wing." He remembers Bill Lane as the "boss." Another favorite was pitcher Manny Salvo, who joined the team in the middle of the 1936 season. "My mother would cook Italian meals for him," said Thompson. George Myatt he recalls as someone who always had a jaw full of tobacco...and a half pouch in his back pocket. Thompson said that the entire team treated him fine.

As for Ted Williams, Thompson said they would go to the movies alone and Ted would pay Ralph's admission. Thompson was not sure why Williams always invited him but thought it might be because Ted was youngest on the team. In any event, Williams always was "very nice" to Thompson. Within a few years, Thompson was following in Williams's footsteps at Hoover High, playing shortstop for the Cardinals.

Les "Cookie" Cook, Padres trainer for many years, was another "father figure" for Thompson, and his favorite along with Hebert.

As mascot, Thompson noted that he did not receive any compensation or tips from the players back then. Occasionally he would accompany the team on a road trip over his years with the team. The fun of being mascot was sufficient reward he felt.

In his last year as mascot, the club gave Thompson a ring shaped like a baseball. He also benefited from the team making the playoffs its first year when he received a letter from owner Bill Lane along with a bonus check. Earl Keller, in the October 1, 1936, edition of *The Sporting News*, noted that "22 players, Trainer Lester Cook and Secretary Spider Baum shared in the $1,250 which was given the Padres for finishing in the first division. Mascot Blondie Thompson also got a small check." Small, indeed--$12.00—but not bad for 1936! In any event, "Blondie" said he appreciated Lane's kindness. The only other form of compensation was free season passes that his father received.

SAN DIEGO'S FIRST PADRES and "THE KID"

APPENDIX A
1936 SAN DIEGO PADRES SEASON STATISTICS

Players	Positions	G	AB	R	H	1B	2B	3B	HR	RBI	SB	AVG
Fred Vaughn	ph	2	2	1	1	1	0	0	0	0	0	.500
Joe Monahan	ph	5	5	2	2	1	1	0	0	0	0	.400
Bobby Doerr	2b	175	695	100	**238**	187	37	12	2	77	30	.342
Gene Desautels	c	148	480	68	153	127	18	5	3	69	4	.319
George McDonald	1b	103	334	36	106	90	11	5	0	52	3	.317
Ernie Holman	3b	174	627	92	197	164	20	7	6	88	17	.314
Ivey Shiver	of	54	191	27	59	37	9	6	7	41	2	.309
Cedric Durst	cf	159	621	71	190	154	32	3	1	81	14	.306
Vince DiMaggio	rf	176	641	109	188	112	43	14	19	102	22	.293
Van Wirthman	lf	132	428	58	123	96	20	6	1	49	6	.287
Ray Jacobs	1b	106	332	42	93	64	23	1	5	46	8	.280
George Myatt	ss	162	652	117	180	151	16	12	1	50	33	.276
Ted Williams	of-p	42	108	18	29	18	9	2	0	11	2	.271
Ash Joerndt	of	12	19	3	5	3	2	0	0	3	0	.263
Jimmy Kerr	c	52	124	9	32	25	4	2	1	17	2	.258
Joe Berkowitz	3b-ss-of-1b	45	97	15	24	20	2	2	0	5	2	.247
Hal Doerr	c	10	27	1	4	4	0	0	0	0	0	.148
Eddie Mulligan	3b-2b-of	39	12	6	1	1	0	0	0	0	7	.083
Les Cook	c	7	7	0	0	0	0	0	0	0	0	.000
Elmer Evert*	c	2	1	0	0	0	0	0	0	0	5	.000

*Record with Padres, also played with Sacramento

SAN DIEGO'S FIRST PADRES and "THE KID"

Pitchers	G	GS	CG	ShO	Sv	W	L	PCT	IP	H	R	ER	SO	BB	ERA
Elmer Hill	1	1	0	0	0	0	0	.000	2	1	2	0	1	2	0.00
Kenny Iverson	1	0	0	0	1	0	0	.000	2	0	0	0	1	1	0.00
Dick Ward***	24	17	10	2	0	12	5	.706	140⅓	114	39	36	67	62	2.31
Howard Craghead**	24	20	16	3	0	14	5	.737	160	133	60	53	80	53	2.98
Wally Hebert	35	30	18	4	0	18	12	.600	229	240	86	77	87	51	3.03
Herman Pillette	31	25	14	3	1	11	8	.579	191	180	80	67	63	37	3.16
Manny Salvo	45	28	14	3	3	15	12	.556	239	244	112	88	145	74	3.31
Ed Wells**	14	12	6	1	0	5	6	.455	91⅔	100	40	35	28	14	3.44
Frank Shellenback	15	12	7	0	0	6	7	.462	102	104	47	40	38	13	3.53
Jack Hile	2	1	0	0	0	0	1	.000	9	10	5	4	3	2	4.00
Trader Horne	38	23	9	3	0	7	14	.333	164	183	110	80	76	78	4.39
Archie Campbell	48	2	1	0	5	6	9	.400	129	143	88	71	45	73	4.95
Bud Tuttle	2	0	0	0	0	0	0	.000	5	5	3	3	2	3	5.40
George Hockette	8	5	1	0	0	0	3	.000	33	48	27	25	4	17	6.82
Ted Williams	1	0	0	0	0	0	0	.000	1⅓	2	2	2	0	1	13.50

** Record with Padres, also pitched for Seattle
***Record with Padres, also pitched for Sacramento

APPENDIX B
TED WILLIAMS GAME-BY-GAME SUMMARY

This Appendix provides a tabular summary of the 1936 game-by-game statistics for Ted Williams for his entire PCL regular season. In compiling this record box scores were reviewed and compared from the following: *The Sporting News, Los Angeles Times, Oakland Tribune, San Diego Evening Tribune, San Diego Union,* and *San Francisco Examiner*.

This research discovered that the Pacific Coast League's "Official" batting statistics for 1936 contained two errors for Ted Williams:
1. The number of his at bats should be 108, not 107.
2. His number of doubles should be 9, not 8.

As a result, Williams' correct batting average for 1936 should be .269, not .271. The corrected numbers are the ones used in this book for Williams' monthly statistics contained in Chapters 8 through 11, and for the season statistics in Appendices A and H.

Date	Pos	Pos in Bat Order	G	AB	R	H	2B	3B	HR	RBI	SB	SAC	BA	Daily Cumulative AB	H	BA
June 27, 1936	PH		1	1	0	0	0	0	0	0	0	0	.000	1	0	.000
	June Totals=		1	1	0	0	0	0	0	0	0	0	.000			
July 3, 1936	RP, LF		1	2	2	2	0	0	0	0	0	0		3	2	.667
July 4, 1936	PH		1	1	0	0	0	0	0	1	0	0		4	2	.500
July 4, 1936	LF	7	1	4	1	1	1	0	0	0	0	0		8	3	.375
July 5, 1936	LF	8	1	3	0	0	0	0	0	0	0	0		11	3	.273
July 5, 1936	LF	7	1	3	0	0	0	0	0	0	0	0		14	3	.214
July 15, 1936	PH		1	1	0	0	0	0	0	0	0	0		15	3	.200
July 17, 1936	PH		1	1	0	0	0	0	0	0	0	0		16	3	.188
July 22, 1936	PH		1	1	0	0	0	0	0	0	0	0		17	3	.176
July 24, 1936	PR		1	0	1	0	0	0	0	0	0	0		17	3	.176
July 26, 1936	LF	7	1	3	0	1	0	0	0	0	0	0		20	4	.200
July 30, 1936	PH		1	1	0	0	0	0	0	0	0	0		21	4	.190
	July Totals=		11	20	4	4	1	0	0	1	0	0	.200			
August 7, 1936	LF		1	0	0	0	0	0	0	0	0	0		21	4	.190
August 7, 1936	LF	8	1	4	1	1	0	0	0	1	0	0		25	5	.200
August 8, 1936	LF	8	1	3	1	2	0	0	0	0	0	0		28	7	.250
August 8, 1936	LF	8	1	3	0	0	0	0	0	0	0	0		31	7	.226
August 9, 1936	LF	7	1	4	0	2	1	0	0	2	0	0		35	9	.257
August 9, 1936	LF	7	1	3	1	1	1	0	0	0	0	0		38	10	.263

(continued on next page)

SAN DIEGO'S FIRST PADRES and "THE KID"

(continued from previous page)

Date	Pos	Pos in Bat Order	G	AB	R	H	2B	3B	HR	RBI	SB	SAC	BA	Daily Cumulative AB	H	BA
August 11, 1936	RF	7	1	3	0	0	0	0	0	0	0	0		41	10	.244
August 12, 1936	LF	7	1	4	0	0	0	0	0	0	0	0		45	10	.222
August 16, 1936	PH		1	1	0	1	0	0	0	0	0	0		46	11	.239
August 16, 1936	RRF		1	1	0	0	0	0	0	0	0	0		47	11	.234
August 19, 1936	PH		1	1	0	0	0	0	0	0	0	0		48	11	.229
August 23, 1936	PH		1	1	0	0	0	0	0	0	0	0		49	11	.224
August 28, 1936	PR		1	0	0	0	0	0	0	0	0	0		49	11	.224
August Totals=			13	28	3	7	2	0	0	3	0	0	.250			
September 1, 1936	LF	8	1	3	1	2	1	1	0	2	0	0		52	13	.250
September 2, 1936	LF	8	1	3	0	0	0	0	0	0	0	1		55	13	.236
September 3, 1936	LF	8	1	3	0	0	0	0	0	0	0	0		58	13	.224
September 4, 1936	LF	8	1	3	1	2	0	0	0	2	0	0		61	15	.246
September 5, 1936	LF	8	1	3	0	1	1	0	0	0	0	0		64	16	.250
September 6, 1936	LF	8	1	4	2	1	1	0	0	2	0	0		68	17	.250
September 6, 1936	LF	8	1	1	0	1	0	0	0	0	1	0		69	18	.261
September 7, 1936	LF	8	1	3	1	1	1	0	0	0	0	0		72	19	.264
September 7, 1936	LF	8	1	3	1	1	0	0	0	0	1	0		75	20	.267
September 9, 1936	LF	8	1	3	0	0	0	0	0	0	0	0		78	20	.256
September 9, 1936	LF	8	1	3	1	1	1	0	0	0	0	0		81	21	.259
September 10, 1936	LF	3	1	4	1	1	0	0	0	0	0	0		85	22	.259
September 11, 1936	LF	3	1	5	0	1	0	0	0	0	0	0		90	23	.256
September 12, 1936	LF	3	1	4	0	0	0	0	0	0	0	0		94	23	.245
September 12, 1936	LF	3	1	6	1	3	0	1	0	1	0	0		100	26	.260
September 13, 1936	LF	3	1	4	1	2	0	0	0	0	0	0		104	28	.269
September 13, 1936	LF	3	1	4	1	1	1	0	0	0	0	0		108	29	.269
September Totals=			17	59	11	18	6	2	0	7	2	1	.305			
1936 Season Totals=			42	108	18	29	9	2	0	11	2	1	.269			

The Governor's Cup

Date	Pos	Pos in Bat Order	G	AB	R	H	2B	3B	HR	RBI	SB	SAC	BA
September 15, 1936	LF	3	1	3	1	1	0	0	1	2	0	0	
September 16, 1936	LF	3	1	4	0	0	0	0	0	0	0	0	
September 19, 1936	LF	7	1	3	1	0	0	0	0	0	0	0	
September 20, 1936	LF	6	1	2	1	0	0	0	0	1	0	0	
September 21, 1936	LF	6	1	4	1	2	0	0	0	0	0	0	
1936 Playoff Totals=			5	16	4	3	0	0	1	3	0	0	.188

APPENDIX C
1936 TEAM ROSTER

	Player		1935-Hollywood Stars	2/7/36-Rec'd Contract	1936-Spring Training	3/15/36-Official Roster	March	April	May	June	July	August	September	Governor's Cup	Uniform No.	Transactions During Season
Pitchers	Archie	Campbell	☒	☒	☒	☒	☒	☒	☒	☒	☒	☒	☒	☒	7	
	Hec	Carroll	-	-	☒	☒	-	-	-	-	-	-	-	-		
	Howard	Craghead	-	-	-	-	-	-	-	☒	☒	☒	☒	☒	18	Joined 6/11/36 in trade for Wells
	Elmer	Donovan	-	-	☒	-	-	-	-	-	-	-	-	-		
	Eddie	Ehil	-	-	☒	-	-	-	-	-	-	-	-	-		
	Don	Elton	-	-	☒	☒	-	-	-	-	-	-	-	-		
	Larry	Gillick	-	☒	☒	☒	-	-	-	-	-	-	-	-		Released 3/16/36
	George	Harris	-	-	☒	-	-	-	-	-	-	-	-	-		
	Wally	Hebert	☒	☒	☒	☒	☒	☒	☒	☒	☒	☒	☒	☒	15	
	Jack	Hile	☒	☒	☒	☒	-	☒	-	-	-	-	-	-		Released 5/29/36
	Elmer	Hill	-	-	-	-	-	-	-	☒	-	-	-	-		Signed 6/27/36; released 6/28/36
	George	Hockette	-	☒	☒	☒	☒	☒	☒	-	-	-	-	-	19	Released 6/4/36
	Trader	Horne	☒	☒	☒	☒	☒	☒	☒	☒	☒	☒	☒	☒	22	
	Kenny	Iverson	-	-	☒	☒	-	☒	-	-	-	-	-	-		Released 5/10/36
	M. K.	Jackson	-	-	☒	-	-	-	-	-	-	-	-	-		
	Hub	Kittle	-	-	☒	-	-	-	-	-	-	-	-	-		
	Herman	Pillette	☒	☒	☒	☒	☒	☒	☒	☒	☒	☒	☒	☒	23	
	Manny	Salvo	-	-	-	-	-	☒	☒	☒	☒	☒	☒	☒	3	Signed 4/13/36
	?	Scaroli (or Scaroldi)	-	-	☒	-	-	-	-	-	-	-	-	-		
	Frank	Shellenback	☒	☒	☒	☒	☒	☒	☒	☒	☒	☒	☒	-	21	
	Stan	Steely	-	-	☒	-	-	-	-	-	-	-	-	-		
	Bud	Tuttle	-	-	☒	☒	-	-	☒	-	-	☒	-	-		
	Dick	Ward	-	-	-	-	-	-	-	☒	☒	☒	☒	☒	22?	Signed 6/1/36
	Ed	Wells	☒	☒	☒	☒	☒	☒	☒	☒	-	-	-	-	18	Traded to Seattle for Craghead 6/11/36
	Allan	Whitlock	-	-	☒	-	-	-	-	-	-	-	-	-		

(continued on next page)

SAN DIEGO'S FIRST PADRES and "THE KID"

(continued from previous page)

	Player		1935-Hollywood Stars	2/7/36-Rec'd Contract	1936-Spring Training	3/15/36-Official Roster	PLAYED (by month, min. 1 game)							Uniform No.	Transactions During Season
							March	April	May	June	July	August	September	Governor's Cup		
Catchers	Max	Bryan	-	-	☒	-	-	-	-	-	-	-	-	-	-	
	Les	Cook	-	-	-	-	-	-	-	-	☒	-	☒	-	-	Signed 7/1/36, released 7/6/36; signed 9/2/36
	?	Curtis	-	-	☒	-	-	-	-	-	-	-	-	-		
	Gene	Desautels	☒	☒	☒	☒	☒	☒	☒	☒	☒	☒	☒	☒	2	
	Hal	Doerr	-	-	-	-	-	-	-	☒	☒	-	-	-	11	Signed 6/29/36; released 7/16/36
	Elmer	Evert	-	-	-	-	-	-	-	-	☒	-	-	-		Signed 6/25/36; released 6/29/36
	Jimmy	Kerr	☒	☒	☒	☒	-	☒	☒	☒	-	☒	☒	-	11	
	Winfred	Pepper	-	-	☒	-	-	-	-	-	-	-	-	-		
	Elmer	Stock	-	☒	☒	☒	-	-	-	-	-	-	-	-		Released 3/16/36
Infielders	John	Appleby	-	-	☒	-	-	-	-	-	-	-	-	-		
	Joe	Berkowitz	☒	☒	☒	☒	☒	☒	☒	☒	☒	☒	☒	☒	5	
	Ritchie	Cooper	-	☒	☒	☒	-	-	-	-	-	-	-	-		Released 5/10/36
	Bobby	Doerr	☒	☒	☒	☒	☒	☒	☒	☒	☒	☒	☒	☒	6	
	Ernie	Holman		☒	☒	☒	☒	☒	☒	☒	☒	☒	☒	☒	14	
	Ray	Jacobs	☒	☒	☒	☒	☒	☒	☒	☒	☒	☒	☒	☒	9	
	Burke	McDonald	-	-	☒	-	-	-	-	-	-	-	-	-		
	George	McDonald	☒	☒	☒	☒	☒	☒	☒	☒	☒	☒	☒	☒	10	
	Joe	Monahan	-	-	☒	☒	☒	☒	-	-	-	-	-	-		Released 4/9/36
	Eddie	Mulligan	☒	☒	☒	☒	☒	☒	☒	☒	☒	☒	☒	-	1	
	George	Myatt	☒	☒	☒	☒	☒	☒	☒	☒	☒	☒	☒	☒	12	
	Red	Williams	-	-	☒	☒	-	-	-	-	-	-	-	-		
Outfielders	Dennis	Crabb	-	-	☒	-	-	-	-	-	-	-	-	-		
	Vince	DiMaggio	☒	☒	☒	☒	☒	☒	☒	☒	☒	☒	☒	☒	4	
	Cedric	Durst	☒	☒	☒	☒	☒	☒	☒	☒	☒	☒	☒	☒	17	
	Bill	Englund	-	☒	☒	-	-	-	-	-	-	-	-	-		Released 3/9/36
	Ross	Gilhousen	-	-	☒	-	-	-	-	-	-	-	-	-		
	Ash	Joerndt	-	-	☒	☒	☒	☒	☒	-	-	-	-	-	20	Released 5/24/36
	Harl	Maggert	-	-	☒	☒	-	-	-	-	-	-	-	-		
	Al	Pignataro	-	-	☒	☒	-	-	-	-	-	-	-	-		
	Ivey	Shiver	-	-	-	-	-	-	-	-	☒	☒	-	-	11	Signed 7/3/36; left on own 9/1/36
	Kenneth	Storms	-	-	☒	-	-	-	-	-	-	-	-	-		
	Fred	Vaughn	-	☒	☒	☒	-	☒	-	-	-	-	-	-		Released 5/10/36
	Ted	Williams	-	-	-	-	-	-	-	☒	☒	☒	☒	☒	19?	Signed 6/26/36
	Van	Wirthman	☒	☒	☒	☒	☒	☒	☒	☒	☒	☒	☒	☒	16	
Unk.	John	Bladel	-	-	☒	-	-	-	-	-	-	-	-	-		
	Robert	Vickers	-	-	☒	-	-	-	-	-	-	-	-	-		
		Total number =	18	24	52	32	19	24	21	25	22	22	21	18		

APPENDIX D
KEY DATES AND GAME-BY-GAME RECORD

1936

Key Dates:

Jan. 28-Lane signs agreement with City of San Diego

Jan. 30-Construction approved for Lane Field

Feb. 1-PCL Board approves transfer

Feb. 20-Padres selected as name, and ballpark named Lane Field

Feb. 23-Spring training starts in Fullerton

Mar. 28 to Sep. 13- PCL season

Mar. 31-1st home game, a win vs Seattle

May 30-News of contract offer to Williams from Lane

Jun. 26-Williams signs

Sep. 15 to Sep. 21- Governor's Cup playoff

Sep. 15-Williams hits 1st pro HR

Sep. 21-Padres lose 7-6 to Oakland, season ends

January
Su	Mo	Tu	We	Th	Fr	Sa
			1	2	3	4
5	6	7	8	9	10	11
12	13	14	15	16	17	18
19	20	21	22	23	24	25
26	27	*28*	29	*30*	31	

February
Su	Mo	Tu	We	Th	Fr	Sa
						1
2	3	4	5	6	7	8
9	10	11	12	13	14	15
16	17	18	19	*20*	21	22
23	24	25	26	27	28	29

March
Su	Mo	Tu	We	Th	Fr	Sa
1	2	3	4	5	6	7
8	9	10	11	12	13	14
15	16	17	18	19	20	21
22	23	24	25	26	27	*28*
29	30	*31*				

April
Su	Mo	Tu	We	Th	Fr	Sa
			1	2	3	4
5	6	7	8	9	10	11
12	13	14	15	16	17	18
19	20	21	22	23	24	25
26	27	28	29	30		

May
Su	Mo	Tu	We	Th	Fr	Sa
					1	2
3	4	5	6	7	8	9
10	11	12	13	14	15	16
17	18	19	20	21	22	23
24	25	26	27	28	29	*30*
31						

June
Su	Mo	Tu	We	Th	Fr	Sa
	1	2	3	4	5	6
7	8	9	10	11	12	13
14	15	16	17	18	19	20
21	22	23	24	25	*26*	27
28	29	30				

July
Su	Mo	Tu	We	Th	Fr	Sa
			1	2	3	4
5	6	7	8	9	10	11
12	13	14	15	16	17	18
19	20	21	22	23	24	25
26	27	28	29	30	31	

August
Su	Mo	Tu	We	Th	Fr	Sa
						1
2	3	4	5	6	7	8
9	10	11	12	13	14	15
16	17	18	19	20	21	22
23	24	25	26	27	28	29
30	31					

September
Su	Mo	Tu	We	Th	Fr	Sa
		1	2	3	4	5
6	7	8	9	10	11	12
13	14	*15*	16	17	18	19
20	*21*	22	23	24	25	26
27	28	29	30			

SAN DIEGO'S FIRST PADRES and "THE KID"

Game No.	Day	Date	Opponent	Score	Record	Notable Events
1	Saturday	March 28, 1936	at Los Angeles	L 7-5	0-1	George Myatt gets 1st Padres hit in 1st inning
2	Sunday	March 29, 1936	at Los Angeles	W 9-2	1-1	1st Padres win by Wally Hebert; 1st Padres HR by Vince DiMaggio
3		March 29, 1936	at Los Angeles	L 9-6	1-2	
4	Tuesday	March 31, 1936	Seattle	W 6-2	2-2	1st home game at Lane Field
5	Wednesday	April 1, 1936	Seattle	W 10-5	3-2	1st home run at Lane Field (Gyselman, Seattle)
6	Thursday	April 2, 1936	Seattle	L 7-4	3-3	
7	Friday	April 3, 1936	Seattle	L 8-4	3-4	
8	Saturday	April 4, 1936	Seattle	L 7-5	3-5	
9	Sunday	April 5, 1936	Seattle	L 7-4	3-6	1st double header at Lane Field
10		April 5, 1936	Seattle	L 2-1	3-7	
11	Tuesday	April 7, 1936	San Francisco	W 2-1	4-7	
12	Wednesday	April 8, 1936	San Francisco	L 5-2	4-8	
13	Thursday	April 9, 1936	San Francisco	L 7-6	4-9	
14	Friday	April 10, 1936	San Francisco	L 6-3	4-10	Ray Jacobs hits 1st Padres home run at Lane Field
15	Saturday	April 11, 1936	San Francisco	W 23-4	5-10	
16	Sunday	April 12, 1936	San Francisco	W 6-5	6-10	
17		April 12, 1936	San Francisco	W 3-2	7-10	
18	Tuesday	April 14, 1936	at Oakland	W 3-2	8-10	Manny Salvo arrives
19	Wednesday	April 15, 1936	at Oakland	L 2-0	8-11	
20	Thursday	April 16, 1936	at Oakland	L 6-2	8-12	
21	Friday	April 17, 1936	at Oakland	L 6-5	8-13	
22	Saturday	April 18, 1936	at Oakland	W 7-2	9-13	
23	Sunday	April 19, 1936	at Oakland	L 6-2	9-14	
24		April 19, 1936	at Oakland	L 7-1	9-15	
25	Tuesday	April 21, 1936	at Seattle	L 5-4	9-16	
26	Wednesday	April 22, 1936	at Seattle	W 12-5	10-16	
27	Thursday	April 23, 1936	at Seattle	W 4-3	11-16	
28	Friday	April 24, 1936	at Seattle	L 7-1	11-17	
29	Saturday	April 25, 1936	at Seattle	W 4-1	12-17	
30	Sunday	April 26, 1936	at Seattle	L 13-1	12-18	
31		April 26, 1936	at Seattle	L 5-2	12-19	
32	Tuesday	April 28, 1936	at Portland	L 11-4	12-20	
33	Wednesday	April 29, 1936	at Portland	W 10-3	13-20	
34	Thursday	April 30, 1936	at Portland	W 6-4	14-20	
35	Friday	May 1, 1936	at Portland	L 1-0	14-21	
36	Saturday	May 2, 1936	at Portland	W 15-4	15-21	
	Sunday	May 3, 1936	at Portland	Rain		Only rain out during 1936
		May 3, 1936	at Portland	Rain		
37	Tuesday	May 5, 1936	at Missions	L 2-0	15-22	1st triple play against Padres
38	Wednesday	May 6, 1936	at Missions	W 7-0	16-22	
39	Thursday	May 7, 1936	at Missions	W 4-0	17-22	
40	Friday	May 8, 1936	Missions	W 5-4	18-22	1st Padres triple play
41	Saturday	May 9, 1936	Missions	W 11-3	19-22	
42	Sunday	May 10, 1936	Missions	L 4-2	19-23	
43		May 10, 1936	Missions	W 5-4	20-23	
44	Tuesday	May 12, 1936	Portland	W 6-5	21-23	
45	Wednesday	May 13, 1936	Portland	L 3-2	21-24	
46	Thursday	May 14, 1936	Portland	L 5-0	21-25	
47	Friday	May 15, 1936	Portland	W 2-0	22-25	
48	Saturday	May 16, 1936	Portland	W 3-2	23-25	
49	Sunday	May 17, 1936	Portland	L 4-3	23-26	Attendance record set with 11,000 fans
50		May 17, 1936	Portland	W 3-1	24-26	

(continued on next page)

APPENDIX D—KEY DATES AND GAME-BY-GAME RECORD

(continued from previous page)

Game No.	Day	Date	Opponent	Score	Record	Notable Events
51	Tuesday	May 19, 1936	at Sacramento	L 6-3	24-27	
52	Wednesday	May 20, 1936	at Sacramento	L 2-1	24-28	
53	Thursday	May 21, 1936	at Sacramento	W 9-6	25-28	
54	Friday	May 22, 1936	at Sacramento	W 11-3	26-28	
55	Saturday	May 23, 1936	at Sacramento	W 5-0	27-28	
56	Sunday	May 24, 1936	at Sacramento	W 7-2	28-28	
57		May 24, 1936	at Sacramento	L 1-0	28-29	
58	Tuesday	May 26, 1936	San Francisco	W 9-3	29-29	
59	Wednesday	May 27, 1936	San Francisco	W 7-6	30-29	
60	Thursday	May 28, 1936	San Francisco	L 4-3	30-30	
61	Friday	May 29, 1936	San Francisco	L 12-0	30-31	
62	Saturday	May 30, 1936	San Francisco	W 5-3	31-31	
63		May 30, 1936	San Francisco	L 12-7	31-32	
64	Sunday	May 31, 1936	San Francisco	L 5-3	31-33	
65		May 31, 1936	San Francisco	L 5-2	31-34	
66	Tuesday	June 2, 1936	Los Angeles	L 5-4	31-35	
67	Wednesday	June 3, 1936	Los Angeles	W 5-1	32-35	
68	Thursday	June 4, 1936	Los Angeles	L 11-2	32-36	
69	Friday	June 5, 1936	Los Angeles	L 8-7	32-37	
70	Saturday	June 6, 1936	Los Angeles	L 5-2	32-38	
71	Sunday	June 7, 1936	Los Angeles	L 4-2	32-39	
72		June 7, 1936	Los Angeles	W 7-2	33-39	
73	Tuesday	June 9, 1936	at San Francisco	W 7-3	34-39	
74	Wednesday	June 10, 1936	at San Francisco	W 8-3	35-39	
75	Thursday	June 11, 1936	at San Francisco	W 5-4	36-39	
76	Friday	June 12, 1936	at San Francisco	L 15-2	36-40	Ed Wells traded for Howard Craghead
77	Saturday	June 13, 1936	at San Francisco	W 6-1	37-40	
78	Sunday	June 14, 1936	at San Francisco	L 7-3	37-41	
79		June 14, 1936	at San Francisco	L 9-3	37-42	
80	Tuesday	June 16, 1936	Oakland	W 16-0	38-42	
81	Wednesday	June 17, 1936	Oakland	W 5-3	39-42	
82	Thursday	June 18, 1936	Oakland	W 6-3	40-42	
83	Friday	June 19, 1936	Oakland	W 1-0	41-42	
84	Saturday	June 20, 1936	Oakland	L 4-2	41-43	
85	Sunday	June 21, 1936	Oakland	W 20-4	42-43	
86		June 21, 1936	Oakland	W 3-2	43-43	
87	Tuesday	June 23, 1936	Sacramento	W 10-4	44-43	
88	Wednesday	June 24, 1936	Sacramento	L 5-2	44-44	
89	Thursday	June 25, 1936	Sacramento	L 6-1	44-45	
90	Friday	June 26, 1936	Sacramento	W 3-2	45-45	
91	Saturday	June 27, 1936	Sacramento	W 7-6	46-45	Ted Williams 1st at bat, as pinch hitter, strikes out
92	Sunday	June 28, 1936	Sacramento	W 14-7	47-45	
93		June 28, 1936	Sacramento	L 4-3	47-46	
94	Tuesday	June 30, 1936	at Los Angeles	L 9-5	47-47	
95	Wednesday	July 1, 1936	at Los Angeles	W 2-0	48-47	
96	Thursday	July 2, 1936	at Los Angeles	L 6-1	48-48	
97	Friday	July 3, 1936	at Los Angeles	L 14-9	48-49	Ted Williams pitches in relief; gets 1st hit as pro
98	Saturday	July 4, 1936	at Los Angeles	L 4-3	48-50	
99		July 4, 1936	at Los Angeles	L 4-3	48-51	Ted Williams gets 1st extra base hit as pro
100	Sunday	July 5, 1936	at Los Angeles	L 3-1	48-52	
101		July 5, 1936	at Los Angeles	L 4-3	48-53	

(continued on next page)

SAN DIEGO'S FIRST PADRES and "THE KID"

(continued from previous page)

Game No.	Day	Date	Opponent	Score	Record	Notable Events
102	Tuesday	July 7, 1936	at Oakland	L 2-0	48-54	
103	Wednesday	July 8, 1936	at Oakland	W 1-0	49-54	
104	Thursday	July 9, 1936	at Oakland	L 1-0	49-55	
105	Friday	July 10, 1936	at Oakland	W 1-0	50-55	
106	Saturday	July 11, 1936	at Oakland	W 7-1	51-55	
107	Sunday	July 12, 1936	at Oakland	W 3-2	52-55	
108		July 12, 1936	at Oakland	W 1-0	53-55	
109	Tuesday	July 14, 1936	Seattle	W 2-0	54-55	
110	Wednesday	July 15, 1936	Seattle	L 2-1	54-56	
111	Thursday	July 16, 1936	Seattle	L 3-2	54-57	
112	Friday	July 17, 1936	Portland	L 4-2	54-58	
113	Saturday	July 18, 1936	Portland	W 3-1	55-58	
114	Sunday	July 19, 1936	Portland	W 7-2	56-58	
115		July 19, 1936	Portland	L 6-4	56-59	
116	Tuesday	July 21, 1936	Missions	W 5-4	57-59	
117	Wednesday	July 22, 1936	Missions	L 3-1	57-60	
118	Thursday	July 23, 1936	Missions	L 6-5	57-61	
119	Friday	July 24, 1936	Missions	W 4-3	58-61	
120	Saturday	July 25, 1936	Missions	W 5-2	59-61	
121	Sunday	July 26, 1936	Missions	L 4-1	59-62	
122		July 26, 1936	Missions	W 3-1	60-62	
123	Tuesday	July 28, 1936	Los Angeles	W 2-0	61-62	Three Angels "tossed"
124	Wednesday	July 29, 1936	Los Angeles	W 5-1	62-62	
125	Thursday	July 30, 1936	Los Angeles	L 10-5	62-63	1st home night game
126	Friday	July 31, 1936	Los Angeles	W 2-0	63-63	"Spanky Day" (kids admitted free)
127	Saturday	August 1, 1936	Los Angeles	W 4-3	64-63	
128	Sunday	August 2, 1936	Los Angeles	W 3-2	65-63	
129		August 2, 1936	Los Angeles	W 5-2	66-63	
130	Tuesday	August 4, 1936	at Seattle	W 7-4	67-63	
131	Wednesday	August 5, 1936	at Seattle	W 4-1	68-63	
132	Thursday	August 6, 1936	at Seattle	W 5-3	69-63	"Ward Night" (in honor of Dick Ward)
133	Friday	August 7, 1936	at Portland	L 3-2	69-64	
134		August 7, 1936	at Portland	W 10-0	70-64	
135	Saturday	August 8, 1936	at Portland	L 9-6	70-65	Boston Red Sox scout Eddie Collins in attendance for the four weekend games
136		August 8, 1936	at Portland	L 8-1	70-66	
137	Sunday	August 9, 1936	at Portland	W 4-1	71-66	
138		August 9, 1936	at Portland	W 4-1	72-66	
139	Tuesday	August 11, 1936	at Missions	W 2-0	73-66	
140	Wednesday	August 12, 1936	at Missions	L 5-1	73-67	
141	Thursday	August 13, 1936	at Missions	W 10-9	74-67	
142	Friday	August 14, 1936	at Missions	W 5-1	75-67	
143	Saturday	August 15, 1936	at Missions	W 15-11	76-67	
144	Sunday	August 16, 1936	at Missions	L 15-4	76-68	
145		August 16, 1936	at Missions	L 6-2	76-69	
146	Tuesday	August 18, 1936	at Sacramento	W 7-6	77-69	
147	Wednesday	August 19, 1936	at Sacramento	L 10-8	77-70	
148	Thursday	August 20, 1936	at Sacramento	W 6-1	78-70	
149	Friday	August 21, 1936	at Sacramento	W 10-0	79-70	
150	Saturday	August 22, 1936	at Sacramento	L 4-2	79-71	
151	Sunday	August 23, 1936	at Sacramento	L 7-3	79-72	
152		August 23, 1936	at Sacramento	W 5-0	80-72	

(continued on next page)

APPENDIX D—KEY DATES AND GAME-BY-GAME RECORD

(continued from previous page)

Game No.	Day	Date	Opponent	Score	Record	Notable Events
153	Tuesday	August 25, 1936	Oakland	L 6-4	80-73	
154	Wednesday	August 26, 1936	Oakland	W 1-0	81-73	
155	Thursday	August 27, 1936	Oakland	W 3-2	82-73	George Myatt wedding at home plate
156	Friday	August 28, 1936	Oakland	W 3-2	83-73	
157	Saturday	August 29, 1936	Oakland	W 7-5	84-73	
158	Sunday	August 30, 1936	Oakland	L 9-1	84-74	
159		August 30, 1936	Oakland	L 4-3	84-75	32,199 attend series; largest crowd in 1936 for PCL
160	Tuesday	September 1, 1936	Sacramento	W 14-3	85-75	Ivey Shiver leaves on 8/31 for football coaching position
161	Wednesday	September 2, 1936	Sacramento	W 11-1	86-75	
162	Thursday	September 3, 1936	Sacramento	L 1-0	86-76	
163	Friday	September 4, 1936	Sacramento	W 13-1	87-76	
164	Saturday	September 5, 1936	Sacramento	W 10-3	88-76	Cedric Durst receives award as most popular Padre
165	Sunday	September 6, 1936	Sacramento	W 15-3	89-76	
166		September 6, 1936	Sacramento	W 1-0	90-76	
167	Monday	September 7, 1936	Sacramento	W 5-1	91-76	
168		September 7, 1936	Sacramento	W 3-0	92-76	
169	Wednesday	September 9, 1936	at San Francisco	L 6-0	92-77	
170		September 9, 1936	at San Francisco	L 3-2	92-78	
171	Thursday	September 10, 1936	at San Francisco	W 8-2	93-78	
172	Friday	September 11, 1936	at San Francisco	L 7-5	93-79	
173	Saturday	September 12, 1936	at San Francisco	L 4-3	93-80	
174		September 12, 1936	at San Francisco	W 4-1	94-80	
175	Sunday	September 13, 1936	at San Francisco	L 5-3	94-81	
176		September 13, 1936	at San Francisco	W 4-0	95-81	

The Governor's Cup

	Day	Date	Opponent	Score	Record	Notable Events
1	Tuesday	September 15, 1936	at Oakland	L 6-3	0-1	Ted Williams hits 1st professional home run
2	Wednesday	September 16, 1936	at Oakland	L 4-3	0-2	
3	Saturday	September 19, 1936	Oakland	L 5-4	0-3	
4	Sunday	September 20, 1936	Oakland	W 7-1	1-3	
5	Monday	September 21, 1936	Oakland	L 7-6	1-4	Padres lose series 4 games to 1

SAN DIEGO'S FIRST PADRES and "THE KID"

APPENDIX E
NOTABLE 1936 PADRES: THOSE HONORED AS MEMBERS OF BASEBALL HALLS OF FAME

National Baseball Hall of Fame

Robert Pershing Doerr
Inducted in 1986

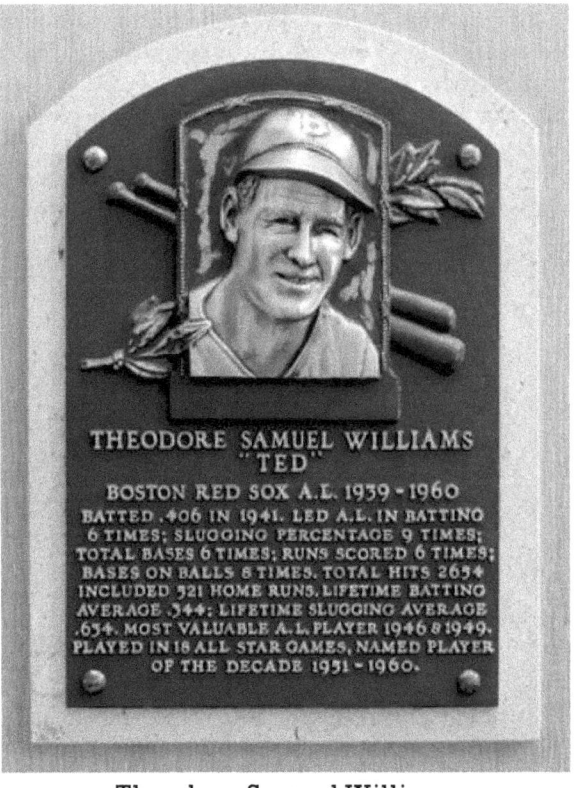

Theodore Samuel Williams
Inducted in 1966

SAN DIEGO'S FIRST PADRES and "THE KID"

Pacific Coast League (PCL) Hall of Fame*

Charles Adrian Baum

Teams:

> Los Angeles Angels (1903-05)
> Sacramento Sacts (1909-12)
> Vernon Tigers (1912)
> Venice Tigers (1913)
> San Francisco Seals (1914-19)
> Salt Lake City Bees (1919-20)

Inducted as a player. Also served as the Club Secretary for the Hollywood Stars and San Diego Padres.

Harry William Lane

Inducted as an executive. Lane was a long-time owner of the Salt Lake cum Hollywood cum San Diego Padre franchise, and PCL Vice President and power broker. Lane claimed to have been miner, explorer and Indian fighter before turning to baseball ownership, first as a partner with the Butte franchise. Lane picked up the nickname of "Hardrock" because of his early career as a miner, and because of his brusque personality and gravelly voice. In 1915, when the first Missions franchise was sold to Salt Lake City interests, Lane took a small stake in the venture. After the league suspended operations in July, 1918, for the duration of World War One, Lane bought up controlling interest in the club for a song. From 1919 through 1925, he ran one of the most exciting franchises in Coast League history. When interest in baseball waned in Salt Lake City, he moved his club to Los Angeles, where he founded the first Hollywood Stars ball club. After yearly disputes with Angel owner P. K. Wrigley over rental fees at Wrigley Field, he moved his club to San Diego, where the San Diego Padres flourished. Under his guidance his clubs discovered and developed such players as Tony Lazzeri, Lefty O'Doul, Earl Sheely, Johnny Frederick, Bobby Doerr, Ted Williams, and many others.

Edward Joseph Mulligan

Teams:

> Salt Lake Bees (1919-20)
> San Francisco Seals (1923-27)
> Mission Reds (1929-32; 1935)
> Seattle Rainiers (1932)
> Portland Beavers (1932-33)
> Oakland Oaks (1934)
> Hollywood Stars (1935)
> San Diego Padres (1936-38)

Inducted as a player. Holder of the PCL record for most clubs played for within the league with eight...Also owns the PCL record for most career sacrifice hits with 390...Won two PCL Championships with the San Francisco Seals (1923 and 1925) and one with the San Diego Padres (1937)...Played in 350 Major League games between 1915 and 1928.

---

* The descriptions for each member are verbatim from the PCL Hall of Fame pages of www.MiLB.com.

APPENDIX E—NOTABLE 1936 PADRES: THOSE HONORED AS MEMBERS OF BASEBALL HALLS OF FAME

Herman Polycarp Pillette

Teams:
- Portland Beavers (1920-21)
- Vernon Tigers (1925)
- Mission Reds (1926-33)
- Seattle Rainiers (1933-35)
- Hollywood Stars (1935)
- San Diego Padres (1936-42)
- Sacramento Solons (1943-45)

Inducted as a player. Member of the PCL Hall of Fame's inaugural class of 1943...His 23 years as pitcher in the PCL is a league record...He also holds the PCL record for number of PCL teams pitched for (7) and most career games pitched in the PCL (708)...Member of the 1937 PCL Champions, the San Diego Padres...Threw a no-hitter on October 5th, 1929 for Mission against Los Angeles in a seven-inning game...Pitched in 107 Major League games between 1917 and 1924.

Frank Victor Shellenback

Teams:
- Vernon Tigers (1920-24)
- Sacramento Senators (1925)
- Hollywood Stars (1926-35)
- San Diego Padres (1936-38)

Inducted as a player. Member of the PCL Hall of Fame's inaugural class in 1943...Named to the PCL All-Centennial Team as a pitcher for the 1903-57 era...His 296 career wins in the PCL are the most ever in league history...Also holds the league record for most innings pitched in a career with 4,184.1...Led the PCL in wins in 1929 and 1932 and in winning percentage in 1929 and 1931...Paced the league in complete games in 1927, 1931 and 1932...Holds the PCL record for most complete games in a career with 364...Was a career .273 hitter (475-for-1743) in the PCL and hit 70 home runs, including a career-high 12 in 1929...Won a PCL Championship with the 1920 Vernon Tigers, 1929 and 1930 Hollywood Stars, and 1937 San Diego Padres...Pitched in 36 Major League games between 1918 and 1919.

SAN DIEGO'S FIRST PADRES and "THE KID"

San Diego Padres (PCL) Hall of Fame

LES "COOKIE" COOK (C, TRAINER, 1936-1968)
Colorful veteran caught for San Jose Prune Pickers in old California League during 23-year career beginning in 1913; friend and confidant of owner Bill Lane, team president Spider Baum and coach Jimmie Reese; became Padres' trainer and traveling secretary (1936-1968).

CLASS OF
— 2004 —

BOBBY DOERR (2B, 1936)
Joined Hollywood Stars with George McDonald in 1934 at age 16; batted .342 for the "new" San Diego Padres in 1936; his 238 hits remain a PCL Padres' record; led league for most assists by second baseman (504) in 1936; best man at shortstop George Myatt's home plate wedding at Lane Field; played for Boston Red Sox 1937-1951; elected to Baseball Hall of Fame (1986); "retired with no enemies."

CLASS OF
— 1966 —

CEDRIC DURST (OF-MGR, 1936-1943)
Original Padre when team moved to San Diego; .297 batting average for six seasons as player and later Padres player-manager (1939-1943); compiled 437-426 record as manager with teams always picked for the bottom in league standings; played 7 seasons in the Major Leagues and was a member of the legendary 1927-1928 New York Yankees; befriended and mentored Ted Williams.

CLASS OF
— 1968 —

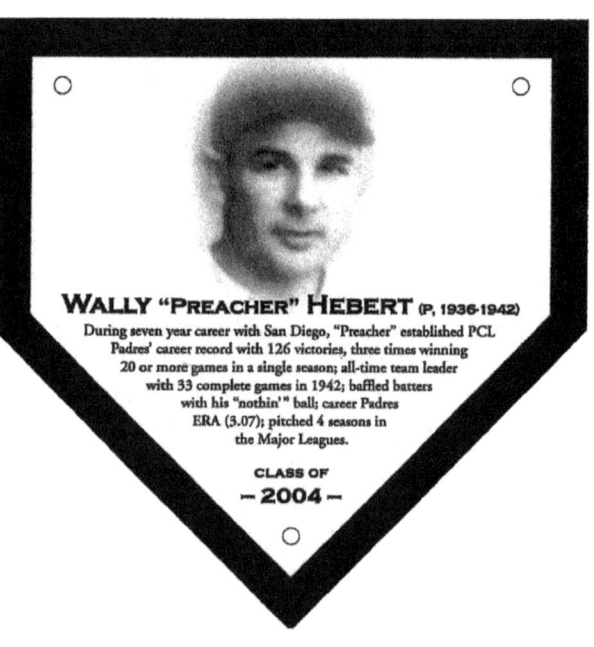

WALLY "PREACHER" HEBERT (P, 1936-1942)
During seven year career with San Diego, "Preacher" established PCL Padres' career record with 126 victories, three times winning 20 or more games in a single season; all-time team leader with 33 complete games in 1942; baffled batters with his "nothin'" ball; career Padres ERA (3.07); pitched 4 seasons in the Major Leagues.

CLASS OF
— 2004 —

178

APPENDIX E—NOTABLE 1936 PADRES: THOSE HONORED AS MEMBERS OF BASEBALL HALLS OF FAME

GEORGE McDONALD (1B, 1936-1944, 1946-1947)
"Mac" was one of the best defensive first baseman in baseball during his era; highest fielding percentage for first basemen in PCL (3 times); averaged .291 in ten seasons as everyday player with Padres; all-time PCL Padres' RBI leader with 545; legend has it he hit longest home run when a PCL ball was found inside a boxcar parked in a Los Angeles train yard (120 miles from San Diego).

CLASS OF
— 2004 —

FRANK SHELLENBACK (P-MGR, 1936-1938)
One of PCL's great right-handers (most victories - 295, most innings pitched - 4,185, most complete games - 361); last of the "legal" spitballers; respected Hollywood Stars and Padres' manager (284-247 San Diego record); led team to 1937 Playoff Championship; played on Chicago White Sox 1918-1919; elected PCL Hall of Fame (1943).

CLASS OF
— 1968 —

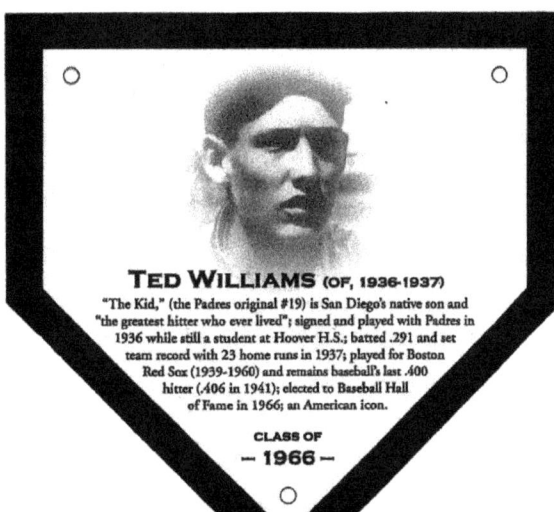

TED WILLIAMS (OF, 1936-1937)
"The Kid," (the Padres original #19) is San Diego's native son and "the greatest hitter who ever lived"; signed and played with Padres in 1936 while still a student at Hoover H.S.; batted .291 and set team record with 23 home runs in 1937; played for Boston Red Sox (1939-1960) and remains baseball's last .400 hitter (.406 in 1941); elected to Baseball Hall of Fame in 1966; an American icon.

CLASS OF
— 1966 —

BILL LANE (OWNER, 1936-1938)
Bill "Hardrock" Lane, PCL owner since 1915, moved his struggling Hollywood Stars to San Diego during the Great Depression; namesake for Lane Field, original home of the Padres; his last game was Dick Ward's 12-2/3 innings of no-hit ball on August 30, 1938; PCL Hall of Fame member.

CLASS OF
— 2004 —

EARL KELLER
"Earl the Pearl" joined the *San Diego Evening Tribune* in 1934 at age 19 writing for the newspaper for 46 years; covered Padres from 1936-1964; close friend of Ted Williams; president National and PCL Baseball Writers Association (1962).

CLASS OF
— 2004 —

SAN DIEGO'S FIRST PADRES and "THE KID"

The San Diego Hall of Champions Breitbard Hall of Fame

Ted Williams
Inducted in 1954

APPENDIX F
THE REAL AND TRUE HISTORY OF THE FRANCHISE THAT BECAME THE SAN DIEGO PADRES

When the Hollywood franchise came to San Diego in the spring of 1936, every schoolboy knew that the team had come down from Los Angeles, where the team had been playing more often than not under the name Stars. The sharper ones knew—or soon learned—that Hollywood had originally been from Salt Lake City, where the owner, Bill "Hardrock" Lane had started out. That, of course, is only partially true. The real story began some eight years prior to Salt Lake City joining the Pacific Coast League. The San Diego franchise began not in Salt Lake City, and not even in the PCL. The Padres franchise began as an expansion franchise in an outlaw league. The following is the true story of the San Diego Padres PCL franchise.

THE SACRAMENTO YEARS, 1906-1914

— 1906 —

In the spring of 1906, Sacramento was given a franchise in the outlaw California State League, which had formed in 1903, when the California League gave up its name and became the Pacific Coast League. The first three years were lean, playing mainly on Sundays in the interior of the state. Oakland and San Francisco had franchises, but were almost exclusively road teams. The schedule ran from early April to late November, generally giving the teams a 30 to 36 game schedule. The towns represented mainly consisted of the towns that had not be able to make it earlier as California League cities. Stockton and San Jose were the mainstays, but teams from Fresno, Alameda, Lodi, Vallejo and Petaluma also contributed teams during that stretch. The military base at the Presidio in San Francisco also supplied a team with a mixture of soldiers and civilians.

Nineteen hundred Six brought Alameda back into the league, along with Sacramento, which was not able to cut it in the Coast League city in 1903. The league gave the Sacramento franchise to Bill Curtin, who had been field manager of the non-California State League Stockton Distillers in 1905. Curtin stocked his club, called the Sacramento Cordovas, with former California League-PCL players, and future major leaguers like Charlie Enwright. Such well-known names as Charlie Graham, Spider Baum, Fred Brown, Jay Hughes, Phil Knell, Bobby McHale, Jimmy Shinn, and Max Muller played for them over the next several years. Future Hall-of-Famer Harry Hooper played two seasons for Sacramento, 1907 and 1908, before joining Boston in the American League. Basically, the California State League depended on released Coast Leaguers and local players on the way up. The Cordovas began the season with former major league 20-game winner Jay Hughes at the helm. The league scheduled some thirty games apiece for the teams, and all were scheduled for Sundays.

SAN DIEGO'S FIRST PADRES and "THE KID"

Opening day was April 7, 1906. The Cordovas' played their games at the former PCL park, Oak Park, in the close in Sacramento suburb. The park was also the venue for the 1898-1902 PCL/ California League.

The following is the first game account and box score of the franchise:

> **Opening Day, April 10, 1906, in the *Sacramento Bee***
>
> With one of the best crowds which ever attended a ball game in this city, and a ball game that could hardly be beaten by any of the big-league teams. The season of the California State League was opened in this city yesterday afternoon at Oak Park. The Cordovas, of Sacramento, and the Presidio team, of San Francisco, were the contesting nines.
>
> With a speech by Manager Curtin, introducing Mayor Beard, the ball game was started. Mayor Beard threw the first ball, and a weird throw it was. The Mayor truly has a glass arm. A brass band discoursed sweet music throughout the game, after having escorted the opposing teams through the city in a street car.
>
> From the opening of the game the contest was a pitchers battle between Brown, of the locals, and Rollander, the soldier pitcher. For the first few innings the teams went out in one, two, three order, and the fans settled back in their seats with the anticipation of witnessing a game which had all the ear marks of going more than the regular nine innings. Neither team was able to earn anything but ciphers in the run column on the score board until the close of the eighth inning, when Burke crossed the rubber for Sacramento with what proved to be the only run of the day.
>
> The visiting team had almost certain chances of scoring in its half of the fifth inning, when they had two men on the bases with nobody out. Gannon hit safely and advanced a station, when Brown gave Fair free transportation to first. Brown attempted to catch Gannon off second and threw the ball into the field. Gannon advanced to third and Fair to second, but both were caught a moment later by poor base running. Oswald hit to Loverich, who fielded the ball to the plate. Gannon attempted to get back to third, but was caught, and Fair was put out in attempting to return to second. Oswald was caught a moment later attempting to steal second.
>
> The lone run of the game came in the closing half of the eighth inning. Burke walked and stole second. But matters looked bad for any chances for a run, as the next two men were easy outs, one by the strike-out route and the other by a short foul which Oswald caught. Enwright came through with a hit to left field, however, and Bruke came tearing to the plate when the visiting left fielder allowed the ball to get away from him.
>
> Manager Curtin has a team that from the showing made yesterday will make a strong bid for championship honors. They play ball all the time; all of them are good fielders; and the majority of them clever batters. If they continue to play the game they did yesterday they will easily be able to hold the attendance of such crowds as were at the game yesterday. Mike Fisher's heart would have been warmed within him had he seen the file passing through the gates.

Cordovas	ab	r	bh	sb	po	a	e
McHale, 3d b	4	0	0	0	2	1	0
Enwright, rf	4	0	2	2	1	0	0
Muller, lf	4	0	0	0	1	0	0
White, cf	2	0	1	1	0	0	0
Neilsen, 2d b	3	0	1	0	2	2	0
McCarthy, ss	3	3	0	0	3	0	0
Loverich, 1st b	3	0	0	0	7	1	0
Burke, c	2	1	0	1	10	4	0
Brown, p	3	0	0	0	1	4	1
Totals	28	1	4	4	27	12	1

Presidios	ab	r	bh	sb	po	a	e
Cameron, cf	4	0	1	0	1	1	0
Gannon, 3d b	4	0	0	0	1	1	0
Fair, ss	3	0	1	1	2	1	2
French, rf	3	0	1	0	1	0	0
Cusack, 2d b	2	0	0	0	2	0	0
Oswald, c	3	0	0	0	10	0	0
Rice, lf	3	0	0	0	1	0	1
Hunter, 1st b	2	0	0	1	5	0	0
Rollander, p	3	0	0	0	0	4	3
Totals	27	0	3	2	23*	7	3

*Brown bunted third strike.

Opening Day, April 10, 1906, Sacramento, California

By Innings	1	2	3	4	5	6	7	8	9	
Presidio	0	0	0	0	0	0	0	0	0	--0
Cordovas	0	0	0	0	0	0	0	1	0	--1

Summary: First base on called balls— Off Brown 1, off Rollander 2. Left on bases— Presidio 1, Cordova 4. Struck out— By Brown 9, by Rollander 6. Hit by pitcher— Hunter. Double play— Loverich to Burke to McHale to Neilson. Time of game— 1:25. Umpire— Walter Henley. Scorer— H. J. McClatchy

APPENDIX F—THE REAL AND TRUE HISTORY OF THE FRANCHISE THAT BECAME THE SAN DIEGO PADRES

But who were these players? The starting lineup for the franchise:

- Bobby "Rabbit" McHale was born in Michigan Bluff, California on February 25, 1872. He was a longtime infielder on various Sacramento teams, in the California League, California State League and PCL, from 1898 through 1909. He got an eleven-game cup of coffee with Washington in the National League in 1898.
- Charlie Enwright was a Sacramento product, born in the city on October 6, 1887. He played briefly for the St. Louis Cardinals in 1909. He played primarily for teams in Sacramento in the California State League.
- Max Muller began his career in 1898, as best we can determine, with Stockton. He played several years with them in the California League. He next moved north to the Pacific Northwest League, then joined Seattle in the PCL for the 1905 season. He also played with Sacramento in 1908.
- White. No information on this player, probably a local sandlotter.
- Neilson. No information on this player, probably a local sandlotter.
- Joe McCarthy. "Little Joe," as he was called, had a career that began, probably, in the Examiner Tournament in 1897 for all the best clubs in the state of California. He played from the Pacific Northwest on down to California's Central Valley. He played in the PCL in 1903. His career probably ended around 1909.
- Joe Loverich. Played for the Sacramento franchise in the California State League in 1904, and was probably local talent
- Jimmy Burke played for Oakland in the PCL, but began his career in Sacramento with the previous franchise in the State League. He played for Sacramento in 1907, and then shows up in the new Sacramento franchise in the Cal State League after the 1908 franchise bolted the league for the PCL.
- Fred Brown may have been the pitcher who got into a California League game with Sacramento in 1901. We are sure that he is the pitcher who began his Coast League career with Sacramento in 1903. In 1904, he stayed in the capital, and pitched for the State League team. He rejoined his original PCL team, which had transferred to Tacoma, in 1905. He joined the 1906 State League team, and continued with them into the PCL. He would up his career in 1910 with the PCL Sacramento Senators.

Despite all of the great expectations generated by their first success, the team did not do as well as hoped, and the manager was changed on July 21. Charlie Graham took over the reins. Graham, who would later become the long-time part owner of the San Francisco Seals, returned to the West Coast from Boston, where he caught some 30 games with the last place Boston Pilgrims. Graham, from Santa Clara, began his pro career as a catcher with San Francisco, a California League club in 1901. In 1902, he joined Sacramento, and at midseason owner Mike Fisher named him manager, or captain in terminology of the time. He stayed with the franchise when it deserted Sacramento for Tacoma. He was drafted by Boston after the 1905 season. He hated the East, and returned to the West Coast right after the quake, and decided to remain at home. Graham righted the team almost immediately, and by the end of the season had become part owner of the franchise.

The 1906 season was interrupted by the Earthquake in San Francisco on May 17th, but the California State League continued their schedule without break. The first two years, 1903 and 1904, were shaky; the league stabilized in 1905 and 1906; and then they made their big push in 1907.

— 1907 —

With the Pacific Coast League weakened by the 1906 Earthquake, its directors decided to drop two teams, Seattle and Fresno, and compete as a four-team circuit for 1907, and had the same number in 1908. Even this skeleton PCL nearly went under in 1907, with the league not drawing as well as it had in the Bay Area prior to the quake, and some of its best players being snatched up by the Cal State League. An argument could be made that the 1907 and 1908 California State League had talent superior to the Coast League. And players found the money better, and every team was stocked with Coast League contract jumpers. The PCL countered by having the California State League declared an outlaw league by the National Association.

Sacramento played excellent ball those two years under the management of Graham, with a number of fine players showing up in the lineup. Hall-of-Famer Harry Hooper roamed the outfield for two years, hitting

.301 and .344. Fred Brown was the stopper with 24-6 and 23-12. The club in those two years had pitchers who would go on to win over 300 games in the minors, Spider Baum and Jimmy Whalen. Whalen went 31-8 for Sacramento in 1908. The team also changed its name from Cordovas to Senators, the name that had been used in the earlier Cal League-PCL era.

— 1908 —

While the California State League may have been the dominant league in California in 1908, the PCL had stabilized its franchises, and was poised to return to preeminence. But after the 1908 season, the two leagues made one last stab at resolving their differences. However, both leagues carved out positions unacceptable to the other—primarily over the Coast League's right to draft State Leaguers and what to do about contract jumpers—and negotiations broke down. Charlie Graham was quoted in the press as having said: "I would sooner throw up the whole thing and retire from baseball than go into Organized Baseball under any such conditions." The Coast League had been threatening to place a franchise back in Sacramento for some time, and it looked like a real fight between the two leagues would begin in earnest. Cy Moreing, the real driving force behind the league, and owner of the Stockton franchise, planned to invade the Bay Area and take the PCL on in Oakland. Graham made one last stab at a compromise, but league directors sided with Moreing who wanted an all-out war with the PCL. When Graham and his partner, Bill Curtin, saw that the gap between the two leagues could not be breached, they took up a standing offer by Coast League to join that circuit. The Coast League also had an implied threat in that they would place a club in Sacramento if Graham and Curtin didn't jump. Thus, an outlaw league team became, overnight, a stalwart in the Pacific Coast League.

— 1909 —

The newly created Vernon team would join Sacramento in the 1909 PCL. In an effort to confront the Coast League's power play, the Cal State league placed a club in San Francisco and Oakland, but couldn't compete with the more established league, so on July 19, the San Francisco club was transferred to Sacramento, where they didn't do much better, and in 1910—when the California State League was in Organized baseball—the club became the farm club of the PCL club.

On March 30, 1909, the Sacramento Senators faced the Vernon Tigers at Oak Park in Sacramento in what was the first Coast League game for both clubs. Sacramento won their first game in the PCL, besting the Tigers by a 6-2 score. Fred Brown, as he had done in the franchise's first game in 1906, pitched a complete game win. The lineup for the Senators was very nearly the same as had taken the field in the Cal State League. Future Hall-of-Famer Harry Hooper had been sold over the winter to the Boston American League team, but had been replaced by future Black Sox, Chic Gandil. The young Gandil hit a credible .282, and Jimmy Whalen won 23 games, but the Sacs finished 4th in the league (97-107 .475). They were not one of the dominant teams—as they had been in the Cal State League—but they showed they could compete in a league considered far superior to the one they had come from. Of course, in Sacramento, winning on the field was what counted for the fans, no matter what league, and the turnstiles didn't click as much as had been anticipated, and the club found itself facing a $5,000 deficit. Charlie Graham, by then the owner of an automobile agency in Sacramento, tried to persuade other businessmen to help the club financially. But when that failed, Graham turned to John Irving Taylor, owner of the Boston American League team, and scion of the *Boston Globe* fortune. Taylor had been looking for a minor-league team in the East where he could send his prospects, but Graham persuaded him to buy controlling interest in the team. Taylor bought 12,000 of the 25,000 shares in the club, with Bill Curtin and Charlie Graham retaining 4,000. The latter two would control the day-to-day operations, Graham as manager, and Curtin taking care of off-the-field matters.

— 1910 —

The infusion of Taylor cash, and a number of Red Sox players did not help, as the Senators finished in the cellar in 1910. It did, however, eliminate the debt incurred by Graham and Curtin. The truth be told injuries played a major role in the poor team showing that season.

— 1911 —

In 1911 the team bounced back on the field, but they still didn't draw enough fans to break even. Patsy O'Rourke was brought in to manage the club, as Graham had to spend ever more time at his automobile dealership, and Curtin to his business interests. But O'Rourke had a running feud with players on other clubs,

APPENDIX F—THE REAL AND TRUE HISTORY OF THE FRANCHISE THAT BECAME THE SAN DIEGO PADRES

and his own team. Then he had a fight with popular player Jimmy Lewis, and that brought everything to a head. The climate on the club got so bad that newspapers began a crusade to get O'Rourke fired, which didn't happen, but on June 25 he handed in his resignation. Graham and Curtin installed veteran Deacon Van Buren, who had been in the PCL since 1903, as manager, O'Rourke remaining with the club as a player. When O'Rourke had enough, the club was in 4th place (out of six teams), but the move to Van Buren didn't help at all, and the club wound up dead last in the league. And Graham and Curtin gave less than their full attention to the team after having recouped all their losses when Taylor became majority owner. Then John I. Taylor unloaded his stock in the club, selling out to Jack Atkin of Spokane. Jack Who they asked in Sacramento, but after the season, Atkin—like many a new owner—came on like gangbusters. He spent money like it was going out of style, and managed to snag highly respected manager, Harry Wolverton, paying him more than he had made leading the Yankees. The team was rechristened the Wolves in honor of their new manager. One problem the club could not solve was to find somebody to play the hot corner.

— 1912 —

Atkin's spreading around of so much cash did succeed in making the club competitive on the field, but the club still failed to draw fans during the week, and, all told, was probably a losing proposition for Atkin. By mid-season, rumors began to spread that Wolverton and a couple of Sacramento insurance men wanted to buy the club. Aiken himself let it be known that he would be interested in selling the club to Sacramento interests. The rumors turned out to be true, but the deal did not conclude until the season ended.

— 1913 —

The Wolves had finished second to the Portland Beavers in 1913, and the new owners, who turned out to be manager Harry Wolverton and Sacramento insurance man Lloyd Jacobs, believed they could improve upon what Jack Aiken started.

— 1914 —

After spending all their cash and credit on buying Atkin's shares, the majority owners had nothing left over for player acquisitions. The club started out poorly, and the club went downhill from there. The Wolves stumbled out of the gate in fourth place, and then settled into fifth, where it remained for the rest of the summer. First, fans didn't come up to see the team during the week, and by the end of August, hardly anybody came out to see the Wolves on the weekends. It got so bad that the league demanded something be done. Opponents lost so much money when playing at Sacramento that they no longer wanted to travel there. First, it was announced that the club would be a traveling team, but the club would still be known as "Sacramento" for the balance of the season. That was on September 2. On Monday, September 6, which was supposed to be a Sacramento home game, the Portland Beavers met the Wolves at Freeman Park in Oakland, then the Venice Tigers came into play the newly crowned Missions in Oakland, though the club didn't become officially the Mission Wolves until September 14. The club played its home games at Freeman's Park in Oakland and Ewing Park in San Francisco.

When league President Alan Baum (brother of the famous pitcher and later Padres club secretary) queried the other owners about what was to be done with the franchise, Wolverton and Jacobs negotiated a lease agreement for Rec Park, where the Seal and Oaks had played until Ewing Filed opened at the beginning of the 1914 season.

While the league struggled with what to do with the bankrupt Missions, other changes were happening in the league. Hen Berry, owner of Los Angeles Angels, bought the San Francisco franchise from Cal Ewing, who had run into financial problems because nobody showed up at his new ballpark, Ewing Field, because it was in what the papers called the "cold zone." Ewing had negotiated a deal with a fight promoter, but the league and his partner Frank M. Ish did not approve of the sale, so Ewing told Ish to sell the club, which he promptly did by selling the team to Berry. Hen Berry sold out his interest in the Los Angeles club to one of his partners, Tom Darmondy.

That solved one of the problems, but he Missions problem lingered. The club had declared that Wolverton and Jacobs had not met their "financial responsibilities" and formally took over the club. Both Wolverton and Jacobs yelled loudly and threatened to sue. Wolverton said he lost all his money, probably over $20,000.

At the PCL Winter Meeting in November, the league announced that the Missions would be sold to the highest bidder. San Jose, Seattle, San Diego and Sacramento submitted formal bids of $25,000 at that time, but, almost immediately, San Jose was deemed too small a city to host a franchise, and Seattle too far away (the league always worried about transportation costs), leaving San Diego and a newly constituted group in Sacramento as the leading bidders. According to press accounts, the San Diego bid was rejected not much later because of some shady characters who formed part of their group.

With only Sacramento left, the press speculated that the club would more than likely go back to the capital city, but under new management. The second choice, according to press accounts, would be to leave the club in the Bay Area.

Then Salt Lake City put in a formal bid. A group was put together by E.(ward) A. Vanderventer, editor of the *Salt Lake City Tribune*. (Bill Lane would later claim that it was he who put the group together.) Vanderventer also hired Cliff Blankenship, whose career in the Coast League began as a player in 1904, and who knew everybody in the league, to spearhead the lobbying effort. Vanderventer sent Blankenship to the Winter Meetings in New Orleans in early December, where he pressed the Salt Lake bid with Allan T. Baum, the President of the PCL, and met with other club representatives. Blankenship was so successful, that on the way back to the coast, Allan Baum made a stop in Salt Lake City to meet with the Salt Lake City group.

It appeared that President Baum had been sold on Salt Lake City coming into the league after his stop in the city, league owners worried about the travel expenses on train trips from California to Utah. Vanderventer did two things that put Salt Lake City over the top: (1) He sent a $20,000 deposit to the league (the other bidders only sent promises; (2) Formally guaranteed every club $2,000 minimum on every series they played in Salt Lake (the last series in Sacramento the year prior generated $26 for the visiting team).

At a special meeting on December 18, the league officially awarded the franchise to Salt Lake. Concurrent to that, Hen Berry announced the signing of Harry Wolverton to manage the San Francisco Seal, and thus splitting the old owners. (Several years later, Lloyd Jacobs widow would sue the league, but the suit went nowhere, or was settled silently.)

After the announcement from the league, the club established a temporary board of directors: George Wasson, President; Reverend Elmer Goshen, Vice President, and Bill Lane as Secretary. Goshen and Wasson would remain stockholders in the club until the Lane Estate sold the club in 1944.

THE SALT LAKE CITY YEARS, 1915-1925

— 1915 —

On January 15, 1915, the board met officially a permanent Board of Directors was elected. The biggest shareholder, lumberman Frank Murphy became president, with Goshen retained as V.P., and Wasson and Lane remaining on the board as directors.

The first thing Murphy did was hire Bill O'Connor, who had run the Salt Lake club in Union Association the year before, as business manager and "assistant secretary" of the club. O'Connor ran the club until he resigned in after the 1916 season. Blankenship became "officially" field manager of the club.

The first thing new business manager Bill O'Connor did was head off to make acquaintance of the other owners and business managers in the Coast League, while Cliff Blankenship went about signing players for the coming season.

On his return, O'Connor spent most of his time looking for a place to play, as the old Majestic Park was deemed unsuitable for a Coast League franchise. On February 1, O'Connor announced that the club had secured a corner area of Bonneville Amusement Park for the ballpark, which would also be called Bonneville Park. Meanwhile, the *Salt Lake City Telegram* newspaper ran a "name that club" contest, with "Bees" being announced as the winning nickname of February 5.

Under Bill O'Connor and Manager Cliff Blankenship, the 1915 club finished in second place, only five games out of first place. The club proved to be a huge success financially as well. No data were published by the league on attendance, but during the first three years, it was well-reported that the club declared a dividend paid out to all subscribers, some 500 shareholders in all.

Another thing that helped with attendance: Nearly three times as many home runs were hit at Bonneville Park, and batting averages were some 50 points higher than the league average.

At one point during 1915, Bill Lane was appointed temporary secretary of the club, but Lawrence Green was shortly named to the permanent position.

APPENDIX F—THE REAL AND TRUE HISTORY OF THE FRANCHISE THAT BECAME THE SAN DIEGO PADRES

— 1916 —

The 1916 season had the club falling back to third place, three games above .500. And there was turmoil, though attendance continued to be strong. Manager Blankenship had trouble controlling his club, and was being undermined by star outfielder Buddy Ryan. On September 5, with the club at 71-70 Cliff Blankenship abruptly resigned, saying that he couldn't take any more backbiting.

Even though the press speculated that Wahoo Sam Crawford would be offered the job, the managerial post went to none other than Buddy Ryan, who had led the player revolt. Quickly, Ryan found that he couldn't control the club any better than Blankenship, with team going at a .371 clip before he gave up the reins on October 9, at which time he said he would continue as a player only. On the tenth of October, Bill Bernhard, the former American League pitcher, met with club directors, and was given a contract for the rest of the season, and for 1917. Bernhard managed the 1914 Salt Lake City club in the Union Association, and had not managed for two seasons, working as a pitching coach and umpire in the Southern Association. The club immediately responded with a 15-4 record for the rest of the 1916 season, which moved the club from fifth to third by the season finale.

Then, just as the club seemed to have righted itself, the business manager Bill O'Connor resigned. His letter of December 20 to President Frank Murphy stated that he formed a group to take over the Bonneville Amusement Park, which included the grounds of the ballpark, and would have to concentrate on that business.

— 1917 —

Frank Murphy worked over the Christmas holidays to find a replacement for O'Connor, and at the January 19, 1917, directors meeting Murphy announced that he had offered the business manager job to William P. "Jack" Cook. Additionally, Cook planned to invest $10,000 in the club. At the time of the offer, Cook was business manager and part owner of the Oakland Oaks, and was considered one of the best in the league. Previously, he had been Alameda County Clerk.

The club made it through the 1917 season, again turning a profit with another third-place finish. The club had three 20-game winners, and third baseman Morrie Rath led the league in hitting with a .341 batting average.

Just prior to the November club's directors meeting, Frank S. Murphy resigned as president of the club, citing his other business interests as compelling his fulltime attention. At that meeting, Bill Lane became president of the club. In short order, he fired manager Bill Bernhard and hired Walt McCredie. McCredie had managed the Portland franchise since 1905 when his uncle bought the floundering club. Judge McCredie—along with the league—that club and the league would be better served by Portland moving into Northwestern League for the duration of the war. Transportation costs and availability caused the club switch leagues. The nephew wanted to remain in the Coast League as a manager.

On December 18, Lane sent out a telegram from the PCL meeting in Los Angeles: "Tell the fans that we have signed for the 1918 season the best manager in minor league baseball—Walter H. McCredie."

— 1918 —

The 1918 season was a financial disaster for the PCL, forcing the league to suspend operations on July 14. The "Work or Fight" order from Washington was the stated reason for closing up shop, but attendance was way down, as a great number of fans felt it unpatriotic to attend baseball games while men went off to war. The Salt Lake club again finished third, this time winning their last game of the season 5-3 to wind up with 49-49 win-loss record.

Off the field, the club lost money for the first time since the club moved to Salt Lake City. Every year prior the club had paid out dividends of some 25% of the original stock value over the first three years of the franchise. Two days after the close of the season, the club announced an assessment $8 a share to stockholders. The league announced that it had suspended operations for the duration of the war, and nobody knew when that might occur. There was much speculation that what would become known as World War One could last for years. A number of stockholders in the club (some 500 people owned shares) felt that they would be throwing good money after bad. The club needed something like $14,000 to right its books, which included improvement to the ballpark. When those balked, Bill Lane picked up the shares of those stockholders over the course of the next few months. (Lane once stated that he got control of the club in 1919, which seems correct. He probably began picking up shares in 1918, and gained control in early 1919. Lane also said that he had put up the $40,000 needed to keep the club going, not the $14,000 in the statement issued by the club after the season closed.)

— 1919 —

With the war over, the league decided to expand to eight teams for 1919, bringing in Seattle, and bringing back Judge McCredie's Portland franchise, which led manager Walt McCredie to resign and head back to managing his uncle's club.

President Lane wasted no time in hiring St. Louis Cardinal scout Eddie Herr–– reputed to be one of the best minds in baseball–– to take the reins of the Bees. The club did no better than before, finishing once again in third place. Bill Lane was less than satisfied with the result, and fired Herr, replacing him with Ernie Johnson as player-manager.

In Lane's first year, there were two scandals, one which only erupted the following season.

On the last day of the season, it was speculated that the Oakland Oaks threw the batting title to Bill Rumler, who had been battling Sam Crawford of the Los Angeles Angels nearly all season. Rumler got four hits in the last game of the season, three of which were bunts. This was, as a lot of the league press stated, reminiscent of the Lajoie-Cobb shenanigans in 1910. When the unofficial stats came out the next day, Crawford was still the league leader in batting. Only when the official stats came out later did Rumler take the title. Nevertheless, historians consider the title suspect because of the season-ending game.

In the wake of the game, the beat reporter who covered the game for the *San Francisco Chronicle* analyzed all of Rumler's hits. On one line drive, Sammy Bohne made no attempt to catch the ball. The other three hits were bunts. The reporter stated that one was not fielded quickly, but even if it had, there was only a 50-50 chance that Rumler could have been thrown out. The other two bunts were unplayable. Therefore, if we take two hits away from Rumler, he would have still won the title.

The other scandal–– much bigger–– did blow up until mid-season the following year. William H. McCarthy, a prominent San Francisco lawyer, was appointed league president to replace Allan T. Baum after the 1919 season, and he went on a rampage against gambling throughout the Coast League, which led to the banning and suspension of a number of players, including Bill Rumler, who was suspended for five years.

The scandal began when Charlie Graham of the San Francisco Seals discovered that two of his pitchers, Tom Seaton and Casey Smith, had thrown games at the behest of gamblers. Graham released both. Then Graham and his partner went to McCarthy and asked him to clean up the gambling mess in the PCL. McCarthy hired detectives to get to the bottom of the gambling scandal.[*]

— 1920 —

Detectives caught Babe Borton of Vernon giving a check to Bill Rumler on July 27, 1920. When confronted with the evidence, Borton stated that Vernon paid a number of players on the Salt Lake City club to "lay down" so they could win the pennant, which they did. The briber named six Salt Lake players, and a number of players around the league when interviewed by McCarthy. In the end, Harl Maggert (who had already quit the club over a disputed fine) and Gene Dale (no longer with the club) were expelled from the league (and baseball) for life. And because the evidence against Rumler was ambiguous he received a five-year suspension. (Rumler said the money received was a "hedge bet" that they would split the money they received for their club finishing in the pennant race, which was common at all levels of baseball back then. Borton admitted that later on.)

Business manager Jack Cook, and president Bill Lane supported his outfielder 100 percent, and with the suspension of Rumler (who hit .459 against Vernon it the last two series when the laying down was supposed to have taken place), the Salt Lake City club lost a sale of Rumler to the Boston Braves for a reported $65,000. With that President McCarthy became the mortal enemy of Bill Lane, and would help pave the way for McCarthy's removal several years later. McCarthy, in 1923, would say that Jack Cook was behind the attempt to oust him. That attempt failed.

---

[*] Gambling on baseball in California was anything but new. Rampant gambling was reported in the press on league games as far back as 1878 during the first season of the first league in the state. And it never stopped. There were gambling sections at every park in the Coast League, and to say it was tolerated is an understatement. As one wag put it, "Who would go to a Tuesday game between Oakland and Sacramento other than gamblers?" Even Ban Johnson, when first told about the Black Sox throwing the World Series, wasn't surprised, after all, saying, "They all came from California," meaning that they were alumni of the PCL, all except Joe Jackson, that is.

APPENDIX F—THE REAL AND TRUE HISTORY OF THE FRANCHISE THAT BECAME THE SAN DIEGO PADRES

With Rumler (hitting .348 at the time of his suspension) and Maggert (who was at .370), the club went from one percentage point behind league-leading Vernon to fifth place at the close of the season.

— 1921 —

Ernie Johnson, who was named as one of the dumpers but never proved, was replaced as manager the following season by Gavvy Cravath, who was replaced by catcher Butch Byer late in the season. The club finished in seventh place.

— 1922-1924 —

Outfielder Duffy Lewis was named manager, and reeled off three straight fifth-place finishes. In 1924, Lewis won the PCL batting title with a .392 BA, barely edging out teammate Lefty O'Doul by .0002 for the championship. Duffy Lewis, after the close of the season, would be sent to Portland, and another teammate, Ossie Vitt, named manager.

Off the field, Jack Cook became ill in 1923, an illness (probably cancer), that would lead to his death in June 1924. Jack Cook hired Spider Baum as a coach of the club and his assistant in January 1924; he would still be with the club in 1936, and beyond, winding up as president of the club. Les Cook, a catcher, joined the club that season, and would likewise remain with the club all the way to San Diego. O'Doul would come back to take the club to its only pennant in 1954.

— 1925 —

With Lane and Baum fully in charge of the club for the 1925 season, they named third baseman Ossie Vitt player-manager. The club jumped from 5th place to second. Additionally, Tony Lazzeri set the record for home runs for both the PCL (that still stands), and for Organized Baseball. There was some question about his last home run of the season, but that only came up years after the fact. None of the reporters covering the game mentioned anything about it being a bogus—or even cheap—home run. It was an inside-the-park blast, but the Sacramento park was a paradise for triples, and Lazzeri probably legged out a home run on what would have been a stand-up triple.

Also, that season Frank Shellenback joined the club. Shellenback would become the all-time leader in wins for the Pacific Coast League with 296. He would remain with the club through the 1938 season, first as a star pitcher, and later as manager and pitcher for the Padres. The pitcher was also quite a hitter, compiling a .273 BA in 19 seasons, coupled with 70 HR.

After the season, the club held its annual meeting on November 15 in Salt Lake City, where plans were discussed for the coming season, and the directors all reelected. The club showed a profit based on the sales of Lazzeri Lefty O'Doul and Bill Piercy. The big sale was that of Tony Lazzeri to the Yankees for $75,000. Nothing was mentioned about moving the club, as a matter of fact, the club discussed improvements to Bonneville Park.

At the annual PCL Winter Meeting in December, dubbed later on as the Battle of Catalina because it took place at William Wrigley's island, Wrigley and four other owners mounted a coup against PCL president William H. McCarthy. Chewing gum magnate William Wrigley, Jr. owned the Los Angeles Angels, and the Chicago Cubs, and wanted to wrest control from the Bay Area owners and their man PCL President William H. McCarthy, and install his man, L.A. Times journalist Harry Williams, and move the power base south to Los Angeles. Bill Lane supported Wrigley full heatedly, and in doing so ingratiated himself with Wrigley, or as one reporter put it: "Salt Lake and Seattle owners do just about as he says." (Years later, Lane would claim that he was behind the canning of McCarthy.

Of course, Wrigley was dead by the time he claimed Wrigley also wanted to get rid of the owner who was sharing his new digs, beer baron Ed Maier, who wound up selling the club to a Wrigley confidante, Hebert Fleishhacker. The league, in a special meeting on January 15, 1926, announced approval of the deal, the club moving to San Francisco-- and one surprise: The Salt Lake City Bees would be moving to Los Angeles to share the new park, Wrigley Field, with the Los Angeles Angels.

Four days later, the stunned reporter for the *Salt Lake City Telegraph* wrote: "H.W. Lane, president of the Hollywood Blues, erstwhile Salt Lake City Bees, arrived in Salt Lake Monday to close up his business here and to move his business interests to Los Angeles. With Secretary C. A. [Spider] Baum he hopes to have everything moved to Los Angeles, where he will make his permanent home, by February 1."

Lane was so excited to get out of Salt Lake City that he announced that he had signed a 20-year lease with William Wrigley to share the gum magnate's new park that had just opened in September of 1925.

SAN DIEGO'S FIRST PADRES and "THE KID"

THE HOLLYWOOD YEARS, 1926-1935

— 1926-1927 —

The Hollywood club was first named the Blues, then Lane thought better of that, and retained the old name the Bees. The Hollywood Bees name lasted throughout most of spring training, but at the behest of Hollywood people, the name was changed officially to Stars. As late as February 21, the *Los Angeles Times* quoted Bill Lane as saying: "I don't see any sense in changing the nickname of Bees." On March 8, the *Times* was still using "Bees" in its headlines, but four days later the *Times* started using "Stars," and the Hollywood Bees ceased to exist.

— 1928 —

Starting in 1928, the nickname "Sheiks" began to be used in the press for several years in the wake of silent movie star Rudolph Valentino's death, though still officially the "Stars."

The Stars dropped to sixth place their first year in Los Angeles, but attendance for the club increased from 137,012 the year prior in Salt Lake City to 212,813 at Wrigley Field. While the attendance was nice, the Angels retained all concessions at the park. That, along with Wrigley's insistence on having ladies admitted free to every game, did not sit well with the Star's owner. Lane also began a feud with the new league president, Harry A. Williams, whom he supported in the ousting of the old president, William McCarthy. Years later, it would also be revealed that he began not speaking to Seals managing partner Charlie Graham. That would last some nine years.

The following season, the club remained in sixth place, and attendance slipped to 164,430. Rumors ran wild that Bill Lane was going to show Ossie Vitt the gate after the club's poor showing, but nothing came of it, and the manager returned for the 1928 season.

The Sheiks rebounded in 1928, both on the field and at the box office. The Hollywood club finished second in the first half of the split season, and third in the second. The club also outdrew their landlords, the Angels for the first time that season. Yet, Bill Lane picked a fight with the Los Angeles Angels, leading to the Angels telling Lane that he should find a new place to play in 1929. What caused the Angels to break with the Stars was Lane's statement to the press that he would no longer honor Wrigley Field's Lady Days policy, which gave free entrance to women on Tuesdays, Saturdays and Sundays. Lane also said the agreement with the Angels amounted to highway robbery. Lane had always claimed that his club should share in the concessions revenue, or at least have a certain percentage on Hollywood home games.

With Lane's rebellion, the Angels sent the sent the following letter to Lane on June 13, 1928:

> *Dear Sir:*
>
> *This is formal notice that the relations between the Angel City Baseball Association and the Hollywood baseball club, as to playing on Wrigley Field will cease at the expiration of the playing season of 1928.*
>
> *We are giving this early notice so that you will be able to find a desirable location before the playing season of 1929.*
>
> *Yours respectfully,*
>
> *ANGEL CITY BASEBALL ASSOCIATION*
>
> *By J.H. Patrick, President*

President Joe Patrick, with Wrigley's full-hearted support, sent a copy of the above letter to the press, and also gave the following statement to the Los Angeles newspapers:

> *Gentlemen:*
>
> *We are inclosing [sic] a copy of a letter written this day to Mr. H.W. Lane, president of the Hollywood Baseball Club.*
>
> *There has arisen a situation between Mr. Lane and ourselves that does not seem capable of solution otherwise than as contained in the inclosed [sic] letter.*
>
> *Mr. Lane came to Los Angeles in 1926. No formal lease was made between Mr. Lane and ourselves. This arrangement was made because the future of baseball in Los Angeles at*

APPENDIX F—THE REAL AND TRUE HISTORY OF THE FRANCHISE THAT BECAME THE SAN DIEGO PADRES

that time was extremely uncertain and we wished to see what the coming years would bring forth before any hard and fast agreement was made.

Mr. Lane paid nothing on account of his removal from Salt Lake City to Los Angeles. Even the payment made to the Oakland Baseball Club for their permission to remove the Vernon Club to San Francisco was paid by the Angel Baseball Association, with the exception of the portion that is now being contributed by each club in the league.

Mr. Lane pays only one-half of the park expenses during the baseball season, nothing at all at any other time. His total expenses last year were approximately 10,500, of which 5350 was for advertising. In other words, Mr. Lane's park expenses for the year 1927 were $7000. Mr. Lane was paid for preseason training trip games over $6000. This reduces his payment to the Angels playing on Wrigley Field to a little over $1000.

Our taxes on Wrigley Field are approximately $20,000; the depreciation on investment, $24,000. (Interest on investment of 1,500,000 not considered in these figures.) Mr. Lane pays no part of these amounts.

Mr. Lane feels, even on this basis, that he has been unfairly treated and the arrangement has not been satisfactory either to Mr. Lane or ourselves.

The recent cause for disagreement between Mr. Lane and ourselves has been our policy of admitting ladies free on Tuesdays, Saturdays and Sundays. We felt that baseball was rapidly deteriorating in Los Angeles. Year after year our attendance and receipts have dropped. We wished to try every possible remedy to again bring back the Los Angeles population to baseball. We are of the opinion that our ladies' day policy has been a success. Each league team has now appeared in Los Angeles and has carried away with it a much larger check than in previous years.

We are not unmindful of the fact that the closeness of the race and broadcasting are contributing factors. We, however, believe that the main reason why more people are attending the games at Wrigley Field is ladies free.

Los Angeles is a peculiar town, the conditions here being very different from any other city in the United States. We have seventy-five miles of beaches, thousands of miles of good roads. Every family owns a "flivver," the percentage of automobiles being larger per capita in Southern California than in any other part of the United States. This is very severe competition and desperate remedies are necessary to meet it; therefore, our experiments in this direction. We are of the opinion that the results show that our policy is correct.

We are willing to pay to the league 32½ cents per lady on the aforesaid days, when the rest of the league charges for ladies.

We are not willing to assume Mr. Lane's proportion of this. We do not think this is just or equitable from the aforesaid figures. We consider that Mr. Lane is paying very little to play baseball in a plant like Wrigley Field and should assume his proportion of the expense of ladies' admissions.

This is the main cause of the termination of Mr. Lane's playing agreement in Los Angeles. We make this explication because we feel it is due to our partners in baseball of the Pacific Coast.

Yours respectfully,

Angel City Baseball Association,

J.H. Patrick, President

Lane seethed, but kept his mouth shut. The press stated that Lane had only two other choices: return to Salt Lake City, or move the club down to San Diego, neither prospect was appealing to other owners in the league. As also noted in the press, Hollywood was part of the Angels' territory, so the Stars would not be able to build a park there.

After two years of spring training in Santa Monica, the Hollywood Stars arranged to train at Navy Field (future site of Lane Field) in San Diego, no doubt with Bill Lane trying to determine if San Diego was ready for Coast League baseball. Spring training went well, but Lane and Spider Baum were not sure if San Diego was ripe for a berth in the PCL.

— 1929 —

The ball club in 1929 did well on the field, with Ossie Vitt helming the team again. The Sheiks started off slow, and finished fourth in the first half. But Vitt brought the club home first in the second half, and then went on to win the playoffs against the Missions, taking the flag in six games. The team got Bill Rumler back from his five-year suspension, during which he played independent ball, primarily in the industrial-backed Midwest League. Rumler hit .386 with 26 HR. On the mound, Shellenback led the club with 26 wins.

The 1929 season was a success for the whole league, and for the Hollywood Stars which finished second to Los Angeles in attendance with 314,243 passing through the turnstiles at Wrigley Field.

After such a successful season ended, Ossie Vitt asked for a raise and a two-year contract. The papers said Lane and Vitt were "on the outs" over the demands of the manager. Finally, Lane told his manager that he would take it up with the club's directors at their annual meeting in Salt Lake City in November. (The club was still a Utah corporation, and would remain so until the club moved to San Diego.)

— 1930 —

In 1930, the club again trained at Navy Field in San Diego, but did not bring the Stars any closer to making a move south. The Depression had not made its full weight felt in Los Angeles, and both clubs drew fairly well at Wrigley Field. Hollywood's attendance dipped to a still respectable 289,131. The Angels again led the league.

In mid-summer, Wrigley Field had lights installed, which helped attendance. At the time, Bill Lane said he would play under the lights, but opined that he didn't think night ball would be more than a passing fad.

The first half ended with the Angels edging out the Stars by 3½ games, but the second half was all Stars. Hollywood had a .650 win-loss percentage, and finished 8 games ahead of Los Angeles. In the playoffs, Hollywood ran off with the title 4 games to one. And at the annual meeting in November 1930, the club did show a modest profit:

— 1931 —

Nineteen thirty-one had the club win the first half by a wide margin, then stumble to under .500, and wind up losing the playoffs to the San Francisco Seals. Yet the club drew over 300,000 fans to Wrigley Field, leading the league by far. The Sheiks had two outstanding individual player-seasons that year. Frank Shellenback had his best season ever with a 27-7, 2.85 record, and Dave Barbee hit a league-leading 47 HRs to go along with 166 RBIs and a .332 batting average.

APPENDIX F—THE REAL AND TRUE HISTORY OF THE FRANCHISE THAT BECAME THE SAN DIEGO PADRES

— 1932 —

The following season, the Stars trained at San Diego for the fourth straight year, though pitchers and catchers reported early to Carlsbad. Both Vitt and Lane were bent on reversing their second-half swoon. The only problem was that Frank Shellenback, coming off a great season, demanded a raise. Bill Lane offered him the same salary that he had the years before, stating that his star pitcher was lucky he didn't cut his salary, as the Depression began to bite hard into Southern California. Hollywood's attendance in 1932, as a matter of fact, was cut in half, the club drawing only 151,292.

Several owners proposed a split schedule for the 1932 season. Since the league began, the schedule had featured a weekly series between clubs. A club would travel to a city and play a seven-game series that week: Tuesday through Saturday games, and a doubleheader on Sunday. Monday would be a travel day. Lane opposed it on cost grounds; i.e., more series meant more travel costs, and was able to convince a sufficient number of owner to nix the idea. Also, Lane always opposed the split-season, and in 1932 he was able to get enough owner to his side to terminate the two-halves schedule that had been in effect since 1928.

The Sheiks finished second, five games behind the Portland Beavers. Nobody ran away with the pennant that season, so Frank Shellenback's 26 wins and Cleo Carlisle's .346 average were enough to power the club in the runner up-spot in the standings. Whatever happened with Shellenback's contract is unknown, but the rest of the club received cuts in salary according to the *Los Angeles Times*.

After the season, Bill Lane had some more disputes. Adding to the Ladies Day dispute, the Angels decided to continue to broadcast games from Wrigley Field. Bill Lane opposed radio broadcasts, but at that time, it was the park rather than the club that controlled over-the-air rights. Lane also took the battle over too many night games to the league winter meetings, but lost on that front also.

In October 1932, Lane and Baum travelled down to San Diego to determine whether Navy Field would be ready for the club when the players were scheduled to report in the first days of March. The two were horrified to find Navy Field converted into a motorcycle track. Even the inside of the track was so bad that couldn't be used for any sort of training, according to Lane. The club quickly made a deal with Shell Oil to use their ballpark for spring training, though pitchers and catcher would still report to Carlsbad for early training.

— 1933 —

Spring training, however, didn't go as planned. An earthquake damaged the Shell Oil Park in Long Beach, and the Sheiks were forced to move to grounds in Sawtelle. The club dropped a notch in 1933, being barely edged out of second place by the Portland Beavers. But there were some fine individual seasons that year. Ray Jacobs, longtime Angel player, joined the club and had arguably the best season of his career: 36 HR and 125 RBI. Also, the club produced four twenty-game winners: Frank Shellenback, Archie Campbell, Tom Sheehan and Vance Page. Attendance at Wrigley Field for the Stars rebounded to 173,501.

Joe DiMaggio's brother joined the club in 1933, after Joe had replaced brother Vince in the outfield for the San Francisco Seals, and would remain with the club until sold to the Red Sox in 1937.

At the winter meeting, Lane successfully lobbied the other owner to rescind the ban on spitballers for the coming season (Frank Shellenback had been grandfathered), and promptly signed Jack Quinn who hand come to the end of the line in Cincinnati in 1933. Quinn would only get in 6 games, going 1-1 with 6.35 ERA.

— 1934 —

Nineteen-thirty-four dawned with the possibility that Portland and Seattle would have to be jettisoned from the PCL because of the once again deteriorating economy. Lane gave an interview to Bob Ray of the *Los Angeles Times* on January 25 in which he stated: "Something has to be done quickly...And the only solution is to plan for a six-club, all-California league." That never happened, and, as a matter of fact, the weak Seattle club outdrew the rest of the league in 1934. On the eve of the 1934 season, Bill Lane had his first heart attack. He recovered somewhat by August, but would always be in delicate health thereafter.

Bill Lane had been right, though, to have worried about the 1934 season. Attendance dropped to 128,140. The 1934 season was the year of the greatest PCL club of all time, the '34 Angels. The team finished with a .733 win-loss record, 35 games ahead of its nearest rivals, the Mission Reds. Hollywood finished third again, some 39½ games back. The Angels were so far ahead that by mid-season (with a .786 winning percentage) the league decided to split the season. It did no good, as the Angels took the second half as well. The '34 Angels, considered by nearly every minor-league historian to be the greatest minor league club ever, drew only a little more than a thousand more fans than the Sheiks. San Francisco, which was beset by strikes, drew under a 100,000 again, and Portland only 50,731.

With Bill Lane back on his feet, Ossie Vitt was gone as manager of the club. As a UP article stated, "Whether Vitt resigned or was ousted by Owner H.W. Lane remained undetermined. Although Lane said his manager quit on his own volition, other baseball sources said the resignation was requested by Lane." That was on October 24, 1934. The next day Lane named Frank Shellenback as his new manager. Days later Ossie Vitt signed to manage the Oakland Oaks.

— 1935 —

The club trained at Fullerton for the first time in 1935, having found Riverside in 1934 not to the Sheiks liking. Just before the season started, Bill Lane told the press that he had dropped $61,000 over the preceding three seasons. When asked about his health, he stated that his health had been completely restored.

While his health may have been restored, that of his club was not. The Hollywood Stars dropped into the cellar for the season. In the first half, Shellenback had the club above .500, but the floor dropped out from under them in the second half. Ossie Vitt? The Oakland Oaks signed him a couple of days after he left the Sheiks. He improved the Oaks from 5th place to 3rd.

Attendance inched up to 135,916 for Hollywood, but was still much under the salad days the late 1920s, and the problems with Angels management and William Wrigley's son, P.K., was not an improvement for Bill Lane. Rumors swirled around the league folding up, forcing Coast League officials to formally deny the rumors. The league went to a split series schedule in 1935 and travelling expenses more than offset any gains in attendance. Lane reappointed Shellenback on October 28.

In November, Hy Baggerly resigned as Coast League president. Bill Lane had been after his scalp for several seasons. Lane said that Baggerly only "beat the league to the punch by resigning."

At the PCL Winter Meeting, Bill Lane was elected First Vice President of the league, though the league presidency remained open. Lane also represented the league at the National Association Winter Meetings in Dayton, Ohio. Lane it was announced would stop in Salt Lake City on his way back to see if it might be "advisable to put a Coast League club back in the Mormon metropolis." The Sacramento franchise was rumored to be the club to be moved. A week later, it became the Hollywood Sheiks that was rumored to be moved. On November 27, Lane stated he was seriously considering a move back to Salt Lake City.

On December 5, the Sacramento Chamber of Commerce offered Lane a chance to move to Sacramento, even though the Solons had been a disaster with only 49,324 in 1935. But the Sacramento disaster was not the only league problem that off-season. The San Francisco Seals faced foreclosure on Seals Stadium, and the Missions might have to be sold. Both the Seals and the Missions resolved their pressing financial problems, and the Sacramento franchise fell into the hands of Branch Rickey and the St. Louis Cardinals.

And on December 18, Will C. Tuttle, novelist and former newspaper reporter and cartoonist, was elected president of the Pacific Coast League.

Yet, as of 11:59 p.m., December 31, 1935, the club remained the Hollywood Stars (or Sheiks), and still domiciled at Wrigley Field in Los Angeles.

APPENDIX F—THE REAL AND TRUE HISTORY OF THE FRANCHISE THAT BECAME THE SAN DIEGO PADRES

A Bogus Padres Franchise History

In Wikipedia, which relied on Bill O'Neal's history of the PCL, and a typo in the 1906 Spalding and Reach Baseball Guides, a fake history of the Padres franchise came into being and has now become the "official history" of the team.

The entry, following the lead of O'Neal, states that the Sacramento PCL franchise was created in 1903. In 1904, it moved to Tacoma, moved back to Sacramento in 1905, then was revived in 1909, as if it had been in suspended animation for the years between 1905 and 1909. After that, the history is more or less correct as to venue changes.

In the 1906 Spalding Guide, Sacramento is listed in the standings as having played the whole second half of the season, and Tacoma the whole first-half of the season. In the Reach Guide, the club standing for the second half is listed as "Tac.-Sac. 43-62 .409." For the Spalding Guide, H.L. Baggerly, Sporting Editor of the San Francisco Bulletin wrote a two-page summary of the 1905 season, in which he only mentioned that "Tacoma was such a dismal failure that several series were transferred in the fall." But none of them was played in Sacramento, nor did Mike Fisher's club get within 75 miles of state capital.

All the transferred series were to the opponent's park, save one. The September 27-October 1 series with Oakland was transferred to Spokane, and both Spokane newspapers referred to the club as the Tacoma club, as did all the major newspapers in league cities. After Tacoma stopped playing home games, the club was invariably referred to as the Tacoma Wanderers.

I've always been guided by the old Chicago reporters' adage: If your mother says she loves you, check it out. Neither Bill O'Neal, nor those that followed him, have ever checked out the Sacramento papers to see what really transpired.

On a separate note, the history of that early Sacramento franchise is interesting in itself. The Sacramento club in the 1903 Pacific Coast League was not created out of whole cloth for the 1903 season. Actually, the club began as an independent club that played in the 1897 San Francisco Examiner Tournament. After being kicked out of the tournament (supposedly for playing an unauthorized exhibition game, which Sacramento disputed), they joined a newly comprised league of supposedly "sore losers." The 1897 California League was a huge success, and Sacramento finished second under Mike Fisher's leadership, only ½ game behind league-leader, Stockton.

The club continued in the league in 1898, but a rival league sprang up, the Pacific States League and after a month the two leagues were forced to combine in an unwieldly structure called the Pacific Coast League that soldiered on to conclusion of the season.

A whole new league was created out of the clubs that played in 1898. Under the direction of long-time San Francisco magnate, Henry Harris, the new California League came into being. The Sacramento franchise of Mike Fisher was one of the six clubs chosen to play in that league. The founders of the PCL considered 1899 as the true beginning of the Pacific Coast League and stated as much until all the old owners had died or retired. At that point, the league president chose to re-write history and give the PCL its 1903 birth.

Mike Fisher remained owner of the club throughout the California League years, and battled through the 1903 PCL season in Sacramento. But the Sacramento fan base did not support the club, so in 1904 Fisher moved the club to Tacoma, which at first appeared to be an improvement. But in 1905, Fisher found out that even the best club in the league couldn't draw flies in Tacoma, so the club went on the road in September, and stayed on the road for the rest of the campaign.

Mike Fisher moved the club to Fresno in 1906, but between the San Francisco Earthquake and the heat of the Central Valley, the club barely made it to the end of the season.

After the 1906 season, the league contracted to four teams, axing both the Seattle and Fresno franchises.

And so ended the history of the original PCL Sacramento franchise.

SAN DIEGO'S FIRST PADRES and "THE KID"

APPENDIX G
A BIOGRAPHY OF H.W. "BILLY" LANE (AS HE WAS CALLED IN SALT LAKE CITY)

When Bill "Hardrock" or "Hardpan" Lane died of a heart attack on October 9, 1938, *The San Diego News*papers listed, collectively, the highlights of his long career:

- He was born in Baton Rouge, Louisiana on February 29, 1860, a leap-year baby, as they said back then.
- He was a life-long bachelor, and left no living relatives.
- He graduated from the Colorado School of Mines with high (or the highest) honors.
- As a mining engineer, he practiced his profession in Idaho, Montana, Nevada, Alaska and Korea.
- He studied law in Salt Lake City in the winters, when his mines were shut down, and joined the bar, though never practiced law.
- He was one of three lawyers that brought about the mining law compromise of the early 1890s.
- He was also a newspaperman for a time.
- He played semipro baseball as a young man.
- He began his ownership career in baseball with the Murray, Utah club in the 1914 Union Association.
- He led a group of businessmen to acquire the bankrupt Mission franchise of the Pacific Coast League, and successfully move it to Salt Lake City.
- In 1919, when the other shareholders of the Salt Lake City club failed to pay off a $40,000 debt, he put up the money himself, and thus acquired controlling interest in the team.
- He was the one who led a coup against President William H. McCarthy of the Pacific Coast League in 1925 that led to journalist Harry A. Williams being named president of the league.

Bill "Hardrock" Lane

When Harry William Lane's will was read shortly after his death, it was noted that he left a $100 monthly stipend to one M.E. Lane of Spokane, Washington. An enterprising Associated Press reporter contacted the mysterious M.E. Lane, and discovered that she was the former wife of Bill Lane. She recounted that they were married on August 7, 1888 on a steamer excursion across Lake Coeur d'Alene in northern Idaho. According to his ex-wife, they remained married for 22 years. Several months later, his brother John Lane, and his nephews, contested the will.

The Colorado School of Mines has no record of a Harry William or of a William Harry or a Harry or a William or even a Bill graduating with high honors, or graduating, or even attending—until a Bill Lane matriculated at the school in 1924.

No lawyer by the name Lane was associated in any way with the mining law compromise, as can be determined by contemporary newspaper accounts available.

The Murray club of the 1914 Union Association was organized by, and owned by, a prominent physician in Murray, Utah, Dr. C.P. Harvielle. He brought in longtime Coast League player, Cliff Blankenship, to manage the club. As Salt Lake formed part of the league in 1914, newspaper coverage was extensive. Never once did Lane's name appear in print as having anything to do with the club, though he did appear in the press from time to time in relation to his mining operations in Nevada. What is interesting is that Lane, when he was elected to the first board of directors of the Salt Lake City Coast League club, there was no mention of his association with Murray club the season prior.

In the *Salt Lake City Telegram*, gave capsules of all the directors of the new Salt Lake franchise:

H.W. Lane

Mr. Lane, elected director of the baseball club today, has not only demonstrated business ability in commercial lines, but he has provided himself to be a capable baseball man as well. He made most of his money in mining, but he also practiced law In Nevada, Idaho and Washington.

He was manager and financial secretary of the Spokane baseball team in the practical charge of the club's affairs. The stock had a par value of $1 a share.

Under Mr. Lane's management the team earned $1.58 a share dividend that year on the stock.

Mr. Lane has been interested in baseball from Alaska to Salt Lake. He was the first one to put up money for the Union Association and contributed liberally when money was needed. He is what red-blooded people call "game to the core" when does anything.

His thorough knowledge of baseball and his legal training and his business ability make him a valuable members [sic] of the board of directors.

Strange that Bill Lane never had a note even appear in the newspapers about his financing the Union Association, or his interest in the Spokane baseball club. Or even when Dr. Harvielle was trying to unload the Murray club for free, Bill Lane's name never came up.

What is known about Bill Lane is that he began showing up in Nevada and Utah newspapers in 1908 as an associate in the Gold Circle Mines outside of Elko, Nevada. Prior to that, we find both Bill Lane and his wife were listed as living in Spokane, Washington in 1896, but at different addresses. Bill was listed as a miner—not a mining engineer—and living in a rented room; his wife May appeared to be renting out rooms in her own private home.

In the 1900 census, H. W. Lane is listed as living in Elko, Nevada. The data lists him as being born in Louisiana, but in 1870 instead of 1860.

Gold Circle Mines--and Bill Lane personally—was listed for years in the Salt Lake City newspapers as having been in arrears on taxes.

Bill Lane, around 1916, shows up as a stockbroker on the Salt Lake City Exchange. Later on, he will form a brokerage house with J. R. Sebree called *Sebree & Lane, Mining and Industrial Stocks and Bonds*.

In 1918, Lane was elected president of the Salt Lake Exchange, and he added oil stocks to the listing of mining stocks.

When Bill Lane died he left a will that stated that the club should be sold as quickly as humanly possible. It took until 1944, when the Bill Starr group

APPENDIX G—A BIOGRAPHY OF H.W. "BILLY" LANE (as he was called in Salt Lake City)

bought the San Diego Padres. First, Lane's brother sued to have the Will broken. He eventually settled with the executors in October 1939, but that put any attempt to sell the club on hold until that date. Then two tentative sales failed to be consummated, one to the owner of the Syracuse International League club, and another by Omaha oilman, M. L. Clark, who suspended his offer to buy the club for an unspecified reason.

Florence Eastwood, Bill Lane's "friend" and housekeeper remained club owner for six years while the hoped-for quick sale never materialized.

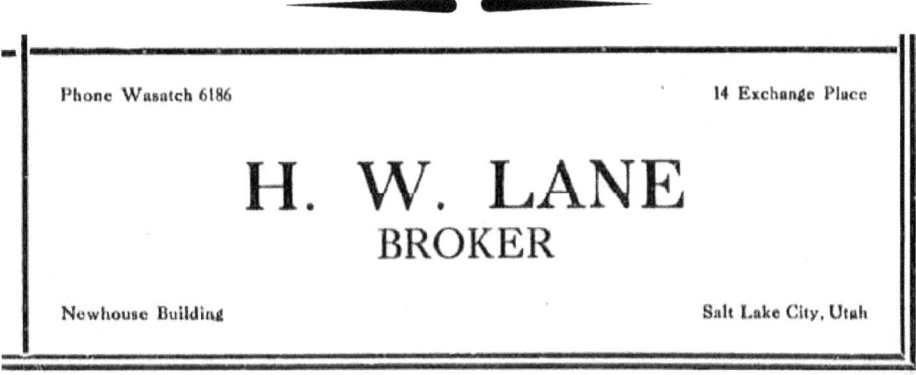

APPENDIX H
BIOGRAPHIES OF THE 1936 SAN DIEGO PADRES

The Supporting Cast

Team Owner	Bill "Hardrock" Lane, Owner and President, San Diego Padres
Team Secretary	Spider Baum, Vice President and Secretary, San Diego Padres
League President	W. C. Tuttle, President, Pacific Coast League
Team Trainer	Les Cook, Trainer (Part-time Catcher), San Diego Padres
Scout	Eddie Collins, Scout, Boston Red Sox
Beat Writer	Earl Keller, Reporter, *San Diego Evening Tribune*
Team Mascot	Ralph Thompson, Mascot, San Diego Padres

The Cast: Players from February Through October

John Appleby	Rosey Gilhousen	George Myatt
Joe Berkowitz	Larry Gillick	Winfred Pepper
John Bladel	George Harris	Al Pignataro
Max Bryan	Wally Hebert	Herman Pillette
Archie Campbell	Jack Hile	Manny Salvo
Hec Carroll	Elmer Hill	? Scaroli (or Scaroldi)
Les Cook (and Team Trainer)	George Hockette	Frank Shellenback
Ritchie Cooper	Ernie Holman	Ivey Shiver
Dennis Crabb	Trader Horne	Stan Steely
Howard Craghead	Kenny Iverson	Elmer Stock
D.H. Curtis	M.K. (or M.H.?) Jackson	Kenneth Storms
Gene Desautels	Ray Jacobs	Bud Tuttle
Vince DiMaggio	Ash Joerndt	Fred Vaughn
Hal Doerr	Jimmy Kerr	Robert Vickers
Bobby Doerr	Hub Kittle	Dick Ward
Elmer Donovan	Harl Maggert	Ed Wells
Cedric Durst	Burke McDonald	Allan Whitlock
Eddie Ehil	George McDonald	Red Williams
Don Elton	Joe Monahan	Ted Williams
Bill Englund	Eddie Mulligan	Van Wirthman
Elmer Evert		

In the order shown above, the biographies of each person are included in the following pages of this Appendix. For the players, their entire professional baseball career records are included.

These biographies include 67 individuals: 61 players (one of whom—Les Cook--played a dual role of Trainer and catcher) and another six men who were in a supporting role in one way or another during the Padres' 1936 season, including spring training. For the regular season, there were 32 players who played in one or more games for the team, and 20 of these players had major league experience either prior to 1936 or afterward.

THE SUPPORTING CAST

THE TEAM OWNER: HARRY WILLIAM LANE

(Born on February 29, 1860 in Baton Rouge, LA, and died on October 9, 1938 in San Diego)

Lane was owner of the San Diego Padres. In 1936 he turned 76 years old. He was called "Hardrock" because of his early work experience as a miner and "his never say-die spirit and his ability to beat hard rock mining, the toughest method of obtaining ore known to the old school miners."[363] The nickname also fit his personality because of the "hard side" he showed others.

Lane was also an explorer and Indian fighter and mixed in state and national politics. Lane was quite a ballplayer on semi-professional mining camp teams. He injured his right arm in a mining accident and then had a fishing accident, which resulted in some bones not healing properly, and Lane was forced to wear a brace the remainder of his life.

He lived at 4106 Alameda Street in Point Loma[364] and according to Bobby Doerr had a "kind of crippled right hand and brace."[365] He died while still team President on October 9, 1938. According to *Tribune* Sports Editor at the time, Tom Akers, "it was his pleasure to match wits with the shrewdest men in his chosen field, that of baseball, and he was famed for his ability to out-think the cleverest of them all."[366]

A more extensive biography of Lane is contained in Appendix G.

THE TEAM SECRETARY: CHARLES ADRIAN BAUM

(Born on May 28, 1882 in San Francisco, CA and died on June 28, 1955 in Renton, WA)

In 1936 "Spider" Baum was age 54 and served as Vice President and Secretary of the Padres. He was hired by Lane in Salt Lake City in 1922 as an assistant secretary, and moved up to be the vice president and secretary for the Hollywood Baseball Club, and subsequently, for the Padres.

Known as "The Matty of the Minors" Baum was a right-handed spitball pitcher who won 267 games in the PCL in a career that started in 1902; this was a record until Frank Shellenback broke it.[367] His overall minor league career record totaled 342 wins over a 20-year period ending in 1921 with Merced in the Central California League. He never pitched in the major leagues, apparently refusing to report to both the Phillies and Red Sox, which had owned his contract. His nickname of "Spider" reportedly was related to his spindly legs.

While in San Diego he first lived at 3036 Elliot Street[368] and later at 3757 Narragansett Avenue. When Bill Lane died in 1938 Baum became club President until ousted in 1939.

SPIDER BAUM Charles Adrian Baum "Soup Bone" "Honk"   6:01 165 BR TR
Born: May 28, 1882 San Francisco, CA   Died: June 28, 1955 Renton, WA

Year	Team	League	G	GS	CG	ShO	SV	W	L	PCT	IP	H	R	ER	K	BB	ERA
1902	SF Bulletins		2	2	2	0	0	0	2	.000	16.0	13	15	9	7	5	5.06
	San Francisco	California	2	2	2	0	0	1	1	.500	18.0	20	10	7	2	7	3.50
	San Jose		1	1	1	0	0	0	1	.000	9.0		3	2			2.00

APPENDIX H—BIOGRAPHIES OF THE 1936 SAN DIEGO PADRES

Year	Team	League	G	GS	CG	ShO	SV	W	L	PCT	IP	H	R	ER	K	BB	ERA
1903	Petaluma		3	3	3	0	0	1	2	.333	26.0	14	16	7	11	3	2.42
	Los Angeles	PCL	3	3	3	0	0	1	2	.333	26.0	29	16	9	4	9	3.12
	Oakland Heesemen	California St	1	0	0	0	1	0	0	.000	1.0	4	3	2	1	1	18.00
1904	Los Angeles	PCL	53	49	40	4	0	25	23	.521	404.0	365	161	119	158	110	2.65
1905	Los Angeles	PCL	57	51	47	9	0	27	28	.491	445.0	381	146	111	221	86	2.24
1906	Altoona	Tri-State	29	27	22	4	0	14	12	.538	218.0	229	93	70	79	36	2.89
	Sacramento	California St	4	4	4	1	0	3	1	.750	35.0	23	9	4	32	5	1.03
1907	Altoona	Tri-State	29	27	27	2	0	15	13	.536	243.3	209	85	65	88	47	2.40
	Sacramento	California St	8	8	7	1	0	4	3	.571	67.7	50	22	16	54	11	2.13
1908	Fresno	California St	41	37	33	7	0	24	14	.632	334.0	263	92	69	158	48	1.86
1909	Sacramento	PCL	54	45	37	6	1	21	21	.500	397.3	**371**	141	106	192	88	2.40
1910	Sacramento	PCL	47	37	31	3	1	18	20	.474	372.0	317	121	90	119	82	2.18
1911	Sacramento	PCL	39	30	25	4	1	17	15	.531	320.0	302	106	78	118	49	2.19
1912	Sacramento/Vernon	PCL	37	28	16	2	2	14	13	.519	227.0	228	89	68	73	54	2.70
1913	Venice	PCL	51	42	30	3	1	23	19	.548	361.3	360	149	113	140	72	2.81
1914	San Francisco	PCL	40			3		21	12	.636	302.7	295	104	68	120	74	2.02
1915	San Francisco	PCL	55			3		30	15	.667	382.0	**393**	162	104	153	65	2.45
1916	San Francisco	PCL	56	41	21	4	5	20	20	.500	327.7	336	134	100	114	95	2.75
1917	San Francisco	PCL	50	42	30	5	2	24	17	.585	352.0	332	144	98	94	86	2.51
1918	San Francisco	PCL	22	17	11	3	0	8	8	.500	155.7	131	55	35	30	42	2.02
1919	SF/Salt Lake City	PCL	36	20	13	3	1	11	17	.393	219.3	238	100	87	68	43	3.57
1920	Salt Lake City	PCL	30			0		7	10	.412	149.0	204	100	84	48	32	5.07
1921	Merced	Central California	25	24	23	0	0	13	10	.565	207.7	214	130	91	122	28	3.94
	Minor League totals		773	538	426	67	15	342	297	.535	5600.7	5308	2191	1603	2199	1173	2.58

THE LEAGUE PRESIDENT: WILBUR COLEMAN TUTTLE

(Born on November 11, 1883 in Glendive, Montana, and died on June 6, 1969 in Los Angeles, CA)

Elected President of the Pacific Coast League in December 1935 Tuttle remained in that position through 1943. He was a former Missoula, Montana, and Spokane newspaperman, cartoonist, photographer and fiction writer who moved to Van Nuys in the San Fernando area of Los Angeles in 1918. Born in 1883 he had no prior professional baseball experience but was active in local semi-pro baseball where he played, managed and umpired. In his adult life he usually went by the name of W.C., but also was commonly referred to by the nickname of "Tut."

He started writing western fiction in 1915 and authored numerous books and short stories. For some reason, most of his books for were published in England. Tuttle was recognized as someone who knows baseball, but also understood the importance of publicity for the sport. He reportedly recommended Gene Lillard to the Angels, who turned out to be the PCL's home run leader in 1935. This apparent ability to recognize baseball talent must have been impressive since it was noted in several articles about his election.

Tuttle was sponsored for the PCL position by the Hollywood and Los Angeles clubs. One of the interesting sidelights of San Diego getting the Hollywood franchise was the relationship between Padres owner Lane and Tuttle. It was reported that Lane took a liking to Tuttle's writings and required his ballplayers to buy every magazine having a Tuttle story in it. Then Lane would buy the magazines from them. Lane eventually found out from Frank Shellenback that Tuttle was a Los Angeles resident and they became close friends. It was Lane who suggested Tuttle to other owners when it came time for selection of a new PCL President.[369] Presumably, this relationship came in handy when the necessary three-fourths vote of owners was needed for the transfer of the Hollywood club.

THE TEAM TRAINER: LESTER SPURGEON COOK

A long-time minor league catcher Cook served as Trainer in 1936 yet played in seven games being called upon in July for back-up purposes. Cook, who turned 41 during spring training, joined Lane back in 1924 with the Stars. He began his career in 1913 and played until 1932 when he turned to devote his time to "looking after the condition and ailments of the athletes."[370] In 1913 he played with Vernon and again in 1915. Then, Cook went to San Antonio in the Texas League for 1916-17 and was sold to St. Paul in 1918. In 1919 he returned to Vernon, and moved on to Seattle and Sacramento until 1924 when he joined Salt Lake City/Hollywood in 1926. He had brief appearances in games from 1937 to 1939 and then remained with Padres as trainer through the 1950s. In 1936 he lived at 208 Grape Street in San Diego. He is a member of the PCL Padres Hall of Fame. An expanded biography of Cook is contained in a 2007 article by Smith.[371]

 *March 20, 1936, The San Diego Union*
LESTER C. [sic] COOK

Lester C. [sic] Cook, "Les" or "Cookie" to the ball club, is the trainer of the San Diego Padres of the Pacific Coast Baseball league.

Cook is a veteran player with the team, formerly the Hollywood Stars, and is one of the oldest men associated with Owner Bill Lane. He has been with the Padres since 1924, a total of 12 years, first joining the team as a catcher. He gradually turned his attention in late years to training activities and three years ago gave up catching entirely to devote full time to looking after the condition and ailments of the athletes.

Cook started in baseball in 1913 as a catcher with the old Vernon Tigers,* then managed by Hap Hogan. He was farmed out to the California State league and in 1915 returned to Vernon. In 1916 Cook went to San Antonio in the Texas league and remained there for two seasons, being sold to St. Paul in 1918. In 1919 Cook returned to Vernon but before the season was out played for Seattle and Sacramento. He remained with the latter team until 1924 when he joined Hollywood.

Next week will mark Cook's 41st birthday. He is married. When playing regularly he was a right hand hitter.

Cook in 1921 with Sacramento

LES COOK Lester Spurgeon Cook 5:09 171 BR TR
Born: March 26, 1895 York, PA Died: July 1, 1968 San Diego, CA

Year	Team	League	Pos	G	AB	R	H	1B	2B	3B	HR	RBI	K	BB	SB	AVG
1913	Stockton	California	c	8	20	0	3	3	0	0	0				0	.150
1914	San Jose	California	c	29	88	9	17	17	0	0	0				2	.193
1915	San Jose	California	c	6	22	1	8	6	2	0	0				2	.364

* Cook actually broke in playing one game with Sacramento in 1912.

APPENDIX H—BIOGRAPHIES OF THE 1936 SAN DIEGO PADRES

Year	Team	League	Pos	G	AB	R	H	1B	2B	3B	HR	RBI	K	BB	SB	AVG
1916	San Antonio	Texas	c	97	289	18	40	33	5	2	0				6	.138
1917	San Antonio	Texas	c	88	265	25	57	52	5	0	0				5	.215
	Vernon	PCL	c	11	28	4	5	4	1	0	0				1	.179
1918	St. Paul	American Assn	c	20	55	4	9	8	1	0	0		2	2	0	.164
1919	Vernon/Seattle/Sac	PCL	c-2b	94	303	23	47	37	8	2	0				3	.155
1920	Sacramento	PCL	c	100	288	23	62	53	7	1	1				3	.215
1921	Sacramento	PCL	c	97	285	29	59	41	11	4	3	29			4	.207
1922	Sacramento	PCL	c	83	237	27	48	36	11	1	0	17			4	.203
1923	Sacramento	PCL	c	21	27	4	9	5	4	0	0	2			0	.333
1924	Salt Lake City	PCL	c	131	345	58	104	64	36	1	3	57			4	.301
1925	Salt Lake City	PCL	c	105	258	29	63	51	11	0	1	29			2	.244
1926	Hollywood	PCL	c-of	93	226	27	47	39	8	0	0	18			2	.208
1927	Hollywood	PCL	c	55	125	14	29	22	7	0	0	11			0	.232
1928	Hollywood	PCL	c	7	9	1	0	0	0	0	0	0			0	.000
1929	Hollywood	PCL	c	41	57	11	14	7	6	0	1	5			0	.246
1930	Hollywood	PCL	ph	14	13	2	4	4	0	0	0	0			0	.308
1931	Hollywood	PCL	ph	6	8	0	0	0	0	0	0	0			0	.000
1932	Hollywood	PCL	ph	6	4	0	1	1	0	0	0				0	.250
1933-1935							**Did Not Play**									
1936		PCL	c	7	7	0	0	0	0	0	0	0			0	.000
1937	San Diego	PCL	c	1	0	0	0	0	0	0	0	0			0	.000
1938	San Diego	PCL	c	1	0	0	0	0	0	0	0	0			0	.000
1939	San Diego	PCL	c	1	5	0	1	1	0	0	0	0			0	.200
Minor League totals				1122	2964	309	627	484	123	11	9	168	2	2	38	.212

THE SCOUT: EDWARD TROWBRIDGE COLLINS, SR.

(Born on May 2, 1887 in Millerton, NY and died on March 25, 1951 in Boston, MA)

Eddie Collins (middle) between Ted Williams and Bill Lane

A member of the National Baseball Hall of Fame, Collin's playing career started in 1906 with two seasons of minor league ball then covered 24 seasons in the major leagues with the Philadelphia A's and Chicago White Sox until his last appearance in three games during the 1930 season with the A's.

Collins coached full-time for Philadelphia in 1931 and 1932 before joining the Boston Red Sox as vice president and general manager when Tom Yawkey purchased the team in early 1933. Collins remained with the Red Sox for the rest of his life. His connection to the 1936 Padres involves the notable scouting trip to California when he signed two future Hall of Famers, Bobby Doerr and Ted Williams.[372]

SAN DIEGO'S FIRST PADRES and "THE KID"

EDDIE COLLINS Edward Trowbridge Collins, Sr. "Cocky"   5:09 175 BL TR
Born: May 2, 1887 Millertown, NY   Died: March 25, 1951 Boston, MA

Year	Team	League	Pos	G	AB	R	H	1B	2B	3B	HR	RBI	K	BB	SB	AVG
1906	Red Hook, NY															
	Plattsburgh/Rutland	Northern	ss	32	113	18	39									.345
	Philadelphia	AL	3b	6	15	2	3	3	0	0	0	0		0	0	.200
1907	Rutland	Vermont	3b													
1907	Philadelphia	AL	ss	14	23	0	8	7	0	1	0	2		0	0	.348
1908	Philadelphia	AL	2b-ss	102	330	39	90	64	18	7	1	40		16	8	.273
1909	Philadelphia	AL	2b	153	571	104	198	155	30	10	3	56		62	67	.347
1910	Philadelphia	AL	2b	153	581	81	188	154	16	15	3	81		49	**81**	.324
1911	Philadelphia	AL	2b	132	493	92	180	142	22	13	3	73		62	38	.365
1912	Philadelphia	AL	2b	153	543	**137**	189	153	25	11	0	64		101	63	.348
1913	Philadelphia	AL	2b	148	534	**125**	184	**145**	23	13	3	73	37	85	55	.345
1914	Philadelphia	AL	2b	152	526	**122**	181	142	23	14	2	85	31	97	58	.344
1915	Chicago	AL	2b	155	521	118	173	137	22	10	4	77	27	**119**	46	.332
1916	Chicago	AL	2b	155	545	87	168	137	14	17	0	52	36	86	40	.308
1917	Chicago	AL	2b	156	564	91	163	133	18	12	0	67	16	89	53	.289
1918	Chicago	AL	2b	97	330	51	91	79	8	2	2	30	13	73	22	.276
1919	Chicago	AL	2b	140	518	87	165	135	19	7	4	80	27	68	**33**	.319
1920	Chicago	AL	2b	153	602	117	224	170	38	13	3	76	19	69	19	.372
1921	Chicago	AL	2b	139	526	79	177	145	20	10	2	58	11	66	12	.337
1922	Chicago	AL	2b	154	598	92	194	161	20	12	1	69	16	73	20	.324
1923	Chicago	AL	2b	145	505	89	182	150	22	5	5	67	8	84	**49**	.360
1924	Chicago	AL	2b	152	556	108	194	154	27	7	6	86	16	89	**42**	.349
1925	Chicago	AL	2b	118	425	80	147	115	26	3	3	80	8	87	19	.346
1926	Chicago	AL	2b	106	375	66	129	92	32	4	1	62	8	62	13	.344
1927	Philadelphia	AL	2b	95	226	50	76	62	12	1	1	15	9	56	6	.336
1928	Philadelphia	AL	ss	36	33	3	10	7	3	0	0	7	4	4	0	.303
1929	Philadelphia	AL	ph	9	7	0	0	0	0	0	0	0	0	2	0	.000
1930	Philadelphia	AL	ph	3	2	1	1	1	0	0	0	0	0	0	0	.500
	Newark	Eastern	2b-ss	4	16	6	7	7	0	0	0				1	.438
	Minor League totals			36	129	24	46	7	0	0	0				1	.357
	Major League totals			2826	9949	1821	3315	2643	438	187	47	1300	286	1499	744	.333

THE BEAT WRITER: EARL RAYMOND KELLER

(Born on March 30, 1915 in San Diego, CA and died on November 13, 1995 in San Diego, CA)

San Diego Evening Tribune,
June 26, 1936

Keller's newspaper career paralleled Ted Williams's. He was 21 in 1936 and his newspaper career had been initiated when he joined the *San Diego Tribune* in November 1934 after working as a high school correspondent for the *San Diego Sun*. In 1936 he was assigned as the *Tribune's* beat writer for the Padres. For the next 28 years, he covered the PCL Padres.[373] Keller also was the region's sports news contributor to *The Sporting News* beginning in 1936. He was there to chronicle Ted Williams's introduction to professional

APPENDIX H—BIOGRAPHIES OF THE 1936 SAN DIEGO PADRES

baseball in 1936 and 1937. San Diego baseball historian, Bill Swank, wrote in detail about Keller's and Williams's 1937 season with Padres and the forging of a friendship between the two men was to last until Keller's death in 1995.[374] In 1936 he lived at 1724 29th Street in San Diego.

THE TEAM MASCOT/BATBOY: ALLEN RALPH THOMPSON

(Born on May 8, 1927 in San Diego, CA and died on December 16, 2003 in Alpine, CA)

Going by the nickname of "Blondie," Thompson was the "mascot," or batboy for the team. A 3rd grade student in 1936 he won a contest to become the team's first batboy, a job he held for four seasons. Thompson lived with his parents at 4587 Terrace Drive in 1936. A resident of Alpine, CA, in 2001, he indicated that he was a good ball player himself, and played at Hoover High School after Ted Williams had departed.[375] His first appearance in uniform would be on opening day. He indicated that he wore uniform number 55. Thompson would continue to serve the ball club for four more years...until, he said, "...he was bigger than some of the players themselves!"

THE PLAYERS

JOHN OROVILLE APPLEBY

Reportedly a left-handed first baseman he was invited down from Los Angeles by Spider Baum. There was only a single reference to him found, as a pinch hitter in one game, and no first name listed.[376] It is very likely that this was John Oroville Appleby, who would have been age 22 during spring training. He attended UCLA where he played both basketball and baseball. No records were found of him playing in organized baseball.

JOSEPH BERKOWITZ

Joe was a 25-year old infielder was from the Los Angeles area. He played for Hollywood in 1935. In 1931 he signed with El Paso of the Arizona-Texas League and moved up to the Oakland club in 1932, and Hollywood in 1933. He played through the 1940 season with the Padres where he ended his professional career. While in San Diego he lived at 1159 6th Avenue.

March 22, 1936, The San Diego Union,
JOE BERKOWITZ

Young in years but a veteran in experience. That's Joe Berkowitz, 25-year old infielder who is expected to put in some heavy licks for the San Diego padres this season.

Berkowitz, calls Los Angeles home, and is a product of Roosevelt High school there. He gained his first baseball experience on vacant lots, but really learned what it was all about as a member of the Roosevelt team, where he put in two years at various spots on the infield, mostly at third base and shortstop.

In 1931, he decided to fare forth and earn his living as a ball player. He signed his first contract with the El Paso club of the Arizona-Texas league, and played both third base and short stop [sic] that year. He showed up so well that he earned a contract with Oakland as a shortstop for the season of 1932, and in 1933 he went to Hollywood in the same capacity.

He has remained there ever since and has earned his spurs as a veteran coast leaguer.

Berkowitz is 25 years of age and single. He is fast on the bases and fields well. His batting mark for last year was .275. He is five feet 10, weighs 162 and bats and throws right handed.

Joe is no stranger in San Diego as he has played with numerous semi-pro teams in Los Angeles winter league baseball. He played with both Pirrone's team and that of Joe E. Brown and appeared in San Diego with both organizations.

JOE BERKOWITZ   Joseph Berkowitz aka Joe Burke   5:10½ 154 BR TR
Born: October 12, 1909 Los Angeles, CA   Died: December 4, 1984 Pico Rivera, CA

Year	Team	League	Pos	G	AB	R	H	1B	2B	3B	HR	RBI	K	BB	SB	AVG
1931	El Paso	Arizona-Texas	ss	25	82	18	12	10	2	0	0				1	.146
1932	Oakland	PCL	ss	33	115	7	24	21	3	0	0	7			1	.209
1933	Hollywood	PCL	ss-3b-2b	83	266	43	81	67	8	5	1	26			4	.305
1934	Hollywood	PCL	2b	112	373	46	104	84	17	0	3	23			4	.279
1935	Hollywood	PCL	ss-3b	71	222	25	51	42	8	1	0	21			4	.230
1936	San Diego	PCL	3-s-o-1	45	97	15	24	20	2	2	0	5			2	.247
1937	San Diego	PCL	ss-2b-3b	126	422	49	107	82	23	2	0	35			3	.254
1938	San Diego	PCL	3b-2b	129	443	72	132	102	23	6	1	52			8	.298
1939	San Diego	PCL	s-3-2-1	132	402	51	105	80	17	8	0	43		32	2	.261
1940	San Diego	PCL	2b-3b	53	100	11	21	15	6	0	0	5		6	0	.210
	Minor League totals			809	2522	337	661	523	109	24	5	217		38	29	.262

JOHN BLADEL

There was only a singled reference found on him which indicated that a player named Bladell was under contract to Brooklyn in 1935.[377] However, no record of any professional player by that name could be found. The player is likely Johnny Bladel who graduated from Inglewood High School in the Los Angeles area in 1930 and had a brief spring stint with Seattle in 1932. He was captain of the baseball team which included Rosy Gilhousen, another player who was in the 1936 Padre spring training camp. Both players also attended Compton Junior College and played baseball together on that team.

MAX ALEXANDER BRYAN

A Long Beach resident in 1936, he was invited to spring training as a catcher to replace Elmer Stock, but then released on March 22, 1936.[378] There is no record of him playing minor league baseball although he was found to be a participant in spring training for the Los Angeles Angels in 1937, and while working in the oil fields at Signal Hill played for the company team.

MAX BRYAN   Max Alexander Bryan
Born: December 23, 1908 Springville, UT   Died: February 22, 1988 Nephi, UT

Year	Team	League	Pos	G	AB	R	H	1B	2B	3B	HR	RBI	K	BB	SB	AVG
1934	Signal Hill		c													
1935	Signal Hill		c													
1936	Signal Hill		c													

APPENDIX H—BIOGRAPHIES OF THE 1936 SAN DIEGO PADRES

ARCHIBALD STEWART CAMPBELL

Archie was a 32-year-old pitcher and had a 12-17 record with the Hollywood club in 1935. His nickname "Ever Ready" came from the fact he thrived on pitching with only two days rest never encountering arm trouble. Campbell began his career in semipro ball in Los Angeles then signed with Wichita of the Western League in 1924 staying there until 1927. In 1928 he went to the Yankees but missed out on the World Series that year by finishing with St. Paul. In 1929 he was drafted by the Washington Senators but remained at St. Paul where he led the American Association with wins and complete games. In 1930 Cincinnati picked him up and was swapped to Columbus with a month to go in the season. Then, it was to Indianapolis until 1933 when Lane picked Campbell up for his Hollywood team.[379] 1936 was the only season that Campbell played for the Padres, but he was in professional baseball off and on through 1947.

 *March 25, 1936, The San Diego Union*
ARCHIE CAMPBELL

Archie Campbell, right-handed hurler who first saw the light of day at Maplewood, N. J., bears the monicker [sic] "Iron Man Archie" throughout the Coast league and has merited it on numerous occasions.

"The Iron Man" thrives on pitching, and has frequently taken his turn on the mound with only two days of rest. He never has any trouble and accounts for that by declaring that he conserves arm strength by taking things easy in the bull pen.

Campbell not only is an iron man on the mound, but can take bumps and hard knocks of the game as well. He has the reputation of having knocked down Flint Rhem, tough major league hurler, five times in a fight on the field while with St. Paul.

Campbell started his career in semi-pro ball in Los Angeles and broke into organized ball in 1924 when he was signed by Wichita of the Western League. Archie played with Wichita until 1927 and then went to the Yankees in 1928. With only six weeks to go, Archie saw visions of a fat World Series check but the Yanks fooled him and sent him to St. Paul. Col. Ruppert, owner of the Yanks, provided balm for his wounded feelings by sending him a personal check for $750.

Campbell was drafted by Washington and returned to St. Paul in 1929, where he led the American association in games won and complete games pitched. He was sold to Cincinnati in 1930 and was swapped to Columbus with only a month left to go that season. He was traded to Indianapolis in 1931 and remained there until 1933, when Bill Lane and Killefer arranged a trade by which Jim Turner went to Indianapolis and Campbell came to Hollywood. He has been with the club ever since.

Campbell is 32 years of age, is six feet, one inch in height, weighs 190 pounds, and is married. He is the father of three children, two girls and one boy.

ARCHIE CAMPBELL   Archibald Stewart Campbell "Iron Man"   6:00   195   BR   TR
Born: October 20, 1903 Maplewood, NJ   Died: December 22, 1989 Sparks, NV

Year	Team	League	G	GS	CG	ShO	SV	W	L	PCT	IP	H	R	ER	K	BB	ERA
1923	"Dads" Thielman Buick Auto																
1924	Sioux City	Tri-State	16					6	6	.500							
	Wichita	Western	19			0		1	5	.167	91.0	104	77	57	34	66	5.64
1925	Wichita	Western	35					9	11	.450	174.0	218	160	114	65	102	5.90
1926	Wichita	Western	44					14	**21**	.400	272.0	345	207	153	134	118	5.06
1927	Wichita	Western	38					19	6	**.760**	200.0	208	106	78	99	57	3.51

Year	Team	League	G	GS	CG	ShO	SV	W	L	PCT	IP	H	R	ER	K	BB	ERA
1928	New York	AL	13	1	0	0	2	0	1	.000	24.0	30	22	14	9	11	5.25
	St. Paul	American Assn	13					3	2	.600	47.0	51	25	21	23	20	4.02
1929	Washington	AL	4	0	0	0	0	0	1	.000	4.0	10	7	7	1	5	15.75
	St. Paul	American Assn	24					15	3	**.833**	174.0	152	63	54	82	53	2.79
1930	Cincinnati	NL	23	3	1	0	4	2	4	.333	58.0	71	38	35	19	31	5.43
	Columbus	American Assn	9		2			2	4	.333	34.0	42	33	25	11	13	6.62
1931	Columbus	American Assn	41					13	15	.464	195.0	221	132	106	63	110	4.89
1932	Indianapolis	American Assn	46					10	19	.345	234.0	233	123	95	146	103	3.65
1933	Hollywood	PCL	51	37	27	2	9	21	15	.583	310.7	308	157	140	135	122	4.06
1934	Hollywood	PCL	42		10	1		12	13	.480	191.0	224	108	102	76	74	4.81
1935	Hollywood	PCL	42		17	0		12	17	.414	241.0	296	156	121	105	99	4.52
1936	San Diego	PCL	48	2	1	0	5	6	9	.400	129.0	143	88	71	45	73	4.95
1937	Los Angeles	PCL	20		0	0		1	3	.250	55.0	80	58	48	17	17	7.85
1938	Fox Studios																
1939	Grass Valley	Sacramento Valley	1	1	1	0	0	1	0	1.000	9.0	14	1	1	3	0	1.00
1940	Grass Valley	Sacramento Valley	11	9	9	0	0	10	0	1.000	88.7	87	33	29	23	20	2.94
1941	Grass Valley	Sacramento Valley	13	7	6	1	0	5	4	.556	84.3	101	47	31	34	17	3.31
1942	Grass Valley	Sacramento Valley	7	2	2	0	0	2	2	.500	33.0	26	7	5	15	4	1.36
1943	Grass Valley	Sacramento Valley						**Did Not Pitch**									
1944	Oakland	PCL	13	0	0	0	0	3	2	.600	33.3	37			9	7	
	Rosabell Plumbers																
1945	Signal Oil																
1946	Signal Oil																
1947	Nevada Turf Club																
	Harrahs Casino																
	Reno	Sunset	9		0	0		1	0	1.000	28.0	37	23	15	15	14	4.82
	Minor League totals		524	59	76	4	14	166	152	.522	2542	2837	1528	1210	1103	1023	4.28
	Major League totals		40	4	1	0	6	2	6	.250	86.0	111	67	56	29	47	5.86

HERMAN E. CARROLL

A pitcher who was from San Pedro, Carroll had no professional experience prior to joining the Padres during spring training on March 2nd. At the time he was on active duty with the U.S. Navy on the USS Tennessee. Carroll was reportedly one of the "most publicized" players in Navy baseball history at the time.[380] The Navy ultimately refused to grant him a special discharge. There is no record of him playing minor league baseball; however, he was recognized as a pitcher on the 1937 National Baseball Congress All-American team (as a member of the Hollywood, CA Painters).

HEC CARROLL   Herman Carroll   5:11 175 BR TR
                    Born: 1913

Year	Team	League	G	GS	CG	ShO	SV	W	L	PCT	IP	H	R	ER	K	BB	ERA
1935	U.S.S. Tennessee																
1936	U.S.S. Tennessee																
1937	U.S.S. Tennessee																
	Hollywood Painters																
1938	U.S.S. Tennessee																
1939	U.S.S. Tennessee																
1940	U.S.S. Tennessee																

APPENDIX H—BIOGRAPHIES OF THE 1936 SAN DIEGO PADRES

LESTER SPURGEON COOK

A former catcher Cook served as Trainer in 1936 and eventually played in seven games being called upon in July for back-up purposes. He served the Padres as trainer through the 1950s. Since Cook's primary role on the 1936 team was as Trainer, his full biography is contained in the initial section of this Appendix (see "The Supporting Cast").

FRANK RITCHIE COOPER

At 21 years old Cooper was going after a utility job given that George Myatt seemingly had the shortstop position wrapped up. He hailed from the Van Nuys area and played semi-pro ball with W. C. Tuttle's team, and had teamed up with Bobby Doerr in 1934 on the Van Nuys Merchants. It was Tuttle who recommended Cooper to Bill Lane as a player who hustled all of the time and could be a replacement for Myatt when the team loses him for the 1937 season.[381] He, along with Iverson and Vaughn, were on the roster in April but played with the Padres "B" team and stayed in San Diego while the team was on the road. The three players were released on May 10, 1936. There is no record of Cooper playing minor league baseball.

 *March 18, 1936, The San Diego Union*
RITCHIE COOPER

Bubbling over with energy, a will to learn and a never-say-die complex, young Ritchie Cooper consistently shines in the San Diego Padres' spring training camp at Fullerton and from all indications will be on deck when the Padres return here to their new home March 31.

Ritchie, short and stocky and a protégé of Coast League President W. C. Tuttle, is 21 years old and is seeking a shortstop's job, or at least a utility infield berth, with the Padres. He's 5 feet 5½ inches of diamond dynamite and his bat has been filled with base hits during early prep sessions.

His home town is Van Nuys in San Fernando valley where he first broke into diamond prominence with Van Nuys High. His first efforts other than prep ball were with Tuttle's Grasshoppers, a group of youngsters banded together by the present league prexy to mop up on southland opposition, something they did in no uncertain fashion.

Following several years of campaigning with the Grasshoppers Ritchie landed a berth on the Twentieth Century Fox Films ball club, playing with many present minor league stars and several big leaguers.

Tuttle recommended the youngster to H. W. Lane, Padre prexy, and from all accounts "Tut" didn't send Lane a "lemon" for Ritchie has won over the entire club with his willingness to learn and hustle.

Then, too, Manager Frank Shellenback and President Lane know that next spring at this time they'll probably be looking for a shortstop to replace George Myatt, who is billed for delivery to the Boston Red Sox, so its [sic] probable that they'll hold on to him or farm him out to some small minor league team for a year's experience in organized baseball.

Unlike a great many infielders Cooper goes at everything banged his way and as a result he has more than his share of the errors, but he's too full of fight to watch hard hit balls go by to save his fielding average.

RITCHIE COOPER

Frank Ritchie Cooper "Sandy" 5:05½ 135 BR TR
Born: January 2, 1914 Chicago, IL Died: July 9, 1966 Ventura, CA

Year	Team	League	Pos	G	AB	R	H	1B	2B	3B	HR	RBI	K	BB	SB	AVG
1933	Van Nuys Merchants		ss													
1934	Van Nuys Merchants		ss		72		24									.333
1935	Van Nuys Merchants		ss													

DENNIS WAYNE CRABB

He was an unknown except it was reported that he was released on the day of the first game. Spelled as "Crab" he was listed in the box score of a game on March 18th as a catcher.[382] There is no record of him playing minor league baseball. However, in addition to this tryout, he participated in another spring tryout in 1939 when he was cut on the last day of spring training for the 1939 Abilene Apaches of the West Texas-New Mexico League and returned to Watsonville, California.

DENNIS CRABB

Dennis Waye Crabb 5:10 175 BR TR
Born: May 23, 1917 Kansas Died: February 13, 1978 Santa Cruz, CA

Year	Team	League	Pos	G	AB	R	H	1B	2B	3B	HR	RBI	K	BB	SB	AVG
1934	Watsonville Pippins		of													
1935	Watsonville Haciendas		of-c													
1936-1937								**No Record**								
1938	Pasadena Merchants		c-of													
1939	Watsonville White's Cardinals		of													
	Watsonville Apple Pickers		of													

HOWARD OLIVER CRAGHEAD

A 27-year old pitcher he began his career in 1926 with Oakland and then was with Cleveland for 15 games during the 1931 and 1933 seasons. In June 1936 he came to the Padres from Seattle in a trade for Ed Wells and remained with the team through 1940 when he retired. He won 209 minor league games in his career.

HOWARD CRAGHEAD

Howard Oliver Craghead 6:02 200 BR TR
Born: May 25, 1908 Selma, CA Died: July 14, 1962 San Diego, CA

Year	Team	League	G	GS	CG	ShO	SV	W	L	PCT	IP	H	R	ER	K	BB	ERA
1926	Oakland	PCL	20	9	4	0	0	2	4	.333	84.3	78	40	29	35	33	3.09
1927	Ogden	Utah-Idaho	9		6	0		4	4	.500	65.0	73	32	29	60	28	4.02
	Oakland	PCL	24		3			4	4	.500	100.0	104	46	38	49	41	3.42
1928	Oakland	PCL	39		21			18	13	.581	282.0	283	122	107	147	104	3.41
1929	Oakland	PCL	52		23	3		21	12	.636	298.0	321	158	134	**190**	128	4.05
1930	Oakland	PCL	47		26	2		21	22	.488	343.0	342	156	139	199	125	3.65
1931	Oakland	PCL	36		16	0		13	15	.464	229.0	233	117	106	156	100	4.17
	Cleveland	AL	4	0	0	0	0	0	0	.000	6.0	8	4	4	2	2	6.00
1932	Toledo	American Assn	41					18	15	.545	253.0	292	157	*121*	112	98	*4.30*

APPENDIX H—BIOGRAPHIES OF THE 1936 SAN DIEGO PADRES

Year	Team	League	G	GS	CG	ShO	SV	W	L	PCT	IP	H	R	ER	K	BB	ERA
1933	Cleveland	AL	11	0	0	0	0	0	0	.000	17.0	19	13	12	2	10	6.35
	Toledo	American Assn	21					5	9	.357	119.0	154	87	78	45	44	5.90
1934	Seattle	PCL	46		16	1		16	21	.432	280.0	339	162	135	145	110	4.34
1935	Seattle	PCL	39		19	0		18	16	.529	276.0	316	149	125	120	101	4.08
1936	Seattle/San Diego	PCL	40		18	3		16	12	.571	235.0	233	109	94	109	83	3.60
1937	San Diego	PCL	42		17	2		16	13	.552	245.0	265	100	89	119	74	3.27
1938	San Diego	PCL	47	34	22	3	3	18	18	.500	271.0	279	132	86	138	79	2.86
1939	San Diego	PCL	34	28	14	1	0	11	16	.407	203.0	239	121	107	94	56	4.74
1940	San Diego	PCL	38	20	6	0	1	8	14	.364	175.0	205	104	95	66	74	4.89
	Minor League totals		575	91	211	15	4	209	208	.501	3458.3	3756	1792	*1512*	1784	1278	3.93
	Major League totals		15	0	0	0	0	0	0	.000	23.0	27	17	16	4	12	6.26

D. H. CURTIS

A Curtis was listed in the box score for a March 5, 1936, intrasquad game as a catcher (but it might have been as a pinch runner for the catcher Desautels in the six-inning game).[383] No reference to his first name could be found, nor any verifiable minor league record. However, there was a D. H. Curtis who had a tryout for the 1935 Hollywood Stars and was found to playing in leagues around Fontana, California, which is near the team's San Bernardino spring training base.[384]

D. H. CURTIS   David Henry Curtis
Born: March 8, 1915 Utah   Died: September 11, 1980 Fontana, CA

Year	Team	League	Pos	G	AB	R	H	1B	2B	3B	HR	RBI	K	BB	SB	AVG
1935	Fontana		p													
1936	Fontana		3b													

EUGENE ABRAHAM DESAUTELS

A 28-year old catcher from Quinebaug, Connecticut, Desautels started his career at Holy Cross College and then was signed by the Detroit Tigers in 1930. He played in limited duty with the American League champion Tigers that year, and remained with them through 1933. He played with Toledo in the American Association in 1934 and joined the Hollywood team for the 1935 season where he hit .265.[385] 1936 was Desautels' only year with the Padres; however, he was active professionally through 1948 where he played with Williamsport in the Eastern League. His major league career totaled 712 games with Detroit, Boston (NL), Cleveland, and Philadelphia (AL). After retiring from active play Desautels managed in the minor leagues into the early 1950s.

 *March 9, 1936*, The San Diego Union
EUGENE DESAUTELS

Eugene Desautels, call him "Gene" or "Red," he answers to both, is the regular catcher for the San Diego Padres of the Pacific Coast Baseball league. He's only 27 now, married, and hails from Quinebaug, Conn.

Desautels is a product of the fine baseball coaching at Holy Cross college. He broke directly into major league baseball from college in 1930, being signed by the Detroit Tigers. He caught 42 games for the now champions of the American league that first season, but was sent to Columbus in the American association the next year for more seasoning, particularly when it came to hitting.

At the end of the 1931 season, Detroit recalled Gene and he played through the 1932 and 1933 seasons with the Tigers. In 1934 he was optioned to Toledo in the American association and last year Owner H. W. Lane of the Hollywood Stars bought him from the Detroit club. Now he shifts scenes to San Diego.

Desautels throws and bats right handed and handles pitchers in fine style.

GENE DESAUTELS

Eugene Abraham Desautels "Red"   5:11 170 BR TR
Born: June 13, 1907 Worcester, MA   Died: November 5, 1994 Flint, MI

Year	Team	League	Pos	G	AB	R	H	1B	2B	3B	HR	RBI	K	BB	SB	AVG
1930	Detroit	AL	c	42	126	13	24	18	4	2	0	9	9	7	2	.190
1931	Columbus	American Assn	c	96	275	45	75	58	16	1	0	32	17	35	3	.237
	Detroit	AL	c	3	11	1	1	1	0	0	0	1	1	0	0	.091
1932	Detroit	AL	c	28	72	8	17	15	2	0	0	2	11	13	0	.236
1933	Detroit	AL	c	30	42	5	6	5	1	0	0	4	6	4	0	.143
1934	Toledo	American Assn	c	88	280	33	75	59	13	3	0	38	17	36	1	.268
1935	Hollywood	PCL	c	129	426	48	113	78	26	3	6	55			6	.268
1936	San Diego	PCL	c	148	480	68	153	127	18	5	3	69			4	.319
1937	Boston	AL	c	96	305	33	74	61	10	3	0	27	26	36	1	.243
1938	Boston	AL	c	108	333	47	97	77	16	2	2	48	31	57	1	.291
1939	Boston	AL	c	76	226	26	55	41	14	0	0	21	13	33	3	.243
1940	Boston	AL	c	71	222	19	50	42	7	1	0	17	13	32	0	.225
1941	Cleveland	AL	c	66	189	20	38	31	5	1	1	17	12	14	1	.201
1942	Cleveland	AL	c	62	162	14	40	35	5	0	0	9	13	12	1	.247
1943	Cleveland	AL	c	68	185	14	38	31	6	1	0	19	16	11	2	.205
1944				**In Military Service**												
1945	Cleveland	AL	c	10	9	1	1	1	0	0	0	0	1	1	0	.111
1946	Philadelphia	AL	c	52	130	10	28	24	3	1	0	13	16	12	1	.215
1947	Toronto	International	c	75	208	16	39	30	3	1	5	28	18	23	0	.188
1948	Williamsport	Eastern	c	16	50	6	15	11	4	0	0	6	2	9	0	.300
1949	Williamsport	Eastern	c	1												
1950-1961				**Did Not Play**												
1962	Indianapolis	American Assn	c	1	0	0	0	0	0	0	0	0	0			.000
Minor League totals				616	1858	227	499	388	83	14	14	241	71	116	15	.269
Major League totals				712	2012	211	469	382	73	11	3	187	168	232	12	.233

VINCENT PAUL DIMAGGIO

Playing for the Padres in 1936 DiMaggio was the 23-year old brother of pro ballplayers Joe and Dom. He started out with the San Francisco Seals in 1932 right out of high school and hit a home run in his first at bat.[386] He also played with the Tucson team in the Arizona-Texas League before being sold to the Stars for the 1933 season.[387] He hit .278 for Hollywood in 1935. His only year in San Diego was 1936. DiMaggio played professionally until 1951 with his last major league season being 1946 with the New York Giants. He also played for Boston (NL), Cincinnati, Pittsburgh, and Philadelphia (NL). DiMaggio also managed several minor league teams.

APPENDIX H—BIOGRAPHIES OF THE 1936 SAN DIEGO PADRES

 *March 21, 1936, The San Diego Union*
VINCENT DI MAGGIO

Vincent "Vince" Di Maggio, regular outfielder with the San Diego Padres in the Pacific Coast league, is an older brother of Joe, the outfielder the San Francisco Seals sold to the New York Yankees late last season. He's not quite as big and powerful as brother Joe, but he is a good fielder and bats with power.

Di Maggio was born in Martinez, but calls San Francisco home. He broke in baseball with the San Francisco Seals in 1932 right out of high school. He was farmed to Tucson in the Arizona-Texas league and when that broke up in July, was recalled by the Seals. He played through part of the next season with the Seals, was released and later joined them again.

An injury to his arm which Di Maggio had in 1932 slowed up his playing then. He was still bothered in 1933, but later that year was sold to Hollywood and since then has been coming along in fine style, earning a berth as a regular outfielder last season.

In spring training camp Di Maggio has been hitting consistently and throwing well. A right-handed hitter and thrower, Vince has played outfield all his professional career, though he was a third baseman and catcher when playing junior and senior ball.

VINCE DiMAGGIO   Vincent Paul DiMaggio   5:11   183   BR   TR

Born: September 6, 1912 Martinez, CA   Died: October 3, 1986 North Hollywood, CA

Year	Team	League	Pos	G	AB	R	H	1B	2B	3B	HR	RBI	K	BB	SB	AVG
1932	Tucson	Arizona-Texas	inf-of	94	398	90	138	82	22	9	25	81			14	.347
	San Francisco	PCL	of	59	200	35	54	33	13	2	6	31			2	.270
1933	SF/Hollywood	PCL	of	96	339	54	113	74	24	4	11	65			7	.333
	San Mateo	California St	of-ss	4	12	2	1	1	0	0	0	0			0	.083
1934	Hollywood	PCL	of	166	587	89	169	124	25	3	17	91			7	.288
1935	Hollywood	PCL	of	174	659	107	183	119	36	4	24	112			15	.278
1936	San Diego	PCL	of	176	641	109	188	112	43	14	19	102			22	.293
1937	Boston	NL	of	132	493	56	126	91	18	4	13	69	**111**	39	8	.256
1938	Boston	NL	of-2b	150	540	71	123	78	28	3	14	61	**134**	65	11	.228
1939	Kansas City	American Assn	of	154	544	122	158	71	32	9	**46**	**136**	**123**	89	21	.290
	Cincinnati	NL	of	8	14	1	1	0	1	0	0	2	10	2	0	.071
1940	Cincinnati/Pittsburgh	NL	of	112	360	61	104	59	26	0	19	54	83	38	11	.289
1941	Pittsburgh	NL	of	151	528	73	141	88	27	5	21	100	100	68	10	.267
1942	Pittsburgh	NL	of	143	496	57	118	78	22	3	15	75	**87**	52	10	.238
1943	Pittsburgh	NL	of-ss	157	580	64	144	86	41	2	15	88	**126**	70	11	.248
1944	Pittsburgh	NL	of-3b	109	342	41	82	49	20	4	9	50	**83**	33	6	.240
1945	Philadelphia	NL	of	127	452	64	116	69	25	3	19	84	**91**	43	12	.257
1946	Philadelphia/New York	NL	of	21	44	3	4	3	1	0	0	1	12	2	0	.091
	San Francisco	PCL	of	43	129	19	34	21	10	2	1	21	23	13	3	.264
1947	Oakland	PCL	of	140	473	80	114	68	20	4	22	81	87	36	7	.241
1948	Stockton	California	of	127	420	108	119	64	24	1	**30**	100	87	98	15	.283
1949	Pittsburg	Far West	of	101	362	108	133	76	19	1	37	117	82	85	11	.367
1950	Pittsburg	Far West	of	125	434	105	153	93	28	6	26	129	79	79	15	.353
1951	Pittsburg	Far West	of	44	127	32	33	19	9	1	4	29	24	35	4	.260
	Tacoma	Western Int	of	74	236	35	53	34	12	2	5	44	41	59	6	.225
Minor League totals				1577	5561	1095	1643	991	317	62	273	1139	546	494	149	.295
Major League totals				1110	3849	491	959	601	209	24	125	584	837	412	79	.249

HAROLD FRANCIS DOERR

Hal was the 22-year old brother of Bobby. He grew up in Los Angeles where he attended George Washington High School. Another Padre, Van Wirthman also attended Washington High and played on the baseball team with Doerr. Upon graduation from high school in 1932, Doerr initiated his professional playing career when he joined the Hollywood Stars and played one game that season. Mostly a part-time player in 1933-1935, he was signed by the Padres in late June 1936 after being released by Houston of the Texas League when Desautels got injured. In his short month with the Padres Doerr managed to get into 10 games and was let go by the team on July 15th.

HAL DOERR Harold Francis Doerr   5:10 175 BR TR
Born: May 15, 1913 Los Angeles, CA   Died: March 2, 1983 San Diego, CA

Year	Team	League	Pos	G	AB	R	H	1B	2B	3B	HR	RBI	K	BB	SB	AVG
1930	Dennis Painters		c													
1931						**No Record**										
1932	Hollywood	PCL	c	1	3	1	1	1	0	0	0				0	.333
1933	Springfield	Miss Valley	c	12	22	0	4	4	0	0	0	1	3	2	0	.182
	Omaha/St. Joseph	Western	c	22	68	9	12	7	4	0	1				0	.176
	Lincoln	Nebraska St	c	11	29	3	6	3	2	0	1		5	4	1	.207
	Seattle	PCL	c	3	9	1	3	3	0	0	0	2			0	.333
1934	Portland	PCL	c	71	199	16	51	42	8	0	1	14			2	.256
1935	Portland/Los Angeles	PCL	c	68	140	17	30	24	4	2	0	18			1	.214
1936	Houston	Texas	c	8	15	2	2	2	0	0	0	0			0	.133
	San Diego	PCL	c	10	27	1	4	4	0	0	0	0			0	.148
1937-38						**No Record**										
1939	El Centro		c													
	Minor League totals			206	512	50	113	90	18	2	3	35	8	6	4	.221

ROBERT PERSHING DOERR

In November 1935, at age 17, Doerr was still attending Fremont High School when he and George Myatt were sold as an option to the Boston Red Sox for "1937 delivery."[388] He had already played in the 1934 and 1935 seasons with the Stars. Myatt and Doerr were referred to as the "million-dollar kid" keystone.[389] His American Legion team won the California state championship in 1932, and his Fremont High School team won the Los Angeles city championship in 1933. He joined the Hollywood Stars at age 16 in 1934 batting .259 in 67 games. Then, in 1935, in all but two games for the Stars he batted .317. Doerr attended school in the winter months and expected to receive his high school diploma in June 1936. He was recognized early by Red Sox scout Ernie Johnson and General Manager Eddie Collins, and it was Collins who negotiated with Bill Lane to make Doerr a future Red Sox. He also played on the same high school baseball team with the Padres first baseman George McDonald. The 1936 season was Doerr's only one with San Diego and he led the PCL in hits with 238. Doerr joined the Boston Red Sox in 1937 and remained there until his last season in 1951. After retiring, he was a coach in the major leagues for eight years. Doerr was elected to the National Baseball Hall of Fame in 1986.

APPENDIX H—BIOGRAPHIES OF THE 1936 SAN DIEGO PADRES

March 15, 1936, The San Diego Union
ROBERT DOERR

One-half of the "million-dollar kid" keystone combination, young Robert Doerr, better known as Bobby, appears to be one of the boys destined to dominate the headlines this summer as San Diego's newly-adopted Padres launch their initial Pacific Coast League campaign representing this city.

Bobby, who doesn't reach 18 until April 7, is a product of California American Legion junior baseball, and from all indications will be heard from as a major leaguer in another year or so.

Doerr first started playing ball as a member of the Leonard Wood post, American Legion team in Los Angeles in 1932. His team swept to the state championship with Bobby playing an important role at second base. In '33 he helped Fremont High win the Angel City prep diamond bunting and then rejoined the Leonard Wood juniors, who again won state laurels.

The spring of 1934 found him finishing his prep school career with Fremont High's team and then joined the Padres, then Hollywood Stars, in June, and before the season ended he had played 67 games, picked up a .259 batting mark and .955 fielding average to show his potentialities.

It was last year that he came into his own, however, for his activities won the attention of major league scouts, the Red Sox finally placing the highest bid to obtain Doerr and his buddy, Georgie Myatt. He played in all but two games, finishing with a .317 bat figure and .960 fielding mark, remarkable inasmuch as he was only 17 and playing his first full season in double A ball.

Bobby resides in Los Angeles during the off season and only recently completed his school work. He managed to make up enough credits during the fall and winter months to earn his diploma and will receive the treasured sheepskin in June.

Success hasn't softened his head and he's popular to a point of being idolized everywhere he goes. He's especially popular with his teammates and the Padres' grizzled old veterans are never too busy to help him along with valuable pointers. Like Myatt, Doerr credits the old warhorse, Eddie Mulligan, with being most responsible for his rise to diamond fame with his helpful playing hints.

BOBBY DOERR

Robert Pershing Doerr 5:11 175 BR TR
Born: April 7, 1918 Los Angeles, CA Died: November 13, 2017 Junction City, OR

Year	Team	League	Pos	G	AB	R	H	1B	2B	3B	HR	RBI	K	BB	SB	AVG
1934	Van Nuys Merchants		2b	30			6									.200
	Hollywood	PCL	2b	67	201	12	52	46	6	0	0	11			1	.259
1935	Hollywood	PCL	2b	172	647	87	205	171	22	8	4	74			5	.317
1936	San Diego	PCL	2b	175	695	100	**238**	187	37	12	2	77			30	.342
1937	Boston	AL	2b	55	147	22	33	25	5	1	2	14	25	18	2	.224
1938	Boston	AL	2b	145	509	70	147	109	26	7	5	80	39	59	5	.289
1939	Boston	AL	2b	127	525	75	167	125	28	2	12	73	32	38	1	.318
1940	Boston	AL	2b	151	595	87	173	104	37	10	22	105	53	57	10	.291
1941	Boston	AL	2b	132	500	74	141	93	28	4	16	93	43	43	1	.282
1942	Boston	AL	2b	144	545	71	158	103	35	5	15	102	55	67	4	.290
1943	Boston	AL	2b	**155**	604	78	163	112	32	3	16	75	59	62	8	.270
1944	Boston	AL	2b	125	468	95	152	97	30	10	15	81	31	58	5	.325
1945						**In Military Service**										
1946	Boston	AL	2b	151	583	95	158	97	34	9	18	116	67	66	5	.271
1947	Boston	AL	2b	146	561	79	145	95	23	10	17	95	47	59	3	.258
1948	Boston	AL	2b	140	527	94	150	94	23	6	27	111	49	83	3	.285

Year	Team	League	Pos	G	AB	R	H	1B	2B	3B	HR	RBI	K	BB	SB	AVG
1949	Boston	AL	2b	139	541	91	167	110	30	9	18	109	33	75	2	.309
1950	Boston	AL	2b	149	586	103	172	105	29	11	27	120	42	67	3	.294
1951	Boston	AL	2b	106	402	60	116	80	21	2	13	73	33	57	2	.289
	Minor League totals			414	1543	199	495	404	65	20	6	162			36	.321
	Major League totals			1865	7093	1094	2042	1349	381	89	223	1247	608	809	54	.288

ELMER DONOVAN

Manager Shellenback wanted to take a look at a Johnny Donovan in spring training as he had played with Seattle and Los Angeles in 1935.[390] Very likely this player was Elmer Donovan, from Venice, California, and a right-handed pitcher who played in the minors in 1934-35, including being with Seattle and Los Angeles.[391]

ELMER DONOVAN Elmer Darrah Donovan TR
Born: October 15, 1913 Van Nuys, CA Died: March 21, 1975 Hesperia, CA

Year	Team	League	G	GS	CG	ShO	SV	W	L	PCT	IP	H	R	ER	K	BB	ERA
1934	Los Angeles	PCL	2	1	1	0		1	0	1.000	10.0	9	1	0	5	2	0.00
	Ponca City	Western Assn	33		21	0		13	15	.464	232.0	286	156	116	120	114	4.50
1935	Los Angeles/Seattle	PCL	18		2	0		0	4	.000	57.0	95	67	61	13	27	9.63
	Minor League totals		53	1	24	0		14	19	.424	299.0	390	224	177	138	143	5.33

CEDRIC MONTGOMERY DURST

Durst played with San Diego from 1936 through 1943 (except for a brief period in 1938 when he was traded to Hollywood) and managed the team from 1939-1943. Durst joined Hollywood in 1933 and played outfield since that time. He broke into professional ball in 1921 with Beaumont of the Texas League. In 1922-24 and 1926, he played for the St. Louis Browns, then for the New York Yankees where he played alongside Babe Ruth in the outfield during 1927-30. Durst finished the 1930 season with the Boston Red Sox when he was traded in May 1930 with $50,000 for Red Ruffing. Ruffing went on to win 231 games for the Yankees and induction into the Hall of Fame. Durst was gone from the Red Sox in 1931, played with St. Paul for a few years before joining up with Hollywood in 1933.[392] After leaving San Diego he managed other minor league teams through 1950. In San Diego, he lived at 2640 Strand Way.

March 6, 1936, The San Diego Union
CEDRIC DURST

Cedric "Syd" Durst is a regular in the outfield for the San Diego padres of the Pacific Coast baseball league. He has been with the club, formerly the Hollywood Stars, since 1933, when he was sold to Owner H. W. Lane's club by the Boston Red Sox. In 1936, this season, of course, he will be with the Padres, but still under the old direction.

Durst, who calls Austin, Texas, home is 35, married and has two children, a boy and a girl. And he likes the prospect of coming to San Diego. He likes beach houses, where the youngsters can be outdoors and swim year round.

It was in 1921 that Durst first broke into organized baseball. He went to Beaumont in the Texas league after playing high school and semi-professional baseball in Texas. At the end of the 1931 season his contract was purchased by the St. Louis Browns of the American league and Durst played in the outfield for the Browns in 1922 and 1923. In 1924 he was farmed to the Los Angeles club of the Coast league and played centerfield.

In 1925 the Browns recalled Durst and sent him to St. Paul in the American association. The 1926 season he was recalled by the Browns and played for them, and in the fall was traded to the New York Yankees. The seasons of 1927, 1928, 1929 and the spring of 1930 saw Durst patrol the outer gardens in the Yankee stadium along with Babe Ruth and company. Late in 1930 he was sold to the Boston red Sox and finished the season with that club. The next year he was sold to St. Paul again and played there in 1931 and 1932. Then came the shift to Hollywood on the sale engineered by the Red Sox.

Durst bats and throws left-handed "I'm left-handed even to thinking," Durst explains.

Almost all of the Texan's baseball career has been as an outfielder, though he has played a little first base.

Durst likes the game and insists he'll keep on playing until they cut the uniform off him.

CEDRIC DURST

Cedric Montgomery Durst 5:11 160 BL TL
Born: August 23, 1896 Austin, TX   Died: February 16, 1971 San Diego, CA

Year	Team	League	Pos	G	AB	R	H	1B	2B	3B	HR	RBI	K	BB	SB	AVG
1921	Beaumont	Texas	of	159	584	80	160	110	38	6	6	63	80	50	1	.274
1922	St. Louis	AL	of	15	12	5	4	3	1	0	0	0	1	0	0	.333
1923	St. Louis	AL	of-1b	45	85	12	18	11	2	0	5	11	14	8	0	.212
1924	Los Angeles	PCL	of-1b	185	705	141	241	151	**59**	14	17	130			16	.342
1925	St. Paul	American Assn	of	168	653	131	227	136	59	25	7	105	36	72	23	.348
1926	St Louis	AL	of-1b	80	219	32	52	37	7	5	3	16	19	22	0	.237
1927	New York	AL	of-1b	65	129	18	32	25	4	3	0	25	7	6	0	.248
1928	New York	AL	of-1b	74	135	18	34	29	2	1	2	10	9	7	1	.252
1929	New York	AL	of-1b	92	202	32	52	42	3	3	4	31	25	15	3	.257
1930	New York/Boston	AL	of	110	321	29	77	51	20	5	1	29	25	17	3	.240
1931	St. Paul	American Assn	of-1b	144	557	88	167	105	43	8	11	98	32	40	12	.300
1932	St. Paul	American Assn	of	117	408	53	128	95	16	11	6	49			4	.314
1933	Hollywood	PCL	of-1b	180	730	116	232	178	39	2	13	80			23	.318
1934	Hollywood	PCL	of-1b	125	438	76	131	109	15	3	4	61			3	.299
1935	Hollywood	PCL	of	167	639	89	207	160	38	3	6	72			9	.324
1936	San Diego	PCL	of	159	621	71	190	154	32	3	1	81			14	.306
1937	San Diego	PCL	of	137	458	52	134	105	25	2	2	57			4	.293
1938	SD/Hollywood	PCL	of	134	474	54	146	120	17	5	4	46			3	.308
1939	San Diego	PCL	1b-of	73	155	12	41	35	6	0	0	18		10	1	.265
1940	San Diego	PCL	1b	47	67	10	19	15	2	1	1	13		6	2	.284
1941	San Diego	PCL	of	30	53	4	13	11	2	0	0	2	2	2	0	.245
1942	San Diego	PCL	ph	2	1	0	0	0	0	0	0	0			0	.000
1943	San Diego	PCL	1b	10	7	0	0	0	0	0	0	0			0	.000
Minor League totals				1837	6550	977	2036	1484	391	83	78	875	150	180	115	.311
Major League totals				481	1103	146	269	198	39	17	15	122	100	75	7	.244

EDDIE EHIL

A pitcher from Missouri, he was invited to spring training but did not stick around long, being cut on March 1, 1936.[393] Various articles at the time had his last name also spelled Ehll. Under either spelling there is no record of him having played professional baseball.

DON LESTER ELTON

A 21-year old pitcher with semi-pro experience, he was apparently property of the Boston Red Sox.[394] He was cut by the Padres in late March 1936 and pitched for Danville of the Bi-State League over the remainder of the season.

DON ELTON   Donald Lester Elton   6:02½   190   BR   TL
Born: September 7, 1913 California   Died: October 24, 1976 Sacramento Co., CA

Year	Team	League	G	GS	CG	ShO	SV	W	L	PCT	IP	H	R	ER	K	BB	ERA
1935	Reading																
1936	Danville	Bi-State	8	3	1	0		2	1	.667	31.0	45	23		13	15	
	Newport News	Tidewater															
1937							No Record										
1938	Santa Curz Alpines																
1939							No Record										
1940	Devey's Demons Oakland, CA																
1940	Reno Garage																
1940	Sperry's of Reno, NV																
1941	Frank Newman	Peninsula St															
1944	Richmond Hubs	Richmond CA City															
	Minor League totals		8	3	1	0		2	1	.667	31.0	45	23		13	15	

WILLIAM EDWARD ENGLUND

An outfielder who was "showing promise"[395] Englund was cut on March 9, 1936. He played a few seasons with Reseda (semi-pro), and may have played in the Western Association. Some of the spring training newspaper articles had his last name spelled as England. A William England was found to have played one season, 1936, with the West Plains/Caruthersville team in the Northeast Arkansas League.[396] However, it is believed that this was a different ballplayer than William Englund.

BILL ENGLUND   William Edward Englund
Born: January 31, 1917 Chicago, IL   Died: September 28, 1987 Oceanside, CA

Year	Team	League	Pos	G	AB	R	H	1B	2B	3B	HR	RBI	K	BB	SB	AVG
1933	Van Nuys Merchants		of													
1934	Van Nuys Merchants		of													
1935	Reseda Athletics		of													
1936							No Record										
1937	Reseda Athletics		of													
1938	Reseda Athletics		of													
1939	Reseda Athletics		of													

ELMER RUSSELL EVERT

Born in Wisconsin, Evert grew up in San Diego and played a limited time with Muskogee in the Western Association, but mainly played in San Diego city leagues from 1928 to 1936. In 1936, Evert had limited PCL experience with San Diego and Sacramento. He was brought up to serve as an emergency catcher in June and let go the same month when Hal Doerr was signed.

APPENDIX H—BIOGRAPHIES OF THE 1936 SAN DIEGO PADRES

ELMER EVERT Elmer Russell Evert 5:11 170 BR TR
Born: December 8, 1905 Arlington, WI Died: April 11, 1966 San Diego, CA

Year	Team	League	Pos	G	AB	R	H	1B	2B	3B	HR	RBI	K	BB	SB	AVG
1927	Muskogee	Western Assn.	c	45	132	13	33	22	7	1	3	11			1	.250
1928	Chula Vista		c													
1929	North Park	SD City	c													
1930	N. Park/Harding Colts	SD City	c													
1931	San Diego		c													
1932	San Diego		c													
1933	Walter Church	SD City	c													
1934	Walter Church	SD City	c													
1935	Tex. Liquor House	SD City	c													
1936	SD Liqour House		c													
	SD/Sacramento	PCL	c	6	14	1	2	2	0	0	0	0			0	.143
	El Centro		c	2	6	0	1	1	0	0	0				0	.167
1937	Paris Inn		c													
	Minor League totals			51	146	14	35	24	7	1	3	11			1	.240

ROSS DICKSON GILHOUSEN

Wall Street Journal,
July 31, 1976

His name appeared in one box score during spring training, on March 4th as a center fielder.[397] He attended Inglewood High in Los Angeles with Johnny Bladel in 1930, then both played at Compton Junior College in 1931. According to his obituary Gilhousen began his professional career in 1931[398] However, the earliest records found with his name were with semi-pro teams in California in 1934. He eventually played two seasons in Alabama-Florida League—1939-1940—and then managed a couple of seasons. However, after ending his playing career Gilhousen went into scouting and remained a scout for over 50 years, mainly the Los Angeles Angels (American League) and Kansas City Royals. Gilhousen was one of the top scouts for Roland Hemond when he headed the scouting bureau for the expansion Angels in 1961.[399] Notably, when scouting for the Royals, he was responsible for the signing of Dan Quisenberry and George. Brett. His obituary stated that he had signed over 100 players who made it to the major leagues. In 1986 he was the named West Coast Scout of the Year.

ROSEY GILHOUSEN Ross Dickson Gilhousen 5:08 175 BL TL
Born: June 7, 1913 California Died: December 20, 1997 Rancho Mirage, CA

Year	Team	League	Pos	G	AB	R	H	1B	2B	3B	HR	RBI	K	BB	SB	AVG
1934	Pasadena Merchants		of													
1935	Covina Merchants		of													
1936	Covina Merchants		of													
1937	San Bernardino Stubbys		of													
1938	San Bernardino Merchants		of													

Year	Team	League	Pos	G	AB	R	H	1B	2B	3B	HR	RBI	K	BB	SB	AVG
1939	Tallassee	Alabama-Florida	of	121	407	66	141	120	17	3	1	63	31	85	20	.346
1940	Tallassee	Alabama State	of	108	396	99	132	93	17	15	7	68	36	106	8	.333
1941	L.A. Railway Clerks		of													
1942							**No Record**									
1943	Northrup Bombers		of													
							No Record									
1945	Signal Oil All-Stars		of													
1946	Bakerfield Elks		of													
	Rosabell Plumbers		of													
	Minor League totals			229	803	165	273	213	34	18	8	131	67	191	28	.340

GEORGE LAWRENCE GILLICK

A pitcher with PCL experience Gillick was 26 years old when he tried to make the club in spring training. He was a Californian from Sutter Creek. He was the only player who played for two San Diego professional baseball teams: the 1929 San Diego Aces of the California State League and the 1936 Padres. Gillick took the loss in the Aces' 2nd game played on April 12, 1929, and ended with a 7-9 record. The league folded in mid-season and he finished 1929 with Sacramento. He played another five seasons in the PCL with Sacramento through the 1933 season, and then signed with the Oakland team in 1934. Gillick was out of baseball in 1935 due to a contract dispute and problems with his teeth. Gillick was married to "petite, blonde" Thelma Daniels a movie actress who appeared in Marx Brothers films and had a leading role in several westerns.[400] He was eventually released on March 16th with the expectation that he has a chance to catch on with a team in the Texas or Western Leagues.[401] However, it appears that he did not play professional baseball again after his 1934 season. After his playing career ended he went into law enforcement, first as an under-Sheriff in Chico, California, and eventually serving 32 years as Butte County Sheriff. He was known to never carry a firearm and on one occasion felled a fleeing criminal with a well-aimed rock.[402] Gillick's son, Patrick, became an accomplished major league baseball executive and is a member of the National Baseball Hall of Fame elected in 2011.

 *March 14, 1936*, The San Diego Union
LARRY GILLICK

Counted on by Manager Frank Shellenback to be one of his chief relief hurlers during the coming campaign, Larry Gillick needs little introduction to local baseball followers for the rotund right-hander first broke into the organized baseball picture here.

Gillick, 25 years old though the record books say 26, hails from one of California's dearest landmarks, Sutter Creek, Amador county. He played prep school ball and in the spring of '29 was given a tryout with the Seattle Indians at their San Clemente camp.

The chunky moundsman didn't have a chance to show his wares there, however, and lasted only one day, before being cut adrift along with about 30 more aspiring youngsters.

However, that was Gillick's good fortune for Sam Agnew, veteran catcher, who was organizing the San Diego Aces for the California State league, knew of his ability and wired that he would be a welcome addition to the local staff.

APPENDIX H—BIOGRAPHIES OF THE 1936 SAN DIEGO PADRES

Larry started off by losing his first three starts for the Aces, and then ran up 14 victories [sic]* before the league broke up. He then headed home and joined the Sacramento club and finished out the season with the Senators. In 1930 the Solons farmed him to Globe in the Arizona State loop. He uncovered enough stuff that the Solons brought him home in '31 and he played with them through that season, 1932 and '33. In 1934 he obtained his papers from the Solons in order to make a deal for himself, signing with Oakland as a free agent.

He turned in a good record there, but last spring couldn't agree with Acorn officials over contract terms and remained out of baseball. It came at an opportune time, for he had been bothered by a sore arm. That ailment has been remedied, however, for he found his teeth had been causing the trouble. The ailing molars have been removed and Gillick claims he feels better now than ever before, for the year's rest came in handy.

He's anxious to return to San Diego, and is confident he'll be what the doctor ordered in the way of relief chucker for the Padres.

Gillick is married, so there is no chance for local girls with leap year ideas to get notions. His wife is Thelma Danfield, a movie actress who has played many bit roles and leads in western films.

LARRY GILLICK   George Lawrence Gillick   6:01½ 205 BL TR
Born: July 25, 1909 Amador Co., CA   Died: October 20, 1988 Long Beach, CA

Year	Team	League	G	GS	CG	ShO	SV	W	L	PCT	IP	H	R	ER	K	BB	ERA
1929	San Diego	Southern California	20	15	9	0	1	7	9	.438	122.7	134	77	58	61	40	4.26
	Sacramento	PCL	20		3	1		3	5	.375	86.0	119	74	60	26	37	6.28
1930	Sacramento	PCL	2	0	0	0	0	0	0	.000	2.3	1	0	1	0	5	3.86
	Globe	Arizona State	23					6	5	.545	85.7	118	84	59	42	42	6.18
1931	Sacramento	PCL	44		8	0		8	11	.421	187.0	209	110	72	62	69	3.47
1932	Sacramento	PCL	38		9	1		10	10	.500	178.0	225	112	93	45	60	4.70
1933	Sacramento	PCL	31	27	11	1	0	11	12	.478	202.3	262	116	108	68	64	4.80
1934	Oakland	PCL	8	3	0	0		3	1	.750	23.3	22	13	12	6	8	4.63
	San Leandro	California State	3	3	2	0	0	0	2	.000	24.3	27	13	11	11	8	4.07
1935	Perfection Bread																
1936	Chico	Sacramento Valley	8	8	6	0	0	4	4	.500	63.7	86	44	29	27	15	4.10
1937	Chico	Sacramento Valley	1	0	0	0	0	0	0	.000	2.0	1	0	0	1	1	0.00
1938	Chico	Sacramento Valley	3	3	2	0	0	3	0	1.000	24.0	18	9	7	12	3	2.63
1939	Chico	Sacramento Valley	5	4	2	0	0	2	3	.400	33.7	39	22	18	16	12	4.81
1940	Chico	Sacramento Valley	2	1	1	0	0	2	0	1.000	13.0	5	2	2	8	3	1.38
1941	Chico	Sacramento Valley	9	4	3	1	0	3	1	.750	44.3	31	12	10	23	15	2.03
1942	Chico	Sacramento Valley	12	6	6	0	0	3	3	.500	79.0	75	38	30	40	12	3.42
Minor League totals			206	74	62	4	1	59	61	.492	1085.7	1254	642	511	406	352	4.24

GEORGE ROSS HARRIS, JR.

A "lanky right-handed hurler," Harris had played semi-pro ball in El Centro.[403] He was born in San Diego, but spent almost all of his life in El Centro where he served as a city councilman in the 1940s and 1950s and owned M.O. King & Co., a men's store started by his father. Harris was cut on March 9, 1936, despite being listed as one the youngsters showing the most promise.[404] Harris played 10 games in 1937 for Kilgore in the East Texas League.[405] His last professional baseball venture was a tryout with Oakland in May 1939 that did not result in a contract.

---

* A review of the 1929 California League records find that Gillick pitched in 20 of the Ace's 60 games winning seven and losing nine. He was the starting pitcher in the Ace's first home game on April 11, 1929, and took the loss, 5-4.

SAN DIEGO'S FIRST PADRES and "THE KID"

GEORGE HARRIS

George R. Harris
Born: July 27, 1916 San Diego, CA   Died: February 12, 1992 El Centro, CA

Year	Team	League	G	GS	CG	ShO	SV	W	L	PCT	IP	H	R	ER	K	BB	ERA
1936	El Centro All-Stars																
1937	Kilgore	East Texas	10					3	3	.500	65.0	62	33	16	51	28	2.22

WALLACE ANDREW HEBERT

Hebert was a 28-year old pitcher of French descent from Lake Charles, Louisiana, Hebert joined the Stars in 1934 going 11-11 that year, and 10-17 in 1935. Hebert started his career in 1930 with Springfield of the Class C Western Association. He then was called up by the St. Louis Browns in 1931 and pitched with them through the 1933 season.[406] Hebert played with the Padres through 1942 and ended his last season with Pittsburgh in 1943 with a total of 21 major league wins in his career. Overall, his statistics for San Diego were 126-95.

March 17, 1936, The San Diego Union
WALLACE HEBERT

Wallace Hebert,...Wally...to his friends and hopes that he can find many in San Diego, is a member of Frank Shellenback's "Big Five" and when the San Diego Padres return home March 31 to launch their Coast league wars as this city's representative for this first time local fans will have an opportunity to see a really first class southpaw twirler in action.

Hebert hails from St. Charles, La., is 27 years old and weighs 187 pounds. He's of French descent and speaks that foreign language fluently. So if you hear some foreign mumbles when the going is roughest, just credit it to Wally and think of the same words you would be tossing in the direction of the umpires if you were in his boots.

Wally landed in the middle of the professional diamond wars in 1930 with the Springfield Western Association club. It was a fast Class C circuit and he worked 251 innings, winning 15 games and losing 16 with a second division club.

He worked so good that the St. Louis Browns called on him in 1931 and he remained there until the 1932 season had been completed. In his first season as a big leaguer he toiled 103 innings, winning six games and losing seven. The next year, 1932, found him working 108 innings with a sixth place club, winning only one game and losing an even dozen. He did much better in 1933, winding up with four wins and six defeats in 88 innings of work with a last-place club.

During the winter of '33 he was sent to Bill Lane, then at Hollywood, and the St. Charles Frenchman let a sigh of relief go up, for he is in no sense of the word lazy and the long sessions of sitting on the bench with the Browns was tiresome to say the least and welcomed a chance to become a regular chucker, even though it meant dropping back into Class double A ball. He won 11 games and lost a like number in '34 with the Stars, and last season he won 10 and lost 17, many by one-run margins, bowing in so many by that margin, that he was rated the league's No. 1 hard-luck chucker.

Managers everywhere like his work, and his chances of returning to the majors is considered bright by many. Last year Montreal, with an eye on the gate receipts through having a real Frenchman on the club, and Hebert's known mound ability, sought to buy him from President Lane, but the old "hardrock miner" said nay, nay.

APPENDIX H—BIOGRAPHIES OF THE 1936 SAN DIEGO PADRES

WALLY HEBERT   Wallace Andrew Hebert "Preacher"   6:01 195 BL TL
Born: August 21, 1907 Lake Charles, LA   Died: December 8, 1999 Westlake, LA

Year	Team	League	G	GS	CG	ShO	SV	W	L	PCT	IP	H	R	ER	K	BB	ERA
1930	Springfield	Western Assn	36		22	1		15	16	.484	251.0	265	151	106	154	83	3.80
1931	St. Louis	AL	23	13	5	0	0	6	7	.462	103.0	128	70	58	26	43	5.07
1932	St. Louis	AL	35	15	2	0	1	1	12	.077	108.3	145	99	78	29	45	6.48
1933	St. Louis	AL	33	10	3	0	0	4	6	.400	88.3	114	58	52	19	35	5.30
1934	Hollywood	PCL	37		10	0		11	11	.500	170.0	200	111	80	53	49	4.24
1935	Hollywood	PCL	39		16	1		10	17	.370	219.0	276	146	120	79	50	4.93
1936	San Diego	PCL	35	30	18	4	0	18	12	.600	229.0	240	86	77	87	51	3.03
1937	San Diego	PCL	39		21	4		17	14	.548	244.0	257	108	82	90	42	3.02
1938	San Diego	PCL	37	31	18	3	1	12	16	.429	243.0	244	98	84	102	58	3.11
1939	San Diego	PCL	39	27	24	3	1	20	10	.667	299.0	295	124	104	104	64	3.13
1940	San Diego	PCL	38	35	23	2	1	15	18	.455	280.0	316	132	122	106	100	3.92
1941	San Diego	PCL	39	35	25	0	0	22	10	.688	279.0	294	114	93	102	58	3.00
1942	San Diego	PCL	40	39	33	5	1	22	15	.595	319.0	324	104	84	125	78	2.37
1943	Pittsburgh	NL	34	23	12	1	0	10	11	.476	184.0	197	75	61	41	45	2.98
	Minor League totals		379	197	210	23	4	162	139	.538	2533.0	2711	1174	952	1002	633	3.38
	Major League totals		125	38	10	0	1	11	25	.306	299.7	387	227	188	74	123	5.65

JOHN R. HILE

A 21-year old pitcher from Shelton, Nebraska, Hile was a resident of Long Beach and pitched for the Long Beach American Legion teams 1927-31, and was on the state championship team in 1930. He played for the University of Santa Clara in 1931 and eventually was signed by the Stars in 1934. In 1935 he went 1-7 for the Stars.[407] Released by the Padres in late May 1936 Hile did not play professional ball the remainder of the year and then attempted to make the 1937 Oklahoma City team. Unsuccessful, he quit professional ball after that

 *March 16, 1936, The San Diego Union*
JACK HILE

Just 21 years old and another product of junior American Legion baseball, Jack Hile is being counted on by Manager Frank Shellenback to go places in Pacific Coast league baseball as a member of the San Diego Padres' pitching staff.

Hile didn't set any worlds afire with his work last year, but showed enough promise to indicate he boasted potentialities. Hile, a 175-pound right-hander, was born in Shelton, Neb., but now calls Long Beach home.

He pitched for Long Beach Poly back in 1930, but didn't start showing anything exceptional until joining Long Beach Post 27's entry in the yearly American Legion junior ball competition.

He played with the junior Legionnaires first in 1929, but it wasn't until 1930 after leaving Poly that he started moving along. During that summer his team won the California state championship, but was beaten in the regional championship by New Orleans' Lee Stine, now pitching in the majors, also played for the Long Beach team at that time.

In 1931 Hile attended the University of Santa Clara and played freshman ball for the Broncos under Walter "The Great" Mails. The next two years found him performing on the mound for George Stovall's Houghton Park team, which has provided "Uncle Bill" Lane with many players, including George McDonald and George Myatt.

SAN DIEGO'S FIRST PADRES and "THE KID"

He showed enough under Stovall to be signed by the Padres, then the Hollywood Stars, in 1934, winding up that season by working 79 innings to win one game against six losses, but Manager Shellenback still has a great deal of faith in his future.

Hile is a 5-foot, 11-inch youngster; good looking and eligible prey for all feminine fans with leap year ideas.

JACK HILE

John R. Hile 5:09 175 BR TR
Born: August , 1914 Shelton NE   Died: February 23, 1995 Reno, NV

Year	Team	League	G	GS	CG	ShO	SV	W	L	PCT	IP	H	R	ER	K	BB	ERA
1934	Hollywood	PCL	28		9	1		1	6	.143	79.0	94	65	37	35	33	4.22
1935	Hollywood	PCL	33		5	0		1	7	.125	148.0	189	126	86	52	51	5.23
1936	San Diego	PCL	2	1	0	0	0	0	1	.000	9.0	10	5	4	3	2	4.00
	Minor League totals		63	1	14	1	0	2	14	.125	236.0	293	196	127	90	86	4.84

ELMER CLYDE HILL

Hill was active in semi-pro baseball around San Diego for years beginning in 1916. He was signed by owner Bill Lane in June and started one game, June 27th, the same game that Ted Williams had his first professional at bat…the at bat was as a pinch hitter for Hill. The two innings he played on that date was his sole appearance for the 1936 Padres. Elmer was a fireman in San Diego and lived at 2143 33rd Street.

ELMER HILL

Elmer Clyde Hill 5:08 150 BR TR
Born: May 21, 1897 De Luz, CA   Died: August 17, 1992 San Diego, CA

Year	Team	League	G	GS	CG	ShO	SV	W	L	PCT	IP	H	R	ER	K	BB	ERA
1916	Hippodrome Theater	SD City	4	4	4	1	0	3	1	.750	36.0	22	7	5	25	18	1.25
1917	Golden Hill Blues																
1918	Golden Hill Blues		3	3	3	1	0	1	2	.333	27.0	16	2	1			0.33
1919	Golden Hill Blues		1	1	1	0	0	1	0	1.000	12.0	5	5	3	11	0	2.25
	Standard Oil		5	5	5	1	0	5	0	1.000	45.0	24	7	6	5	16	1.20
	Gas Company	SD City	2	2	2	0	0	1	1	.500	17.0	11	11	6	16	11	3.18
1920	Vernon	PCL	5	0	0	0	0	0	1	.000	19.7	20	14	10	5	16	4.58
	Yakima	Pacific Coast Int	32					8	11	.421	193.0				88	107	
1921						**No Record**											
1922	Beaumont/Dallas	Texas	10	0	0	0		2	1	.667	34.0	42	22	16	18	30	4.24
	Amarillo	West Texas	9					5	1	.833	65.0				45	22	
1923	Canadienns	E. Canada	4														
	Syracuse	International	33		7	0		7	11	.389	145.0	189	115	82	39	68	5.09
1924	Syracuse	International	1	0	0	0	0	0	0	.000	0.0	1	2	2	0	2	∞
	Harrisburg	NY-Penn	28		14	1		8	13	.381	187.7	196	108	80	89	90	3.84
1925	Binghamton	NY-Penn	34		18			11	11	.500	203.0	229	117	90	73	93	3.99
1926-1927		**Played Semi-pro Ball at Ft. Stockton, TX**															
1928	Amarillo	Western	5					0	2	.000	14.0	21	13	10	2	14	6.43
	Miami	Arizona St.	23					6	9	.400							
1929	Miami	Arizona St.	13					5	5	.500	79.0	88	62	50	43	62	5.70
1930						**No Record**											
1931	San Diego		1	1	1	1	0	1	0	1.000	9.0	8	0	0	6	1	0.00
	California Cab	SD City	1	1	1	0	0	1	0	1.000	10.0	7	4	3			2.70

APPENDIX H—BIOGRAPHIES OF THE 1936 SAN DIEGO PADRES

Year	Team	League	G	GS	CG	ShO	SV	W	L	PCT	IP	H	R	ER	K	BB	ERA
1932-1933							No Record										
1934	Arterburn Auctioneers		22	22	21	5	0	16	5	.762	296.7	125	53	38	191	66	1.15
	North Park		3	3	2	0	0	1	2	.333	22.0	26	14	10	16	15	4.09
	Texas Liquor House		1	1	1	0	0	0	1	.000	6.0	5	5	3	4	2	4.50
1935	Cramer's Bakery	SD City	13	13	13	0	0	12	1	.923	116.0	80	35	21	122	46	1.63
1936	Cramer's Bakery		3	1	0	0	1	1	0	1.000	18.0	11	8	6	17	7	3.00
	San Diego	PCL	1	1	0	0	0	0	0	.000	2.0	1	2	0	1	2	0.00
	El Centro		2	2	1	0	0	2	0	1.000	14.0	11	4	2	8	1	1.29
	Minor League totals		218	21	59	2	0	69	68	.504	1121.3	907	512	375	566	581	4.22

Note: 1922 Amarillo stats are for first half only; 1931-34 stats incomplete.

GEORGE EDWARD HOCKETTE

Hockette, turned 28 during the season, came to the Padres via the Red Sox organization where he was with Kansas City of the American Association in 1934. He then finished the 1935 season with Syracuse where he was the winning pitcher in the International League championship game. He pitched for the Red Sox in 26 games during the 1934-35 seasons and was part of the deal between Eddie Collins of the Sox and Bill Lane in which the Sox received an option to obtain Bobby Doerr and George Myatt for the 1937 season. Hockette broke into professional ball in 1929 with Gadsen of the Georgia-Alabama League. He then went to Anniston in 1930 of the same league. He finished 1930 with Buffalo and in 1931-33 also pitched for New Haven and Hazleton. He was acquired by Kansas City in 1933 and played there in 1934.[408] He played a partial year in San Diego in 1936 and finished his career in 1941.

 *March 13, 1936, The San Diego Union*
GEORGE HOCKETTE

Batters of the Pacific Coast Baseball league are going to be looking at a lot of left handed slants from the good arm of George Hockette when the San Diego Padres open the season here March 31. He is one of the three southpaw hurlers who will be regulars on the mound staff of the club.

Hockette, 26 next month, joined the team this year, coming by way of the Boston Red Sox and Owner Bill Lane and Manager Frank Shellenback look for him to do some fancy twirling. He seems to do well in tight spots. Last season, the Red Sox recalled him from Kansas City in the American association late in the season after he had won 16 games, and sent him to Syracuse, then embroiled with Montreal in a play-off for the International league championship. He arrived in time to get into the final game of the series and pitched Syracuse to the title, winning a 2 to 1 game and allowing only four hits.

The southpaw first broke into baseball in 1929 with Gadsden in the Georgia-Alabama league. The next season he was with Anniston in the same circuit and after he won nine straight games, was sold to Buffalo, New Haven and Hazleton and in 1932 was sent to Reading where he won 20 games. That record caused the Boston Red Sox to reach out and buy his contract. In 1933 he was farmed to Kansas City and from there came the jump to Syracuse late in the 1935 season.*

Hockette bats left handed as well as pitching from that side of the plate. He is married.

---

* There are several inaccuracies in this write-up: Hockette actually broke in with Gadsen in 1928; he went to Reading in 1933, not 1932, and won 18 games, not 20; and it was 1934 when Hockette went to Kansas City.

SAN DIEGO'S FIRST PADRES and "THE KID"

GEORGE HOCKETTE George Edward Hockette "Lefty"   6:00 174 BL TL
Born: April 7, 1908 Perth, MS   Died: January 20, 1974 Plantation, FL

Year	Team	League	G	GS	CG	ShO	SV	W	L	PCT	IP	H	R	ER	K	BB	ERA
1928	Gadsen	Georgia-Alabama	23		9			6	10	.375	148.0	160	86	65	37	25	3.95
1929	Gadsen	Georgia-Alabama	22					8	9	.471	139.0	145	72	53	45	16	3.43
1930	Anniston	Georgia-Alabama	26					11	8	.579	177.0	239	116	91	68	30	4.63
	Buffalo	International	2	0	0	0	0	0	0	.000	3.0	8	4	3	0	1	9.00
1931	New Haven	Eastern	3														
	Hazelton	NY-Penn	33					6	14	.300	194.0	233	125	103	65	38	4.78
1932	Hazelton	NY-Penn	32					15	11	.577	217.0	241	106	89	46	43	3.69
1933	Reading	NY-Penn	39					18	7	.720	214.0	243	103	84	62	50	3.53
1934	Kansas City	American Assn	39					16	15	.516	260.0	299	139	111	57	35	3.84
	Boston	AL	3	3	3	2	0	2	1	.667	27.3	22	5	5	14	6	1.65
1935	Boston	AL	23	4	0	0	0	2	3	.400	61.0	83	43	35	11	12	5.16
	Syracuse	International	5	4	2	1	0	2	2	.500	24.7	27	11	7	4	2	2.55
1936	San Diego	PCL	8	5	1	0	0	0	3	.000	33.0	48	27	25	4	17	6.82
	Syracuse	International	23	16	7	2		4	11	.267	102.0	130	72	64	27	29	5.65
1937	Syracuse	International	26	18	7	2		11	6	.647	132.0	144	68	49	35	35	3.34
1938	Birmingham/Knoxville	Southern	16	11	3	0		3	10	.231	73.0	102	61	52	13	18	6.41
1939	Hazelton	Interstate	6		5			2	3	.400	42.0	43	19	15	18	10	3.21
1940	Ft. Lauderdale	Florida E. Coast	22		15			12	8	.600	164.0	180	74	58	33	33	3.18
1941	Bristol	Appalachain	6		2			1	3	.250	25.0	46	29	20	5	6	7.20
	Ft. Lauderdale/Miami	Florida East Coast	17		10			5	10	.333	121.0	123	65	55	15	27	4.09
1942-45							**In Military Service**										
1946	West Palm Beach	Florida Int	1	1	0	0	0	0	1	.000	3.7	4	7	7	3	5	17.18
	Minor League totals		327	33	52	5	0	109	116	.484	1930.7	2228	1074	870	509	379	4.06
	Major League totals		42	29	10	2	0	14	16	.467	205.0	246	129	101	48	53	4.43

WALTER ERNIE HOLMAN

Holman, a 30-year old third baseman, was traded from Tulsa over the 1935-36 offseason. He had 12 seasons of professional ball coming into 1936. He started out with Texarkana of the East Texas Class D League in 1924 then went to Monroe with the Cotton states Class D League in 1927. From 1928-35 he was with the Shreveport/Dallas/New Orleans/Tulsa of the Class A Texas and Southern Leagues. He was reported as a "lackadaisical sort of guy, appearing to be sleeping around the hot corner when balls are flying the other direction, but once a play comes his way, or flying feet are needed on the bases, he's Johnny-on-the-spot."[409] He hit .294 with Tulsa in 1935. Holman stayed with the Padres through 1938 and finished that season with Tulsa. He lived at 4476 Oregon in San Diego.

March 10, 1936, The San Diego Union
ERNIE HOLMAN

Ernest Holman, well known in the southern and southwest portions of the United States, but a stranger in Pacific coasters, will be making his western debut when he comes to San Diego late this month to open the Coast league wars with the Padres at Lane Field.

Twenty-nine years old with a record of 12 seasons of active professional playing behind him, Ernie appears to be "what the doctor ordered" for third base on the San Diego club.

APPENDIX H—BIOGRAPHIES OF THE 1936 SAN DIEGO PADRES

Known as "Sleepy Ernie" when he played in the Texas league, he comes to San Diego boasting an impressive record. His last stopping off place was Tulsa, in the Texas league, coming to the Padres in the deal which saw Jim Levey transferred to the Oklahoma club.

Holman hails from Amarillo, Tex., where he graduated from high school in 1924. He lost no time entering organized ball and joined the Texarkana East Texas league club and played in 74 games, batting .297 and fielding .916. He remained with the Texarkana Class D league team until 1927 when he transferred his third basing activities to Monroe of the Cotton States league another D circuit. He pounded the "apple" for a .317 average in his first year there.

He stepped into Class A company in 1928, being purchased by Shreveport of the Texas league. He remained there until 1931 when he joined Dallas of the same circuit. He was garbed in a Dallas uniform until 1934 and during his sojourn there won the Texas league third base fielding laurels in '31 and '32. His next stopping off place was New Orleans in 1934, helping the Pelicans win the Southern Association pennant that year, batting .369*
and leading the league in fielding for his position around the hot corner.

Last year he was transferred to Tulsa and after a great season, climbed from Class A to Double A ball with the Padres.

Ernie is one of the most popular members of the Padre crew in Fullerton and should win a big following among San Diegans. He's a lackadaisical sort of a guy, appearing to be sleeping around the hot corner when balls are flying the other direction, but once a play comes his way, or flying feet are needed on the bases, he's Johnny "on-the-spot."

ERNIE HOLMAN   Walter Ernie Holman   5:10½ 168 BR TR
Born: December 17, 1905 Claude, TX   Died: November 8, 1965 Los Angeles, CA

Year	Team	League	Pos	G	AB	R	H	1B	2B	3B	HR	RBI	K	BB	SB	AVG
1924	Texarkana	East Texas	3b	74	263	50	78	52	16	0	10		57	34	8	.297
1925	Texarkana	East Texas	3b	105	425	82	137	96	18	1	22		68	37	26	.322
1926	Texarkana	East Texas	3b		457	101	150	103	24	3	20				9	.328
1927	Monroe	Cotton States	3b	104	363	69	115	76	22	11	6	47	55		7	.317
1928	Shreveport	Texas	3b	155	539	84	154	93	35	13	13	73	90	59	5	.286
1929	Shreveport	Texas	3b	151	522	112	160	99	30	6	25	98	83	79	15	.307
1930	Shreveport	Texas	3b	147	484	95	148	87	29	5	27	99	94	108	23	.306
1931	Dallas	Texas	3b-2b	124	428	68	126	82	30	4	10	53	71	55	13	.294
1932	Dallas	Texas	3b	143	495	66	139	103	21	6	9	98	69	77	5	.281
1933	Dallas	Texas	3b	152	537	86	149	102	30	9	8	78	74	84	12	.277
1934	New Orleans	Southern Assn	3b	156	583	76	158	125	16	12	5	63	50	52	7	.271
1935	Tulsa	Texas	3b	**162**	598	96	176	118	37	8	13	98	67	68	11	.294
1936	San Diego	PCL	3b	174	627	92	197	164	20	7	6	108			17	.314
1937	San Diego	PCL	3b	94	305	38	68	58	6	3	1	28			2	.223
1938	San Diego	PCL	3b	8	17	0	2	2	0	0	0	2			0	.118
1938	Tulsa	Texas	3b	121	398	52	105	87	13	2	3	38	56	41	6	.264
	Minor League totals			1870	7041	1167	2062	1447	347	90	178	836	826	749	166	.293

BERLYN DALE HORNE

Horne was a 36-year old pitcher for the Padres having gone 13-7 with the 1935 Hollywood team. He started with Jacksonville in 1917 and in 1919 joined up with Battle Creek. He then went to Port Huron in the M & O League for 1921-22. Horne played for Saginaw in 1923 and was sold mid-season of 1924 to Rochester/Jersey City of the International League where he stayed through 1927. In 1928 he was the International League's Most Valuable Player while with Jersey City. He played with the Chicago Cubs for 11 games in 1929. In 1933 Horne

---

* This .369 average is in error, the actual figure was .271.

SAN DIEGO'S FIRST PADRES and "THE KID"

joined the Oakland team, then went to Sacramento, and finally Hollywood in 1935.[410] His only season for San Diego was 1936 and he followed that with two more minor league seasons before retiring. His minor league wins totaled 231.

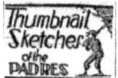 *March 11, 1936, The San Diego Union*
BERLYN HORNE

He was short and stocky, but Berlyn Horne was a winning pitcher for the Hollywood Stars of the Pacific Coast Baseball league and he hopes to better his mark of 13 victories against seven defeats in the uniform of the San Diego Padres this season.

Horne joined the Stars last season after a year with Sacramento and his right-handed slants worked well. "Berly" is the nickname the fans have tacked onto him: "Berly" not "Burly."

Horne, right handed pitcher, hits from either side of the plate, switching according to what pitching he is facing. He broke into baseball first in 1919 with Battle Creek,* Mich., playing there two years. In 1921 he went with Port Huron, Mic., in the M. & O. league and played there two years. He went to Saginaw in 1923 and on July 1, 1924, was sold to Rochester of the International league. He played with Rochester through 1927, when the franchise was transferred to Jersey City. Of course, Horne went along and in 1928 was sold to the Chicago Cubs.

Horne was with the Wrigley clan in 1929 and in 1930 was farmed to Los Angeles. In 1931 the Cubs recalled Horne and later sold him to Indianapolis. He played for the American Association team until 1933 when he joined Oakland. The season at Sacramento followed and then with the Stars.

TRADER HORNE Berlyn Dale Horne "Sonny" 5:09 155 BB TR
Born: April 12, 1899 Bachman, OH Died: February 3, 1983 Franklin, OH

Year	Team	League	G	GS	CG	ShO	SV	W	L	PCT	IP	H	R	ER	K	BB	ERA
1917	Jacksonville	Sally	25					11	11	.500	177.3	161	74	55	93	74	2.79
1918		**In Military Service**															
1919	Battle Creek	Michigan-Ontario	34					19	9	.679	245.0	239	107	71	119	62	2.61
1920	Battle Creek	Michigan-Ontario	33					8	15	.348	223.0	242		76	114	67	3.07
1921	Port Huron-Sarnia	Michigan-Ontario	33					16	13	.552	233.0	208		85	97	111	3.28
1922	Port Huron-Sarnia	Michigan-Ontario	16					6	7	.462	104.0	135		51	44	41	4.41
1923	Saginaw	Michigan-Ontario	27					7	8	.467	149.0	186	90	64	63	62	3.87
1924	Saginaw	Michigan-Ontario	22					11	4	.733	132.0	134	67	41	57	51	2.80
	Rochester	International	20		8			3	11	.214	112.0	127	71	57	30	51	4.58
1925	Rochester	International	40		20			13	12	.520	252.0	282	142	108	93	97	3.86
1926	Rochester	International	42		16			15	16	.484	241.0	269	144	114	111	87	4.26
1927	Rochester	International	37		15			18	10	.643	199.0	212	117	106	67	82	4.79
1928	Jersey City	International	44		24			16	17	.485	266.0	258	146	89	137	140	3.01
1929	Chicago	NL	11	1	0	0	0	1	1	.500	23.0	24	20	13	6	21	5.09
	Los Angeles	PCL	9		3	0		5	4	.556	49.0	63	35	33	27	24	6.06
1930	Los Angeles	PCL	31		9	0		13	7	.650	175.0	185	100	87	98	107	4.47
1931	Jersey City	International	7					2	4	.333	46.0	43	24	21	15	20	4.11
	Indianapolis	American Assn	30					9	9	.500	136.0	149	87	68	66	61	4.50

---

* He actually played his first season in 1917 with Jacksonville.

APPENDIX H—BIOGRAPHIES OF THE 1936 SAN DIEGO PADRES

Year	Team	League	G	GS	CG	ShO	SV	W	L	PCT	IP	H	R	ER	K	BB	ERA
1932	Indianapolis	American Assn	4					1	0	1.000	10.0	12	9	7	4	4	6.30
	Knoxville	Southern Assn	9					2	1	.667	33.0	40	30	29	12	30	7.91
	Scranton	NY-Penn	7					2	4	.333	44.0	42	24	20	10	18	4.09
	Omaha	Western	7					3	3	.500	58.0	68	36	25	23	23	3.88
1933	Oakland/Sacramento	PCL	23	18	11	1	1	9	7	.563	141.3	140	63	55	86	50	3.50
1934	Sacramento/Missions	PCL	44		16	1		7	7	.500	114.0	116	88	55	52	38	4.34
1935	Missions/Hollywood	PCL	39		13	1		13	7	.650	174.0	196	97	77	73	50	3.98
1936	San Diego	PCL	38	23	9	3	0	7	14	.333	164.0	183	110	80	76	78	4.39
1937	Seattle	PCL	26		0	0		1	3	.250	64.0	69	35	32	40	36	4.50
	Wenatchee	Western Int	4		2			2	1	.667	24.0	18	15	7	18	7	2.63
1938	Yakima/Vancouver	Western Int	29		14			12	8	.600	184.0	220	108	80	108	58	3.91
	Minor League totals		680	41	160	6	1	231	212	.521	3749.7	3997	1819	*1593*	1733	1529	3.82
	Major League totals		11	1	0	0	0	1	1	.500	23.0	24	20	13	6	21	5.09

KENNETH THEODORE IVERSON

1936 was Iverson's only year in professional baseball. On March 11th it was reported that Iverson, "a short southpaw from Tacoma" had "turned in a sparkling game." He, along with Cooper and Vaughn, remained on the roster in April but played with the Padres "B" team and stayed in San Diego while the team was on the road. The three players were released on May 10, 1936.

KENNY IVERSON   Kenneth Theodore Iverson   5:08 163 BL TL
Born: July 17, 1915 Stanislaus Co., CA   Died: May 13, 1990 Stanislaus Co., CA

Year	Team	League	G	GS	CG	ShO	SV	W	L	PCT	IP	H	R	ER	K	BB	ERA
1936	San Diego	PCL	1	0	0	0	1	0	0	.000	2.0	0	0	0	1	1	0.00
	Hutchinson	Western Assn	3		0			0	2	.000	9.0	15	11	10	8	16	10.00
	Bentonville	Ark-Missouri	24					4	8	.333	111.3	119		61	52	31	4.93
	Minor League totals		28	0	0	0	1	4	10	.286	122.333	134	11	71	61	48	5.22

M. K. (or M.H.) JACKSON

Jackson was a pitcher invited to spring training and did get into a February 27th intrasquad game but was cut, along with Ehil and Whitlock, on March 1, 1936. No reference to either an M.H. or M.K. Jackson having played professional baseball was found.

RAYMOND F. JACOBS

Born and raised in Salt Lake City Jacobs was 34 in 1936. He had hit .296 with Hollywood in 1935. He started with the Ogden team of the Utah State League in 1923 and then joined the Los Angeles Angels as shortstop in 1923 through 1927. He signed with the Chicago Cubs for the 1928-29 seasons playing two games in 1928 for them, then returned to the Angels through 1931. In 1932 Jacobs played for Portland before going to Hollywood in 1933. Jacobs last played in 1942 with Spokane but 1936 was his only season in San Diego. His 198 home runs rank 6th all-time in the PCL.[411]

Ray Jacobs, 1st Baseman when he was with the L.A. Angels (1930)

SAN DIEGO'S FIRST PADRES and "THE KID"

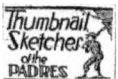 *March 23, 1936, The San Diego Union*
RAY JACOBS

Fourteen years in organized baseball and still going strong is the record of Ray Jacobs, veteran first sacker for the San Diego Padres.

Despite his long service in the national game, Jacobs is by no means old or decrepit, as his record discloses that he is only 31.

Jacobs was born in Salt Lake City, but now calls Los Angeles his home. Ray made a name for himself on Salt Lake City sand lots in 1923, and decided to capitalize on his talent by going into organized baseball. He earned a trial with the Ogden club of the Utah State league and made the grade. He succeeded so well that Doc Crandall signed him to a Los Angeles contract in September of that year.

Jake played with the Angels as a shortstop in 1924 and remained with them in that capacity until 1927 when he fractured a leg sliding into a base. He came back strong in 1928 and was signed by the Chicago Cubs where he remained until 1929. Then he came back to Los Angeles and remained with the Angels until 1932, going to Portland. In 1933 he came to Hollywood where he made himself over into a first baseman. He has been with the club ever since and is so versatile that he can play first, third, short, or take a post in the outfield at a moment's notice. He is a long driving hitter, and batted .298 last season.

He is 6 feet tall, weighs 180, married, and has three boys who share their dad's enthusiasm for baseball.

RAY JACOBS Raymond F. Jacobs 6:00 160 BR TR
Born: January 2, 1902 Salt Lake City, UT Died: April 5, 1952 Los Angeles, CA

Year	Team	League	Pos	G	AB	R	H	1B	2B	3B	HR	RBI	K	BB	SB	AVG
1923	Los Angeles	PCL	ss	15	45	6	16	12	3	0	1	8			1	.356
1924	Los Angeles	PCL	3b	147	517	73	143	90	44	0	9	76			2	.277
1925	Los Angeles	PCL	ss-3b-1b	150	539	116	167	98	53	3	13	75			18	.310
1926	Los Angeles	PCL	1-3-s-2	178	580	91	148	84	39	4	21	102			12	.255
1927	Los Angeles	PCL	1b-2b-ss	97	359	70	116	71	25	7	13	64			9	.323
1928	Los Angeles	PCL	1b	36	111	8	23	18	5	0	0	11			1	.207
	Chicago	NL	ph	2	2	0	0	0	0	0	0	0	1	0	0	.000
	Toledo/Minneapolis	American Assn	ss-2b	40	141	23	47	34	5	4	4	24			2	.333
1929	Los Angeles	PCL	2b-1b-3b	178	591	84	196	128	40	8	20	118			11	.332
1930	Los Angeles	PCL	1b	196	710	128	216	147	41	8	20	130			11	.304
1931	Los Angeles	PCL	1b-3b	124	386	78	115	65	29	3	18	73			5	.298
1932	Portland	PCL	1b	40	149	15	43	32	5	1	5	34			2	.289
	Galveson	Texas	1b	27	88	7	11	7	3	0	1	5	8	13	1	.125
1933	Hollywood	PCL	1b-3b	159	564	107	160	89	35	0	36	129			7	.284
1934	Hollywood	PCL	1b-2b	178	597	93	172	119	28	1	24	112			9	.288
1935	Hollywood	PCL	1b	115	402	62	119	86	17	3	13	69			11	.296
1936	San Diego	PCL	1b	106	332	42	93	64	23	1	5	46			8	.280
1937	Yakima	Western Int	1b-3b	118	432	82	139	91	37	3	8	78	78	70	4	.322
1938	Yakima	Western Int	1b	90	291	48	88	56	24	3	5	44	46	59	9	.302
1939	Yakima	Western Int	1b	95	321	49	78	49	15	0	14	48	56	49	4	.243
1940	Twin Falls	Pioneer	1b	13	31	2	6	4	0	0	2	8	5	5	0	.194
1941	Spokane	Western Int	1b	24	37	4	9	6	3	0	0	3	4	13	1	.243
1942	Spokane	Western Int	1b	24	39	6	11	8	2	0	1	9	7	12	1	.282
	Minor League totals			2150	7262	1194	2116	1358	476	49	233	1266	204	221	129	.291
	Major League totals			2	2	0	0	0	0	0	0	0	1	0	0	.000

APPENDIX H—BIOGRAPHIES OF THE 1936 SAN DIEGO PADRES

HENRY ASHLEY JOERNDT

A San Diegan who came up through San Diego High School in 1928-29, and played at San Diego State College, as well. He got his professional start playing for Beatrice of the Nebraska State League in 1934 and 1935, when he won the batting title hitting .334. The *Union* reported that he was "23 years of age and single, so there is a chance for the feminine fans who have promised themselves to improve their own batting averages during leap year."[412] Joerndt played a limited time for the Padres in 1936 and the Padres released him on May 24th because of his "trick knee." He subsequently played for Tacoma and Spokane in 1937 and 1938, respectively. He lived at 3571 Herman Avenue in San Diego.

March 22, 1936, The San Diego Union
ASHLEY JOERNDT

When the Padres come home to San Diego, there will be at least one player in the fold who will need no introduction to home towners. He is Ashley Joerndt, fromer [sic] San Diego High school player, whose aggressive spirit, willingness to learn and all around ability apparently have combined to clinch a steady berth with the club.

Joerndt needs little introduction to San Diego, for he was one of the shining lights of the Hilltop varsity team in 1928 and 1929. In addition, he has played with many local sandlot and semi-pro clubs and his fame as an outfielder of ability spread.

Last season, Ash turned to professional baseball and signed with the Beatrice club of the Nebraska State league as an outfielder. His first year was a winning one for him, as he led the league with a batting average of .331.* He also topped the circuit in the total number of base hits.

Joerndt is six feet in height and weighs 175 pounds. He is 23 years old and single, so there still is a chance for the feminine fans who have promised themselves to improve their own batting averages during leap year.

ASH JOERNDT   Ashley Joerndt   6:00 175 BR TR
Born: May 28, 1912 San Diego, CA   Died: September 2, 1964 El Cajon, CA

Year	Team	League	Pos	G	AB	R	H	1B	2B	3B	HR	RBI	K	BB	SB	AVG
1931	California Cab	SD City	of													
1932						No Record										
1933	Walter Church	SD City	of													
1934	Beatrice	Nebraska St	of	101	425	52	106	79	17	6	4		47	21	6	.249
1935	Beatrice	Nebraska St	of	104	458	65	153	111	26	10	6	59	32	24	13	**.334**
1936	San Diego	PCL	of	12	19	3	5	3	2	0	0	3			0	.263
1937	Tacoma	Western Int	of	107	437	56	112	85	22	2	3	61	36	20	3	.256
1938	Spokane	Western Int	of	60	248	30	72	57	13	2	0	28	24	12	2	.290
Minor League totals				384	1587	206	448	335	80	20	13	151	139	77	24	.282

JAMES E. KERR

A 22-year-old catcher with the Padres, Kerr joined the Hollywood team in 1935 from the local Marine Corps Base in San Diego.[413] Kerr, from Baltimore, started with the Baltimore Athletic club in 1930 then joined the Marines at Quantico in 1932, and came to San Diego in 1933. He played the one year for the 1936 Padres and then with some Texas minor league through 1939, his last year playing professional baseball.

---

* This average is in error, Joerndt actually finished with an average of .334.

March 7, 1936, The San Diego Union
JAMES E. KERR

James E. Kerr, Jimmy to baseball fans of San Diego, will be coming back home when he takes the field with the San Diego padres of the Pacific Coast league here March 31 at Lane Field. For Jimmy went to the then Hollywood Stars for his first start in organized baseball from the local Marine Corps Base.

Just 22 now—and single, girls—Kerr first joined the Stars regularly last season as a catcher. He stuck the full season and now is the chief understudy of Eugene Desautels, the regular catcher, who hails from Holy Cross.

Kerr got his first baseball training with the Baltimore Athletic club in his home city in 1930. It was a fast outfit. The next year he joined the Marine Corps and played with the Quantico Marines, starting in 1932. He played baseball and football both at the Virginia Marine Corps camp and in 1933, when transferred to the San Diego base, added basketball to the list. He followed his career in 1934, getting in a few games with Owner Bill Lane's Stars.

Kerr throws right-handed, but hits from the left side of the plate.

JIMMY KERR James E. Kerr   6:01 191 BL TR
Born: July 9, 1911 Baltimore, MD   Died: May 6, 1999 Towson, MD

Year	Team	League	Pos	G	AB	R	H	1B	2B	3B	HR	RBI	K	BB	SB	AVG
1935	Hollywood	PCL	c	66	193	24	52	39	9	0	4	31			0	.269
1936	San Diego	PCL	c	52	124	9	32	25	4	2	1	17			2	.258
1937	Kilgore	East Texas	c-of	111	409	69	117	83	23	8	3	46	53	46	12	.286
1938	Shreveport/Dallas	Texas	c	63	130	12	17	12	3	0	2	10	21	13	0	.131
1939	Midland	WT-NM	c	95	350	76	115	80	22	4	9	59	42	43	12	.329
	Minor League totals			387	1206	190	333	239	61	14	19	163	116	102	26	.276

HUBERT MILTON KITTLE

Spelled as Kettle in the local news, Hub Kittle was a recruit brought in for a tryout on February 24, 1936.[414] In a biography written by Ross, he noted that Kittle attended Fairfax High School in Los Angeles, and that their baseball team won the city championship in 1934. After that Hub received a scholarship to the Army and Navy Academy in San Diego. On weekends he was playing with a semi-pro team called Walter Church Service Stations, the same one that Ted Williams patrolled right field.[415] He was in organized baseball from 1937 through the end of his life as a player, coach, scout, and manager.

HUB KITTLE Hubert Milton Kittle   6:01 195 BB TR
Born: February 19, 1917 Los Angeles, CA   Died: February 10, 2004 Yakima, WA

Year	Team	League	G	GS	CG	ShO	SV	W	L	PCT	IP	H	R	ER	K	BB	ERA
1935	Walter Church																
1936	Santa Catalina Junior Angels																
1937	Ponca City	Western Assn	47		12			9	15	.375	214.0	250	158	126	155	119	5.30
1938	Ponca City	Western Assn	37		14	1		18	8	.692	209.0	200	113	74	150	123	3.19
1939	Yakima	Western Int	32		20			20	10	.667	238.0	207	104	91	156	95	3.44

APPENDIX H—BIOGRAPHIES OF THE 1936 SAN DIEGO PADRES

Year	Team	League	G	GS	CG	ShO	SV	W	L	PCT	IP	H	R	ER	K	BB	ERA
1940	San Francisco	PCL	17	4	1	0	0	3	3	.500	55.0	56	33	32	15	26	5.24
	Yakima	Western Int	17		12	2		9	5	.643	119.0	129	52	39	63	28	2.95
1941	San Francisco	PCL	20	1	0	0	1	2	3	.400	44.0	46			14	13	
1942	Oklahoma City	Texas	8		2			1	4	.200	40.0	39	20	14	13	20	3.15
	Spokane	Western Int	35		20	3		15	14	.517	229.0	233	107	85	99	83	3.34
1943	Oakland	PCL	14	3	1	0	0	2	1	.667	59.0	56	30	18	30	22	2.75
1944-1945							**In Military Service**										
1946	Bremerton	Western Int	32		15	2		15	10	.600	216.0	187	96	89	138	103	3.71
1947	Bremerton	Western Int	35		19	7		13	14	.481	216.0	192	84	67	130	69	2.79
1948	Yakima	Western Int	38		18	0		7	18	.280	204.0	223	127	108	115	85	4.76
1949	Klamath Falls	Far West	17		21	0		7	2	.778	78.0	77	41	32	85	22	3.69
1950	Klamath Falls	Far West	24		0	0		10	0	1.000	55.0	48	26	24	59	23	3.93
1951	Salt Lake City	Pioneer	22		0	0		4	2	.667	45.0	36	20	9	46	12	1.80
1952	Salt Lake City	Pioneer	36		0	0		6	6	.500	79.0	64	31	17	35	25	1.94
1953	Terre Haute	Three I	14	1	0	0		2	1	.667	27.0	27	11	5	20	9	1.67
1954	Terre Haute	Three I	7	0	0	0		1	0	1.000	17.0	18	10	10	7	7	5.29
1955	Yakima	Northwest	1	0	0	0		0	0	.000	1.3	6	6	3	1	1	20.25
1956-1957							**Did Not Play**										
1958	Yakima	Northwest	1	0	0	0		0	0	.000	2.0	0	0	0	1	0	0.00
1959-1965							**Did Not Play**										
1966	Austin	Texas	1	1	0	0	0	0	0	.000	1.0	1	0	0	0	1	0.00
1967-1968							**Did Not Play**										
1969	Savannah	Southern	1	0	0	0		0	0	.000	2.0	4	3	2	1	0	9.00
1970-1979							**Did Not Play**										
1980	Springfield	American Assn	1	1	0	0	0	0	0	.000	1.0	0	0	0	0	0	0.00
	Minor League totals		457	11	155	15	1	144	116	.554	2151.3	2099	1072	845	1333	886	3.54

HARL WARREN MAGGERT

Maggert was a 21-year old outfielder with some early limited experience in 1932-33 with Seattle and was brought to camp by the Boston Red Sox "to get in condition."[416] Maggert's father, Harl Vestin Maggert, played professional baseball for 15 years and in the major leagues for Pittsburgh in 1907 and Philadelphia (American) in 1912. The younger Maggert was productive during spring training but it was noted that "the big blonde is of no use...as he is in the San Diego camp getting in condition to report to the Boston Red Sox."[417] He eventually was sent to the Rocky Mount club in late March 1936 and proceeded to hit 30 home runs in a full season there. He went on to play major league ball with one season with the Boston Braves in 1938 then going on to finish his career in 1939 with Oklahoma City.

HARL MAGGERT Harl Warren Maggert 6:00 195 BR TR
Born: May 4, 1914 Los Angeles, CA   Died: July 10, 1986 Citrus Heights, CA

Year	Team	League	Pos	G	AB	R	H	1B	2B	3B	HR	RBI	K	BB	SB	AVG
1932	Seattle	PCL	of	61	219	32	56	36	10	0	10	57			2	.256
1933	Seattle	PCL	ph	1	1	0	0	0	0	0	0	0			0	.000
	San Mateo	California St	of	6	17	3	9	7	1	0	1				0	.529
1934	San Mateo	California St	of	18	73	13	28	17	6	5	0				1	.384
1935	San Mateo	California St	of	19	73	19	26	22	2	0	2				0	.356
1936	Rocky Mount	Piedmont	3b-of	135	505	105	171	108	28	5	30	119	68	50	3	.339
1937	Sacramento	PCL	ph	1	1	0	0	0	0	0	0	0			0	.000
	Ashville	Piedmont	3b	138	555	112	191	115	47	6	23	139	45	41	3	.344

Year	Team	League	Pos	G	AB	R	H	1B	2B	3B	HR	RBI	K	BB	SB	AVG
1938	Boston	AL	of-3b	66	89	12	25	19	3	0	3	19	20	10	0	.281
1939	Hollywood	PCL	3b-of-2b	43	99	13	24	15	6	0	3	12		6	0	.242
	Oklahoma City	Texas	of-3b	87	299	39	74	49	13	2	10	58	46	24	4	.247
	Minor League totals			509	1842	336	579	369	113	18	79	385	159	121	13	.314
	Major League totals			66	89	12	25	19	3	0	3	19	20	10	0	.281

FRANCIS BURKE MCDONALD

The San Diego papers used several different first names for McDonald: Burt, Bruce, and Berkeley. It was Burt in the *San Diego Union*, February 23, 1936. Then, it was Bruce when it was reported in the *San Diego Union* on February 26 and 28, 1936, that the "yannigan infielder from Wyoming packed his bags and went home." Finally, in the March 2 *Union*, it was reported that Berkeley McDonald "promising young Cody, Wyoming, infielder left camp the other day leaving a note for Mgr. Shellenback: 'A couple of days of training and I'm convinced I should go back to work. So I'm back to boots and saddles.'"[418] There is no evidence of a Burt/Berkeley/Bruce from the 1936 era having played professional baseball. Francis Burke "Snooks" McDonald, 6'2" and 220 pounds in 1940,[419] was born on March 8, 1919 in Casper, Wyoming, and died in Cody, Wyoming, on September 17, 1972.[420]

GEORGE THOMAS MCDONALD

McDonald was a teammate of Bobby Doerr's for six years starting together in junior high school, American Legion, and then Fremont High in Los Angeles. Only 18 at the start of the 1936 season, he joined the Hollywood team in 1934 and hit .255 in 1935 for them.[421] McDonald played with San Diego through 1944 and then again in 1946 and 1947. His last season in the minor leagues was 1951.

March 26, 1936, The San Diego Union
GEORGE T. McDONALD

George T. McDonald is one of the real youngsters of the San Diego team of the Pacific Coast Baseball league, but he's not a newcomer to baseball. He has been playing since he was 4 years of age, the first time he was big enough to handle a ball.

When the season opens Saturday in Los Angeles, McDonald will alternate at first base with Ray Jacobs, the veteran, and he will get his innings when the club opens its home season against Seattle here on Tuesday of next week.

Seattle, Wash., is McDonald's home. He will reach his 18th birthday April 12 and playing in the Padre infield for him is like home for he and Bobby Doerr, second baseman, have been playing together for six years. They started together in junior high school, played on an American Legion junior team together and then went through Fremont High in Los Angeles. George played two years on the varsity team there. Later they joined semi-pro outfits together.

McDonald first joined a professional team when he went to Hollywood in 1934. He was with the team last season, playing first base and batting well, until he was taken ill. He was out of uniform for 13 weeks, but looks for a big season this year.

The youngster stands six feet in height and weighs 170 pounds. He bats left handed and throws the same.

APPENDIX H—BIOGRAPHIES OF THE 1936 SAN DIEGO PADRES

GEORGE McDONALD George Thomas McDonald   6:00½ 185 BL TL
Born: April 12, 1917 Seattle, WA   Died: May 12, 2011 Palm Desert, CA

Year	Team	League	Pos	G	AB	R	H	1B	2B	3B	HR	RBI	K	BB	SB	AVG
1934	Hollywood	PCL	1b	19	46	6	9	9	0	0	0	8			0	.196
1935	Hollywood	PCL	1b	68	212	16	54	42	9	3	0	23			1	.255
1936	San Diego	PCL	1b	103	334	36	106	90	11	5	0	52			3	.317
1937	San Diego	PCL	1b	163	632	95	197	164	22	7	4	102			5	.312
1938	San Diego	PCL	1b	143	549	49	147	117	26	4	0	61			7	.268
1939	San Diego	PCL	1b	134	490	53	112	88	17	6	1	50		18	4	.229
1940	San Diego	PCL	1b	141	537	56	155	128	20	5	2	63		31	3	.289
1941	San Diego	PCL	1b	157	611	80	173	146	23	3	1	58	23	25	4	.283
1942	San Diego	PCL	1b	70	272	25	73	59	10	4	0	19	9	9	0	.268
1943	San Diego	PCL	1b	112	391	42	129	95	24	10	0	50	19	15	5	.330
1944	San Diego	PCL	1b	85	313	32	97	77	18	2	0	34	10	24	5	.310
1945	Seattle	PCL	1b	151	552	81	183	151	26	5	1	69	30	48	26	.332
1946	Seattle/San Diego	PCL	1b	142	506	55	140	113	21	5	1	56	28	42	7	.277
1947	SD/Sacramento	PCL	1b	10	26	5	5	4	1	0	0	1			0	.192
	San Antonio	Texas	1b-of	30	105	11	26	19	4	3	0	9	1	5	2	.248
1948	Seattle	PCL	1b	31	99	10	23	20	3	0	0	11	3	9	3	.232
	New Orleans	Southern Assn	of-1b	62	246	42	92	78	10	2	2	48	10	25	4	.374
1949	New Orleans	Southern Assn	of-1b	142	514	63	161	120	34	4	3	111	18	53	6	.313
1950	Chattanooga	Southern Assn	of	40	137	17	45	33	11	1	0	22	5	14	1	.328
	Jersey City	Southern Assn	1b-of	11	20	1	3	3	0	0	0	1	1	1	0	.150
	Minneapolis	American Assn	1b-of	21	60	6	15	11	4	0	0	4	3	2	0	.250
1951	Salem	Western Int	1b-of	52	184	24	54	48	6	0	0	21	12	19	1	.293
	Minor League totals			1887	6836	805	1999	1615	300	69	15	873	172	340	87	.292

JOSEPH PATRICK MONAHAN

The son of a major league scout Monahan was 18 years old in 1936. He hailed from Springfield, Illinois, and lived most of his life in St. Louis. His professional career began with the 1936 season and extended through 1940 with that initial season—and only five games—being only time in San Diego. He was released on April 9th and ended the year playing with Dothan in the Alabama-Florida League.

JOE MONAHAN Joseph Patrick Monahan   6:00½ 185 BL TL
Born: March 13, 1918 St. Louis, MO   Died: August 30, 1973 St. Louis, MO

Year	Team	League	Pos	G	AB	R	H	1B	2B	3B	HR	RBI	K	BB	SB	AVG
1936	San Diego	PCL	ph	5	5	2	2	1	1	0	0	0			0	.400
1936	Dothan	Alabama-Florida	1b	54	196	23	66	54	3	5	4	36	21	22	1	.337
1937	Dothan	Alabama-Florida	1b	44	161	20	40	29	8	2	1	28	27	24	2	.248
	Meridian	Southeastern	of	12	46	7	9	3	4	1	1	3	8	4	0	.196
1938							**No Record**									
1939	Newport News	City League	of-1b													
1940	Moline	Three I	1b													
	Fond du Lac	Wisconsin St	1b	104	372	80	112	73	15	5	19	74			9	.301
	Minor League totals			219	780	132	229	160	31	13	25	141	56	50	12	.294

EDWARD JOSEPH MULLIGAN

Mulligan served as a coach and utility player for the 1936 Padres and remained with the club for three years before ending his professional career in 1939 with Salt Lake City. At 41, the oldest of the Padres, he was part-time coach and utility infielder who hit .257 for Hollywood in 1935. 1936 was his 23rd year in organized baseball. Mulligan started with Galesburg, Illinois, and Davenport, Iowa, in 1914 and then was picked up by the Chicago Cubs in 1915 and played 69 games for them in 1915-16. Subsequently he played, in order, with the Kansas City Blues, Salt Lake City (for Bill Lane), Chicago White Sox, San Francisco Seals, Pittsburgh Pirates, Mission Reds, Seattle Indians, Portland, Oakland, and finally, Hollywood. Mulligan also played professional soccer in St. Louis for 12 seasons and was selected as an All-American several times.[422] He was acting President of the Padres for a short time in 1945, plus managed three teams, before becoming President of the California League from 1956-75.

March 19, 1936, The San Diego Union
EDWARD J. MULLIGAN

A gamester of the old school with a heart of gold and a will to win; every inch a battler and one who never has cried quits. That's Senor Edward J. Mulligan, better known throughout the baseball world as Eddie.

Mulligan will be on the coaching lines when the San Diego Padres open their Pacific Coast league wars here late this month, being Manager Frank Shellenback's chief aide-de-camp. He doesn't remain on the coaching lines all the time, however, for he has few peers in the art of running the bases and will handle general utility infield duties for he has long been one of the game's classiest infielders.

Eddie is 41 years young and though age in [sic] beginning to take its toll, still can battle and run with the best of the youngsters. Whereas most players are slowed up by ailing limbs at 41, Mulligan can still flit around the bases like a streak of lightening, but his batting eye isn't so good these days and there are too many youngsters around to allow him to be a regular.

Mulligan is the No. 1 tutor to all aspiring youngsters. He appears from the stands to be a gruff old gent who would scorn all younger players encroaching on all his good nature, but appearances are deceiving, so the old gamester loves the game like a kid and is never too busy to take time out and give playing hints to his juniors.

He's now starting his 23rd year in baseball, that is organized baseball, for he says he can't remember the day he wasn't thinking or playing the sport. Probably if you tossed in his school-day activities you would find he had started playing corner-lot ball when just out of diapers.

He broke into baseball with Davenport, Iowa, in 1914 and was purchased by the Chicago Cubs in 1915. He was optioned to the Kansas City Blues in 1915 and played there until 1917, quitting baseball to enter the World war in '16.

The year following the war, 1919, found him toiling under Bill Lane for the first time when the Padre owner was operating the Salt Lake City team. He remained there until the close of the 1920 campaign when he was sold to the Chicago White Sox along with Ernie Johnson and Earl Shelly. He spent 1921 and '22 there, and then re-entered the Coast league with the Frisco Seals, remaining there five years before climbing back to the majors, this time with the Pittsburgh Pirates in 1928.

He came back to the coast in '29 with the Missions and played there for a four-year stretch, then went to the Seattle Indians in '33.* He then joined Portland and wound up with

---

* The year Mulligan joined Seattle was 1932, ended up that season with Portland which is where he played in 1933.

APPENDIX H—BIOGRAPHIES OF THE 1936 SAN DIEGO PADRES

Oakland, and early last season was signed by Lane at Hollywood when Jim Levey suffered a broken arm. Mulligan was born in St. Louis, Mo., but now calls San Francisco home.

EDDIE MULLIGAN Edward Joseph Mulligan 5:09 152 BR TR
Born: August 27, 1894 St. Louis, MO   Died: March 15, 1982 San Rafael, CA

Year	Team	League	Pos	G	AB	R	H	1B	2B	3B	HR	RBI	K	BB	SB	AVG
1914	Galesburg	Central Assn	3b	82	310	36	83								11	.268
	Davenport	Three I	of-ss	2	7	0	1	1	0	0	0	0			0	.143
1915	Davenport	Three I	ss	124	463	58	129	96	24	7	2		63		40	.279
	Chicago	NL	ss-3b	11	22	5	8	7	1	0	0	2	1	5	2	.364
1916	Chicago	NL	ss	58	189	13	29	22	3	4	0	9	30	8	1	.153
	Kansas City	American Assn	ss-of	55	189	20	45	35	10	0	0		24	18	6	.238
1917	Kansas City	American Assn	ss	100	348	35	88	76	7	3	2		54	20	15	.253
	Mobile	Southern Assn	ss	20	75	10	16	14	1	0	1		13	7	10	.213
1918								**In Military Service**								
1919	Salt Lake City	PCL	3b-ss-of	135	460	66	122	88	22	6	6				21	.265
1920	Salt Lake City	PCL	3b-ss	179	662	116	198	146	35	11	6				50	.299
1921	Chicago	AL	3b	152	609	82	153	119	21	12	1	45	53	32	13	.251
1922	Chicago	AL	3b	103	372	39	87	65	14	8	0	31	32	22	7	.234
1923	San Francisco	PCL	3b	155	620	94	204	163	26	6	9	77			30	.329
1924	San Francisco	PCL	3b	199	**820**	150	251	185	51	2	13	114			28	.306
1925	San Francisco	PCL	3b	180	751	143	215	152	45	8	10	77			12	.286
1926	San Francisco	PCL	3b-ss	181	711	110	186	149	30	4	3	52			8	.262
1927	San Francisco	PCL	3b	170	665	128	182	129	46	1	6	65			23	.274
1928	Pittsburgh	NL	2b-3b	27	43	4	10	8	2	0	0	1	4	3	9	.233
1929	Missions	PCL	3b	181	734	144	205	163	34	5	3	56			42	.279
1930	Missions	PCL	3b	201	828	141	248	205	35	3	5	56			27	.300
1931	Missions	PCL	3b	94	390	57	109	86	17	6	0	27			12	.279
1932	Miss/Seattle/Portland	PCL	3b	139	548	83	162	134	23	2	3	42			15	.296
1933	Portland	PCL	3b	177	694	135	203	163	33	5	2	56			38	.293
1934	Oakland	PCL	3b	184	722	118	194	157	32	5	0	44			45	.269
1935	Hollywood/Missions	PCL	3b	82	245	31	63	55	7	1	0	21			11	.257
1936	San Diego	PCL	3b-2b-of	39	12	6	1	1	0	0	0	0			7	.083
1937	San Diego	PCL	3b	35	86	13	22	18	4	0	0	5			2	.256
1938	San Diego	PCL	3b	8	12	3	3	1	2	0	0	1			0	.250
1939	Salt Lake City	Pioneer	ph	3	2	0	0	0	0	0	0	0			0	.000
	Minor League totals			2725	10354	1697	2930	2217	484	75	71	693	154	45	453	.283
	Major League totals			351	1235	143	287	221	41	24	1	88	120	70	32	.232

GEORGE EDWARD MYATT

Myatt and Doerr were part of a deal with the Boston Red Sox that gave the Sox an option for "delivery" in 1937 (see Bobby Doerr reference). Turning age 22 for the 1936 season Myatt was from Denver. At age 18 in 1933 he played for San Antonio of the Texas League. He signed with the Stars in 1934 and finished the 1935 season with a .311 mark. Like Doerr, he attended winter school and expected to have a diploma by the end of 1936.[423] He was a fast runner and Eddie Collins was quoted as saying that "he can move down to first base faster than Archdeacon could when he was at his peak."*[424] His career included 407 games in the major leagues with New York (NL) and Washington, and concluded in 1949. Myatt played for the Padres in 1936 and 1937,

---

* The reference to Archdeacon was because he was felt to be the fastest man in baseball by the article's author.

and was married at home plate in Lane Field during the 1936 season. He also was a manager for the Philadelphia Phillies in 1968 and 1969, and coached in both major leagues for 23 years.

 *March 15, 1936, The San Diego Union*
GEORGE MYATT

"The big leagues or bust." That's the baseball motto of young George Myatt, Georgie to his friends, and if his 1935 performance is any criterion, the name George Myatt will be commonplace in the American league in another year or so.

Myatt, just 19, turning 20, is regarded as one of the fastest, if not fleetest, players in baseball today and his ability at shortstop, which he covers for the San Diego Padres, is of the A No. 1 class.

Five feet 10½ inches and 165 pounds dripping wet, Georgie is one half of Bill Lane's prized keystone combination, and is slated to report next spring along with his buddy, Bobby Doerr, to the Boston Red Sox.

He was born in Deenver [sic], Colo., but he now calls El Segundo, Calif., his home. He started playing early, performing with the El Segundo Firemen when only 13. When only 17 Willis Butler, big league scout, sent him to San Antonio in the Texas league and he remained there two months.

That was in 1933. In '34 he signed with the Padres, then the Hollywood Stars. He joined the club last spring and became a regular from the very start and in his first season found Pacific coast hurlers for a nice .311 batting average.

He makes no bones about his ambitions, for he says that if he can't make good in major league ball, there's no use continuing to play.

He stepped from George Stovall's Houghton Park club to the Padres last spring and looks to be about the finest shortstop developed in the coast circuit in many a moon.

Georgie took up baseball in order to lessen the financial burdens of his family, for his father, a contractor, became an invalid and he was forced to quit school to help out.

Like his keystone partner, Doerr, he has continued to attend school in the winter months and lacks only one credit of receiving his diploma and he plans to have that by the time he reports to manager Joe Cronin of the Red Sox next spring.

GEORGE MYATT

George Edward Myatt "Stud"   5:11 167 BL TR
Born: June 14, 1914 Denver, CO   Died: September 14, 2000 Orlando, FL

Year	Team	League	Pos	G	AB	R	H	1B	2B	3B	HR	RBI	K	BB	SB	AVG
1933	San Antonio	Texas	ss	1	3	0	0	0	0	0	0	0			0	.000
	Baton Rouge	Dixie	ss-3b	3	10	1	1	1	0	0	0	0			0	.100
1934	Hollywood	PCL	2b-ss	2	2	2	0	0	0	0	0	0			0	.000
1935	Hollywood	PCL	ss	135	530	82	165	143	16	5	1	33			22	.311
1936	San Diego	PCL	ss	162	652	117	180	151	16	12	1	50			33	.276
1937	San Diego	PCL	ss-3b	155	565	102	159	130	17	6	6	51			**33**	.281
1938	Jersey City	International	ss-3b	116	464	82	129	106	17	5	1	36	57	54	**45**	.278
	New York	NL	ss-3b	43	170	27	52	46	2	1	3	10	13	14	10	.306
1939	New York	NL	3b	22	53	7	10	8	2	0	0	3	6	6	2	.189
	Jersey City	International	ss-3b-2b	15	57	12	18	16	2	0	0	6	8	5	4	.316
1940	Jersey City	International	3b	6	8	2	2	1	1	0	0	0			0	.250
	Knoxville	Southern	ss-3b	116	415	65	111	80	22	9	0	28	51	67	16	.267
1941	Columbus	American Assn	2b	110	402	84	119	99	17	2	1	33	55	44	24	.296
1942	Columbus	American Assn	2b-of	116	322	60	90	69	11	10	0	35	39	54	**32**	.280

APPENDIX H—BIOGRAPHIES OF THE 1936 SAN DIEGO PADRES

Year	Team	League	Pos	G	AB	R	H	1B	2B	3B	HR	RBI	K	BB	SB	AVG
1943	Washington	AL	2b-3b-ss	42	53	11	13	10	3	0	0	3	7	13	3	.245
1944	Washington	AL	2b-ss-of	140	538	86	153	128	19	6	0	40	44	54	26	.284
1945	Washington	AL	inf-of	133	490	81	145	120	17	7	1	39	43	63	30	.296
1946	Washington	AL	2b-3b	15	34	7	8	7	1	0	0	4	3	2	1	.235
1947	Washington	AL	2b	12	7	1	0	0	0	0	0	0	4	4	0	.000
	Jersey City	International	3b-ss	110	383	63	116	90	20	5	1	50	22		11	.303
1948	Chattanooga	Southern	2-3-s-p	97	262	30	68	52	13	3	0	27	21	26	5	.260
1949	Chattanooga	Southern	p-2-o-3	22	33	6	3	3	0	0	0	4	4	7	0	.091
	Orlando	Florida St	3b-ss-of	63	189	39	61	39	17	1	4	27	17	40	7	.323
	Minor League totals			1229	4297	747	1222	980	169	58	15	380	274	297	232	.284
	Major League totals			407	1345	220	381	319	44	14	4	99	120	156	72	.283

WINFRED EDWARD PEPPER

Pepper was a catcher from Fullerton who received a spring tryout. He was a three-sport letterman at Fullerton Junior College, and followed that starring at the University of Oregon in football. He was released on March 9th "on his own request" indicating that he "had been offered a well-paying job in the east."[425] He eventually played one year (1938) for Hobbs in the West Texas-New Mexico League.[426]

WIN PEPPER Winfred Edward Pepper 6:00 190 BR TR
Born: December 11, 1915 Oklahoma Died: April 6, 1984 Riverside, CA

Year	Team	League	Pos	G	AB	R	H	1B	2B	3B	HR	RBI	K	BB	SB	AVG
1938	Hobbs	WT-NM	c	22	58	8	11	8	3	0	0	9	2		2	.190

ALBERT PIGNATARO

An outfielder, Pignataro was an 18-year old living in Salt Lake City with semi-pro experience who was invited to spring training. He remained with the club through March and was released at the start of the season. The next year Pignataro caught on with the Greenville team in the Coastal Plain League and afterward played for several years in Salt Lake City leagues. After ending his playing career, he became a long-time employee with Cudahy Packing Co. in Salt Lake City and, eventually, as its top manager in San Francisco.[427]

AL PIGNATARO Albert Pignataro 5:09 166 BR TR
Born: March 21, 1918 Idaho Died: November 26, 1988 Sacramento Co., CA

Year	Team	League	Pos	G	AB	R	H	1B	2B	3B	HR	RBI	K	BB	SB	AVG
1935	Holsum Bakers	Utah Industrial	of													
1936	Pinney Beverage	Utah Industrial	of													
1937	Greenville	Coastal Plain	of-3b	45	159	16	38	33	4	1	0	25			4	.239
1938	Ayden	Coastal Plain	of													
	Pinney Beverage	Utah Industrial	of													
1939	McClanahan's	Salt Lake City	of													
1940	Cudahy Packing	Salt Lake Metro	of													
	Minor League totals			45	159	16	38	33	4	1	0	25			4	.239

HERMAN POLYCARP PILLETTE

At the age of 40 Pillette had 18 years of professional ball experience coming into the 1936 season, beginning in 1917 with Richmond of the Central League and Tacoma of the Northwest League, plus one game for the Cincinnati Reds that year. From 1918-21 he played for Tacoma and Vancouver, and toured around with Des Moines and Regina, then Portland before being sold to the Detroit Tigers in 1922. Pillette was with the Tigers from 1922-24 and from there he went to Vernon/Missions/Seattle of the PCL. For the Tigers in 1922, he went 19-12. He pitched a no-hitter for the Mission club in 1929. In 1933 Seattle sold him to the Hollywood team and he went 14-15 in 1935.[428] Pillette pitched for San Diego beginning in 1936, lasting through 1942, and ended his career with Sacramento in 1943-45. He racked up 264 career minor league wins and pitched a record 23 years in the PCL.[429] Pillette's brother, Ted, was a minor league pitcher, and his son, Duane, pitched in the Major Leagues in 1949-56.

March 12, 1936, The San Diego Union
HERMAN F. PILLETTE

Herman P. Pillette, 18 years in baseball, is "Old Folks" to veteran baseball fans, but in the spring training camp of the San Diego Padres at Fullerton the veteran right handed pitcher shows as much life as the average recruit.

Pillette is 40, a veteran as pitchers go, but still has many a good game in his right arm and he intends to show it this season. He has been in baseball since 1917. He broke in that season with Tacoma in the old Northwest League, going right into the circuit from a farm. He still calls Portland, Ore., home, though his travels have taken him to a lot of points in his baseball career.

The veteran played part of two years for Tacoma and then went to San Francisco in 1919. He was farmed to Des Moines, but was injured and released. The next season he started out again with Regina in the Western Canadian circuit and the following year joined Portland.

The Beavers sold Pillette to the Detroit Tigers in 1922 and he served the now American League champions for three years. In 1925 he joined Vernon in the Pacific Coast League and moved with the team to San Francisco when it became the Missions. He was with the Reds until 1933 when he was sold to Seattle. After two seasons there he joined the Hollywood Stars, which team now becomes the San Diego Padres.

Pillette is married and has two children.

HERMAN PILLETTE Herman Polycarp Pillette "Old Folks"   6:02 190 BR TR
Born: December 26, 1895 St. Paul, OR   Died: April 30, 1960 Sacramento, CA

Year	Team	League	G	GS	CG	ShO	SV	W	L	PCT	IP	H	R	ER	K	BB	ERA
1917	Richmond	Central	12					1	5	.167	65.0	65	33	22	22	22	3.05
	Tacoma	Northwestern	20		15			12	6	.667	166.0	130	57	39	81	49	2.11
	Cincinnati	NL	1	0	0	0	0	0	0	.000	1.0	4	2	2	0	0	18.00
1918	Tacoma-Vancouver	Pacific Coast Int	11		7			5	4	.556	72.0	54	25	20	42	24	2.50
1919	Des Moines	Western	16					6	5	.545	84.0	83	26	19	53	43	2.04
1920	Regina	Western Canada	26			5		14	9	.609	234.0			56	146	82	2.15
	Portland	PCL	5			0		0	3	.000	17.0	24	18	14	6	8	7.41
1921	Portland	PCL	55			0		13	**30**	.302	275.0	**378**	216	152	141	104	4.97
1922	Detroit	AL	40	37	18	4	1	19	12	.613	274.7	270	110	87	71	95	2.85

APPENDIX H—BIOGRAPHIES OF THE 1936 SAN DIEGO PADRES

Year	Team	League	G	GS	CG	ShO	SV	W	L	PCT	IP	H	R	ER	K	BB	ERA
1923	Detroit	AL	47	36	14	0	1	14	19	.424	250.3	280	138	107	64	83	3.85
1924	Detroit	AL	19	3	1	0	1	1	1	.500	37.7	46	30	20	13	14	4.78
1925	Vernon	PCL	42		19			11	26	.297	285.0	323	160	116	78	71	3.66
1926	Missions	PCL	47	41	25	2	1	21	16	.568	321.3	344	143	108	101	72	3.02
1927	Missions	PCL	46		19			13	20	.394	297.0	**373**	**186**	**155**	74	63	4.70
1928	Missions	PCL	42		23	3		16	18	.471	301.0	332	122	104	71	59	3.11
1929	Missions	PCL	41		20	3		23	13	.639	273.0	299	120	109	82	52	3.59
1930	Missions	PCL	39		19	2		18	14	.563	261.0	350	154	126	66	58	4.34
1931	Missions	PCL	33		21	2		16	11	.593	273.0	334	150	107	68	44	3.53
1932	Missions	PCL	35		13	1		11	12	.478	209.0	277	127	100	52	40	4.31
1933	Missions/Seattle	PCL	35	34	16	1	0	13	14	.481	252.3	327	165	132	73	57	4.71
1934	Seattle	PCL	36		21	**5**		17	11	.607	260.0	278	99	75	87	45	2.60
1935	Seattle/Hollywood	PCL	32		15	0		14	15	.483	201.0	279	135	104	63	40	4.66
1936	San Diego	PCL	31	25	14	3	1	11	8	.579	191.0	180	80	67	63	37	3.16
1937	San Diego	PCL	36		1	0		4	5	.444	126.0	137	85	53	38	29	3.79
1938	San Diego	PCL	26	0	0	0	0	2	2	.500	78.0	92	52	23	29	18	2.65
1939	San Diego	PCL	25	5	3	1	1	8	6	.571	89.0	75	39	23	22	21	2.33
1940	San Diego	PCL	22	11	8	0	1	7	2	.778	89.0	95	39	28	31	18	2.83
1941	San Diego	PCL	15	0	0	0	2	1	2	.333	20.3	17	11	6	4	10	2.66
1942	San Diego	PCL	11	0	0	0	1	1	1	.500	24.3	34	13	12	7	9	4.44
1943	Sacramento	PCL	28	1	0	0	0	2	3	.400	41.0	47	30	26	7	13	5.71
1944	Sacramento	PCL	20	0	0	0	2	3	2	.600	36.7	34	12	10	9	8	2.45
1945	Sacramento	PCL	7	0	0	0	2	1	1	.500	12.0	12	5	5	3	1	3.75
	Minor League totals		794	117	259	28	11	264	264	.500	4554.0	4973	2302	*1811*	1519	1097	3.58
	Major League totals		107	76	33	4	3	34	32	.515	563.7	600	280	216	148	192	3.45

MANUEL SALVO

A 22-year old pitcher who started with Phoenix in 1931, then joined Sacramento in in 1932-35, and was eventually drafted by the Boston Red Sox. He was part of the deal that would send Bobby Doerr and George Myatt to the Sox in 1937. He played with San Diego in 1936-38, joining the team in June 1936. In 1939 Salvo joined the New York Giants and subsequently played for Boston (NL) and Philadelphia (NL), with his last season being with Sacramento in 1949.

MANNY SALVO Manuel Salvo "Gyp" 6:04 210 BR TR
Born: June 30, 1912 Sacramento, CA   Died: February 7, 1997 Vallejo, CA

Year	Team	League	G	GS	CG	ShO	SV	W	L	PCT	IP	H	R	ER	K	BB	ERA
1931	Phoenix	Arizona-Texas	12					1	4	.200	51.0	77	61	43	24	28	7.59
1932	Sacramento	PCL	28		5	0		7	4	.636	127.0	147	98	64	28	38	4.54
1933	Sacramento	PCL	19	15	7	1	1	5	11	.313	114.0	138	62	49	49	19	3.87
1934	Sacramento	PCL	45		21	2		15	18	.455	271.0	283	138	100	112	82	3.32
1935	Sacramento	PCL	44		16	**4**		11	17	.393	248.0	244	119	92	121	83	3.34
1936	San Diego	PCL	45	28	14	3	3	15	12	.556	239.0	244	112	88	145	74	3.31
1937	San Diego	PCL	46		22	**8**		19	13	.594	278.0	275	114	95	**196**	107	3.08
1938	San Diego	PCL	40	33	20	3	0	22	9	.710	239.0	205	87	69	**191**	82	2.60
1939	New York	NL	32	18	4	0	1	4	10	.286	136.0	150	84	70	69	75	4.63
1940	Jersey City	International	12		5			4	3	.571	60.0	56	27	20	17	16	3.00
	Boston	NL	21	20	14	**5**	0	10	9	.526	160.7	151	63	55	60	43	3.08
1941	Boston	NL	35	27	11	2	0	7	16	.304	195.0	192	103	88	67	93	4.06

Year	Team	League	G	GS	CG	ShO	SV	W	L	PCT	IP	H	R	ER	K	BB	ERA
1942	Boston	NL	25	14	6	1	0	7	8	.467	130.7	129	52	44	25	41	3.03
1943	Bost/Philadelphia	NL	22	14	5	1	0	5	7	.417	99.0	101	50	39	26	32	3.55
1944	Oakland	PCL	27	26	20	6	0	18	7	.720	210.0	192	60	50	58	38	2.14
1945																	In Military Service
1946	San Diego	PCL	13	13	6	0	0	3	6	.333	92.0	96	43	34	20	20	3.33
1947	San Diego	PCL	34		14	2		14	13	.519	200.0	215	91	85	77	44	3.83
1948	SD/Sacramento	PCL	36		1	0		5	7	.417	121.0	122	76	59	59	46	4.39
1949	Sacramento	PCL	30		2	0		5	5	.500	75.0	70	39	31	47	26	3.72
	Minor League totals		431	115	153	29	4	144	129	.527	2325.0	2364	1127	879	1144	703	3.40
	Major League totals		135	93	40	9	1	33	50	.398	721.3	723	352	296	247	284	3.69

? SCAROLI (OR SCAROLDI)

The local newspapers spelled his name two different ways. He was mentioned as a tall right handed pitcher and appeared in the box score of an intrasquad game played on February 27th.[430] There is no record of a player with the name spelled either way as having played professional baseball.

FRANK VICTOR SHELLENBACK

Shellenback served as full-time team Manager and part-time pitcher. He was one of the last legal spitball pitchers (in 1919 the use of spitballs was prohibited except for those few using it at the time). 1936 was his second season managing and kept active as a player, too, pitching and pinch-hitting at times. His first professional season was 1916 with Los Angeles, and joined the Chicago White Sox for the 1918-19 seasons where his two-year record was 10-15. The 1936 season would be the 11th with Bill Lane. In 1935 he won 14 games, and held the PCL record for wins with 289 going into this season (his 295 wins in the PCL remain a record).[431] His overall minor league record totaled 318 wins. Shellenback played and managed in San Diego for three seasons, 1936-38. He was popular with his players, but that did not keep them from pulling a fast one on him every now and then. George McDonald recalled that they would put a blanket on a table in the hotel room and play poker all night. The blanket's purpose was to keep Shellenback, who would check the halls regularly, from hearing the money hit the table. The players would sometimes stay up until morning.[432] He also coached in the major leagues for 15 years, through 1955.

March 5, 1936, The San Diego Union
FRANK SHELLENBACK

Frank V. Shellenback, one of the last of the spitball pitchers in organized baseball will begin his second season as manager, when he leads the San Diego Padres onto the field for the opening of the Pacific Coast baseball season at Lane Field here March 31.

Shellenback took over the direction of the team last year when Oscar Vitt shifted to Oakland and made a fine record. He pitched in a number of games and pinch hit as well at times, to aid the team in the campaign. And he will pitch and pinch hit again this season when the occasion demands.

The rangy hurler is 37 now, married and has six children, some of them coming baseball players and the rest rooters.

APPENDIX H—BIOGRAPHIES OF THE 1936 SAN DIEGO PADRES

Shelly, as he is known around the circuit, first broke into organized baseball in 1916 with the Los Angeles team of the Pacific Coast league.* He had no previous professional experience, but made good at once and the next year he went up to the Chicago White Sox as a youngster only in his teens. He remained with the Sox until 1920 when he was sent to Vernon in the Coast league. He remained there through the 1924 season, then was sold to Sacramento. After one season, there he joined the then Hollywood Stars, just brought in from Salt Lake by Owner H. W. Lane and he's been with them ever since.

The rule banning spitball pitchers from the majors caught Shellenback at a bad time. It was made in the fall of 1919. Shellenback then was on the reserve list of the White Sox but never was able to get by that rule and return to the majors, although many clubs wanted him. As late as 1930 Connie Mack made a big effort to land Shellenback in a deal to bolster his pitching staff of Grove, Earnshaw and Walberg, and the no-spitball rule prevented that although Shellenback always felt he was entitled to a chance again.

But Shelly has no regrets. He's been with Lane for 10 seasons and feels great starting the 11th in San Diego as boss of the Padres.

Shellenback pitches and bats right handed.

FRANK SHELLENBACK

Frank Victor Shellenback   6:02   192   BR   TR
Born: December 16, 1898 Joplin, MO   Died: August 17, 1969 Newton, MA

Year	Team	League	G	GS	CG	ShO	SV	W	L	PCT	IP	H	R	ER	K	BB	ERA
1917	Providence	International	24					9	6	.600	139.0	148		47	53	55	3.04
	Milwaukee	American Assn	8					3	3	.500	62.0	68	35	32	32	31	4.65
1918	Minneapolis	American Assn	3				0	1	2	.333	20.7	16	8	4	9	6	1.74
	Chicago	AL	28	21	10	2	2	9	12	.429	182.7	180	77	54	47	74	2.66
1919	Chicago	AL	8	4	2	0	0	1	3	.250	35.0	40	24	20	10	16	5.14
	Minneapolis	American Assn	20					7	3	.700	109.0	114	58	39	39	25	3.22
1920	Vernon	PCL	47			4		18	12	.600	298.7	262	106	90	104	79	2.71
1921	Vernon	PCL	39			3		18	10	.643	268.0	286	111	95	84	64	3.19
1922	Vernon	PCL	5	2	1	1	0	2	0	1.000	10.3	13	11	9	1	12	7.86
	Fresno	San Joaquin Valley	3	2	1	0	0	1	1	.500	20.7	19	12	9	9	10	3.92
	Kingsburg	Raisin Belt	1	1	1	0	0	1	0	1.000	9.0	14	8	6	5	2	6.00
1923	Vernon	PCL	43		23	2		19	19	.500	286.0	362	173	139	98	53	4.37
1924	Vernon	PCL	29		18			14	7	.667	212.0	273	118	86	55	38	3.65
1925	Sacramento	PCL	38		23			14	17	.452	264.0	297	133	96	91	61	3.27
1926	Hollywood	PCL	33	30	22	7	2	16	12	.571	236.3	219	96	73	89	49	2.78
1927	Hollywood	PCL	34		24			19	12	.613	265.0	271	115	90	106	68	3.06
1928	Hollywood	PCL	38		21	3		23	11	.676	272.0	274	124	101	125	66	3.34
1929	Hollywood	PCL	46		28	1		26	12	.684	335.0	365	175	148	163	68	3.98
1930	Hollywood	PCL	36		22	0		19	7	.731	252.0	304	151	130	111	59	4.64
1931	Hollywood	PCL	36		34	5		27	7	.794	306.0	305	118	97	127	61	2.85
1932	Hollywood	PCL	36		35	0		26	10	.722	322.0	343	133	112	119	48	3.13
1933	Hollywood	PCL	38	37	28	1	1	21	12	.636	314.0	373	170	157	122	77	4.50
1934	Hollywood	PCL	34		18	3		14	12	.538	229.0	259	127	106	80	50	4.17
1935	Hollywood	PCL	26		16	0		14	9	.609	200.0	236	102	76	82	33	3.42
1936	San Diego	PCL	15	12	7	0	0	6	7	.462	102.0	104	47	40	38	13	3.53

---

* Shellenback might have had a tryout with the Los Angeles team in 1916 but his first year was 1917 with Providence in the International League.

Year	Team	League	G	GS	CG	ShO	SV	W	L	PCT	IP	H	R	ER	K	BB	ERA
1937	San Diego	PCL	6					0	1	.000	16.0	23	15	10	7	7	5.63
1938	San Diego	PCL	3	0	0	0	0	0	0	.000	2.0	4	4	3	1	1	13.50
	Minor League totals		641	84	322	30	3	318	192	.624	4550.6	4952	2150	*1795*	1750	1036	*3.55*
	Major League totals		36	25	12	2	2	10	15	.400	217.7	220	101	74	57	90	3.06

IVEY MERWIN SHIVER

A 29-year old outfielder he had played for the Detroit Tigers in 1931 and the Cincinnati Reds in 1934. Shiver's career began in 1929 with Fort Worth and Evansville, and concluded in 1936 with the Padres when he was brought up in early July from Indianapolis. However, his season came to an abrupt end at the start of September when he decided to leave and take a position as Athletic director and head coach at Armstrong Junior College in Georgia. He was an All-American end for the University of Georgia in 1927.

IVEY SHIVER   Ivey Merwin Shiver "Chick"   6:01½ 190 BR TR
Born: January 22, 1906 Sylvester, GA   Died: August 31, 1972 Savannah, GA

Year	Team	League	Pos	G	AB	R	H	1B	2B	3B	HR	RBI	K	BB	SB	AVG
1929	Ft. Worth	Texas	of	1	4		1	0	0	1	0					.250
	Evansville	Three I	of	142	496	97	156	104	20	14	18	98	87	72	26	.315
1930	Beaumont	Texas	of	122	414	95	126	69	18	13	26	93	88	58	34	.304
1931	Toronto	International	of	115	434	69	134	82	25	14	13	89	80	34	10	.309
	Detroit	AL	of	2	9	2	1	1	0	0	0	0	3	0	0	.111
1932	Montreal	International	of	152	531	95	166	90	33	16	27	110	87	82	17	.313
1933	Montreal	International	of	145	450	69	140	92	19	6	23	82	82	68	3	.311
1934	Cincinnati	NL	of	19	59	6	12	9	1	0	2	6	15	3	1	.203
	St. Paul	American Assn	of	108	383	68	109	65	18	7	19	75	105	35	12	.285
1935	St. Paul	American Assn	of	144	555	107	176	110	25	10	31	125	**109**	49	5	.317
1936	St. Paul/Indianapolis	American Assn	of	50	165	29	43	25	10	0	8	34	30	20	3	.261
	San Diego	PCL	of	54	191	27	59	37	9	6	7	41			2	.309
	Minor League totals			1033	3623	656	1110	674	177	87	172	747	668	418	112	.306
	Major League totals			21	68	8	13	10	1	0	2	6	18	3	1	.191

STANLEY C. STEELY

Spelled with an extra 'e' in the local papers, this player was likely Stan Steely a Californian from Moraga who was brought in for a tryout. A right-handed pitcher, he attended St. Mary's College and had a professional career that started in 1936 when he played for Danville of the Bi-State League. Steely went on to play for three more seasons as high as Class B.[433]

STAN STEELY   Stanley C. Steely   6:00 170 BR TR
Born: September 3, 1914 San Joaquin Co., CA   Died: September 15, 2000 San Joaquin Co., CA

Year	Team	League	G	GS	CG	ShO	SV	W	L	PCT	IP	H	R	ER	K	BB	ERA
1936	Danville	Bi-State	30	15	7			12	5	.706	149.0	186	98		59	59	
1937	Canton	Middle Atlantic																
1938	Rocky Mount	Piedmont	34		3			7	10	.412	114.0	124	75	51	62	50	4.03
1939	Rocky Mount	Piedmont																
	Centerville	Eastern Shore																
	Minor League totals		64		10			19	15	.559	263	310	173	51	121	109	*4.03*

APPENDIX H—BIOGRAPHIES OF THE 1936 SAN DIEGO PADRES

ELMER T. STOCK

Stock was a 21-year old catcher from Canoga Park, California, who had some semi-pro experience and was invited to spring training. He was released on March 16, 1936.[434] While active in semi-pro ball around Los Angeles, no record was found of Stock playing in organized leagues.

ELMER STOCK Elmer I. Stock 5:11 174 BR TR
Born: February 28, 1913 Ohio Died: April 13, 1967 Los Angeles Co., CA

Year	Team	League	Pos	G	AB	R	H	1B	2B	3B	HR	RBI	K	BB	SB	AVG
1935	Reseda Athletics		c													
1936	Canoga Park		c													

KENNETH P. STORMS

A Kenneth Storey was brought in for tryouts but his name was reported only one time at the start of training.[435] In a March 6 box score a Storms was listed as playing left field. However, an article in the *Union* indicated that a Storms was released on March 9th, and *The Sporting News* reported that it was Kenneth Stroms who was released.[436] Searching minor league records found that there was an outfielder named Ken Storms who would been 24 years old in 1936 and born in California. This player was with Fresno in the California State League in 1936 and was at the spring training camp with the San Francisco Seals in 1937.

KEN STORMS Kenneth P. Storms
Born: August 6, 1911 California Died: February 22, 1995 Colorado

Year	Team	League	Pos	G	AB	R	H	1B	2B	3B	HR	RBI	K	BB	SB	AVG
1934	Frenso Brownies	Twilight	of													.375
1935	Fresno Hollywood Jrs.	Twilight	of													
1936	Fresno	California St	of	14	56	9	21	14	5	2	0				1	.375
1937-1939							**No Record**									
1940	Los Baños	San Joaquin Val.	of													

GENE EDWARD TUTTLE

Tuttle was the son of 1936's PCL President, W. C. Tuttle. A bespectacled 22-year old semi-pro pitcher he pitched in one game for Hollywood in 1935 and saw limited duty with the 1936 and 1937 Padres. Interviewed some 60+ years later he said his contract with the Padres in 1936 was $75 a month. However, he also added that the players would get free meals in restaurants because they loved the Padres. "The hotel was fifty cents a day, so I was able to make it on $75."[437]

BUD TUTTLE Gene Edward Tuttle 6:03 ½ 190 BR TL
Born: March 15, 1914 Spokane, WA Died: November 1, 2007 New Haven, IN

Year	Team	League	G	GS	CG	ShO	SV	W	L	PCT	IP	H	R	ER	K	BB	ERA
1933	Van Nuys Merchants																
1934	Van Nuys Merchants																
1935	Hollywood	PCL	1		0			0	1	.000	2.0	7	7	7	1	3	31.50

Year	Team	League	G	GS	CG	ShO	SV	W	L	PCT	IP	H	R	ER	K	BB	ERA
1936	San Diego	PCL	2	0	0	0	0	0	0	.000	5.0	5	3	3	2	3	5.40
1937	San Diego	PCL	2		0			0	0	.000	3.0	4	4	4	3	3	12.00
	Minor League totals		5	0	0	0	0	0	1	.000	10.0	16	14	14	6	9	*12.60*

FREDERICK THOMAS VAUGHN

Vaughn was a 17-year old with semipro experience when he joined the 1936 Padres. He and Red Williams were referred to as "the Santa Paula rookies." He was also a professional "crooner."[438] 1936 was his first year in professional baseball and he appeared in two games for San Diego, but finished that year with Hutchinson of the Western Association. Vaughn eventually played in the major leagues with Washington for two years and ended his career in 1950. He, along with Cooper and Iverson, were on the roster in April but played with the Padres "B" team and stayed in San Diego while the team was on the road. The three players were released on May 10, 1936.

FRED VAUGHN   Frederick Thomas Vaughn "Muscles"   5:10 185 BR TR
Born: October 18, 1918 Coalinga, CA   Died: March 2, 1964 Lake Wales, FL

Year	Team	League	Pos	G	AB	R	H	1B	2B	3B	HR	RBI	K	BB	SB	AVG
1936	San Diego	PCL	ph	2	2	1	1	1	0	0	0	0			0	.500
	Hutchinson	Western Assn	3b	67	258	50	59	31	17	7	4	31	52	34	7	.229
1937	Hutchinson	Western Assn	ss-2b-3b	132	536	119	182	112	34	**21**	15	**123**	89	53	15	.340
1938	Binghamton	Eastern	2b	132	479	93	135	90	17	11	17	99	84	56	10	.282
1939	Indianapolis	American Assn	2b	45	149	25	48	35	8	3	2	21	25	20	2	.322
1940	Birmingham	Southern Assn	2b	27	106	16	30	20	5	2	3	6	13	11	1	.283
1941-1942								**No Record**								
1943	Ind'apolis/Minneapolis	American Assn	2b	119	376	47	90	58	11	12	9	53	64	46	6	.239
1944	Minneapolis	American Assn	2b	125	445	73	143	93	24	9	17	62	70	39	16	.321
	Washington	AL	2b-3b	30	109	10	28	24	2	1	1	21	24	9	2	.257
1945	Washington	AL	2b-ss	80	268	28	63	51	7	4	1	25	48	23	0	.235
1946								**No Record**								
1947	Hollywood	PCL	2b-3b	104	380	64	114	79	19	4	12	56	49	31	0	.300
1948	Hollywood	PCL		8	27	7	10	8	2	0	0	4				.370
	New Orleans/Nashville	Southern Assn	3b-2b	85	324	57	88	51	24	8	5	55	55	48	0	.272
1949	Greensboro	Carolina	2b	129	456	96	132	74	33	3	22	85	57	48	1	.289
1950	Greensboro	Carolina	2b-3b	104	363	81	116	71	16	2	27	88	40	75	2	.320
	Minor League totals			1079	3901	729	1148	723	210	82	133	683	598	461	60	.294
	Major League totals			110	377	38	91	75	9	5	2	46	72	32	2	.241

ROBERT D. VICKERS

He was brought in for tryouts and the papers reported his name without giving a first name. His a last name was spelled with an 'h' (as Vichers) in one story.[439] No professional record for a Vickers or Vichers from this time period could be found. However, it appears this was Robert Vickers born May 24, 1915, and the son of a famous Coast league chucker of former days, Rube (Harry P.) Vickers.[440] He was brought in for tryouts and did not participate very long in spring training. No professional record for Vickers could be found.

APPENDIX H—BIOGRAPHIES OF THE 1936 SAN DIEGO PADRES

RICHARD OLE WARD

Ward was a 27-year old pitcher who played in several games with the Chicago Cubs in 1934 and had one appearance with the St. Louis Cardinals in 1935. Ward's career began in 1930 and concluded in 1939. He was with the Padres for parts of four seasons, 1936 through 1939. His Padres stint started when he was acquired on June 1, 1936, from the Boston Red Sox with Salvo and Shiver as part of the original Doerr/Myatt transaction.

DICK WARD　　　Richard Ole Ward　　　6:01　198　BR　TR
Born: May 21, 1909 Herrick, SD　　　Died: May 30, 1966 Freeland, WA

Year	Team	League	G	GS	CG	ShO	SV	W	L	PCT	IP	H	R	ER	K	BB	ERA
1930	North Platte/Norton	Nebraska St	21					4	7	.364	113.0	158	116	87	45	40	6.93
1931	Ft. Smith	Western Assn	19		6	2		7	6	.538	107.0	94	70	42	53	48	3.53
1932	Wichita	Western	34					8	9	.471	150.0	176	133		86	93	0.00
	Los Angeles	PCL	9		4	0		4	3	.571	61.0	66	34	33	32	27	4.87
1933	Los Angeles	PCL	43	35	25	1	0	25	9	**.735**	284.7	258	127	103	176	119	3.26
1934	Chicago	NL	3	0	0	0	0	0	0	.000	6.0	9	6	2	1	2	3.00
	Los Angeles	PCL	20		13			13	4	.765	137.0	136	43	40	54	53	2.63
1935	St. Louis	NL	1	0	0	0	0	0	0	.000	0.0	0	0	0	0	1	∞
	Rochester	International	7	7	2	2	0	3	3	.500	43.3	37	20	14	13	28	*2.91*
	Seattle	PCL	1		0			0	0	.000	1.0	0	0	0	0	0	0.00
1936	Sac/San Diego	PCL	37		11	3		15	7	.682	184.0	160	67	70	100	83	3.42
1937	San Diego	PCL	42		24	0		18	18	.500	284.0	308	136	140	116	92	4.44
1938	San Diego	PCL	30	26	13	3	0	9	12	.429	174.0	200	102	97	55	65	5.02
1939	SD/Los Angeles	PCL	6	4	0	0	0	1	3	.250	17.3	27	16	15	3	14	7.79
	Minor League totals		269	72	98	11	0	107	81	.569	1556.3	1620	864	641	733	662	3.71
	Major League totals		4	0	0	0	0	0	0	.000	6.0	9	6	2	1	3	3.00

EDWIN LEE WELLS

Wells was 36 when he came to the Padres with 14 seasons of professional baseball experience. He started playing organized ball in 1922 with the Detroit Tigers organization. His nickname of 'Hardluck' happened upon him because he lost nine 3-2 decisions in 1935.[441] He spent time with the Tigers off and on from 1923 through 1927, with his best season being 1926 when he went 12-10. In 1928 he went to Birmingham of the Southern Association and was sold to the New York Yankees in 1929 and remained there for four years, through 1932, with an overall record of 37-20. In 1933 Wells was sold to the St. Louis Browns where he played two years (7-21) and then Lane picked up his contract for the 1935 season.[442] In June 1936 he was traded to Seattle for Craghead. He won 68 games in the major leagues; his last professional season was in 1937.

March 24, 1936, The San Diego Union
EDWIN L. WELLS

The 1935 season found Edwin L. "Ed" Wells, southpaw hurler of the San Diego Padres, the hard luck man of the then Hollywood Stars' pitching staff. He lost more games by one-run margins than anyone else on the club. The team just could not seem to get runs behind him but he looks for his luck to change this season with the squad performing in a new park and under a new name.

SAN DIEGO'S FIRST PADRES and "THE KID"

Wells has been through the baseball mill and the big powerful hurler knows his slants. He started in the game in 1922 with the Detroit Tigers after playing some at Bethany, West Virginia. He was farmed out to Ludington for a time and the next season recalled by Detroit and sent to Birmingham in the Southern association. But in 1924 the Tigers called him into action and he remained in Detroit through the 1927 season. In 1928 he went to Birmingham again and in 1929 was sold to the New York Yankees, remaining there for five years.* In 1934 he was sold to the St. Louis Browns and last year Owner Bill Lane of the Hollywood Stars acquired his contract.

Wells' home is Ashland, O. He is married and bats left handed along with his pitching.

ED WELLS
Edwin Lee Wells "Satchelfoot" 6:01½ 183 BL TL
Born: June 7, 1900 Ashland, OH Died: May 1, 1986 Montgomery, AL

Year	Team	League	G	GS	CG	ShO	SV	W	L	PCT	IP	H	R	ER	K	BB	ERA
1922	Ludington	Central	24		16			13	10	.565	177.0	149	54	38	111	43	1.93
1923	Birmingham	Southern Assn	16	13	13			8	7	.533	135.0	125	41	36	60	32	2.40
	Detroit	AL	7	0	0	0	0	0	0	.000	10.0	11	6	6	6	6	5.40
1924	Detroit	AL	29	15	5	0	4	6	8	.429	102.0	117	58	46	33	42	4.06
1925	Detroit	AL	35	14	5	0	2	6	9	.400	134.3	190	106	93	45	62	6.23
1926	Detroit	AL	36	26	9	4	0	12	10	.545	178.0	201	101	82	58	76	4.15
1927	Detroit	AL	8	1	0	0	1	0	1	.000	20.0	28	16	15	5	5	6.75
	Birmingham	Southern Assn	15		9			13	1	.929	114.0	92	36	27	57	40	2.13
1928	Birmingham	Southern Assn	38		28			25	7	.781	291.0	296	110	90	129	71	2.78
1929	New York	AL	31	23	10	3	0	13	9	.591	193.3	179	102	93	78	81	4.33
1930	New York	AL	27	21	7	0	0	12	3	.800	150.7	185	91	87	46	49	5.20
1931	New York	AL	27	10	6	0	2	9	5	.643	116.7	130	68	56	34	37	4.32
1932	New York	AL	22	0	0	0	2	3	3	.500	31.7	38	19	15	13	12	4.26
1933	St. Louis	AL	36	22	10	0	1	6	14	.300	203.7	230	113	95	58	63	4.20
1934	St. Louis	AL	33	8	2	0	1	1	7	.125	92.0	108	60	49	27	35	4.79
1935	Hollywood	PCL	39		22	0		9	20	.310	264.0	297	136	127	80	55	4.33
1936	San Diego/Seattle	PCL	30		13	2		9	13	.409	196.0	238	106	94	62	60	4.32
1937	New Orleans	Southern Assn	3	2	0	0	0	0	0	.000	8.0	15	9	5	0	2	5.63
	Minor League totals		165	15	101	2	0	77	58	.570	1185.0	1212	492	417	499	303	3.17
	Major League totals		291	140	54	7	13	68	69	.496	1232.3	1417	740	637	403	468	4.65

ALLAN MYERS WHITLOCK

He was described as a tall right-handed pitcher who was with Brooklyn in 1934 and in the North Carolina State League in 1935.[443] His last name was spelled with and without the 'e' during his short time with the team. On March 2nd the *Sun* reported that Whitelock [sic] had tossed two balls and "complained of a sore arm, packed his grip and bid pro baseball a sad adieu for at least another season."[444]

ALLAN WHITLOCK
Allan Myers Whitlock 6:03 180
Born: September 15, 1914 California Died: May 2, 1971 Los Angeles Co., CA

Year	Team	League	G	GS	CG	ShO	SV	W	L	PCT	IP	H	R	ER	K	BB	ERA
1935	Burlington	Central Carolina																

---

* Tenure with Yankees and Browns is in error. Wells played for Yankees for four years, not five, and was with the St. Louis Browns in 1933 and 1934.

APPENDIX H—BIOGRAPHIES OF THE 1936 SAN DIEGO PADRES

LESLIE A. WILLIAMS

A 19-year old with semi-pro experience he was with the team only in spring training and described as a "husky southpaw first baseman and outfielder."[445] Together with Fred Vaughn, they were referred to as "the Santa Paula rookies." On March 1 it was reported that Williams was "slapping the ball with regularity."[446] Later in 1936 Williams was able to get in some game with Augusta in the Sally league, played a full 1937 season with three different teams, and concluded his career in organized ball with a short stint in Tacoma in 1938.

RED WILLIAMS   Leslie Williams   6:00 190 BL TL
Born: 1917

Year	Team	League	Pos	G	AB	R	H	1B	2B	3B	HR	RBI	K	BB	SB	AVG
1936	Augusta	Sally	1b	13	45	2	10	8	1	1	0	0	7	6	0	.222
1937	Peoria	Three I	1b	46	177	16	35	27	5	3	0				2	.198
	Durham	Piedmont	1b	22	68	5	11	9	1	1	0	8	24	0	0	.162
	Muskogee	Western Assn	1b	33	137	17	34	21	7	2	4	22	50	6	1	.248
1938	Tacoma	Western Int	1b	4	9	0	0	0	0	0	0					.000
	Minor League totals			118	436	40	90	65	14	7	4	30	81	12	3	.206

THEODORE SAMUEL WILLIAMS

1936 was his first season in professional baseball and he joined the team in June directly from San Diego Hoover High School. Williams played the 1937 season with the Padres then went to Minneapolis for the 1938 season before joining the Boston Red Sox in 1939 where he remained through 1960 when he retired from baseball. After retiring, Williams also managed the Washington Senators/Texas Rangers for four years. He was elected to the Hall of Fame in 1966. Ted completed his professional baseball career with 589 home runs, 68 in the minors and 521 in the majors. His first professional baseball plate appearance for the Padres was on June 27, 1936, as a pinch hitter which resulted in a strikeout. Williams lived with his family at 4121 Utah Street.

March 18, 1937, The San Diego Union
TED WILLIAMS

From high school to a regular outfield berth with the San Diego Padres in one season is the record of Ted Williams, the San Diego boy who is making good in organized baseball in a big way.

Williams was born in San Diego Oct. 30, 1918, [sic]* and took to baseball like a duck to water. He attended Herbert Hoover High where he was the star pitcher and batting hero. He won the batting trophy in his school two years in a row, and also won the batting crown in the Pomona tournament. He batted .430 for Hoover in three seasons, the highest mark ever recorded there.

In his first trip to the plate as a member of the Padres, Ted struck out while pinch hitting, but it only made him more desirous of succeeding. He got his chance late in the season when Chick Shiver left the club overnight. Ted stepped into his shoes and played the position even better

---

* Note that Williams's actual birth date is August 30, 1918. The reason for October being cited in this 1937 article was covered in the book *The Kid: Ted Williams in San Diego*, page 225. Essentially, so the story goes, Williams did not want anything to interfere with baseball during the season, least of all, his birthday...so he gave it as being in October rather than August.

SAN DIEGO'S FIRST PADRES and "THE KID"

than Chick. The high spot of his first year was the time he hit a home run off Wee Willie Ludolph, the Oakland Ghost, in the Shaughnessy play-offs in Oakland.

Ted batted .271 [sic] in his first year of professional ball, but is expected to go places this year. He hit the ball at a lively clip in last Sunday's exhibition game with Portland, chalking up a homer and three singles in five times up.

Ted is six feet, two inches tall and weighs 170 pounds. His chief love is baseball, but he also loves hunting, fishing and eating, and spends much of his off time in the field.

TED WILLIAMS Theodore Samuel Williams "The Kid" "The Splendid Splinter"   6:03 205 BL TR
Born: August 30, 1918 San Diego, CA   Died: July 5, 2002 Inverness, FL

Year	Team	League	Pos	G	AB	R	H	1B	2B	3B	HR	RBI	K	BB	SB	AVG
1935	Walter Church	SD City	of-p	6	21	4	5	4	0	0	1				0	.238
1936	Benninghoven's Cubs		of-p	2	8	1	1	0	0	0	1	2			0	.125
	San Diego	PCL	of-p	42	108	18	29	18	9	2	0	11			2	.269
1937	San Diego	PCL	of	138	454	66	132	83	24	2	23	98			1	.291
1938	Minneapolis	American Assn	of	148	528	**130**	193	111	30	9	**43**	142	75	**114**	1	**.366**
1939	Boston	AL	of	149	565	131	185	99	44	11	31	145	64	107	2	.327
1940	Boston	AL	of-p	144	561	**134**	193	113	43	14	23	113	54	96	4	.344
1941	Boston	AL	of	143	456	**135**	185	112	33	3	**37**	120	27	**145**	2	**.406**
1942	Boston	AL	of	150	522	**141**	186	111	34	5	**36**	137	51	**145**	3	**.356**
1943-1945							**In Military Service**									
1946	Boston	AL	of	150	514	**142**	176	93	37	8	38	123	44	**156**	0	.342
1947	Boston	AL	of	156	528	**125**	181	100	40	9	**32**	114	47	**162**	0	**.343**
1948	Boston	AL	of	137	509	124	188	116	**44**	3	25	127	41	**126**	4	**.369**
1949	Boston	AL	of	**155**	566	**150**	194	109	**39**	3	**43**	159	48	**162**	1	.343
1950	Boston	AL	of	89	334	82	106	53	24	1	28	97	21	82	3	.317
1951	Boston	AL	of	148	531	109	169	107	28	4	30	126	45	**144**	1	.318
1952	Boston	AL	of	6	10	2	4	2	0	1	1	3	2	2	0	.400
1953	Boston	AL	of	37	91	17	37	18	6	0	13	34	10	19	0	.407
1954	Boston	AL	of	117	386	93	133	80	23	1	29	89	32	**136**	0	.345
1955	Boston	AL	of	98	320	77	114	62	21	3	28	83	24	91	2	.356
1956	Boston	AL	of	136	400	71	138	84	28	2	24	82	39	102	0	.345
1957	Boston	AL	of	132	420	96	163	96	28	1	38	87	43	119	0	**.388**
1958	Boston	AL	of	129	411	81	135	84	23	2	26	85	49	98	1	**.328**
1959	Boston	AL	of	103	272	32	69	44	15	0	10	43	27	52	0	.254
1960	Boston	AL	of	113	310	56	98	54	15	0	29	72	41	75	1	.316
	Minor League totals			336	1119	219	360	216	63	13	68	253	75	114	4	.322
	Major League totals			2292	7706	1798	2654	1537	525	71	521	1839	709	2019	24	.344

APPENDIX H—BIOGRAPHIES OF THE 1936 SAN DIEGO PADRES

TED WILLIAMS   Theodore Samuel Williams "The Kid" "The Splendid Splinter"   6:03 205 BL TR
Born: August 30, 1918 San Diego, CA   Died: July 5, 2002 Inverness, FL

Year	Team	League	G	GS	CG	ShO	SV	W	L	PCT	IP	H	R	ER	K	BB	ERA
1935	Walter Church	SD City	3	3	2	0	0	2	0	1.000	23.0	20	6	5	19	11	1.96
1936	Benninghoven's Cubs		1	1	1	0	0	1	0	1.000	9.0	10	2	2	14	3	2.00
	San Diego	PCL	1	0	0	0	0	0	0	.000	1.3	2	2	2	0	1	13.50
1940	Boston	AL	1	0	0	0	0	0	0	.000	2.0	3	1	1	1	0	4.50
	Minor League totals		4	3	2	0	0	2	0	1.000	24.3	22	8	7	19	12	2.59
	Major League totals		1	0	0	0	0	0	0	.000	2.0	3	1	1	1	0	4.50

VANDER E. WIRTHMAN

A 22-year old, Wirthman was from Los Angeles and attended Washington High there along with Hal Doerr. After high school, he played semi-pro ball in the area before trying out with, and making, the Hollywood team in 1935. He played his only season with San Diego in 1936, and that was his last season in professional baseball.

March 27, 1936, The San Diego Union
VANCE WIRTHMAN

From high school to Coast league baseball in one jump is the record of Vance Wirthman, young outfielder who broke into the lineup with Hollywood last year and conducted himself like a veteran

Wirthman, who answers to the name of Van, is 21 years of age, six feet tall, and tips the beam at 175 pounds. He is unmarried.

Wirthman started his baseball career with the Washington high school team of Los Angeles, and played with the club during the years 1930, 1931, and 1932. Curiously enough, Van's best work with the Washington High team was as a pitcher. He also was a member of the football eleven.

After leaving high school, he played several years with semipro teams in and around Los Angeles and then decided to make his bid in organized baseball. He appeared at the Hollywood camp in 1935 and managed to stick. He found himself in the lineup frequently and ended the season with a batting average of .278.[*]

Wirthman was born in Los Angeles and still calls it his home town.

His favorite winter sports are hunting and fishing and he spends much of his spare time following those pastimes.

VAN WIRTHMAN   Vander E. Wirthman   6:00 175 BR TR
Born: March 3, 1914 Los Angeles, CA   Died: April 28, 1965 Los Angeles, CA

Year	Team	League	Pos	G	AB	R	H	1B	2B	3B	HR	RBI	K	BB	SB	AVG
1935	Hollywood	PCL	of	57	131	26	34	24	8	1	1	9			1	.260
1936	San Diego	PCL	of	132	428	58	123	96	20	6	1	49			6	.287
1940	Walker Roofing															
	Standard Oil Bakersfield															
	Minor League totals			189	559	84	157	120	28	7	2	58			7	.281

---

[*] Average is in error, his correct batting average in 1935 was .260 not .278.

SAN DIEGO'S FIRST PADRES and "THE KID"

REFERENCES

The Baseball Encyclopedia: The Complete and Definitive Record of Major League Baseball, 10th ed. New York: Macmillan Publishing Company, 1996.

Bauer, Carlos. *The Coast League Cyclopedia: An Encyclopedia of the Old Pacific Coast League, 1903-57*. 3 vols. San Diego: Baseball Press Books, 2003.

Benson, Michael. *Ballparks of North America, A Comprehensive Historical Reference to Baseball Grounds, Yards and Stadiums, 1845 to Present*. Jefferson, NC: McFarland, 1989.

Bradlee, Ben, Jr. *The Kid, The Immortal Life of Ted Williams*. New York: Little, Brown and Company, 2013.

Brandes, Ray, and Swank, Bill. *The Pacific Coast League San Diego Padres,* Vol 1, *Lane Field: The Early Years, 1936-1946,* Vol. 2, *Lane Field: The Later Years, 1947-1957*. San Diego: San Diego Padres and the San Diego Baseball Historical Society, 1997.

Cataneo, David. *I Remember Ted Williams: Anecdotes and Memories of Baseball's Splendid Splinter by the Players Who Knew Him*. Nashville, TN: Cumberland House, 2002.

Cobbs, Chris. "Down Memory Lane with Vintage (PCL) Padres." Presented at the 23rd Society for American Baseball Research National Convention, San Diego, CA, June 24-28, 1993.

Cramer, Richard Ben. *Ted Williams, The Seasons of the Kid*. Upper Saddle River, NJ: Prentice Hall, 1991.

———. *What Do You Think of Ted Williams Now?* New York: Simon & Schuster, 2002.

Dobbins, Dick. *The Grand Minor League: An Oral History of the Old Pacific Coast League*. Emeryville, CA: Woodford Press, 1999.

Ferkovich, Scott. "Lane Field (San Diego)." SABR. https://sabr.org/node/27043.

Gabriel, S. *Who's Who in San Diego*. 1936.

Green, John F. "George Myatt." SABR. https://sabr.org/bioproj/person/0b0d19f5.

Greschke, Jim. "San Diego: A Great Baseball Tradition 1936-1986." In *1986 Padres Yearbook*.

Halberstam, David. *The Teammates: A Portrait of Friendship*. New York: Hyperion, 2003.

Hiro, Brian, "Padres' 75th Anniversary: Franchise Roots Run Much Deeper Than Just Major League Club." *North County Times-The Californian*, March 28, 2011.

Holway, John B. *The Complete Book of Baseball's Negro Leagues: The Other Half of Baseball History*. New York: Hasting House, 2001.

———. *The Last .400 Hitter: The Anatomy of a .400 Season*. Dubuque, IA: Wm. C. Brown, 1992.

———. *TED, the Kid*. Springfield, CA: Scorpio Books, 2008.

Internet sites—various, including: Ancestry.com; BaseballReference.com; MiLB.com; Newspapers.com; SABR.org.

Johnson, Dick, and Glenn Stout. *Ted Williams: A Portrait in Words and Pictures*. New York: Walker, 1991.

Johnson, Lloyd, and Miles Wolff, eds. *The Encyclopedia of Minor League Baseball*. Durham, NC: Baseball America, 1993.

SAN DIEGO'S FIRST PADRES and "THE KID"

Kaup, John T. "San Diego Ballparks as a Reflection of Urban Patterns in the City: 1936-1968." Unpublished manuscript, 1994.

Keller, Earl. "Padres PCL History." Presented at the 23rd Society for American Baseball Research National Convention, San Diego, CA, June 24-28, 1993.

———. "San Diego: A Rich Baseball Tradition." Presented at the 23rd Society for American Baseball Research National Convention, San Diego, CA, June 24-28, 1993.

Kernan, Kevin. "Down Memory Lane, Old Stadium Still Draws Smiles, Yearnings." *San Diego Union-Tribune*, June 9, 1996.

Lieb, Frederick G. *The Boston Red Sox*. New York: G. P. Putnam's Sons, 1947.

"Life in San Diego." *Official Monthly Publication of the Hotel Greeters of America*, 24, no. 10, (October 1936).

Linn, Edward. *Hitter: The Life and Turmoils of Ted Williams*. New York: Harcourt Brace, 1993.

———. *Ted Williams, The Eternal Kid*. Bartholomew House, 1961.

Lorge, Barry. "Padres Championships." *Padres Magazine*, 1996.

Mann, Arthur. "Baseball's Bad Boy." *Liberty*, May 9, 1940.

Maracin, Paul R. "Double-A Dago: When the Padres Played the Bush League." *The San Diego Reader*, July 11, 1991.

McDonald, Johnny. "Play Ball." *Old San Diego Gazette*, March 1999.

Montville, Leigh. *Ted Williams: The Biography of an American Hero*. New York: Doubleday, 2004.

Newspapers—various, including: *Boston Post, Fullerton Daily News Tribune, Los Angeles Examiner, Los Angeles Times, San Diego Union, San Diego Evening Tribune, San Diego Herald, San Diego Sun, Santa Ana Register, The Sporting News*.

Norris, Frank. "San Diego Baseball: The Early Years." *The Journal of San Diego History* 30, no. 1 (Winter 1984).

Nowlin, Bill, ed. *The Kid: Ted Williams in San Diego*. Cambridge, MA: Rounder Books, 2005.

Olsen, Ed. "How Professional Baseball Developed in San Diego." Unpublished manuscript, May 26, 1967.

O'Neal, Bill. *The Pacific Coast League, 1903-1988*. Fort Worth, TX: Eakin Press, 1990.

Pallos, Vic. "History of San Diego Ballparks." Presented at the 23rd Society for American Baseball Research National Convention, San Diego, CA, June 24-28, 1993.

Pope, Edwin. *Ted Williams, The Golden Year 1957*. Upper Saddle River, NJ: Prentice-Hall, 1970.

Prime, Jim, and Bill Nowlin. *The Pursuit of Perfection: Ted Williams*. Champaign, IL: Sports Publishing, 2002.

Robinson, Ray. *Ted Williams*. New York: G. P. Putnam's Sons, 1962.

Salin, Tony. *Baseball's Forgotten Heroes: One Man's Search for the Games' Most Interesting Overlooked Players*. Chicago: Masters Press, 1999.

Sampson, Arthur. *Ted Williams: A Biography of The Kid*. New York: A.S. Barnes, 1950.

Sandoval, Jim, and Bill Nowlin, eds. *Can He Play? A Look at Baseball Scouts and Their Profession*. Phoenix, AZ: SABR, 2011.

Schoor, Gene. *The Ted Williams Story*. New York: Julian Messner, 1954.

Seidel, Michael. *Ted Williams: A Baseball Life*. Chicago: Contemporary Books, 1991.

Showley, Roger. "Slow Pitch." *San Diego Union-Tribune*, November 10, 1996.

Smith, James D., III. "Bobby Doerr in 1934, His Reflections on Life in the Pacific Coast League at 16." *The National Pastime* 25 (2005): 86-88.

———. "Lester Spurgeon Cook, Catcher, Trainer, PCL Legend." *The National Pastime* 27 (2007): 39-42.

Snelling, Dennis. *The Pacific Coast League: A Statistical History, 1903-1957*. Jefferson, NC: McFarland & Company, 1995.

Society for American Baseball Research (SABR). "Various Players." Baseball Biography Project. https://SABR.org.

Stevens, Chuck, and Roger Osebbaugh. *The Early Coast League Statistical Record, 1903-1957*. San Diego: Baseball Press Books, 2004.

Swank, Bill. *Echoes from Lane Field, A History of the San Diego Padres 1936-1957*. Nashville, TN: Turner Publishing, 1997.

———. "Ted Williams, Earl Keller and the 1937 San Diego Padres." Unpublished manuscript, 2003.

Swank, William G., and James D. Smith III. "This Was Paradise, Voices of the Pacific Coast League Padres, 1936-1958." *Journal of San Diego History* 41, no. 1 (Winter 1995).

Tomlinson, Gerald, ed. *How to Do Baseball Research*. Phoenix, AZ: Society for American Baseball Research, 2000.

Underwood, John. *It's Only Me: The Ted Williams We Hardly Knew*. Chicago: Triumph Books, 2005.

Updike, John. *Hub Fans Bid Kid Adieu: John Updike on Ted Williams*. London: Penguin, 2010.

Williams, Ted, and David Pietrusza. *My Life in Pictures*. New York: Total Sports Publishing, 2001.

Williams, Ted, and John Underwood. *My Turn at Bat: The Story of My Life*. New York: Simon & Shuster, 1988.

Zingg, Paul J., and Mark D. Meadows. *Runs, Hits, and an Era: The Pacific Coast League 1903-1958*. Champaign: University of Illinois Press, 1994.

Zuckerman, Larry. *Ballparks of the PCL*. Baseball Press, 2007.

SAN DIEGO'S FIRST PADRES and "THE KID"

PHOTO CREDITS

Baseball-Reference.com, pp. 205, 209, 214, 216, 227, 234, 235, 239, 245, 246, 249, 251
Herbert Hoover High School, pp. 27, 37
Collection of Andy Strasberg, pp. 36, 55, 65, 107, 108, 113, 205, 240
Tom Larwin, pp. vii, viii, 141, 197, 203(2), 204, 207, 208, 211, 216, 218, 220, 221, 226, 231, 236, 241(2)
Mark Macrae, pp. 151, 157, 207, 224, 225, 230, 231, 233(2), 236, 247(2)
National Baseball Hall of Fame, p. 175
Alan O'Connor, p. 222
James D. Smith III, pp. 204, 238, 242
Bill Swank, cover (2), pp. 45, 46, 48, 152, 156, 202(2), 204, 206, 212, 213, 218, 228, 243, 244, 249, 252, 253
Ralph Thompson, pp. 44, 51, 160, 161, 207
Larry Zuckerman, pp. 139, 140

SAN DIEGO'S FIRST PADRES and "THE KID"

ENDNOTES

1 *The San Diego News*, March 26, 1936.
2 *San Diego Evening Tribune*, February 10, 1936.
3 *San Diego Evening Tribune*, March 31, 1936.
4 *Life in San Diego*, October 1936.
5 *Los Angeles Times*, November 27, 1935.
6 *The Sporting News*, November 28, 1935.
7 *Los Angeles Times*, November 28, 1935.
8 Bob Ray, *Los Angeles Times*, December 4, 1935.
9 Ray, *Los Angeles Times*, December 6, 1935.
10 *The Sporting News*, December 6, 1935.
11 *San Diego Union*, December 13, 1935.
12 Ray, *Los Angeles Times*, December 13, 1935.
13 Ted Steinmann, *San Diego Union*, December 13, 1935.
14 *San Diego Union*, December 16, 1935.
15 *San Diego Sun*, December 16, 1935.
16 Russell J. Newland, *San Diego Union*; and *San Diego Sun*, December 16, 1935.
17 *San Diego Sun*, December 16, 1935.
18 Newland, *San Diego Union*, December 17, 1935.
19 *San Diego Union*, December 18, 1935.
20 *San Diego Sun*, December 19, 1935.
21 *San Diego Union*, December 20, 1935.
22 *San Diego Sun*, December 20, 1935.
23 *San Diego Union*, December 20, 1935.
24 Steinmann, *San Diego Union*, December 21, 1935.
25 *San Diego Union*, December 22, 1935.
26 *San Diego Union*, December 25, 1935.
27 *San Diego Union*, December 27, 1935.
28 *San Diego Union*, December 30, 1935.
29 Steinmann, *San Diego Union*, December 31, 1935.
30 *San Diego Union*, January 2, 1936.
31 Nelson Fisher, *San Diego Sun*, January 8, 1936.
32 *San Diego Union*, January 10, 1936.
33 *San Diego Sun*, January 10, 1936.
34 Fisher, *San Diego Sun*, January 10, 1936.
35 *San Diego Sun*, January 11, 1936.
36 Tom Akers, *San Diego Evening Tribune*, January 17, 1936.
37 Ray, *Los Angeles Times*, January 17, 1936.
38 *San Diego Sun*, January 22, 1936.
39 *Los Angeles Times*, January 22, 1936.
40 *San Diego Union*, January 22, 1936.
41 Fisher, *San Diego Sun*, January 22, 1936.
42 Steinmann, *San Diego Union*, January 22, 1936.
43 *San Diego Sun*, January 22, 1936.
44 *Los Angeles Times*, January 22, 1936.
45 *San Diego Sun*, January 23, 1936.
46 *Los Angeles Times*, January 23, 1936.
47 *San Diego Evening Tribune*, January 22, 1936.

48 *San Diego Evening Tribune*, January 22, 1936.
49 *San Diego Sun*, January 28, 1936.
50 *San Diego Evening Tribune*, January 28, 1936.
51 *San Diego Union*, January 28, 1936.
52 *San Diego Union*, January 29, 1936.
53 Ray, *Los Angeles Times*, January 29, 1936.
54 Ray, *The Sporting News*, February 6, 1936.
55 *Los Angeles Times*, February 1, 1936.
56 *San Diego Evening Tribune*, February 1, 1936.
57 *San Diego Union*, February 2, 1936.
58 *San Diego Sun*, December 20, 1935.
59 Steinmann, *San Diego Union*, December 21, 1935.
60 *San Diego Sun*, December 21, 1935.
61 Steinmann, *San Diego Union*, December 21, 1935.
62 *San Diego Sun*, January 3, 1936.
63 *San Diego Union*, January 5, 1936.
64 *San Diego Union*, January 23, 1936.
65 Steinmann, *San Diego Union*, January 28, 1936.
66 *San Diego Sun*, January 29, 1936.
67 Bill Nowlin, *The Kid: Ted Williams in San Diego*, 110.
68 *San Diego Union*, April 13, 1935.
69 Ted Williams, *My Turn at Bat, The Story of My Life*, 36.
70 John Updike, *Hub Fans Bid Kid Adieu*, 6.
71 Arthur Mann, "Baseball's Bad Boy," *Liberty*, May 9, 1940: 14.
72 David Cataneo, *I Remember Ted Williams*, 12-13.
73 Jim Sandoval and Bill Nowlin, *Can He Play? A Look at Baseball Scouts and their Profession*, 38.
74 Williams, *My Turn at Bat, The Story of My Life*, 37.
75 *San Diego Union*, January 13, 1936.
76 *San Diego Union*, January 19, 1936.
77 Jack Malaney, *Boston Post*, November 22, 1935.
78 Ray, *Los Angeles Times*, November 23, 1935.
79 *The Sporting News*, November 28, 1935.
80 Malaney, *Boston Post*, November 22, 1935.
81 *The Sporting News*, November 28, 1935.
82 Ray, *Los Angeles Times*, January 12, 1936.
83 Steinmann, *San Diego Union*, February 8, 1936.
84 *San Diego Union*, February 14, 1936.
85 Bill Swank, *Echoes from Lane Field, A History of the San Diego Padres 1936-1957*, 17.
86 Ray, *The Sporting News*, February 27, 1936.
87 *San Diego Sun*, January 29, 1936.
88 *San Diego Union*, February 6, 1936.
89 *San Diego Union*, February 7, 1936.
90 *San Diego Union*, February 8, 1936.
91 *San Diego Union*, February 9, 1936.
92 *San Diego Union*, February 11, 1936.
93 *San Diego Union*, February 10, 1936.
94 *San Diego Union*, February 11, 1936.
95 *San Diego Union*, February 15, 1936.
96 *San Diego Union*, February 18, 1936.
97 *San Diego Union*, February 19, 1936.
98 *San Diego Union*, February 20, 1936.
99 Steinmann, *San Diego Union*, February 21, 1936.
100 Steinmann, *San Diego Union*, February 21, 1936.
101 Earl Keller, *The Sporting News*, February 27, 1936.
102 Tom Akers, *San Diego Evening Tribune*, February 21, 1936.
103 *San Diego Union*, February 26, 1936.
104 *San Diego Union*, March 31, 1936.
105 Steinmann, *San Diego Union*, January 22, 1936.
106 *Fullerton Daily News Tribune*, February 19, 1936
107 Common advertisements in daily editions of the *Santa Ana Register* in 1934-35.

ENDNOTES

108 Renamed Amerige Park in 1937; *Los Angeles Times*, April 22, 1927.
109 *Fullerton Daily News Tribune*, February 22, 1936.
110 *Fullerton Daily News Tribune*, February 24, 1936.
111 *San Diego Union*, February 23, 1936.
112 *Fullerton Daily News Tribune*, February 22, 1936.
113 *San Diego Union*, February 25, 1936.
114 *Fullerton Daily News Tribune*, February 24, 1936
115 *San Diego Union*, February 26, 1936.
116 *San Diego Union*, February 27, 1936.
117 *San Diego Union*, February 28, 1936.
118 Frank Haven, *San Diego Sun*, March 1, 1936.
119 *San Diego Union*, February 2, 1936.
120 Harry Hache, *San Diego Union*, February 2, 1936.
121 *San Diego Union*, February 4, 1936.
122 *San Diego Union*, February 14, 1936.
123 *San Diego Union*, February 23, 1936.
124 Haven, *San Diego Sun*, March 2, 1936.
125 Steinmann, *San Diego Union*, December 31, 1935.
126 Bill Swank and James Smith, "This Was Paradise: Voices of the Pacific Coast League Padres 1936-1958," *Journal of San Diego History*, Winter 1995: 9.
127 *San Diego Union*, February 23, 1936.
128 *San Diego Union*, March 2, 1936.
129 *San Diego Union*, March 3, 1936.
130 *Santa Ana Register*, April 3, 1935.
131 *Fullerton Daily News Tribune*, March 3, 1936.
132 *San Diego Union*, March 4, 1936.
133 Keller, *The Sporting News*, March 5, 1936.
134 *San Diego Union*, March 5, 1936.
135 *San Diego Union*, March 10, 1936.
136 *San Diego Union*, March 11, 1936.
137 *San Diego Union*, March 15, 1936.
138 *San Diego Union*, March 16, 1936.
139 *San Diego Union*, March 18, 1936.
140 Jack Guenther, *San Diego Sun*, March 18, 1936.
141 Keller, *The Sporting News*, March 19, 1936.
142 *San Diego Union*, March 21, 1936.
143 *San Diego Union*, March 22, 1936.
144 *San Diego Union*, March 23, 1936.
145 *San Diego Sun*, March 21, 1936.
146 Monroe McConnell, *San Diego Union*, March 25, 1936.
147 Haven, *San Diego Sun*, March 26, 1936.
148 *The Sporting News*, April 2, 1936.
149 Haven, *San Diego Sun*, March 27, 1936.
150 Steinmann, *San Diego Union*, March 28, 1936.
151 Haven, *San Diego Sun*, March 28, 1936.
152 Ed Olsen, "How Professional Baseball Developed in San Diego": 14.
153 *San Diego Union*, March 15, 1936.
154 *San Diego Union*, March 25, 1936.
155 Steinmann, *San Diego Union*, March 26, 1936.
156 Interviews conducted by Tom Larwin on September 29 and November 10, 2001.
157 *San Diego Evening Tribune*, March 27, 1936.
158 *San Diego Union*, March 29, 1936.
159 Keller, *The Sporting News*, March 19, 1936.
160 *San Diego Union*, March 24, 1936.
161 Frank Haven, *San Diego Sun*, March 24, 1936.
162 Earl Keller, *San Diego Evening Tribune*, March 7, 1936.
163 Keller, SABR, *History of San Diego Baseball*, 12-13.
164 Jim Greschke, "San Diego: A Great Baseball Tradition 1936-1986," *1986 Padres Yearbook*, 3.
165 Olsen, "How Professional Baseball Developed in San Diego": 15.
166 Olsen, "How Professional Baseball Developed in San Diego": 15.

167 *San Diego Sun*, March 29, 1936.
168 *San Diego Sun*, March 31, 1936.
169 *San Diego Union*, March 31, 1936.
170 *San Diego Sun*, March 30, 1936.
171 *San Diego Evening Tribune*, March 31, 1936.
172 *San Diego Union*, April 1, 1936.
173 *San Diego Evening Tribune*, April 1, 1936.
174 *San Diego Evening Tribune*, April 1, 1936.
175 *San Diego Herald*, April 2, 1936.
176 *San Diego Sun*, April 1, 1936.
177 *San Diego Sun*, April 1, 1936.
178 Nowlin, *The Kid, Ted Williams in San Diego*, 71.
179 *San Diego Union*, March 15, 1936.
180 *San Diego Union*, March 19, 1936.
181 *San Diego Union*, March 22, 1936.
182 *San Diego Evening Tribune*, April 2, 1936.
183 *San Diego Evening Tribune*, April 6, 1936.
184 Tony Salin, *Baseball's Forgotten Heroes*, 155.
185 *San Diego Evening Tribune*, April 11, 1936.
186 Swank and Smith, "This Was Paradise: Voices of the Pacific Coast League Padres, 1936-1958," *Journal of San Diego History*, Winter 1995: 8.
187 *San Diego Evening Tribune*, April 20, 1936.
188 Edward Linn, *Hitter: The Life and Turmoils of Ted Williams*, 56.
189 Swank and Smith, "This Was Paradise: Voices of the Pacific Coast League Padres, 1936-1958," *Journal of San Diego History*, Winter 1995: 7.
190 *San Diego Union*, April 23, 1936.
191 *San Diego Union*, April 25, 1936.
192 *San Diego Union*, April 27, 1936.
193 *San Diego Union*, April 14, 1936.
194 *San Diego Union*, April 13, 1936.
195 Nowlin, *The Kid: Ted Williams in San Diego*, 78.
196 *San Diego Union*, April 26, 1936.
197 *San Diego Union*, May 2, 1936.
198 *San Diego Union*, May 4, 1936.
199 *San Diego Union*, May 6, 1936.
200 *San Diego Union*, May 12, 1936.
201 *San Diego Union*, May 14, 1936.
202 *San Diego Union*, May 16, 1936.
203 *San Diego Union*, May 16, 1936.
204 *San Diego Union*, May 18, 1936.
205 *San Diego Evening Tribune*, May 22, 1936.
206 *San Diego Evening Tribune*, May 23, 1936.
207 *San Diego Evening Tribune*, May 24, 1936.
208 *San Diego Evening Tribune*, May 25, 1936.
209 *San Diego Evening Tribune*, May 28, 1936.
210 *San Diego Evening Tribune*, May 28, 1936.
211 *San Diego Evening Tribune*, June 1, 1936.
212 *San Diego Union*, May 4, 1936.
213 *San Diego Union*, May 8, 1936.
214 *San Diego Union*, May 23, 1936.
215 *San Diego Union*, May 31, 1936.
216 *San Diego Evening Tribune*, June 1, 1936.
217 McConnell, *San Diego Union*, June 1, 1936.
218 Bill King and Fitchberg Sentinel, "Johnny Welch's Death Recalls Pitching Grief," September 4, 1940.
219 McConnell, *San Diego Union*, June 2, 1936.
220 *San Diego Union*, June 2, 1936.
221 *San Diego Union*, June 4, 1936.
222 *San Diego Union*, June 7, 1936.
223 *San Diego Union*, June 9, 1936.
224 Steinmann, *San Diego Union*, June 12, 1936.

225 *San Diego Union*, June 12, 1936.
226 *San Diego Union*, June 14, 1936.
227 *San Diego Union*, June 14, 1936.
228 Steinmann, *San Diego Union*, June 19, 1936.
229 McConnell, *San Diego Union*, June 18, 1936.
230 McConnell, *San Diego Union*, June 20, 1936.
231 Steinmann, *San Diego Union*, June 23, 1936.
232 Steinmann, *San Diego Union*, June 19, 1936.
233 Steinmann, *San Diego Union*, June 22, 1936.
234 *San Diego Union*, June 22, 1936.
235 McConnell, *San Diego Union*, June 24, 1936.
236 McConnell, *San Diego Union*, June 24, 1936.
237 McConnell, *San Diego Union*, June 25, 1936.
238 *San Diego Union*, June 27, 1936.
239 Williams, *My Turn at Bat, The Story of My Life*, 35.
240 Nowlin, *The Kid: Ted Williams in San Diego*, 111-112.
241 Williams, *My Turn at Bat, The Story of My Life*, 36.
242 Williams, *My Turn at Bat, The Story of My Life*, 37-39.
243 *San Diego Evening Tribune*, June 1, 1936.
244 Jim Prime and Bill Nowlin, *Ted Williams The Pursuit of Perfection*, 15-16.
245 *San Diego Evening Tribune*, June 26, 1936.
246 Steinmann, *San Diego Union*, June 27, 1936.
247 Williams, *My Turn at Bat, The Story of My Life*, 39.
248 Swank, *Echoes from Lane Field, A History of the San Diego Padres 1936-1957*, 24-25.
249 Swank, *Echoes from Lane Field, A History of the San Diego Padres 1936-1957*, 24-25.
250 McConnell, *San Diego Union*, June 28, 1936.
251 McConnell, *San Diego Union*, June 30, 1936.
252 Steinmann, *San Diego Union*, June 30, 1936.
253 McConnell, *San Diego Union*, June 30, 1936.
254 Steinmann, *San Diego Union*, June 30, 1936.
255 Michael Seidel, *Ted Williams*, 18.
256 Williams, *My Turn at Bat, The Story of My Life*, 40-41.
257 *San Diego Union*, July 3, 1936.
258 Steinmann, *San Diego Union*, July 4, 1936.
259 *San Diego Union*, July 3, 1936.
260 *San Diego Union*, July 18, 1936.
261 Steinmann, *San Diego Union*, July 31, 1936.
262 *San Diego Union*, July 2, 1936.
263 Steinmann, *San Diego Union*, July 7, 1936.
264 Steinmann, *San Diego Union*, July 14, 1936.
265 Steinmann, *San Diego Union*, July 17, 1936.
266 Steinmann, *San Diego Union*, July 12, 1936.
267 Steinmann, *San Diego Union*, July 12, 1936.
268 McConnell, *San Diego Union*, July 15, 1936.
269 McConnell, *San Diego Union*, July 16, 1936.
270 McConnell, *San Diego Union*, July 16, 1936.
271 *San Diego Union*, July 19, 1936.
272 Steinmann, *San Diego Union*, July 21, 1936.
273 *Los Angeles Times*, July 20, 1936.
274 Jack Powell, "Umpire Insists Durst Out," *Los Angeles Examiner*, July 21, 1936.
275 *Los Angeles Times*, July 20, 1936.
276 McConnell, *San Diego Union*, July 21, 1936.
277 *Los Angeles Examiner*, July 18, 1936.
278 *Los Angeles Times*, July 21, 1936.
279 Hunter, *Los Angeles Examiner*, July 19, 1936.
280 McConnell, *San Diego Union*, July 22, 1936.
281 Connolly, *Los Angeles Examiner*, July 22, 1936.
282 Connolly, "Yours Confidentially," *Los Angeles Examiner*, July 22, 1936.
283 *Los Angeles Times*, July 21, 1936.
284 Ray, *Los Angeles Times*, July 23, 1936.

285 McConnell, *San Diego Union*, July 23, 1936.
286 *San Diego Union*, July 28, 1936.
287 McConnell, *San Diego Union*, July 28, 1936. Note: This article incorrectly noted the most recent series as 6-1 in favor of the Angels when it was actually 7-1. Ted Steinmann's column on July 29 lists the Angels record versus San Diego coming into this series as 14-4.
288 James, *Los Angeles Examiner*, July 29, 1936.
289 McConnell, *San Diego Union*, July 29, 1936.
290 Steinmann, *San Diego Union*, August 1, 1936.
291 Ray, *Los Angeles Times*, July 30, 1936.
292 Ray, *The Sporting News*, November 5, 1936.
293 James, *Los Angeles Examiner*, July 30, 1936.
294 Ray, *Los Angeles Times*, July 30, 1936.
295 Ray, *Los Angeles Times*, July 30, 1936.
296 Ray, "The Sports X-Ray," *Los Angeles Times*, July 30, 1936.
297 James, *Los Angeles Examiner*, July 30, 1936.
298 *San Diego Union*, July 24 and 25, 1936.
299 Steinmann, *San Diego Union*, July 29, 1936.
300 Steinmann, *San Diego Union*, August 1, 1936.
301 Steinmann, *San Diego Union*, August 4, 1936.
302 Steinmann, *San Diego Union*, August 4, 1936.
303 *San Diego Union*, August 8, 1936.
304 Steinmann, *San Diego Union*, August 8, 1936.
305 *San Diego Union*, August 8, 1936.
306 *San Diego Union*, August 9, 1936.
307 McConnell, *San Diego Union*, August 11, 1936.
308 *San Diego Union*, August 10, 1936.
309 McConnell, *San Diego Union*, August 11, 1936.
310 Steinmann, *San Diego Union*, August 9, 1936.
311 Swank and Smith, "This was Paradise: Voices of the Pacific Coast League Padres, 1936-1958," *Journal of San Diego History*, Winter 1995: 4.
312 Siedel, *Ted Williams*, 20.
313 *San Diego Union*, August 12, 1936.
314 *San Diego Union*, September 1, 1936.
315 Byrne, *San Diego Union*, August 16, 1936.
316 *San Diego Union*, August 19, 1936.
317 Steinmann, *San Diego Union*, August 15, 1936.
318 Steinmann, *San Diego Union*, August 21, 1936.
319 *San Diego Union*, August 21, 1936.
320 Steinmann, *San Diego Union*, August 23, 1936.
321 Steinmann, *San Diego Union*, August 25, 1936.
322 Steinmann, *San Diego Union*, August 23, 1936.
323 Steinmann, *San Diego Union*, August 27, 1936.
324 *San Diego Union*, August 28, 1936.
325 *San Diego Union*, August 28, 1936.
326 Swank, *Echoes from Lane Field, A History of the San Diego Padres 1936-1957*, 17.
327 Interview conducted by Tom Larwin on November 20, 2001.
328 McConnell, *San Diego Union*, August 28, 1936.
329 Steinmann, *San Diego Union*, August 29, 1936.
330 McConnell, *San Diego Union*, August 30, 1936.
331 *San Diego Union-Tribune*, December 14 and 23, 1999, Currents and Arts section.
332 Keller, *The Sporting News*, October 1, 1936.
333 McConnell, *San Diego Union*, September 6, 1936.
334 *San Diego Union*, September 1, 1936.
335 *San Diego Union*, September 1, 1936.
336 *San Diego Union*, September 2, 1936.
337 Steinmann, *San Diego Union*, September 3, 1936.
338 McConnell, *San Diego Union*, September 5, 1936.
339 Steinmann, *San Diego Union*, September 5, 1936.
340 McConnell, *San Diego Union*, September 6, 1936.
341 Ray Brandes and Bill Swank, *The Pacific Coast League San Diego Padres, Lane Field: The Early Years, 1936-1946*, 56.

ENDNOTES

342 *San Diego Union,* September 7, 1936.
343 Ray, *Los Angeles Times*, "The Sports X-Ray," September 9, 1936.
344 McConnell, *San Diego Union*, September 10, 1936.
345 Steinmann, *San Diego Union*, September 11, 1936.
346 Steinmann, *San Diego Union*, September 9, 1936.
347 Steinmann, *San Diego Union*, September 11, 1936.
348 *San Diego Union*, September 13, 1936.
349 Steinmann, *San Diego Union*, September 15, 1936.
350 McConnell, *San Diego Union*, September 16, 1936.
351 McConnell, *San Diego Union*, September 18, 1936.
352 McConnell, *San Diego Union*, September 18, 1936.
353 *The Sporting News*, October 1, 1936.
354 Steinmann, *San Diego Union*, September 17, 1936.
355 *The Sporting News*, October 1, 1936.
356 Steinmann, *San Diego Union*, September 22, 1936.
357 Steinmann, *San Diego Union*, September 22, 1936.
358 Brandes and Swank, *The Pacific Coast League San Diego Padres, Lane Field: The Early Years, 1936-1946*, 59.
359 Ted Williams with John Underwood, *My Turn at Bat*, 39-40.
360 Interview conducted by Tom Larwin on January 25, 2000.
361 Interview conducted by Tom Larwin on November 20, 2001.
362 Interviews conducted by Tom Larwin on September 29 and November 10, 2001.
363 McConnell, *San Diego Union*, October 10, 1938.
364 Brandes and Swank, *The Pacific Coast League San Diego Padres, Lane Field: The Early Years, 1936-1946*, 44.
365 Brandes and Swank, *The Pacific Coast League San Diego Padres, Lane Field: The Early Years, 1936-1946*, 65.
366 *San Diego Tribune*, October 10, 1938.
367 Ray, *The Sporting News*, January 16, 1936.
368 Brandes and Swank, 44.
369 *San Diego Union*, February 21, 1936.
370 *San Diego Union*, March 20, 1936.
371 James D. Smith III, "Lester Spurgeon Cook, Catcher, Trainer, PCL Legend," *The National Pastime*, Number 27.
372 Paul Mittermeyer, "Eddie Collins," *SABR Baseball Biography Project*, https://sabr.org/bioproj/person/c480756d.
373 Excerpted from Keller's obituary by Jack Williams, *San Diego Union-Tribune*, November 15, 1995.
374 Swank, "Ted Williams, Earl Keller and the 1937 San Diego Padres," 2003.
375 Interviews by Tom Larwin in September and November 2001.
376 *San Diego Union*, March 10, 1936.
377 *San Diego Union*, February 26, 1936.
378 *San Diego Union*, March 17 and 26, 1936.
379 *San Diego Union*, March 25, 1936.
380 *San Diego Union*, March 16, 1936.
381 *San Diego Union*, March 18, 1936.
382 *San Diego Union*, March 19, 1936.
383 *San Diego Union*, March 6, 1936.
384 *Santa Ana Register*, March 4, 1935.
385 *San Diego Union*, March 9, 1936.
386 SABR, *Minor League Baseball Stars, Vol. III*, 1992.
387 *San Diego Union*, March 21, 1936.
388 *The Sporting News*, November 28, 1935.
389 *San Diego Union*, March 15, 1936.
390 *San Diego Sun*, March 3, 1936.
391 Baseball-Reference.com.
392 *San Diego Union*, March 6, 1936.
393 *San Diego Union*, March 1, 1936.
394 Earl Keller, *San Diego Evening Tribune*, March 28, 1936.
395 *San Diego Union*, March 5, 1936.
396 Baseball-Reference.com.
397 *San Diego Union*, March 5, 1936.
398 *The Desert Sun*, December 24, 1997.
399 Mark Starr, *Wall Street Journal*, July 30, 1976.
400 Frank Haven, *The San Diego Sun*, March 10, 1936.
401 *San Diego Union*, March 17, 1936.

402 *Los Angeles Times*, October 22, 1988.
403 *San Diego Union*, March 1 and 8, 1936.
404 *San Diego Union*, March 5, 1936.
405 Baseball-Reference.com.
406 *San Diego Union*, March 17, 1936.
407 *San Diego Union*, March 16, 1936.
408 *San Diego Union*, March 13, 1936.
409 *San Diego Union*, March 10, 1936.
410 *San Diego Union*, March 11, 1936.
411 SABR, ed. by Bauer and Hoie, *The Minor League Baseball Research Journal, Vol. II*, 1997.
412 *San Diego Union*, March 22, 1936.
413 *San Diego Union*, March 7, 1936.
414 *San Diego Union*, February 23, 1936.
415 Ken Ross, "Hub Kittle," *SABR Baseball Biography Project*, https://sabr.org/bioproj/person/4d152362.
416 *San Diego Union*, February 23, 1936.
417 *San Diego Union*, March 11, 1936.
418 *San Diego Union*, March 2, 1936.
419 World War II Draft Registration.
420 *Cody Enterprise*, September 20, 1972.
421 *San Diego Union*, March 26, 1936.
422 *San Diego Union*, March 22, 1936.
423 *San Diego Union*, March 15, 1936.
424 Malaney, *Boston Post*, November 22, 1935.
425 *San Diego Union*, March 10, 1936.
426 Baseball-Reference.com.
427 *The Salt Lake Tribune*, August 12, 1959.
428 *San Diego Union*, March 12, 1936.
429 SABR, *Minor League Baseball Stars*, 1978.
430 *San Diego Union*, February 28, 1936.
431 *San Diego Union*, March 5, 1936.
432 Swank and Smith, "This Was Paradise: Voices of the Pacific Coast League Padres, 1936-1958," *Journal of San Diego History*, Winter 1995: 8.
433 Baseball-Reference.com.
434 *San Diego Union*, March 17, 1936.
435 *San Diego Union*, February 23, 1936.
436 *San Diego Union*, March 10, 1936; and *The Sporting News*, March 19, 1936.
437 Swank, *Echoes from Lane Field, A History of the San Diego Padres 1936-1957*, 26.
438 Earl Keller, *San Diego Evening Tribune*, March 28, 1936.
439 *San Diego Union*, February 23, 1936
440 *Fullerton Daily News Tribune*, February 22, 1936
441 *San Diego Sun*, March 10, 1936.
442 *San Diego Union*, March 24, 1936.
443 *San Diego Union*, March 1, 1936.
444 *San Diego Sun*, March 2, 1936.
445 *San Diego Union*, February 27, 1936.
446 *San Diego Union*, March 1, 1936.

www.ingramcontent.com/pod-product-compliance
Lightning Source LLC
Chambersburg PA
CBHW040929240426
43667CB00027B/2996